INCAPITATED

sex • power • money • control

Evelyn C. Dahab

WESTCOM PRESS
Washington DC

Incapitated
by Evelyn C. Dahab

ISBN - 978-1-938620-03-4

Published by:

Westcom Press
2101 N Street, NW
Suite T-1
Washington DC 20037

westcom.press@mac.com

18 17 16 15 14 13 12 1 2 3 4 5

Dedication

To my eighth-grade English teacher, Mrs. Dorothea Osmun, without whom this book would not exist.

Mrs. Osmun selflessly sacrificed her lunch period to tutor her most thick-skulled student throughout the year. Although I couldn't construct the most basic sentence from a vocabulary list, she recognized the storyteller in me. *Incapitated* is a tribute to her insight and patience.

Thank you, Mrs. Osmun, for teaching me to put thoughts into words, string words into sentences, build paragraphs from those sentences, and create a book that I can share with the world. Please know how precious those lunchtime writing sessions were to a young girl and how invaluable the lessons are to the woman she became.

One

She knew that her mind was resilient, but she had never tested the theory. Most people described her as strong willed, and she believed that her strength was an asset. She did fear that one day she would snap; her younger self had been prone to unprovoked sobbing. But as she settled into her twenties, the crying spells subsided. She felt generally content in her busy life as a single woman in the Yorkville neighborhood, on the upper east side of New York City. In all, she was well liked and relatively happy.

In college, she had made the rounds as a cheerleader and as a junkie—at different times, of course. Ironically, her sober years earned her lower academic marks. She took pride in her inability to monitor balance in her life. In all four years, she attended every party, and sometimes stayed out for a week at a time. Her warped reasoning—to consume all that the metropolis offered—kept her from questioning her hedonistic lifestyle.

By the time she graduated, she had angled herself as a live-in nanny in one of the most remarkable prewar buildings on Fifth Avenue, and she silently gloated about her bedroom's tree-saturated Central Park view. Her wards spent the bulk of that first summer in the Hamptons, and she settled into the sky mansion alone most nights. Often, she collapsed into bed, readying herself for her minimum-wage, high-profile job as a personal trainer at one of the city's poshest gyms.

Personal training earned her the respect and the eye of talent managers, and soon her enviably solid body led to modeling jobs and television roles. This was not how she had intended to use her Ivy League education, but the lifestyle was steady, and her days were never routine. She hated routine.

By the time she moved into her own large, dilapidated railroad apartment on the fourth landing of a building with no elevator, she had grown bored with the gym and was ready for something else. Anything else, really. Watching people expend huge amounts of energy running on machines that never transported them anywhere depressed her. She was happy to expend energy, but only if she ended up somewhere other than where she began.

⤜❧

Her first relationship was forced on her. Many men fell for her, but usually she was able to fend them off. Phil was different. She didn't like him more than anyone else particularly, but he was emotionally aggressive, and when he wouldn't let up, she eventually gave in. He convinced her to leave her life of fitness and follow him on a new financial venture in the then-budding world of hedge funds. Other than the fact that she didn't want to, she couldn't think of another reason why she shouldn't.

Phil insisted that they live together and told her that she loved him. She had never been in love, so she convinced herself that he must know better. After all, he had been married twice. In fact, he was still married, but even his pregnant wife and two young sons were not reason enough in his mind for him to stay with his family. She was a vixen of sorts, but because she was unaware of her prowess, it often caused more harm than good for both her and her weak suitors.

Phil was twice her age, but he was good looking and accomplished, and he treated her well. He had a tendency to interrogate her and was prone to jealousy, but she figured that since he was cheating on his wife, he assumed everyone else was untrustworthy, too.

Sometimes Phil's guilt consumed him, and he would beg her to hit him. She only obliged once, but his crying afterward disgusted her so much that she refused to do it again.

Eventually Phil's desire for money and success overpowered his desire for her, and when his wealthy wife threatened to revoke both, he went home with his tail between his legs.

She had no shortage of interested men in her pursuit, and she quickly sought out the latest technology in electronic personal organizers to manage her dating life. Often, she would cancel one date when a seemingly better offer came up.

There was only one metropolitan personals website back then, and she had to delete her membership when the other users voted her "top profile." The responses were so overwhelming that at one point her laptop froze when she accessed her inbox.

By then, however, she had given out her phone number to a select many interested parties, so she was still in communication with plenty of potentials. Some of the guys seemed eager to impress her, and some were self-deprecating. There seemed to be no middle ground, but at least the eager ones were amusing, if sometimes delusional.

Mitchell regularly sent her photos of himself with wild animals, claiming they were snapshots taken during the safari he was currently traveling. She would chuckle at the thought that he was so desperate to know her that he had created an alias persona, but she had heard that lonely people would spend hours on the Internet formulating their alter egos—the men they secretly longed to be.

When Mitchell called her, she never answered the phone. He was persistent, but not stalking; he left a message maybe once a week. After several months, she decided finally to return his call. She thought she would call his bluff. But he called hers.

She had a date that night, a second date she wasn't particularly looking forward to. But she wasn't not looking forward to it either. Mitchell was in town that night, and he insisted that she allow him to take her anywhere. In the interest of scaring him off, she requested the truffle-tasting menu at Alain Ducasse, a meal she knew would exceed several thousand dollars and was not for the faint of heart. Mitchell sent a car for her at 7:00 p.m.

In the car ride to retrieve Mitchell (she had insisted that they arrive together; she was not a woman to be stood up), she called her original date to cancel. An emergency, a prior obligation, some sort of vague excuse. The car pulled up in front of Mitchell's Park Avenue residence, and a large, oddly dressed man with unruly chin-length salt-and-pepper hair and an ungroomed goatee joined her in the backseat.

He was carrying a big gift-wrapped package and a tiny Goyard man clutch. He saw her eyes drift toward the small purse, and he made her smile by beseeching her not to "make fun of the fag bag."

Mitchell was strong and thick, composed and confident. He seemed socially polished and aware, yet apathetic toward his physical appearance. She was intrigued, and he knew it.

The two entered the vestibule at Ducasse, and he immediately checked the gift package. He assured her that it was for her, but not until the end of the meal. She checked her coat and scarf, but he had no top clothing to check. Even though it was the first week in February, he was wearing nothing more than a tattered, navy blue emblemed blazer and an open-collared French-cuff pink shirt.

As they followed the maître d' to their table with the intimate U-shaped banquet, Mitchell reminded her to place her handbag on the little stool adjacent to the booth, and not on the floor, as at lesser-civilized venues.

The wine list was carefully studied, and several bottles were chosen. She was known in most circles as a gifted student of oenology, but Mitchell was clearly far better versed. She enjoyed being in the presence of a gentleman who was capable of ordering the wine, since in most cases, guys just handed her the list and deferred to her expertise.

Her knowledge of wine came from the same source as all her hedonistic traits. She felt and experienced all sensuous stimuli more than the average person. A sunrise gave her chills, a shrill voice caused her physical pain, a massage made her shudder, and wine—wine made her toes curl and her throat literally purr in transcendence.

Mitchell knew this and pandered to her weakness. He plied her with wine and ordered her excessive quantities of decadent foods. He even sent a course back when it wasn't to his impeccable standards. She was enthralled.

He encouraged her to eat and drink excessively, and at one point, en route to the ladies' room, she tripped on her high-heeled sandals and fell on her swollen belly to the floor. She quickly righted herself, and no one in the restaurant seemed to register the fall.

At the end of the meal, he had the captain bring the package for her to open. Inside, she found an electric pink leather and suede Burberry satchel. It had small handles but no strap to support the deep sack.

"It's a laundry bag," he explained. Considering that the bag cost more than any laundry she might put inside it, she could not think of a more frivolous gift idea. It was brilliant; an outrageously expensive gift, but so bizarre she had no excuse for not being able to accept it. After all, everyone has laundry. And the bag wasn't really useful for any other purpose.

She thanked him for the gift, and he explained that he had bought it specifically for her that day, knowing that she would call him and that they would finally meet. He at once flattered her, embarrassed her, and elevated her.

After dinner, he invited her to his apartment to try on an Armani shell he had recently purchased. He lived only a few blocks from the restaurant, so she obliged. His apartment was under construction, but he had her step over the drop cloths and model the coat in front of the wall-sized gold-framed mirror. The Armani piece fit her well, but she was confused. Was it hers to keep? It was far more valuable than the laundry bag, and a gift she would have to refuse.

But he laughed at her. He only wanted to see it on her, he explained, as though she were crazy for thinking otherwise. He quickly handed her a few fifty-dollar bills for cab fare and showed her the door, explaining that he had a date the next day, but he'd love for her to drop by afterwards. She had a lunch date too, but she had a sneaking suspicion that it was Phil assuming an alias. Because she had considered canceling her standing date anyway, she agreed. Unable to peg Mitchell, she was curious to see what would happen next.

Two

In the early afternoon, she returned to Mitchell's apartment. The doormen had her name on file, and the private elevator operator shuttled her the many flights up to the high floor.

Mitchell was standing in his foyer, yelling at his staff in a voice that unsettled her. But upon seeing her, his voice quickly turned warm and inviting, and he showed her into his kitchen, where two glasses and several bottles of wine were set on the counter.

"I know that you had said that Marcassin is your favorite New World wine, but I couldn't find it anywhere in this city. I hope that you'll enjoy one of the Mersaults or Chassagnes that I purchased instead."

She was a little taken aback by his attention to detail. They opened the first bottle of wine and shared a sip before he scurried off into the master suite for a few minutes. He returned with an unwrapped gift—a black Burberry shoulder purse. She thanked him, and he playfully admonished her for not looking inside. She opened the bag and found a brand new pair of Armani pumps.

"Your heels last night seemed to have given you a bit of a challenge—I hope these fit you better. I guessed at your size, but I've never been wrong."

The shoes did indeed fit perfectly, and she thanked him. The next day happened to be her twenty-third birthday, so she rationalized the gifts as part of her celebration. But she thought the entire experience was far too indulgent, and logic dictated her desire to quit while she was ahead.

"Where do you live exactly?" he asked.

"Excuse me?"

"Your house. Your home. Your apartment. Whichever, my dear. Where exactly is it?"

"I don't—"

"I have a car. An old BMW. Marvelous, actually. I don't use it enough. I'm going to drive it to you tomorrow morning. You know, to take you to a salon for your birthday. You're going to need a salon visit to look perfect in the red Versace pantsuit you're going to wear. You know, for your birthday dinner at Daniel. A Saturday night at Daniel deserves a makeover! Do you want to fly to Greece Sunday? Never mind. Don't answer. I'll pick you up at 7:00 a.m. Here's cab fare. Go home!"

"But, well, . . ."

"Is that not enough cab fare?"

"No, it's fine, . . . I just—"

"Goodbye! See you tomorrow morning!" And with that, he closed the door.

❧

"Good morning, beautiful! I'm downstairs. Hurry down!"

"Oh, I, okay, yes, coming."

She ran down the flights of stairs and into Mitchell's idling car.

"Oh good, you're carrying the new purse! It's magnificent, isn't it?"

"Yeah. . . . I guess. . . . Um, . . . Where are we going?" She was almost embarrassed that she was carrying the new bag, but she didn't dare not to.

"Privé! Privé! At the Soho Grande. Surely you know it." Mitchell was at once both patronizing and effusive. A strange blend.

"Well, I spent my twentieth birthday at the Soho Grande, but I didn't make it to the salon."

"You don't wear makeup, do you, my dear? Well, you don't need it. But we'll have it done anyway! Happy birthday, by the way!"

"Thank you. Wow. This is so unexpected." She hadn't anticipated Mitchell to be all that he had promised.

"No. It's exactly what you expected. You've just been with too many pussy men. Anyway, I'm going to get you settled in at Privé for the works. I'll come get you when you call toward the end."

"Okay. Wow. So, haircut and makeup?"

"And waxing. Ask them to do waxing. You've never been waxed. You haven't—I can tell." Mitchell had a gift for both building her up and slashing her down in one sentence.

It was true, she had never been waxed, but she wasn't a very hairy woman. Her mother was a WASP who, as far as anyone knew, had never even shaved under her arms, because she had no body hair to speak of.

"Okay, I'll ask if they'll wax me. What do I need waxed, exactly?" She tried to be obliging.

"Poor gorgeous young lady. Everything, of course!"

"Oh, okay, well—"

Mitchell cut her off mid-question. "We're here. Privé! You're going to love this. You'll be fabulous for dinner at Daniel! I forgot to ask, any particular requests?"

"Well, in the few times I've been, I've never had a private dining canopy. That would be a treat. Very civilized." She was trying to see how far she could push Mitchell to accommodate absurd requests. Why not?

"My dear, you've got it. Call me when you're through here." And with that, he left her with an open tab at a salon where a haircut cost more than her rent.

She called him later to apprise him of her progress. "I'm almost finished. It was funny; while I was getting a pedicure, my parents called to say 'happy birthday' and—"

"Invite them."

"What?"

"Invite them. To Daniel tonight. We have a private room; invite your parents!"

She called her parents, but her mother told her they had prior obligations that evening. When she called Mitchell back to tell him, he was incredulous.

"On your birthday?! What horrible parents have prior commitments on *your* birthday! They know I'm paying, right?"

"I don't know. They don't like me much. It's no big deal." She tried to dismiss the comment before Mitchell pressed to know more about her family.

"It's a very big deal. They're assholes who don't realize how amazing you are. And on your birthday! What's more important? Have they always been like this?" Mitchell was forceful in his attempt to exhibit empathy.

"I guess. They're not very family oriented. Don't make a big deal. Please." She hoped that he'd change the subject. "We'll have a good time."

"That's right. You deserve an incredible time. Happy birthday, by the way, beautiful."

"Thanks, Mitchell."

"Madam, may I take your coat?" the nebbish maître d' at Daniel asked.

"You look incredible; every eye in this place is on you," Mitchell hissed into her ear.

"I suppose. I really do like this haircut, don't you?" She had to admit that she felt glamorous after her makeover.

"Of course I do. But that makeup they put on your tab—they took advantage of me through you. Never let people do that!"

Was Mitchell admonishing her? "I'm sorry, I didn't—"

He cut her off. Again. "That's enough. Smile. We're here."

They were seated in a canopy in the front corner entrance to the main dining room. It was the perfect location; private, yet every common person had to walk past to shuttle into the open tables in the center of the floor. In New York, real estate is paramount, and restaurant seating is a microcosm of status.

"We'll begin with a Château d'Yquem!" Mitchell announced.

"Sauternes? Surely you aren't suggesting we begin with sauternes! Not to start the evening."

"My dear, you may know much about wine and food, but you don't know everything about chefs. At least, not yet. Chef Boulud begins his lengthy tasting menus with rich foie gras. He does not wait for the middle of the meal. It's his signature quirk, I suppose. Do you trust me?"

"Well, if you say so, but—"

"Château d'Yquem!" He bellowed at no one in particular.

Immediately following an unremarkable amuse bouche, a plate of composed foie gras and brioche was set before each of them. At the same time, the bottle of sauternes arrived.

"Wow, you were right! Foie at the beginning? Who does that?" She was anxious to delve into the course.

"Daniel does that. I told you."

"This brioche is incredible, too."

"Then we'll have to get you more. Captain! More brioche and keep it coming. Make sure her bread plate always has brioche!" Mitchell's personality was glowing. He was truly in his element.

"Yes, sir." The tuxedo-clad man scuttled away.

"You're going to give the baker the ride of his life. He'll never want to make brioche again." Mitchell laughed a forced, yet infectious, belly laugh. There was something at once disturbing and comforting about his composure, so she opted to focus on the comfortable and keep aware of the disturbing, just in case.

The meal continued at a steady pace. Five courses, ten courses, twenty-five courses—it seemed to never end. She was enthralled.

"I'm still thinking Greece." Mitchell made the non sequitur.

"What?" She asked quizzically and hopefully at the same time.

"Tomorrow. Greece. It's been ages since I've been to Greece. Have you been?"

"No. I thought I'd been a lot of places, but now I'm realizing I haven't. I'd love to go to Greece tomorrow!" She hoped that he wasn't kidding.

"Great. After dinner, I'll send you home in a taxi and give you enough fare to return tomorrow morning, packed, to my apartment. I have luggage for you, but bring the Burberry sack and purse as well. I'll go through your clothes when you get here, to see what's appropriate. You inherited some mink, did you not? A nice WASP girl like you? Bring that too. Yes, definitely bring that."

"Okay, right after dinner I'll—"

"No, right after dinner you'll come back to my house and take off that suit. You didn't think it was yours to keep, did you?" He pointed up and down at the bright red Versace pantsuit that she wore.

"Of course not!" she lied, embarrassed.

They shared a bottle of Marcassin during the evening, at her request and his insistence. "I don't like it. No, I don't like it at all. But you, my dear, enjoy it. I suppose my tastes are more refined than yours. I'll just have some sparkling water; no reason to dull my palate with this."

No one had ever questioned her wine expertise so harshly, and she was a bit titillated. She liked being challenged, but so few people ever challenged her.

As he sipped his water and they anticipated another course, he returned to the subject of her parents. "So you left home very young. Because they're assholes?"

"No, because I wanted to experience more of the world than just what exists behind the white picket fences of suburbia."

"But, they are assholes."

"No, I wouldn't—"

"No, my dear, no. You're confused. I'm not asking; I'm telling you: they're assholes. You invited them to the meal of their lifetime on your birthday, and they told you they had something better to do. Or maybe I'm wrong. They hate fine dining?"

"They love fine dining. My mother is even more enthralled by food than I am. She studied at the Cordon Bleu!"

"Ugghhkk." He scoffed, "I loathe the Cordon Bleu. But, that's not the point. They love dining, but they refused your invitation? And on your birthday. What terrible people!"

"I wouldn't call them terrible. They just had some other place to be."

"Don't make excuses. It's embarrassing. They're terrible people. I'm letting you know that. Their behavior is disgusting. Disgusting. Oh well. Anyway, let's get you home and ready for Greece."

They returned to his apartment, and she quickly removed the valuable suit and returned to her unremarkable jeans and sweater set. Mitchell seemed anxious to get her out the door, and in her haste, she forgot to remove the cashmere tank top that accompanied the suit. At least, she thought she had forgotten; perhaps she had no faith that she would see him the next day and wanted to have a token of the bizarre birthday extravaganza.

Mitchell called her the next morning at 10:00. "Hurry over, gorgeous. Don't forget your passport!"

With a bit of guilt and shame, she placed the tiny cashmere top into the sleeve of her coat; she'd replace it somewhere in his home before he noticed it was missing.

She ran downstairs carrying the pink satchel filled mostly with the gifts he had bestowed upon her in the past two days and flagged down a cab. As she rode in the backseat, she at once beamed and chided herself for indulging in such a luxury. After all, Mitchell's address was only one stop away on the downtown express train, and it was difficult to rationalize taking a taxi. But perhaps this was her new life, and she should embrace it.

When she arrived at Mitchell's building, she was quickly seen to the elevator without inquiry or announcement; clearly, he had apprised the doormen of her identity. Carrying the cumbersome pink bag, she pushed open the door to Mitchell's apartment. It was already set ajar in anticipation of her arrival. She found Mitchell lounging in his robe and boxer shorts in an armchair in the corner of his bedroom.

"So, this trip. I was thinking that maybe we should go to the Caribbean instead. Jet Blue has flights to Puerto Rico, and we can head there today."

She looked at him with a blank expression. She had anticipated his bait and switch, but she fancied herself too smart to fall for it. "No, I don't have any warm-weather clothes. I thought we were going to Greece."

"You really want to go to Greece, my dear?" Mitchell sighed, feigning exasperation. "Then we will go to Greece. But I want a blowjob while I'm on the phone booking the flights."

She was caught off guard, but not surprised. As she fell to her knees in front of the armchair, she removed his flaccid cock from his shorts. His lack of basic hygiene produced a strong odor, but she fought her instinct to gag and systematically began to service him.

After about three minutes, he stood up and made a fleeting comment regarding her poor technique. "We'll work on that," he stated matter-of-factly.

"Don't you want me to finish?" She was not used to being denied.

"Not if that's your technique. You have quite a bit to learn. Don't worry, I'll teach you. But I'm happy to see that you're willing to try. Our flight to Athens leaves at 7:15. We'll leave for the airport at 5:00 or so."

She wasn't thrilled that he had rejected her attempt to fellate him, but she understood that the request was fundamentally a test of her will, and clearly, she had passed.

He removed the contents of the pink satchel and repacked them in a gorgeous Louis Vuitton roller bag. While he did this, she clandestinely threw the cashmere tank top under the bed and hoped he didn't notice. It appeared that he did not.

On the flight, Mitchell spared no time in ordering two glasses of each champagne and scotch; both scotches were for her, and the champagnes were for both.

Together, they quickly consumed the contents of the glasses before the crew returned to prepare the cabin for takeoff. Once in the air, Mitchell ordered yet more drinks as well as extra meals for her. "I saw you eat at Daniel; you can't possibly be content with just one small airplane meal."

She smiled and thanked him. By the end of her fourth drink, and before the food had arrived, she was speaking at an elevated volume. Though she could not hear the difference, Mitchell became irritated, and he raised the divider between their seats. She was confused but chose not to register any emotion or reaction in particular.

After about ten minutes, and as the meal was being served, Mitchell lowered the barrier, and the two continued in banter where they had left off.

Three

They arrived in Athens in the mid-morning, slightly drunk and very tired. She dozed in the backseat of the taxi they took to the hotel, where the desk clerk informed them that their suite would not be ready for several hours. He offered a room in the interim for them to refresh and rest, which she was quick to accept. Mitchell bit his lip and refrained from scolding her until they had reached the room.

"You never take the interim room, fool. You wait until your suite is ready, and you make your presence a manageable nuisance." He glanced about the room disdainfully and then settled his gaze back on her. "Do you really want to stay in this sty?" He scoffed.

The room seemed gorgeous to her. But she was tired, and her judgment was tainted, so she deferred to his. "No, it's awful. I'm sorry. Let's go back downstairs."

"We're here already, you fool. The damage is done. Just rest, and I'll wake you when it's time for you to fight for the suite that is rightfully ours. Rest, my dear."

The message and connotation were confusing, but she was too tired to decipher them, so she landed face first on the feather duvet and disappeared into hangover reverie for the next several hours.

In the mid-afternoon, he aggressively shook her and announced that it was time to procure a nicer base for their trip to Greece, however long it may be. She obliged and groggily called the front desk.

"Hello, Mrs. Durman. How may we be of assistance?"

She smiled at the reference to her status as wife, but knowing that Mitchell was expecting results, she played along. "Mr. Durman and I were wondering if our suite was finally available. We're anticipating our imminent move from this claustrophobic cube." She glanced at Mitchell to seek his approval, and he smiled radiantly and signaled for her to carry on the aggressive dialogue.

"Madam, but of course. Your room is ready, and you may head toward the penthouse suites now. A bellman will be along shortly with your bags. We are truly sorry to keep you waiting. Please accept our deepest apologies."

She reported the course of the conversation to Mitchell, and he nodded at her approvingly. The two moved to their nicer quarters on the top deck, and Mitchell once again became warm and friendly.

"You did a great job! This suite is gorgeous." Indeed it was, complete with a 200-square-foot corner balcony overlooking the Parthenon and other ruins. She wasn't happy about her forced hostility toward the hotel staff; her manner of speaking tended to be firm, but not demanding. Mitchell, however, seemed thrilled with her change in character and the results it garnered. She accepted his offer of a glass of champagne from the minibar and joined him on the balcony. After finishing the bottle, the two welcomed the dusk and headed into the room to take a nap before dinner.

"Are you happy, beautiful?"

"Yes! Very. This is a lovely trip. Thank you."

"Don't thank me. Just enjoy it. Your incessant gratitude sounds like begging. You *deserve* this lifestyle. Remember that."

She smiled out of one corner of her mouth as she quickly fell asleep.

~❧~

"Where would you take your wife if you were going out for a wonderful taverna dinner?" Mitchell prodded the concierge.

"Well, sir, we recommend—"

"Not what the hotel recommends! Why would I want to dine among tourists? I asked, and I repeat, where would you take your wife?"

The prostrating concierge cautiously scribbled the name and address of a venue within walking distance of the hotel. Mitchell briskly thanked him, in the same moment placing his hand in the small of her back and gently guiding her toward the street.

"Where are we going, Mitchell?"

"That nice concierge directed us toward a restaurant he swears is his favorite kept secret in town. For the moment, I'm going to feign trust in his judgment. But let's just see where our hotel friend has sent us."

Carefully studying the street names and glancing hopefully down back alleys for a hidden restaurant gem, the two arrived at a large eatery on a main corridor that was clearly geared toward tourists.

"That idiot. He would never eat here. Look, there's a clipped newspaper photo of George W. Bush eating here. This place is disgusting. Come, we're going in."

She was confused but decided that Mitchell was either that hungry or took a sardonic thrill in moving toward certain disappointment.

The restaurant was brightly lit and smelled of chemical disinfectant. There was no atmosphere but for a few shoddy murals that must have been commissioned to a local artist. They were seated, quickly ordered a bottle of wine, and then sat back to ridicule the American-influenced menu.

"This place is overpriced and uninspired. My dear, that man at the concierge desk took advantage of us. He's getting a kickback from our reservation, and I won't stand to be used by little people. We'll order something to nosh just to get us through our wine."

She nodded. The menu was boring and in English—always a bad sign. And the prices did look high, but the dollar was strong against the new Euro, and she didn't think much of it.

They shared some meze and had some small lamb and fish dishes. Practically before they had swallowed the last bites, Mitchell signaled for the check. He paid quickly and leaned in to promise her that they would find a decent dinner in Athens that night if it killed him. She liked that he knew how to keep her anticipating more pleasure, and she was eager to see what the streets of Athens had in store.

"It's almost midnight, which is good because nobody here eats before 2 a.m. We're actually in better shape than we thought." Mitchell was looking all about, trying to find a venue that excited him. "Are you still hungry, my dear?"

"Always." She wasn't hugely hungry, but she was really looking forward to an authentic dining experience that night.

As they strolled through a back alley, Mitchell noticed a treacherously steep flight of stairs descending toward a dim light wafting through a doorway. Muted strains of cheering and belly laughs came from within.

"That's it! That's our taverna. Oh, my dear, you have not lived until you've spent an evening in an Athenian taverna. Come, come!"

They carefully took to the steps and were greeted by a small, slender elderly gentleman with disheveled clothing and a welcoming, drunken smile. Walking through the small concrete box of a room, she took in the sights of the food in the display cases and the geriatric cooks slowly constructing peasant food. Their table rocked, and the chair legs dug into the dirt floor. She beamed at Mitchell.

"Give me your mink. We must save the mink!" His speaking voice was getting a bit animated. The effects of days of drinking were starting to kick in. He carefully folded the beautiful antique fur so that the lining was exposed and all the fur was protected. "Remember, my dear, the proper way to stow a coat."

The waiter approached them, but with no language in common, the best Mitchell could do was point to the large metal jugs being passed around other tables to signal that they, too, would like some wine. His sign language worked, and the table was soon filled with two large vessels and four glasses. They each had a glass of red and a glass of white. Since they had been drinking for over twenty-four hours at that point, quality was not as relevant as quantity, and they were both happy.

She started to feel more comfortable with him, and he seemed to let his guard down with her. The roaring laughter filling the cramped space was contagious, and soon they were laughing wildly at bad jokes they shared.

At one point, Mitchell became physically charged and spoke with great sweeping arm gestures. Timing intervened, and a passing waiter was accidentally struck by a wayward hand. An entire jug of red wine covered Mitchell. She was about to gasp at the notion of his ridiculously expensive tailored shirt being destroyed by this cheap Greek wine, but his next action stopped her response: Mitchell grabbed a pitcher of white wine that the waiter held with his other hand and, without skipping a beat, poured it all over himself. Like magic, the entire red wine stain disappeared. She watched in awe.

"Let that be a lesson to you. The only thing on this planet that can eliminate a red wine stain is white wine. But you have to act fast."

"That's amazing. I mean, wow." She hardly noticed the waiter in her periphery who was standing frozen, a look of unmitigated shock overwhelming his composure.

Mitchell laughed it off, then asked her if she'd like any dessert before they headed back to the hotel. She explained that she had no fondness for sweets, but that she'd love to try some Greek cheese.

"Okay, well, go to the display case and point to what you'd like." She staggered over to the cases of food and pointed vigorously to the blocks of cheese. The man behind the counter nodded, and she returned to the table. "Did you find what you want?"

"I just pointed to the cheese in general. We'll see what comes out."

They settled back into conversation, most of which was focused on her excitement for learning the new stain removal trick. Mitchell asked for some more wine, and as they enjoyed, she speculated on what was taking the cheese so long to arrive. As though on cue, the waiter appeared with a plate in his hands. He placed it in front of her, and Mitchell and she almost lost their balance from such deep laughter. The plate contained a solitary unsliced apple.

Through tears of comedy, she questioned aloud what had gone wrong. She knew her Greek was bad, but she was surprised that apparently her sign language skills were worse. Pushing the apple plate away, she announced to Mitchell that she was ready to leave as soon as she had used the ladies' room.

The path to the outdoor bathrooms was winding and uneven, but she walked it without incident. While turning to flush the toilet when she was finished, she saw one of the funniest picture signs she had ever seen. She contemplated stealing it but quickly shook off the thought and opted to memorize it in detail to relate back to Mitchell.

The sign was similar to those found in women's bathrooms internationally: a red circle with a slash through it indicating what not to flush. Usual items behind the slash were sanitary napkins or tampons. But this sign had a wine bottle. As in, *Please don't flush your empty wine bottles.* In her mind, she could not even imagine what plumbing trauma in this taverna's history had demonstrated the need for this sign. She couldn't wait to tell Mitchell about it on the walk back.

The next day, Mitchell chartered a taxi and they sped through the city, quickly taking in sites. As time grew closer to noon, they began discussing destination options. They decided on a hilltop accessible by tram. The view from the mountaintop was gorgeous, but Mitchell was out of shape, and a long walk was clearly not in their future. Instead, not surprisingly, they settled at a table on the roof deck of a small café and ordered a bottle of wine.

As they waited for the waitress to return, Mitchell began to school her in the lore of Grecian wine. She was an avid student of oenology, but even her knowledge base was limited in reference to the many varietals unique to Greece that few Americans had the opportunity, or desire, to sample.

The rest of the afternoon was wasted in wine and conversation, and when they grew bored, they took the tram back to the waiting taxi. For a fleeting moment, she thought it odd that Mitchell had paid the driver to wait all those hours instead of hiring a new cab, but she didn't dare question his logic.

At the hotel, Instead of heading right to the room, the two decided to take tea in the grand parlor and enjoy a little champagne. As they chatted, Mitchell steered the conversation toward their environs and the fact that they hadn't even known each other a full week. He then leaned in close to her and asked, "Do you want this?"

"Want what?"

"All of this. The life. The pageantry. Travel. Do you want to be my Jackie O?"

She wasn't sure how to respond to such a direct question, and she hesitated. Perhaps, in the deepest layer of her subconscious, she knew she was making a pact with Satan, but her myopia overtook her, and she quietly whispered, "Yes."

"My dear, you are going to have a life you've never dreamed possible. The best of the best, a true jet setter, a socialite. Women will want to be you; women will fuck you to be close to you."

His crass statement took her by surprise, but he was quite serious. She was morbidly curious.

"You, my dear, are now a lady of means. A woman of status. An elegant tour de force. A beacon of refinement, and the embodiment of sex and power." He spoke so convincingly that she felt the excitement palpitate in her chest. She had no idea what to expect, and she was scared to find out. But she knew her life had just changed.

"Pick up the waitress."

"How do you mean?"

"Pick up the waitress. Make her beg you to fuck her."

"You want me to fuck the waitress?" She was confused, but her interest was piqued.

"No, silly girl, I want the waitress to *want* you to fuck her. You're not going to, but I want you to learn how to capture women to bring them to me. I want

you to pick up the waitress. Be hard and strong. Trust me, women respond.
I know."

The waitress returned with a round of drinks and set the wine down in
front of him and a scotch down in front of her. Mitchell looked at the waitress
with both longing and contempt, and then returned his gaze to his companion. The waitress scurried off, and Mitchell began his lesson.

"You see, my dear, you are young and rich and beautiful. I am old and fat.
So if I want to get my cock sucked, I need to know that you can deliver fucktoys to me. Do you understand?" She nodded, as though she did, and waited
for him to continue. "When the waitress returns, you mince no words. You
tell her you want to fuck her; you pretend that you care to know more about
her; you feign interest." Mitchell noted her apprehension and tried to reassure
her. "You look worried. But trust me, all you have to say is that. She'll come to
you. They always fall for the powerful, gorgeous rich girl."

"But I'm not rich."

"You are now."

The waitress returned to replenish the nuts, and the freshly minted rich
girl began to hunt her prey. She followed Mitchell's instructions exactly and
assertively announced, "I want to fuck you."

The waitress blushed and in broken English stuttered her reply, "You want
. . . to . . . fuck me?"

"Yes. I want to fuck you. You are beautiful, and graceful, and a perfect toy."
A glance toward Mitchell ensured she was efficiently delivering the dialogue.

"Yes. . . . Okay. . . . You I want fuck me. . . . What room do you staying in?"
the waitress replied.

Mitchell intervened. "No, sweet girl, you are just a waitress in a hotel in
Greece. I am the family lawyer sent along on my lady's travels to chaperone
her. You are not of the caliber of pussy that warrants fucking. We'd like the
check please." Embarrassed and confused, the waitress scampered off.

"Why did you do that? Why did you ask me to get you the waitress if you
were going to insult her?" The situation felt both uncomfortable and frivolous.

"My dear, I did not insult her. She insulted you by thinking that she was
worthy to be your fucktoy. I just wanted to make sure that you were able to
take instruction and that you were ready and willing to make things happen.
Thank you."

"Oh. Okay. Well. Hmmm. Just let me know when and what, and I'll do my
best to make you happy."

"I know you will, my dear. I really know you will." Mitchell reclined and
smiled an evil, infectious grin.

They retreated to their room and Mitchell seemed still energized from their
encounter with the waitress. "Let's keep the momentum going."

"What do you mean?"

"Do you have any gorgeous friends back in New York whom you can line up for a fucking session when we return? You need a bit of practice, and it's always best to practice with a prequalified friend."

She thought hard. With one of her college roommates, she had once experienced a failed threesome. Maybe that was a good choice? "Well, I can contact my college roommate, Amy."

"Was she submissive to you?"

"I don't know. She always seemed to look up to me. And Amy mostly followed what I said."

"Do you have her email address?"

"I think. Somewhere online." She racked her brain, trying to think where she had stored Amy's address.

"My computer is over there." Mitchell pointed to the bureau. "Email Amy and set something up."

Obediently, she turned on Mitchell's computer and searched her email database to find Amy's address. It took less time than she had anticipated, and she quickly composed a note.

In Greece. Returning next week. Swing by for dinner? Up for playtime? xxx

The note was short and to the point. Either Amy would respond or not. Surprisingly, a response came within moments.

Sure. Let me know when and where. Btw, Greece? Wow. Why? Tell me when I see you. Can't wait. Kisses, Amy

"Amy's on board. She wants to get together." She was careful not to introduce any false hope into the equation. She didn't know what Mitchell expected of a visit from Amy, but she didn't want to anger or disappoint him.

"Amy responded already?" Mitchell laughed. "What a slut."

The short vacation week progressed, and Mitchell and his new companion spent hours eating, drinking, and fancifully planning future excursions. The Greek Isles; no. The Seychelles; perhaps next week. South Africa; definitely before winter set in there.

She was apprehensive that any of it would happen, but they *were* in Greece, so Mitchell had been true to his word so far. As she settled in for a massage in the luxurious hotel spa, she allowed herself to release her doubts and get lost in the decadence of that moment in time.

❦

After they returned to New York, Mitchell insisted that the cab return them to his apartment because her belongings were in his luggage. She quickly unpacked, and they shared a bottle of wine. She wanted to go home; it had been a tiring trip, and an exhausting, drunken trip home. Mitchell seemed to ignore her not-so-subtle gestures toward the door.

"Let's order some takeout!"

She looked around his tarped apartment and declined.

"Then let's go out!"

"Mitchell, I'm really tired. Plus, it's getting late."

"Fine, fine. Here's money for a taxi." He handed her two fifty-dollar bills and held the front door open. "I'll call you in the morning."

She put the money in the zipper compartment of the Burberry handbag and walked toward the uptown subway, which was only a block away.

Four

"Good morning, beautiful!"

She held the telephone receiver groggily. "Good morning, Mitchell." It was 10 a.m., but she hadn't gotten home until close to midnight, and she was hoping for a little more sleep. She rolled over in her bed, still keeping the phone close to her ear.

"Come over!" Mitchell sounded cheerful and playful, and she was happy that he was in good spirits.

"When?"

"Now, foolish girl! Oh, and I want you to stop and get me a *New York Times* on your way. I'll pay you back."

"Now?"

"Now. Take a taxi. I'll pay for that, too." Clearly, she had no say in the matter, and he knew exactly how he'd like the morning to unfold. "I'll see you in a half hour!"

With no time to shower, she quickly threw on some clothes that he would want her to wear, put a comb through her hair, and walked briskly to the subway. On the way, she purchased a newspaper from a kiosk.

At around 11 a.m., she arrived at Mitchell's building. The doorman was expecting her and called Mitchell from the in-house lobby phone to alert him to her arrival while simultaneously gesturing her toward a waiting elevator.

"Good morning, Mrs. Durman," the elevator operator greeted her.

She thought briefly of correcting him, but then realized that Mitchell had clearly not been residing in the building for long, and that the staff was only just getting to know him.

Mitchell's apartment door was left ajar in anticipation of her arrival, and as she entered, he immediately inquired about the newspaper.

"I have it."

"Good girl."

She hated to be referred to as "good girl"; it conjured up memories of her father's patronizing tone. But she brushed it off.

"Yes, sir, I have the *Times*. I'm leaving it on the coffee table."

Mitchell was in the bathroom at the time and speaking to her through the door.

"Good. Okay, my dear, I want you to go into my fag bag and find my ATM card. Please withdraw one thousand dollars. Buy a case of wine—use your judgment."

"Okay, Mitchell," she spoke through the bathroom door. "What's your PIN?"

"It's my son's name."

She had forgotten that Mitchell had briefly mentioned a seven-year-old son. But she looked at the key pad on her cell phone and figured out the numerical code for the four-character name without questioning him further, and she headed down the street with the ATM card in her pocket.

The code worked, and she retrieved one thousand dollars, making sure to obtain a receipt. She then walked over a block to Lexington Avenue and ventured into the wine shop. She picked out twelve reasonably priced, high-quality bottles.

When she returned to his apartment, Mitchell was lounging in his boxers on the leather sofa. He jumped when she entered.

"Oh good, my dear, you found the wine. Sit. I'll bring you a glass."

"Okay, yeah, thanks. I have your change, too."

"Oh, my dear, that's yours. 'Girl walking around money,' I call it. You use it, keep it, whatever. Girls never have any money, do they? So convenient!" Mitchell laughed, and she apprehensively put the eight hundred dollars-plus into her handbag. It more than covered the cost of the subway down and the newspaper purchased en route. He seemed genuine, but she really couldn't tell.

"Come, my dear, let's watch Fox News together."

She laughed; he couldn't be serious. But he was, and he couldn't understand why she was laughing.

"Okay. Really, you watch Fox News?"

"Is there any other station?"

"Well, you're Jewish. . . . I'm just surprised you're Republican."

"My dear, you have much to learn. Come sit by me. Drink your wine. Learn. Learn."

She glanced at the clock on the cable box; it was still morning. But she figured that this was one of those small fish to fry and just listened to the newscast.

After a half hour or so, Mitchell asked her if she was ready for lunch. She wasn't sure if there was a right or wrong answer, but he jumped in before she could decide anyway. "We'll go to Tino's!" Mitchell exclaimed. "You can have run of the menu! Anything you want! You love to eat, right?"

"Ummm, I guess."

"Ummm. Ummm. Only low class people say 'ummm.' You sometimes make me sick, beautiful. Anyway, get ready, look beautiful—we're going to Tino's."

She went into the bathroom, fixed her hair, and adjusted her bust in her bra. She didn't quite understand Mitchell's priorities, but they all seemed to mesh with hers, so she didn't think too hard. Mitchell had asked her to wear the clothing she normally reserved for formal occasions, and even though she felt uncomfortable traipsing around town in her nice clothes in the middle of a weekday, he assured her that she looked dynamic. His opinion meant more to her than her own, although she didn't know why.

She had never been to Tino's, and when they entered, she realized why. She was the youngest, and certainly the poorest, of all the clientele. Mitchell fit in, just barely. They were seated in the best seat in the house; out of the way of foot traffic but visible to all staff and other customers.

The menu was expansive, with some of her favorite foods—calves' brain, sweetbreads, calamari, veal chop; she was happy enough. Mitchell ordered a bottle of wine, and the food began to arrive.

"My dear, I think we will eat here for lunch every day that we are in New York. Brains every day!" Mitchell threw his head back in almost a patronizing laugh. "You do love your offal!"

"Offal?"

"Offal. Organ meats. Oh no, my dear, you're twenty-three years old. You can't love something and not know everything about it. So much to learn, so much to learn." Mitchell sighed, and she felt embarrassed. Most people thought she was intelligent, but Mitchell made her feel inadequate.

The waiter was a nice-looking middle-aged Frenchman who was clearly well versed in the art of fine service. He was available, yet not hovering, and helpful, yet not overbearing. She liked him.

The meal was fine, not memorable, and she and Mitchell began to wander into various topics.

"My son and his mother are coming into town this weekend," he said.

She nodded but was surprised that he referred to the mother of his child as "my son's mother," and not "my ex."

"I'm not happy about it. She is a horrible woman who wants to destroy me. Nothing is enough for her, and she's trying to bleed me dry and make me miserable in the meantime."

She made a mental note that they were on the third bottle of wine; perhaps that was the catalyst for his moaning. But she brushed off the notion and feigned sympathy.

"I'm sorry, Mitchell. But aren't you excited to see your son?"

"I love my son. He's amazing. A wonderful little guy. But his mother is a monster. A goddamn monster." Mitchell pounded his fist forcefully on the table, and she was startled by his angst. How had a simple little lunch turned into such an emotionally powerful event?

"My son's mother is going to be here tomorrow. On Valentine's Day. *She* is not my valentine. *You*, my dear, are my valentine. Ugh. Do we have more wine?"

"Of course, Mitchell." She refilled his glass with the remaining Chianti and half-heartedly tried to raise his spirits. In all honesty, she didn't really care much about his complaining since it sounded to her as though he were being a bit of a drama queen. "Aren't you excited to see your son?" She repeated, ignoring his previous outburst.

"Uuuuck." Mitchell snarled. "Let's get home. Are we finished here?"

She hoped that Mitchell meant *her* home and not his; she was tired and hadn't spent any time at home in an entire week. But she knew that she would be stuck at *his* home, patiently waiting for his cue to let her leave. It became oddly apparent that she had somehow surrendered her ability to delegate her own time; not that she had much else to do. Hopefully, the presence of his visitors would give her a bit of a reprieve.

❧

"Can I go home now?" She was exhausted and looking forward to a good night's sleep. It was early in the evening, but she just couldn't imagine staying awake much longer. A combination of drinking and jetlag was doing her in.

"Contact Amy," Mitchell commanded.

"What?"

"Amy. Amy. You said that you'd have her come over when we were back from Greece." Mitchell threw up his arms and motioned around his freshly painted apartment. "We're home! Have her come over."

Without questioning him, she went into Mitchell's study and logged into her email account to send a message to Amy. A message came back quickly asking for an address and a time.

She called out to Mitchell in the living room. "Amy wants the address and a time. What do I write back?"

"Tell her to come as soon as she can and give her my address," Mitchell responded curtly, as though the answer were obvious.

Amy sent a note saying that she worked only a couple of blocks away, and she would be there as soon as possible.

"Amy's on her way," she reported, as she took a seat on the couch.

"Good," Mitchell replied, his eyes glued to the television. "It will do you some good to reconnect with your old friends."

It wasn't long before the doorman buzzed the intercom to report a visitor. Amy must have really been nearby.

Amy looked the same as she had in college; maybe a little heavier, but smartly dressed and very much the New York sophisticate. The girls kissed each other on both cheeks, and she led Amy into the living room to meet Mitchell.

After all the pleasantries were exchanged, Mitchell asked Amy, "So I believe that you may be submissive to our friend here?"

Amy blushed; Mitchell was being very direct. "How do you mean?"

Mitchell continued the interrogation, "Would you do anything she asked?"

"Anything? Like what?" Amy was coy.

Mitchell turned his attention to his female companion. "Make her do something. Have her get naked."

Amy had been a dear friend, and though they hadn't been close in some time, this was a very strange situation. Taking a deep breath, she took Mitchell's cue and commanded, "Take your clothes off."

As though entranced, Amy disrobed.

"Now go into the bedroom and lie on the bed," she instructed.

Amy marched into the bedroom and threw herself onto Mitchell's bed.

Not knowing what to do next, she turned to Mitchell. He motioned exasperatedly toward the naked woman on his bed. "Get a dildo out of my closet."

She found a large red vibrator sitting on one of the middle shelves and brought it to the bed.

"Now have Amy put it in her pussy."

With her voice shaking, she handed off the red dong and said in a monotone, "Put this in your pussy."

"Say it like you mean it!" Mitchell barked.

"Put this in your pussy!" She repeated, with oomph.

Amy quickly obliged, without hesitation. There Amy lay, gyrating around a big rubber cock.

"Now tell her to put it in her asshole," Mitchell commanded.

"Put it in your asshole!" She dictated.

"Now, I'm going to pull out my cock." Mitchell undid his trousers. "Tell Amy to suck it."

"Suck Mitchell's cock!"

Amy obliged, and horrified, she watched as her dear college friend fellated Mitchell and gyrated around a fake appendage lodged in her ass.

Mitchell didn't cum. Instead, he removed his cock from Amy's mouth and zipped his pants. To Amy, he said, "You liked that, didn't you!"

Amy nodded.

"Good. Clean yourself up." Mitchell spat in her direction. "You little whore."

She and Mitchell seated themselves in the living room while Amy put herself back together. After only a few minutes, Amy reemerged.

"How would you girls like to go to dinner?" Mitchell asked. "There's a very hot restaurant slash nightclub around the corner. A real hotspot. They love me there."

"Sounds great!" Amy exclaimed.

Amy's friend was less than enthusiastic. She wasn't hungry at all, and she had now lost respect for one of the few friends she still had from college. But she just nodded in unison with Mitchell and Amy and went to put on her coat.

The trio sat in a corner booth in the sushi lounge of one of New York's hottest new restaurants, just around the corner from Mitchell's building. Amy was seated in the middle, and Mitchell ignored the girls as he ordered bottles of both wine and sake, and a feast of food from the chef.

Trying to take charge, she draped her arms over the back of the booth, in a commanding position that almost looked as though she were about to take flight. Amy seemed oblivious to her role as sandwich meat while delving into the food that began to arrive.

"Let's all kiss," Mitchell suggested, as though the idea had just come to him.

Without a second thought, Amy turned toward her former roommate and jammed her tongue in her mouth. They were exposed in the restaurant, but she wanted Amy to be comfortable, and she decided that if she kissed Amy with confidence, the other diners would just think it was a typical event. This was New York City after all.

After the girls kissed, Amy turned to kiss Mitchell. The passing of the kisses repeated several times, and then all three turned their attention to the food.

While Amy was leaning over the table eating, Mitchell twisted his neck behind her back and said to his companion, "Take her into the ladies' room and make out with her in a stall."

"What?" She was confused. They had just made out at a table. Wasn't that good enough?

"I want you to learn that all action takes place in the ladies' room. Trust me." Mitchell nodded in a way that suggestively shooed the girls out of the booth.

"Amy, let's go to the girls' room."

Amy stood up, and the two went up the stairs and into the cramped, two-stall ladies' room.

When a stall became available, she took Amy by the hand, and they squished into the narrow space together. Four feet were exposed in the stall next to them, and she realized that Mitchell was right; there was a lot of action in the ladies' room. She and Amy made out for a few minutes, and when she thought that enough time had elapsed, she led Amy back to the table.

Mitchell grinned and opened his arms benevolently. "Did you girls have fun in the ladies' room?" He winked in hyperbole.

"Mitchell, you know that all action happens in the ladies' room." She returned his wink.

The girls sat down to finish the meal. Amy seemed happy. Mitchell seemed happy. But she? She was counting the moments until this nightmare evening was over.

Five

"I'm downstairs! Wake up! Come down!"

She blinked her eyes and yawned while reaching one arm out from under her duvet to find the clock on her nightstand. It was only 8 a.m., which wouldn't have been a hardship except that Mitchell hadn't allowed her to return home the night before until nearly 2 a.m. Lack of sleep was mounting.

"Yeah, Mitchell?"

"Yeah? *Yeah*? Do young ladies say *yeah*?"

"No, sir."

"Mitchell. Not 'sir.' Don't patronize me."

"I'm sorry."

"Right, beautiful." The tone of his voice returned to crooning. "You love it when I call you 'beautiful.' And you are beautiful. You are! Now, get dressed and come downstairs. *Now*."

"Yes, Mitchell."

"Oh, and dress like a real person." And with that, he ended the call.

She was confused by the entire situation, but at least she knew how to dress. When Mitchell referred to "real people," he was targeting a particular sort of everyday formal attire. She rummaged through her tiny standing wardrobe and found a pair of Joseph slacks and a Theory button-down shirt to pair with it. And, of course, she put on the new Armani shoes.

Carefully moving quickly down the flights of stairs, she realized that she had forgotten to do as much as her hair. She shrugged off the moment and scurried into his waiting car, where he sat reading his newspaper for a moment before acknowledging her presence.

Eventually, Mitchell leaned over to kiss her a greeting. Then he glanced over her ensemble and sarcastically smirked. "My, *that's* an interesting look."

"Oh, I'm sorry. I can change." She spoke earnestly, and in a way that she noted was a bit out of character.

"No, no. That's fine. No time. Besides, you look far better than any other of your fellow Americans."

She thought it odd that he referred to Americans almost as though he weren't one himself. But she supposed that disdain for one's own was a fairly common sentiment, and one that had been repeated throughout history— granted, mostly by fascist dictators, but commonly so nonetheless.

"So, we are very busy. My son and my son's mother are coming in to town later today, and first I need to pick up the dry cleaning, go to the bank, and go to the Sprint store to get a new Trio. Mine broke, see?" Mitchell handed her several pieces of a former PDA cell phone, and she chose not to question how it fell apart.

"Okay. Why do you need me?"

"What? Why do I need you? You don't want to come? Fine! You have something better to do?"

"No, I'm sorry, I just meant—"

"I know what you meant, my dear. I *need* you to come so that you can sit in the car when I idle it in case you have to move it out of a no-standing zone."

"Okay." She convinced herself that his logic actually made sense.

They sped down Second Avenue, and he pulled over into a bus-only zone and left her in the car while he ran in to pick up his clean garments. He then sped around the block and pulled into another bus-only zone close to his bank. He returned moments later, sat in the driver's seat for a moment counting his cash into his Goyard "fag bag," and unceremoniously handed her six fifty-dollar bills. "Girl walking around money," he said to her. And then, to no one in particular, "No, girls never seem to have any money when they're walking around. 'Girl walking around money.' Ha!"

He turned the car around and sped up Third Avenue, back toward where they had started. "We're going to the cell phone store. For *my* cell phone. We're not buying anything for you, got it?"

"Uh, yeah. Sorry, yes. I know that." She couldn't figure out why he had said that, but she didn't really care. She just wanted to go home, and she was happy that the Sprint store was in her neighborhood and not his. That increased her odds of getting to take off her ridiculously formal outfit and relax in peace and quiet.

"Can I park here?"

"What?" She looked around, confused.

"Can. I. Park. Here. Can I park here? Read the sign. Don't be an imbecile."

"Sorry. Right. Ummm. . . ." She strained her neck to angle her eyes around the blind spot in the car windshield and read the traffic directional tacked to the signpost. "Yes. Yes, you can park here. It's Saturday morning; that's not one of the no-parking times listed."

"Good. Then you can get out with me. Come on, move. Move! Let's go."

She hopped out of the car and stood on the sidewalk awaiting his next instruction. He paused to read the sign she had just read to him, which was sort of offensive. But she had already realized he had little faith in her, even though she knew for certain that she had never given him any reason not to.

Satisfied with what he read, he barked at her, "Come, come, to the Sprint store. Move it!"

She half walked, half jogged behind him; it was hard enough to keep up with the strides of his incredibly long legs, but it was even more difficult in her sling-back heels. Several times, he turned to glower at her for not moving more quickly. But he still made it into the Sprint store nearly thirty seconds before she did, and as he spoke to a staff member, he shot her a look of disapproval as she slid through the door.

She knew enough not to get in his way while he conducted his business, so she tried to make herself scarce as she wandered through the display racks and pretended to play with the phones. He finished rather quickly, although she couldn't help but notice that the young black man assisting Mitchell seemed a bit shaken by the time the transaction concluded. His attitude toward people in serving roles, his booming voice, and his affected manner of speaking was intimidating.

Mitchell walked toward the door, turned to give her a saccharin-sweet smile, and silently held the door as he motioned her through. Out on the sidewalk, he bemoaned, "Now, that man was an incompetent. Through and through. I'll teach you to manage losers like that. Anyway, at least I have a new phone." Mitchell quickened his pace toward nowhere in particular. "Do you know anywhere for lunch?"

"Sure, there are a few nice places in the area if we go toward—" She was cut off as Mitchell abruptly turned north on Lexington Avenue. "Oh, okay, I was going to name some places the other direction, but I guess we'll go this way."

She quickened her pace, and in doing so, accidentally pierced the back seam of her slacks with her sharp heels. She hoped that Mitchell hadn't noticed, and she made a mental note to have the large hole repaired by the tailor immediately; she didn't have many nice pieces of clothing, and she didn't want to be chastised for her lack of presentability.

The two passed a running store, and she playfully expressed that a pair of sturdy sneakers rather than high heels would be more suitable for following such a tall man through city passageways.

Mitchell sneered at her. "Then, my dear, we will by you some . . . sneakers." Mitchell coughed an elitist scoff and held the door to the running store open for her to pass through.

"Are you being serious, or are you teasing me?" She had yet to learn his signals, and for some reason, she feared his wrath, or worse, his loathing.

"My dear, I am always serious. I said that I would buy you sneakers, and now I will. So go—go pick out your shoes."

She chose a pair of red running sneakers, which fit perfectly, and before she could shop around to compare, Mitchell had already paid for them and announced that she would be wearing them home. "And remember who buys you things, my dear. Remember who cares about you. I do. Who else? I do." Mitchell sternly insisted.

"Yes, Mitchell. Thank you."

"That's right. Come along"

Much more comfortable in the running shoes, she walked beside Mitchell as he led her along Eighty-Sixth Street back toward Second Avenue. He passed his car, nodded in approval that it had not been cited for a parking violation, and made a quick move to walk south. She followed, unsure of where they were headed. She was hungry, but she was always hungry.

For years, she had been the self-made victim of compulsive exercise, and even though she no longer slaved to her daily constitutional, her metabolism and digestive tract still bore the scars. She was often famished, even faint and dizzy. But when she ate to contentment, she was often plagued with diarrhea or unwilled, graceful regurgitation of the bulk of her meal. It was her own private demon, one she hoped to keep secret, though her slight frame and anxious appetite betrayed her silence. Still, she knew there was little she could hide from Mitchell. He would address any issues he felt pertinent to attack.

They walked down Second Avenue, and Mitchell pointed out an Italian restaurant that she had often passed but had never entered. "Let's see the wine list, shall we?" It was less of a question than a discourse, and she obviously voiced no objections.

Once seated, she ordered some fried calamari while Mitchell read over the list. At once, he became excited and almost seemed as though he were going to fly out of his chair. "They have a '96 Gaja Chardonnay for eighty-eight dollars. A '96! That's unheard of! They have no idea what a gem they have. Remember, my dear, the secret to a wine list is *value*. Not price. Value. And this. Well, this is a value!"

They ordered a bottle of the Gaja, and then another, as they settled into an otherwise unremarkable meal. Mitchell leaned toward her and whispered, "When a wine is this well priced, it's as though they've given you the meal for free with the bottle. And that, my dear, is value." Changing the subject, he asked her if she'd ever had mozzarella en carozza. "You'll love the sardine-caper sauce. Ugh!" He chided, to himself it seemed, "You'll love it!"

She did, in fact, enjoy the meal and the time spent that day with Mitchell, but she knew his family had to have been in town by then, and she wondered why he was stalling in going home to them.

Eventually, the meal ended, and he sent her home. Thankful, she arrived home and quickly freed herself from her oppressive clothing and slipped into some at-home loungewear. She settled in for a quiet Valentine's Day at home—alone.

❧

"Beautiful? Are you awake? I want to take my valentine out for dinner!"

She focused her eyes on her clock; it was 11:45 p.m. She tried to rouse herself from her slumber and attempt a coherent conversation. "Why are you calling, Mitchell?"

"You're my valentine! I want to take you out. I'm tired of being at my apartment with my son and my son's mother. I want to be out with someone I care about." Mitchell paused. "Are you ready to go out?"

"Sure," she lied.

"Great!" He seemed genuinely excited. "I'll be downstairs in two minutes. I'm just coming up Third now!"

Crap, she thought, as she thrust her tired body out of bed. So much for her quiet night at home. She quickly dressed, donning a similar outfit to the one she had worn earlier that day. But she altered it by putting on a different top and this time remembering to comb her hair.

She sprinted down the stairs with her high heels in hand and opened her front door just as Mitchell pulled up.

"So, where to?" Mitchell asked, without the faintest trace of sarcasm.

"What?"

"Where *to*?" he repeated, as though she would now magically have an answer.

She was just barely awake and certainly had not put any thought into the venue for a valentine's dinner she had not anticipated. "Oh, I don't know. Anywhere, I guess. Wherever the kitchen's still open." She made a deliberate motion of looking at her wrist, staring at the watch on it.

Mitchell smiled at her smugly. He knew that he had awakened her, and he was proud that she was not complaining.

"Okay, we'll drive down Second Avenue and see what looks hot. Sound good?"

"Sounds great," she agreed, although she really just wanted to go back to bed.

They drove slowly past a Mediterranean restaurant several blocks away that seemed to be bustling in its late-night service. Mitchell turned toward her and asked, rhetorically, "This looks perfect, don't you think?"

At just a little before midnight, they were seated in the restaurant. "We need some champagne now, while it's still Valentine's Day," Mitchell instructed the hostess who seated them. As she scurried off, he turned toward his exhausted companion and explained, "In an establishment such as this, you expect poor selection, garbage quality, and loser clientele." He used his head to motion toward the other diners. "See? Losers. All of them." And then, as though realizing a plan on the spot, Mitchell said, "Actually, I'm going to teach you how to steal a woman from another man or couple!"

Mitchell seemed genuinely excited, but as she sipped the champagne, she really wasn't eager for another lesson in world-mental domination. Certainly not at this late hour.

"Do you see that thin, bleached, fake-tit blonde with that couple?" Mitchell pointed at a distant table. "Let's steal her!" He then lowered his volume. "Remember, we don't want to fuck her; she's a dirt bag loser. But you need to learn how to steal a fucktoy. She's all primed, after all. Why should that bitch go home with that couple when she thinks she can come back to fuck us? I'm more rich, after all." He laughed demonically.

She looked over at the three overly made up, naturally ugly people in their mid-thirties. They were clearly from out of town—probably New Jersey—and their attempts to fit in to New York society only made them look bizarre and stand out even more. It was clear to her which of the women was the third wheel and which belonged in a couple with the man. The man beamed with pride that two women were going to suck his cock that night after dinner. Never mind that neither woman was even remotely worth a second glance.

She turned back toward Mitchell in confusion. It was truly a mystery to her as to why he would want to break up a group of clearly boring and unworthy bridge-and-tunnel folks for mere sport. And though she didn't want to sound crass, she truly had no desire to mingle with any of them. In all honesty, the idea of picking up any woman was unsavory to her, but the thought of picking up an over-the-hill bottle blonde was about as unappealing a vision as she had fought out of her mind.

"My dear, the art of picking up a woman is boring. Easy. Women are needy and desperate. *But* to take one from a man with whom she is already aligned is a skill. A game. A victory." Mitchell laughed, as though remembering a previous encounter in his life. "I learned a long time ago that when you're out with pussy, you never, ever go to the bathroom. Some dirt bag will always steal your bitch. I know. I've done it. Both lost and stolen." He laughed harder. "The men are dicks in St. Tropez. Remember that I've warned you. And," his voice became dark and void of its previous playful character, "if you ever leave with another man from somewhere to which I've brought you, I will hunt you down, and," now Mitchell hissed, "I will squash you like a bug. Like a *bug*."

Mitchell was so overly dramatic and drunk that she just shrugged him off. She was tired and had little energy to spare in even paying attention to what he said, let alone how he said it. Her apathy seemed to calm him and diffuse the situation. Mitchell settled back into his chair and gnawed at his lamb chops, gripping the tiny bones tightly with his large, strong hands. And he never took his eyes off the three-top.

In a moment that truly took her by surprise, she realized that Mitchell was speaking with the platinum blonde. The transition into conversation was so smooth that she almost missed it. The woman was giggling and playfully tossing her overly treated locks. Mitchell feigned interest to the degree that his observant companion almost believed that he really wanted to go home with the woman.

Eventually, Ms. B&T moved her seat from her former lovers' table to theirs and began to swoon over Mitchell and his elegant valentine.

It was late at night, and Mitchell's young valentine just wanted to go to sleep. But Mitchell was working to prove a point, and so she chugged champagne and used her index fingers to prop her eyelids open as her chin rested on her palm, with her elbow on the table bearing most of the weight. Mitchell seemed not to notice the effort she exerted to remain present, and he continued his bizarre conquest of the tramp.

Eventually, she and Mitchell were alone with the woman; the friends had abandoned the bitch when it appeared that the bitch had abandoned them. Mitchell's companion repeatedly checked her watch, bored as the B&T whore threw herself at them, patiently waiting for Mitchell to agree that he had grown bored as well.

Finally, the bottle-blonde tramp blatantly threw herself at Mitchell and his companion, and this was enough to disgust him.

Mitchell was a powerhouse in the art of blank expression, and his companion could only hope that he recognized that it was well after 3 a.m. and that she was craving the warmth of her bed.

He dramatically dismissed the B&T conquest and turned his attention back toward his companion. "You'd fuck her in the ass, right?"

"Sure. Anything. After a good night's sleep. Can I go to sleep?"

"Ha!" Mitchell smirked at her antagonistically.

"Why is that funny?" She was honestly confused. "It's four in the morning; I just want to sleep, but I'm trying to follow your lead. And, well, honestly, Mitchell, I'm confused. What are we? Where are we? Who am I?"

"Sit, imbecile! Quiet!" Mitchell demanded. Obviously, he was actively avoiding being at his apartment with his son's mother, but she did not appreciate being used as a pawn in the excuse. And she most certainly did not want to fuck the old hag from the suburbs in the ass. Or anywhere else for that matter.

She stifled a sigh, but Mitchell saw the sigh register in her eyes.

"I'm sorry, my dear. My valentine. You look gorgeous this evening; I wanted to make sure that I told you that again."

"Thank you, Mitchell."

"Come, come, we'll get you into bed. You've been a good little girl tonight."

"Thank you, Mitchell."

They returned to his car, which was now one of the only cars still parked on Second Avenue at that time of night. He swung around the block, raced up First Avenue, turned again, and idled in front of her house. Then, he cut the engine and told her that he'd like to see her apartment.

Mitchell hadn't yet expressed interest in seeing where she lived, and she blushed as though flattered, although she couldn't imagine why. They climbed all the flights of stairs, and Mitchell, as out of shape and drunk as he was, managed to get to her door without breathing too heavily. He peered in, and she welcomed him inside.

"No, thank you. I've seen enough." Mitchell sneered at her home as though fearing infection. "Goodnight. I'll call you in the morning, my dear. Oh, and happy Valentine's Day."

Completely confused, and thoroughly tired, she turned back toward her bathroom to get ready for bed. She caught her own pained expression in the mirror, then shrugged it off and cut the lights, preferring to pee in the dark rather than face her own judgmental reflection.

Six

She had a couple of days respite as Mitchell spent time with his son. She met him for lunch every day, but her presence was mostly kept to a minimum. He had her come to his apartment to meet the boy and to observe the progress of the wall-painting job. His apartment renovations were almost complete; his art deco furniture had arrived, and he was having his walls and ceiling finished in gold leaf to match.

His bedroom set looked a bit like something a wealthy grandmother would own, but she never let him know her opinion. His living room, on the other hand, had oversized black leather sofas, a large glass coffee table, and a huge plasma TV. She figured that its masculine energy offset the femininity of the bedroom set and thought little more of it.

Mitchell's office study had a large gorgeous bankers' desk set in front of a window with a slightly obstructed, yet impressive, view of Central Park. He had purchased a big home safe, and he kept his computer on top of it as though it were meant as furniture. She had helped to program the combination to the safe, and he had made her promise to remember it; he drank heavily, and was clumsy handed, which made slim his chances of opening the complicated mechanism himself. In his safe, he kept hundreds of thousands of dollars worth of foreign currency, as well as jewelry and important paperwork. However, the flimsy closet in the office had a padlock on it, and the combination and contents were a secret to her, which she thought odd.

Mitchell's son was a charming, well-behaved little boy with a round face and dimples. He was polite and playful and didn't question her relationship with Mitchell. In fact, he was almost unsettlingly comfortable with a strange young woman in Mitchell's presence. The boy's mother had never been married to Mitchell, so the boy never thought of himself as the product of a broken home; rather, the boy had never really had a home at all.

The boy's mother and he lived in San Francisco, in a house that Mitchell rented for them. The mother was a strikingly beautiful blonde in her mid-thirties with an outgoing personality and a radiantly pleasant demeanor. The woman was kind and friendly toward Mitchell's new companion and seemed to think nothing of that fact that she was just twenty-three and had known Mitchell for less than two weeks.

The interaction between his son's mother and Mitchell's companion was brief, yet amicable, and the young woman thought in the back of her mind that if they had been the same age, she and the mother would have been fast friends. Their personalities seemed similar, and the two were cool, strong, beautiful, and charismatic in the same way. Mitchell clearly had a type when it came to female companions.

❧

"Tomorrow is my brother's birthday."

"It is? How marvelous! What are you going to do for him?" Mitchell exclaimed on the phone.

"Well, I hadn't really planned anything. My family's not very close. Why?"

"Oh! You should take him out. Bring him into the city!"

"Ummm, well, he goes to school in Princeton. I'm not sure he's up for a trip to the city." She didn't know her brother well and doubted that he'd come up just to spend his birthday with her.

"Of course he is! Family is the most important thing you have in life. You must, *must* do something for your brother on his birthday."

Tim's birthday was exactly ten days after hers, which made the date easy to remember. So he was four years and ten days younger than she. She had been a bit advanced in school, so she had always been substantially older in terms of placement, but Tim was an intelligent, nice-looking boy who had just begun the second semester of his freshman year at Princeton. She was proud of him, but he didn't seem to care.

"Call him. *Call him,*" Mitchell insisted.

"What do you get a boy for his nineteenth birthday?" She really had no idea.

"Oh, silly girl. That's easy. You get him a blowjob."

She laughed into the telephone receiver. "I can't give my brother a blowjob!"

"Listen again. I didn't say that you *give* him a blowjob. I said that you *get* him a blowjob. Take him out to dinner. Send him home with a waitress."

"Take him to dinner?" She couldn't imagine where a young man would want to go on his nineteenth birthday, least of all why he would spend it with his practically estranged sister.

"There must be a place in your neighborhood that's appropriate. Young girls, big tits, greasy food. Think, my dear."

"I know! There's a rib shack near my home that's filled with Hooters-type waitresses and horny men. I bet Tim would love that."

"I bet he would. Invite him there. My treat. Okay?"

"Okay!" She hung up the phone and turned on her computer. She found her brother Tim logged on to his instant messenger account and invited him to dinner on his birthday night. She was a little surprised, yet thrilled, when he accepted the invite.

She called Mitchell to tell him the news. Tim was taking a train up to Manhattan on his birthday and would join her for dinner at the rib joint.

"See? I knew if you reached out to your family, not everyone would be an asshole. I'd love to meet him. What's his name?"

"Tim."

"Timothy?"

"I guess so, but we've always called him Tim."

"Well," Mitchell emphasized, "his name is *Timothy*, and as he is a man, you should call him by his full and proper name."

"My father's name is also Mitchell, but he goes by Mitch."

"Your father has no class, my dear. You know that."

"Ummm. Okay. Anyway, Tim is coming to my apartment at six o'clock tonight, and we're going to the rib joint. Do you really want to join us?"

"I have to stay here with my son and his mother for a while, but let me know the address, and I'll come before the main courses arrive. And remember, it's my treat."

"Okay. Thank you, Mitchell. I'll see you tonight."

Tim arrived only fifteen minutes late, which surprised her, since he truly didn't seem particularly eager to travel the two hours into New York on his birthday. But there he was.

It was an uphill hike to the rib shack, since she lived at the foot of Manhattan's Carnegie Hill, but Tim didn't seem to notice. He had inherited their mother's tall frame and ridiculously long legs. He stood more than a half foot above her and walked with a strong and determined gait that actually impressed her. She took note of his attire: khaki slacks with dirty bucks, a French-cuffed shirt with the sleeves rolled meticulously, a blue blazer, and a large, imposing corduroy brown overcoat that muffled the icy wind. His appearance was almost comical; he looked like the quintessential Princeton preppie. But she kept these thoughts to herself.

In actuality, she was proud of the strong-looking, handsome man that her brother had become. He played football at Princeton, and his broad shoulders and lean frame echoed his athletic accomplishments. Tim had been a nerd his whole life, with thick glasses, imposing orthodontia, terrible bowl haircuts, and hideous clothes. He had clearly found his stride, and with the help of Lasik surgery, a growth spurt, and a shot of good taste, he was now a magnificent man.

"May I see your ID, please?" The bouncer boomed at the entrance to the restaurant.

"Well, he's—"

"Not his. *Yours.*" The bouncer glared at her.

She found it amusing that her baby brother looked older than she, and she was happy to present her driver's license as Tim casually entered the establishment.

"So, what do you think?" she asked Tim, once they were both inside.

"I might like it. You said they have ribs?"

"Yep. Ribs and really hot waitresses. You'll have fun!"

"Okay," Tim answered, neither thrilled nor particularly disappointed. Tim didn't seem to have much of a personality.

They were seated at a small picnic table with a hideous checkerboard table-cloth and a large roll of paper towels sprouting upward at the center of the table. There was a basket filled with barbecue sauce squeeze bottles of varying degrees of heat. The view from the table was over a large projection screen that was playing some ESPN event. Tim looked around and seemed happy. For the first time that night, he smiled.

As the plates from the appetizer course were removed, she sipped her bourbon and called Mitchell again.

"I'm on my way. Heading to pick up my car now."

"Mitchell, why are you getting your car out of the lot? Just grab a cab."

"I like my car. I'll be there soon. You're on Third Avenue, right?"

"Yes, Third Avenue. The entrees are coming soon, so don't take too long, okay?"

"I'm on my way, beautiful. Tell Timothy I'm coming."

She turned back toward her brother, who was focused on a waitress serving the next table. "Tim? Tim? Tim!"

"What?"

"What are you looking at?"

"Nothing."

"Really?"

"Really. Where are my ribs? Where's your boyfriend?" Tim rolled his eyes. "Mitchell."

"He's not my boyfriend. He's my friend. And be nice to him when he gets here. Okay?"

"Uh huh."

Mitchell arrived a few minutes later and sat next to Tim on the picnic table bench. She chuckled to herself because the two men were dressed nearly identically. Clearly, the quality of Mitchell's clothing was better, but the style was exactly the same.

"Hello, Timothy. I'm Mitchell."

"Hello," Tim replied flatly.

The waitress arrived with drink and food menus, and Mitchell dismissed them. "I'd like a beer," Mitchell snarked.

"Okay, sir. What kind of beer?" The waitress stood ready with her pen to paper.

"I would like a beer. In a bottle."

"Right. But which beer?"

"In a *bottle*," Mitchell repeated.

"Sir, we have a large variety of bottled beers."

"Really? How can there be that much of a market for bottled beer?" Mitchell's attitude seemed dismissive and condescending. "Do you have Amstel light?"

"Yes. Would you like one?"

"Now, please. Thank you." And with that, Mitchell turned his focus back toward Tim. "You like that waitress, don't you?"

"What?" Tim seemed caught off guard as he lowered his Heineken from his lips.

"The waitress. You want to *fuck* her." Mitchell smirked.

"Um. What?" Tim desperately turned his eyes back toward his sister, who offered him no consolation. "She's pretty. I guess."

"Watch this," Mitchell taunted. The waitress returned with Mitchell's beer, and he began to speak with her. In hearing his soft, powerful words, she began to flirt with him. Mitchell beckoned her closer, and whispered into her ear. She giggled and walked away. "You're welcome," Mitchell said to Tim.

"For what?" Tim was clueless.

"You'll see. Excuse me, I have to brave the men's room."

As Mitchell stood and exited, Tim turned toward his sister. "I don't like him."

"What?"

"I don't like Mitchell. He's a pretentious asshole." Tim looked seriously concerned. "'Beer in a bottle,' 'beer in a bottle.' Who says that? What a jackass."

She looked at her brother in disbelief. The two men were dressed the same, and in all fairness, Tim was just as condescending as Mitchell. With a feeling of contempt, she replied, "He invited you to dinner on your birthday. Don't be critical. Be nice. Okay? Be nice."

"Uh huh." Tim rolled his eyes again.

Mitchell returned from the bathroom and instructed Tim to go to the men's room immediately.

"I don't have to go," Tim said.

"Yes, you do, boy. *Yes,* you do."

Confused, but intrigued, Tim got up from the table and disappeared.

"I got your brother his birthday present," Mitchell said to her.

"Isn't this dinner his birthday present?" She had no idea what Mitchell meant.

"No, don't be stupid," Mitchell scoffed. "The waitress is his birthday present."

She didn't quite know what Mitchell meant, but she knew better than to ask too many questions. Mainly because she didn't want to know the answers.

Tim returned about fifteen minutes later, looking radiant. He was smiling from ear to ear and thanked Mitchell profusely for the birthday dinner. After the plates were cleared, Mitchell paid the check and offered Tim a ride to wherever he was going.

"I'm staying at my parents'." Tim looked at his sister and corrected himself. "Oh, I meant *our* parents' apartment on Fifty-Ninth Street."

"Our parents have an apartment on Fifty-Ninth Street?" This was the first she had heard of it.

"Yeah. They're just subletting something for now. Mom wants to be in the city. Always has," Tim stated matter-of-factly. Obviously, he was more in tune with their family than she.

"Well," Mitchell interjected, "I'm happy to give you a ride." He looked back at his companion. "Ready to go?"

"Yes. Let's, please. Thank you," she said and prompted Tim to do the same.

"Thank you, Mitchell," Tim said robotically.

They dropped Tim off in front of an obscure doorway, and Mitchell idled the car until Tim found his key and gained access.

"You really didn't know that your parents had an apartment in the city?" Mitchell asked her, once Tim was out of sight.

"I really didn't know," she conceded. "And why the fuck does Tim have a key?"

"Guess they don't love you," Mitchell said.

"Guess not." She wasn't joking.

"Positive note now." Mitchell became playful. "Where would you like to go?"

"I'm easy. Just happy spending time with you," she patronizingly replied. "Where do you want to go?"

"Well, I definitely do not want to go home. My son and his mother are there, and she is a beast." Mitchell pretended to think. "Let's have a drink."

"Okay, let's."

They sat in front of a fireplace at the Library Bar, and she sipped scotch while he plowed through a bottle of wine.

"How is your scotch?"

"Very nice, thank you."

"Your brother doesn't like me." Mitchell changed the subject with no segue.

"What?"

"Your brother. The pretentious asshole. He doesn't like me."

"Mitchell, he's nineteen. Today. He doesn't like anyone."

"He's a dick. And what's this about your parents having an apartment? How did you not know that?"

"They don't tell me these things. Anyway, why is my brother an asshole?"

"Because, my dear, your brother is an asshole. That's why."

"Wait. Mitchell, you can't say that."

"I can if it's true." Mitchell repeated, "Your brother is an asshole."

"Well, fine. If it means anything to you, he doesn't care for you much either."

"Uh huh. Whatever. Who got him laid at the rib shack?"

"What?"

"Who *paid* for dinner?"

"But wait. You offered. You wanted to pay."

"That's true. But your brother is still an asshole."

She stared at Mitchell in disbelief as he settled into his cozy leather arm-chair in front of the burning fireplace. "He might be an asshole, but you knew that going into it."

"Well, I thought he might be difficult, being a Princeton man and all, but I didn't think he'd be so insufferable." Mitchell chuckled to himself. "You know, we should set him up with that monster of my son's mother. They can be awful to each other and leave us alone." He laughed, but to her, Mitchell seemed more drunk than serious.

"You know what I was thinking?" Mitchell leaned in. "I think I'll get a room here at the hotel for us. That way I don't have to go home, and you don't have to go to that terrible little apartment of yours."

"I like my—" She stopped herself from defending her home. "Okay, we'll stay in the hotel."

Mitchell jumped up from his chair and strode over toward the reception desk. He returned to the small round drinks table and dropped the keys.

"Take your key, my dear. Don't want you to be locked out." Mitchell laughed menacingly. He then stood near his chair and signaled to her that she was fin-ished and that it was time to head to the room. She looked longingly at the remainder of scotch in her glass, which she knew provided more safety and pleasure than sober moments with Mitchell. But she reminded herself that she was exploring the ride, and that she was going to continue to tough it out to interpret the progression of this situation with Mitchell.

They entered a rather banal New York City hotel room, and Mitchell scoffed. "Athens was better, my dear, no?"

"Of course Athens was better. This hotel is not particularly one of New York City's best."

"Hmmmm." Mitchell thought aloud, "Well, I suppose it's still better than suffering through another excruciating night with my son's mother."

"She didn't seem so bad, Mitchell."

He quickly turned his head and sneered at her. "Watch your mouth!" he hissed, "You don't know from which you speak!"

"I'm sorry, sir."

"Don't call me 'sir.'"

"I'm sorry, Mitchell."

"Don't apologize, either."

She was fast asleep when at about 5 a.m., she felt Mitchell pressing up against her. It was the first time he had been physically aggressive or affec-tionate with her, and she was a bit taken aback.

"You want a cock in your asshole?" Mitchell panted into her ear.

She was naïve enough to think this was a question. But she quickly realized that it was an order. "Yes, sir."

"Mitchell."

"Yes, Mitchell."

"Tell me you want a cock in your ass."

"I want a cock in my ass." Her voice cracked and faded. She was nervous and insincere.

"Why do you deserve a cock in your ass? Suck my cock first." Mitchell seemed to be scripting a bad porn sequence.

Exhausted, and substantially hung over, she reached for his member and attempted to fellate him.

"Do it like you mean it!" He seemed angry. But she was startled, and exhausted, and had no idea how to respond.

"Yes, okay, sorry."

"Don't talk. *Suck*," Mitchell commanded.

"Umm-mm-mm-mm."

"That's it. Good girl." Mitchell groaned a bit, and his toes began to wag. In a way, she was proud of herself that she was finally capable of providing him with an enjoyable experience. Never mind the strong musky scent of urine and bad hygiene. If he didn't mind, she didn't mind.

"Now, sit on my cock with your asshole." This was about the least sexy moment she could have imagined. "Sit on my cock! Quickly!"

As virginal as she mainly was, she attempted to force his ability to fuck her. It was as though it were more important to prove it to herself than to prove it to him. This was a new experience for her, and it would be great if she thought she had mastered it.

"Now, get off my cock, and put it in your mouth."

"What?"

"Put. It. In. Your. Mouth." He was glaring at her in the most intimidating way, and she was frightened. Not that she thought that he would harm her, but truly, she didn't know what atrocities Mitchell was capable of.

"Oh. Mmmm. Okay." She looked at his cock; it looked fine. She tasted it; it actually tasted better with sex on it than it had with masculine poor hygiene as it had before. She fellated him for a while, and then Mitchell demanded that she put his cock back in her asshole. She obliged, but at some point, he grew bored and ordered her to the shower.

"I'm leaving, to go back to my son's mother. You have a key. Have breakfast. Enjoy. Goodbye, my dear." Mitchell put on his pants and left.

Seven

The phone rang at exactly 10 a.m.

"Good morning, beautiful!" Without pausing for her response, "I need a *Times* and an *International Herald Tribune*. Quickly, *please*. I'll pay for the taxi so that just maybe you'll get here at a reasonable speed. See you soon! That is all."

She was not getting used to these abrupt dismissals and hostile instruction giving. But she couldn't imagine what choice she had in the matter. Mitchell repeatedly emphasized that the most wonderful ladies in the world had the same life: Jackie O, Grace Kelly—all great affected socialites had sacrificed a certain amount of autonomy for the sake of tyranny.

Mitchell had not been in her life even two weeks, but already she felt weaker physically and in spirit and had acquiesced to the notion that it was just easier and more sensible to follow his direction. After all, Mitchell seemed committed to his dictates and truly believed what he relayed as truth. She was barely twenty-three; he was almost twice her age and clearly more experienced. Who was she to question?

She stumbled into her bathroom and clumsily applied a small amount of makeup, trying her best to recreate what she had been taught during her birthday session at Privé. She actually put a lot of thought into the application; she knew that her complexion and coloring was perfect and not to be fooled with, but she had some ethnic physical deformities. Her biggest challenge was the large bags under her eyes, which had less to do with sleep deprivation than with a strong Syrian background. All her cousins had the same large puffy pockets under their exotic almond-shaped eyes, but that was not an effective strategy in speaking with Mitchell. Even though he was Jewish, he placed emphasis on her WASPness. As a strict Jew, Mitchell believed that a child was the origin of the mother, not the father. Even though her father was descended on all sides by founding rabbis of Sephardic Judaism, it was more impressive in the world at the time that her WASP family descended from the money originating with Queen Victoria that had trickled into the founding of the American Red Cross. Mitchell was at once proud and ashamed of his Jewish heritage, and he used her as a combination platter to bridge the gap.

She, however, was proud of her heritage and almost embarrassed by Mitchell's hijacking of her Jewish identity. Yes, she was a WASP and had no way of disguising that fact: she had long, thin bones, tiny hips, broad shoulders, a miniscule waist, notable large breasts, long, long legs, a smooth head of hair with random ringlets, and bright, striking green eyes. She naturally had little body hair, except for a low forehead line about which Mitchell frequently teased her. It was the green eyes, in fact, that made her not "Arab" to most people. Her last name was telltale, and many of her features invited assumption. She wasn't Jewish, but she supported Mitchell in his quest for equality of what she referred to as Hebes.

Her mother was a strong woman, with the sort of personality that Mitchell referred to as "too big." He didn't mean in size; in fact, her mother shared her long, lean figure and was actually quite a few inches taller than she, towering to almost six feet. Her maternal grandmother had been more than a little insane before passing away, yet the Harvard degree and polished finishing-school refinement defied Granny's seeming lack of rational cognitive thought.

The grandmother had been prone to torturing the mother, and as a young girl, Mitchell's companion had witnessed the harshest of cruelty. She had often seen her mother weeping in the presence of the grandmother but knew better than to try to intervene. The grandmother had tried to be cruel to her, too, but she had matter-of-factly dismissed her, sometimes in a condescending tone, and the grandmother seemed to respond positively to rejection.

Money was always a topic of great turmoil in her family life. The grandmother claimed to be too poor to treat the mother to a meal, yet Granny had taken both grandchildren on multiple luxury vacations when they were too young to fully appreciate them. Tim had been both on safari in Kenya and diving in the Great Barrier Reef with the grandmother, and his sister secretly resented him for traveling to the more exotic locations. Now that she was with Mitchell, however, she had no doubt that she, too, would traverse that terrain.

The mother's family had always been small, and as more members died off, the number remaining dwindled to near extinction. Those still alive were relative strangers to each other; never congregating, never communicating, silently loathing one another for reasons that WASPs were wont to disclose. She never asked for fear that her questions would be answered with both wrath and defensiveness from her rather private mother. She made the decision early in life to leave bad enough alone.

Her father's family, on the other hand, was large, extended, and often got together to celebrate obscure milestones. There was always a wedding, shivah, or bar mitzvah to attend, and the entire clan would gather. Her father's father had a seemingly endless stream of younger sisters, and her father and his many cousins were close in age and enjoyed perpetuating tradition. It was not unusual to have four generations together at a simple holiday like Thanksgiving, a day that was more an event than a celebratory meal.

Though his roots were stronger, her father was a weak man. Granted, he was well educated and fancied himself to be of superior intelligence to, well, everyone on Earth. But he was weak, almost nebbish. He was shorter than her mother and a bit stockier. He carried himself with slumped shoulders, and his head seemed to bob when he slouched along. He had no desire or ability to challenge her mother, and he was happy to acquiesce all power in an attempt to avoid her screaming. He was even apt to beat his children at the goading of his wife.

"She's an abuser," Mitchell had said about her mother. "And your father is a wimp."

She tended to agree with Mitchell and found it almost refreshing to hear someone else state what she had deemed obvious years ago. Other people had said it, too, including her parents' friends when she was a child. But Mitchell spoke authoritatively, and his opinion seemed to carry more weight than those of others.

"*I* care about you," Mitchell stated warmly. "*I* care about you. Those other people are beasts. Horrible to you. Evil. *I* care about you."

"Thank you, Mitchell."

❧

"Come over here and suck my cock."

"Oh, I, what?" She stammered.

"Grab a pillow. I don't want you to hurt your knees."

She had just walked into Mitchell's apartment and found him in his bedroom wearing a beautiful Brunelli shirt, naked from the waist down, sitting in the armchair in the corner.

"You look beautiful today, my dear. Positively stunning. Now, suck my cock."

She took off the mink coat she had inherited from her maternal grandmother and placed it on the bed. Mitchell had a brown Versace mink duvet, and her puffy white mink looked beautiful on top of it. The image was radiantly luxurious.

"*Now*, beautiful." Mitchell was lightly stroking himself and was already completely hard.

She knelt before him and took his cock in her hands.

"My god, your hands are freezing! Did you pack them in ice before coming in here?"

"What? No, I'm sorry. It's February. It's cold outside."

"Mm-hmmm. Well, I'm soft now. You've ruined it. Never mind. Go into the bathroom and run your hands under hot water. I'll be in the living room."

She found him in the living room, sitting on the large black leather armchair, watching Fox News but not really paying attention.

He fumbled through the newspaper, idly throwing sections onto the hardwood floor beside the chair. Without looking at her, he said matter-of-factly, "You have no idea how to suck a cock. I'll have to teach you from the beginning." He sighed. "I've had to teach so many girls how to do this properly. Their future husbands have all come back to thank me. All of them. So appreciative." Mitchell chuckled to himself in short, breathless heaves, with a beaming smile aimed somewhere toward his memory.

After skimming through his paper a bit more, he looked over toward her sitting quietly on the couch. "My dear, you are very, very lucky to have a friend like me. I care about you, and no one else does. I want to make you a better person. You're my girl, after all, right?"

"Yes, Mitchell."

"What?"

"Yes, Mitchell. I'm your girl." She was a little scared of him and only hoped to keep him in his currently pleasant mood. But she had seen his mood change radically and quickly, and when his voice boomed, she cowered.

"Come." He beckoned her. "Come, sit on my lap. Give me a kiss-e-la. MUAH!" He planted a wet, fat kiss over her mouth and then squeezed her shoulders into his chest. "Now a hug-e-la!" He then propped her back onto her feet. "Okay, back to your couch."

She looked at him in confusion. She often felt confused around him. He seemed to care for her; he was generous and patient. But at the same time, he seemed to loathe her.

Mitchell sensed her stare and turned his head to catch her eyes. "You love it when I'm nice to you. You love it when I'm sweet. You love when I call you my girl."

These seemed to be less rhetoric than orders, so she said nothing.

He continued to hold her gaze, and she thought she saw a tear in one of his eyes. He quickly turned his head back toward the television.

"We. Need. Wine. We definitely need wine." He turned back toward her. "My dear, please go into my fag bag and get my credit card. Run out to the wine shop on Madison Avenue and pick out a case for them to deliver. But carry one of the bottles back yourself so that we can comfortably wait for the delivery man."

"Okay, Mitchell." She was relieved to have an excuse to be out of his presence for a little while. "Any particular wines you'd like?"

"My dear, you're the expert. I trust your judgment. I'll see you soon." With that, he flicked the back of his hand to dismiss her toward the door, picked up the front page of the newspaper, and no longer acknowledged her presence.

She walked around the corner to the wine store and, once inside, found a sales associate to follow her around with a pen and paper to record the bin numbers of her selections. She chose several Mersaults and Chassagne-Montrachets, a Puligny-Montrachet, a couple of bottles of champagne, and an assortment of sauternes, choosing a bottle of Mersault to take with her.

His doormen greeted her fondly, as though she truly belonged there.

The elevator operator escorted her up to Mitchell's floor, and she walked down the hallway to find his door open in anticipation of her return.

"Hello, my dear. Did you find us anything good?"

There were already wine glasses set out on the glass coffee table.

"I'm carrying a Mersault, but a case will be arriving soon."

"Very well done, my dear. Please open the bottle, as you're the expert."

She could never tell when he was mocking her and when he was sincere, but at the very least, she knew that he wanted a glass of wine posthaste. She uncorked the bottle and poured them each a generous glass.

"I'm thinking sushi. Why don't you order us up a feast of sushi to enjoy with our wine?"

"That will be very nice. I'll do that in a half hour or so."

"Very well. Come, sit here by me."

She walked over to Mitchell, who was sprawled out on the couch, and he gestured her to squeeze in next to him.

Mitchell whispered into her ear, "My dear, remember your role as my girl. You have to find me pussy. I'm not sure that your heart is in it. It is, isn't it?"

She had no idea how to answer this line of questioning, so she lied, "Of course."

He gently shoved her off the couch and reached for his glass of wine. He kept his eyes on Fox News and began speaking to her without looking at her. "You really do love to travel, don't you? I have to pick up a pair of shoes that I left in my apartment in Paris. And you," he turned his head and animatedly swept his gaze up and down her body, "you could use some healing."

"Okay—"

"I'm not finished. Don't interrupt me, my dear. Don't be a rude little girl."

"Sorry."

"Right. Anyway, I think that this week we should go to Karlovy Vary to heal you. We can stop through Paris to pick up my shoes, and then we'll fly on to Prague. Or maybe the other way around. You can start making phone calls to investigate itineraries after lunch." *BUZZ.* "Oh, good, our wine is here."

The doorman escorted the young Ghanese deliveryman in Mitchell's vestibule and the deliveryman asked no one in particular where he should place the heavy box. Mitchell began speaking to the man in a foreign language, and the two laughed as she looked on in amazement. She had no idea how many languages Mitchell spoke, and she had the feeling that he would never tell her if asked. So as the men chatted, she opened the box in the vestibule and began to remove bottles.

Three at a time, she carried them into the living room and placed them in the wine refrigerator. When she had finished the task, she turned in time to watch Mitchell hand the man a fifty-dollar bill and close the door behind him. She said nothing.

"So, my dear, let's see what you've brought us." Mitchell knelt in front of the wine fridge and smirked. He quickly studied each bottle. "You've done a fine job. Very well. Please order lunch."

He sprawled back over the couch and resumed staring blankly at Fox News. She went into the kitchen and sifted through the takeout menus in search of a Japanese restaurant.

"Look for a lunch special," Mitchell shouted from the other room. "I always like a bargain."

She found what looked to be acceptable and ordered several different lunch specials. At the point at which the woman on the other end of the line requested the credit card number and address, she walked with the phone back into the living room and handed the unit to Mitchell.

"What are you doing?" He snarled at her.

"The woman at the restaurant needs the information for delivery."

Mitchell sneered at her and grabbed the phone. As he brought the handset to his ear, his entire demeanor changed. He sat upright, smiled at no one in particular, and pleasantly said, "Hello, this is Mr. Durman. What would you like to know?" He paused as the other voice responded, and then exclaimed, "Of course! Of course you need the card number and address. How silly of me. It's American Express. American Express. American Express! What? Yes, I know English is difficult. And we here in New York speak so quickly! I'm so sorry. Please accept my apologies. Are you ready now?" He proceeded to cite the pertinent information, and then inquired as to the estimated delivery time. "Twenty-five minutes? My, you're so fast! Your sushi chef must be amazing!...No, thank you. Thank you!" He pressed the end button on the handset and handed it back.

"Okay, so twenty-five—"

"Don't speak. Listen." His face was red with anger. "Never do that to me again. You are my girl. You serve me. Do not put me in the position of speaking to the help. Especially that help from a *Chinese* sushi bar. I would have spoken to her in Japanese, but it was apparent that *they* are not Japanese." He sighed emphatically. "Sometimes you are such an imbecile. Go, go now into my office and retrieve a pen and paper. I'll dictate."

She went into his office and searched his desk for a pad and a pen. As she removed a sheet from the printer, she saw out of the corner of her eye a Post-it note next to his computer. She palmed the sheet of white paper, never removing her gaze from the note. A lump grew in her throat as she recognized all the information on the small yellow square. It contained her social security number, email handle, bank account numbers, Internet dating website handles, credit card numbers, and all her access passwords.

She was shocked but didn't want to linger for too long, to bring attention to her absence from the living room. She took a deep breath and walked back toward Mitchell. She absently scribbled the address and credit card number that he dictated onto the sheet of printer paper and, as instructed, placed it in her purse so that she would not put him in the horrible position of having to once again speak to the help on the phone. Her expression was blank. She was moving almost like a zombie. Mitchell didn't seem to notice, as he never removed his gaze from the television. It occurred to her to confront him, but the thought quickly vanished. She'd take a little more time to process the situation. But she knew that there was something she didn't know. And she was scared.

"I want you to get American on the phone and begin to look into our trip to Europe. I'm thinking we'll leave tomorrow."

"Yes, Mitchell."

She picked up the handset and walked back into the office, trying not to look at the disturbing Post-it note. She found the number to American Airlines and called through to their more exclusive concierge booking extension. As she spoke with a representative about various itineraries, she heard the door buzz. There was a split second to decide whether to continue on the phone call or to answer for the lunch delivery. Because the buzzer was such an offensive sound, she opted to prioritize the delivery and told the airline representative that she would call back later in the afternoon.

A cowardly looking, small-framed Chinese man stood at the door carrying several plastic bags holding paper sacks filled with food. She signed for the food and tipped ten dollars.

"What did you get?"

"An assortment. I think you'll be happy."

"Ummm. Let me see the receipt." She handed it over, and his expression dropped. "Ten dollars? You tipped that little man ten dollars? How dare you have no respect for my money!"

Considering it was a hundred dollar order, and she had just seen him tip the wine deliveryman a fifty, she was sincerely confused. But she said nothing of the sort. Instead, she forced out, "I'm sorry, Mitchell."

"Yeah, yeah. You're always sorry. Right now, I just want you to get some plates and napkins to set the coffee table. Then display the lunch. While we're eating, I want you to tell me what you learned from the airline."

She quickly scrambled to bring dinner plates into the living room. Carefully, she removed the food from the sacks. Several soups, salads, soy sauce cups, dressings, and California rolls filled an entire sack.

"What's all that?"

"I guess it came free with the lunch specials, Mitchell."

"Really? Ah, that's good. You're maybe not such an imbecile after all. Hand me a soup, thank you."

She quickly removed the lid from one of the pints of soup, rummaged for a plastic soup spoon and a napkin, and handed it all to Mitchell. He nodded in appreciation, and she returned to removing lunch from the bags.

"It looks good, doesn't it, beautiful?" She was caught off guard by his affectionate moniker.

"Yes, it does. It looks wonderful." She glanced at his empty wine glass, and the empty bottle next to it. "May I serve you some more wine?"

He smiled at her sincerely. "Yes, yes you may. Thank you. And please," he gestured toward her empty glass, "please enjoy yourself."

"Thank you, Mitchell."

"Right. Hand me one of those containers." He pointed with one finger in a wagging gesture.

She handed him the first of many boxes of food, and he began to devour. She noted that in public, his manners were impeccable, but at home, he was little more evolved than a beast. He had rice caught in his goatee and sauce running down his expensive button-down shirt. Food dripped on the couch, and ran onto the floor. But Mitchell seemed so strong, so sure of himself; she thought perhaps that his boorish ways indicated that he was comfortable around her.

When he finished, he watched her as she ate slowly and contemplatively. Then he chastised her.

"Don't eat so slowly. We're at home. Eat quickly so you can clean the garbage." He waved his arm over the empty plastic boxes and the paper bags filled with mangled napkins. "And you're going to eat all of it."

"Um hmm," she acknowledged while chewing.

"Um hmm? *Um hmm*?"

She swallowed. "Sorry. Yes."

"Good."

She kept eating, though she was uncomfortably full. Mitchell continued to fill her wine glass to the top, and she drank quickly and often while he watched her critically. She never knew when he was going to yell at her, so she tried to always play by his rules.

When she finished, she cleared the garbage, put the plates in the sink, and wiped down the coffee table. Mitchell stopped her to explain how she was doing it badly. He then grabbed his hand vacuum and proceeded to reclean the floor and all the surfaces. She had to admit that he did a better job than she did, but that only meant she was going to have to work that much harder to satisfy his standards.

She went into the kitchen to wash the plates in the sink, but she felt pressure in her abdomen from the exorbitantly large quantity of food and drink she had assaulted it with in a short period. She stumbled into the bathroom adjacent to the kitchen and threw up most of lunch, maybe all of lunch; she felt a little hungry afterward. Checking the bowl to make sure there was no sign, she left the bathroom feeling much better, if not a little angry at Mitchell.

"What were you doing in the bathroom?"

"What?"

"I asked, What were you doing in the bathroom?"

"Nothing, why?" She didn't want to tell him the truth in fear that he would perceive it as weakness. She walked into the living room.

"Really? Nothing?" He looked at her sternly. She had regurgitated, not retched, so there had been no sound to tip him off. In fact, she wondered if he was forcing her to binge with him. "Very well." Mitchell turned his attention back to the television.

She sat down on the couch, and Mitchell looked at her as though she were confused.

"Why are you sitting? You should be finding me pussy. I want you to wear your mink, go to Barney's, and find me pussy."

"How do I do that?"

"My god." Mitchell raised his eyes and hands to the sky. "She knows nothing." He turned back toward her and said, "You find a fucktoy. You say, 'I want to fuck you.' Then you bring the toy to me. I'll teach you from there."

"Really?"

"Really."

She had no idea what to say or do, so she put on her mink and her Armani heels.

"Wait." Mitchell beckoned her back from the foyer. "Drink this glass of wine. Quickly."

With Mitchell watching closely, she chugged an entire glass of Mersault, which seemed to her like a waste of great wine. She then gave him a peck on the cheek and walked over to Barney's.

She walked into the ground floor of the department store, ignored the doorman who greeted her, and strolled in as if she owned the place. Mitchell would have been proud. But once inside, she had no idea what to do.

Mitchell had been very clear in his instructions. There was no chance to waste an opportunity. Mitchell expected her at his apartment within the hour with a beautiful girl, and she somehow had to make that happen. She blew the strands of hair in her eyes away from her face and got into the elevator. It made sense to her that she would start at the ninth, and highest, floor and slowly make her way down. Hopefully she would arrive at street level with "something interesting," as Mitchell would say.

The elevator door closed, and she turned to find herself traveling upward with a gorgeous, 5' 10" Eastern European woman about her age. She knew that she had about fifteen seconds before reaching the destination, so she had to act fast. There was really nothing to lose, she figured. She wondered if girls really slapped you in the face or if that only happened in movies. Nothing ventured, nothing gained.

She turned to the modelesque beauty and in the sternest and most confident of tones announced, "I want to fuck you."

She braced herself for the backlash. But she was shocked by the response. "Excuse me? Really? You want fuck me?" The girl replied earnestly, in a thick accent.

"Yes. I might fuck you. We'll see. Let's go to my apartment where a friend is chilling some wine. We'll have a drink."

"Okay, yes. Thank you!"

She was astonished. She knew that men fell for her quickly, but she sort of understood that. This was something new altogether. It was as though she had a strange power over women. Mitchell had told her this before, but she was really experiencing it now.

The two girls walked in silence back to Mitchell's apartment. She was dressed as though she owned the whole building, and the tall beauty walked beside her, looking all about in awe.

"Please announce to Mr. Durman that I'm arriving, and I've brought a guest," she told the doorman.

"Yes, madam, of course."

She spoke with confidence, but the message to Mitchell really was *I'm coming upstairs with a girl. Put your pants on, button your shirt, comb your hair, and turn off the television!*

They had the time span of rising eighteen floors for Mitchell to prepare his lair. But she wasn't sure he could move that fast. There was a large chance that this encounter would end in disaster.

The front door was ajar when they reached the apartment, and she could hear light techno music coming from within. As she pushed the door open, Mitchell swung it the rest of the way, grinning ear to ear.

"Hello, my dear! Hello! And who is your friend?"

"This is Sascha from Russia."

"Russia! Oh, I love Russia. Remind me to tell you about the crazy night I had in St. Petersburg once!"

"You know Russia?" Sascha seemed surprised.

"Oh, my, yes. Oh, I've been, maybe, one hundred times?" Mitchell always spoke slowly and with great enunciation when he spoke to foreigners. But this time he also threw in a few Russian words.

The girl giggled. Mitchell grinned, then turned to his special friend. "I'm sorry. That was so rude of us!" He turned back toward Sascha. "She doesn't speak Russian, but she speaks so many other languages, who can keep up?" He laughed, and so did Sascha. His companion chuckled feebly. She had no idea what was going on. Mitchell was a totally different person.

"I'm sorry, I'm so rude! Please let me take your coat." Mitchell removed both girls' coats. "I'm supposed to be taking care of the lady of the house, and instead, I forget my manners."

"The lady?" Sascha asked.

"Come, come sit on the sofa. We'll talk there." Mitchell led everyone to the living room, where three clean wine glasses were ready and waiting to be filled. His companion noticed that the whole apartment had been cleaned up; even the Versace throw was on the bed. She couldn't believe how fast Mitchell could move when motivated by sex.

They sat on the L-formation leather sofa, with Mitchell in the armchair, Sascha in the middle of the sofa, and "the lady" at the end. This appropriately placed Sascha as "sandwich meat." Mitchell clandestinely shot his companion a look of approval.

"So, you see. . . . My, you are beautiful; which city are you from?" Mitchell was focusing all his attention on Sascha as though she were a princess. Sascha loosely held her wine glass and seemed to enjoy the moment.

"Oh, I'm from a small village. You've never heard of it."

"Try me."

Sascha said some incomprehensible combination of consonants, and as the lady looked on, pretending to understand, Mitchell actually did.

"Oh, it's marvelous there! You have that one strange type of grass that—"

"You know it? You really know it?"

"Well, of course! I've been everywhere. Although," Mitchell directed the attention back toward his companion, "I'm not nearly as well traveled as she."

Sascha turned her head around and asked the lady of the house, "Really? You've been everywhere?"

"The lady" really had no idea how to answer, since this was clearly a game in which Mitchell was a far better player.

"Of course! She's been everywhere. That's what I'm doing here. I'm a family friend slash lawyer sent to stop by, cater to her, and make sure that she's not squandering her substantial trust fund."

Sascha looked excited. "Really? Are you famous?"

"Am I?" Mitchell scoffed. "No, no. But she is. Well, she is in certain elite international circles."

"Really? Wow. I've only seen this life in movies."

"Oh, well, real life is much different than movies. And I have to constantly watch this one," he nodded toward his companion, "to make sure she doesn't spend too much money on her biggest vice."

"Big vice?"

"Oh, the usual. Handbags, shoes, pretty girls."

Sascha blushed, then turned her attention back to the other side of the sofa. "You like pretty girls? You have very wonderful life. Girls are very lucky to have you."

This was her first time being in a situation like this, and although everything seemed to be going well, she had no idea what to do next, or how to even process what came next.

"Yes. Well, I like pretty girls, but I don't like most girls at all."

"That's right," Mitchell jumped in. "She's very powerful. Very dominant over women."

"You are?" Sascha was wriggling on the couch as though she were extremely turned on.

The lady almost felt bad, because it was apparent that both Mitchell and Sascha were excited, and she was totally not interested. But she chose to play along to see where this strain of dialogue was headed.

"She is," Mitchell said. "I bet if you kiss her right now, she'll turn you away."

"You will?"

"I might."

"Try it," Mitchell suggested, but it was more of a command.

Sascha leaned in for a kiss, in a very submissive stance. The lady forcefully took her head with one hand and teased, bit, and sucked a provocative kiss before flinging Sascha back.

Sascha's eyes were still closed, and her mouth was still open. Clearly, the Russian tramp wanted more; craved more. But it was better to keep her longing than let her desire rule the moment.

"Now pass that kiss to Mitchell," she instructed Sascha.

Mitchell looked at his companion with pride, as though she were finally understanding how this worked.

Sascha seemed apprehensive. Mitchell was not a great-looking guy, and by his own admission, he was the lady's employee. But she was a submissive taking instruction, so she obliged. She kissed Mitchell passionately, and when he released her, Sascha turned back to kiss the lady.

After a few rounds of relay kissing, the lady knew that it was time to raise the stakes. But she had no idea what she was supposed to say and how she was supposed to say it. In her "training," she and Mitchell had not yet covered this. Mitchell was holding back; he didn't want to be the creepy guy who came on too strong. In fact, his role was to play the accessory to his lady's desires.

She invited Sascha into the bedroom, although she had no idea what she would do with her in there. But perhaps she was not as forceful or as smooth as she could have been, and thankfully, Sascha declined and rose off the sofa to collect her belongings.

Mitchell glared at his companion but remained smiling and radiant when Sascha caught his eye.

"My dear, would you mind terribly if I gave your friend some cab fare from your purse?"

"No, of course not." She wasn't really sure what was happening.

"Please get the money bag."

She knew he meant his fag bag, so she grabbed the blue purse and handed it to him.

"Here you are, sweet Russian beauty." Mitchell stood and handed Sascha two hundred dollars as he escorted her to the door. "Get yourself back home safely."

Everyone kissed, and Sascha walked into the hallway toward the elevator. Mitchell closed the door, and when they heard the distant ping of the elevator arriving, he turned his attention back to his companion.

"So. Let's see. What did you do wrong?" His tone had changed.

"I don't know. I don't even know what I did right."

"Don't be fresh." He gestured back toward the living room. "Let's sit and talk."

"Okay." She nervously walked back toward the sitting area.

They both sat. Mitchell took a generous swig of wine, then looked at her intently.

"You brought a nine over. That was good. That was great. I'm impressed."

"Thank you."

"I'm not finished."

"Sorry."

"You are. My dear, you are sorry. You brought great pussy over and left it to me to carry the play. I don't appreciate that."

"I had no idea what I was doing."

"I know, I know. I'm not angry with you. I'm merely trying to get through to that dense imbecile brain of yours so that you won't fuck it up next time."

"Okay. What did I do?"

"What did you do? You didn't do anything. I'm very disappointed." Mitchell sighed and took another large swig of wine. "You had the girl in play. She would have done anything for you. She followed you home from Barney's in . . . how long?"

"Instantly."

"Right. Instantly. She would have licked your asshole, and mine, if you told her to. You know that, right?"

"I guess."

"You guess. *You guess?*" Mitchell's upper lip curled into a snarl. "I'm telling you. Do you understand?"

"Yes."

"Okay. Right. Anyway. You had the girl . . . what was her name? Petra?"

"Sascha."

"Whatever. She was a fucktoy. Sandwich meat. She would have happily sucked my cock if you were fucking her from behind with a strap-on. Do you understand?"

"Not really."

"FUCK!" Mitchell quickly stopped himself from yelling further. He took a deep, long breath and released a sigh. "You are an idiot. A complete fucking idiot. I like you because girls fall to you. Girls want you. You are a pussy magnet. A pussy magnet! You need work. You need guidance. But your power over women—that can't be taught."

"Oh."

"Oh. Oh, she says." Mitchell rolled his eyes dramatically upward. "You have a gift of attracting pussy. And I am trying to cultivate that gift. Not just for me, but for any man you meet later in life. You will own all pussy, and all men. But you have to stop being an imbecile and learn, damn it. Do you want to learn?"

"Yes."

"Yes. You say yes, but show me yes. Get me sandwich meat. Seal the deal. I guarantee that if you had met that girl a month from now, she would be gyrating her asshole on my cock right now. Right now."

She sheepishly looked downward. Mitchell talked her back up.

"My dear, you did an excellent job today. You worked hard, you went out there, and you delivered. I'm investing my time and effort in training you because you, I hope, will never disappoint me."

"I'll try."

"I know you will. Come here. Give me a kiss-e-la." Mitchell held her close to him and whispered in her ear, "You did a good job. Thank you. I'm proud to have you as my girl." He planted an uncomfortably wet kiss on her and released her to her feet.

She stood there, silent, and Mitchell handed her forty dollars.

"Here's cab fare. Go home. Get some sleep. Think of what you did wrong. And promise to fix it."

"Yes, sir."

"What?"

"Yes, Mitchell."

"Goodnight, beautiful."

"Goodnight." She grabbed her purse and walked out into the hall, closing and locking the front door behind her.

Eight

The next morning, after Mitchell's usual wake-up call, she stumbled out of bed and opened the Burberry laundry sack. Not knowing where they were eventually headed, she packed the two pairs of pants that Mitchell approved of and also tossed in the Armani shoes and a couple of blouses. She wore her mink coat and the red sneakers. She hoped he wouldn't yell at her about the sneakers. She really hoped he wouldn't yell at her.

Mitchell had a pile of clothes and toiletries scattered throughout the foyer, and he was manically running through his apartment in his boxer shorts. She wasn't sure if he noticed her come in, and she tentatively called out his name.

"Come! Come! We're going to Karlovy Vary. We're going to make you healthy and even more beautiful than you are." He paused for a moment and eyed her up and down. "Sneakers? Really? Sneakers?" He shook his head in disappointment and ran off into his office.

"Mitchell?"

"Yes, my dear?"

"What is Karlovy Vary?"

"What is Karlovy Vary?" He seemed genuinely surprised that she didn't know. He spoke warmly and attentively, even as he rummaged through his desk. "Karlovy Vary is a city in the Czech Republic that was built around spas that serviced all of the high society of Europe for centuries. It is a healing place, with healing facilities, and healing people. And you, my dear . . ." Mitchell clucked his tongue. "Well, let's face it; you need healing."

He set down his papers, walked over to her, and grabbed her face with both his hands. "You're my girl!" He gave her a kiss on the lips, and then squeezed her cheek painfully between his thumb and forefinger.

"Oooooh." She winced.

"That's an Aunt Runya! You got an Aunt Runya!" He laughed. "It's out of love, my dear. Don't be a baby."

She caught her reflection in the wall mirror and saw a swelled purple and red circle on her cheek. She wondered if he knew how rough he was with her physically. Mitchell was, after all, almost three times her size.

"So we're going to Karlovy Vary?"

"Yes, yes! It's your reward for doing so well in bringing home pussy." He smiled at her. "See? When you do well and perform your girl duties, you get properly acknowledged for your work." He paused. "That reminds me. Come into the bedroom and suck my cock. You have to thank me for staying on the phone all night with those imbeciles at the airline. Did you know they're in prison?"

"What?"

"Suck my cock."

"No, I heard that. Who's in prison?"

"You didn't know? It's common knowledge that the people who answer the phones for American Airlines at night are prisoners performing their work detail. That's why they're so unhelpful."

She wrinkled her forehead and stared at him for a minute. For an intelligent man, he seemed frequently paranoid and detached from reality.

"Don't look at me that way. I'm trying to teach you how the world works. You can either be an imbecile, or you can learn from me. Do you want to learn?"

"Yes, Mitchell. I want to learn."

"Good. Now come and suck my cock."

❧

They landed in Prague, a bit drunk and very tired. Mitchell considered staying there for the day, but it was raining and cold, and Prague seemed dreary and depressing. They rented a Smart car, and Mitchell seemed very excited to drive it.

There was a honk that sounded more like a beep, and she looked out through the glass doors to a ridiculous sight. Giant Mitchell was crammed into a tiny little two-seat car. His head was bent down to fit, and the back of his neck touched the roof. He was smiling radiantly.

"Isn't this a great car? They're not getting it in the U.S. for years yet, but we're going to zip along in it now! Grab the bags! Come in, come in!"

She was happy that they had packed so lightly. There was no room for excess luggage.

"Don't you love it? It's the most practical car in the world!"

She found that hard to believe. Especially with Mitchell twisted up like a pretzel in the driver's seat.

"Yes, Mitchell. It's a great car." She paused. "Doesn't your neck hurt?"

"No, no! This car is great. It's zippy! See?" He threw the car into gear, and they sped off.

"So, navigator, where is Karlovy Vary?" Mitchell asked, pointing toward the map in her lap.

She stared at the map for a few moments, and then looked at Mitchell shamefully. "Mitchell, I don't even know how to spell Karlovy Vary. Where on the map should I be looking? Which direction from Prague?"

"I forgot." Mitchell sighed. "I forgot that you're the product of American public school."

"I went to Barnard." She was proud of her education.

"Yeah, yeah, Columbia. Finely educated." He snorted. "Ha! I went to Yale. At Yale, they taught geography."

She opted to ignore the snub and asked again. "Where do I look for Karlovy Vary?"

"My dear, we're going there for you. Don't make me play tour guide."

She didn't want to anger him, and it occurred to her that he might not actually know where Karlovy Vary was. She studied the map, and then saw the small writing off to the west of Prague. It looked like a tiny village on the map.

"We're going the right way."

"Good. I thought so." Mitchell looked at the dashboard. "Hey! We're going 150 kilometers per hour! Can you believe this car can go so fast?"

Judging by her nausea, she could. The car didn't handle speed very well, and the roads in the Czech Republic were not well paved.

"That's great, Mitchell."

"It's wonderful!"

They turned off the highway at the signs indicating Karlovy Vary and carefully negotiated a steep winding road leading into a valley.

"This is worse than San Francisco." Mitchell thought for a moment. "That reminds me, I have to take you to my house in San Francisco. My son likes you, by the way."

"That's nice. I like him too."

The steep road down the mountainside seemed endless, but it might have been because they had to drive so slowly. Eventually, they reached the bottom and drove through the village.

"Look for parking!" Mitchell shouted as he wound the car through the streets.

They found a place to leave the car, which wasn't very difficult considering how incredibly small the car was. Mitchell carefully untangled himself from the confines of the driver's seat, and the two stood and stretched.

Walking, they reached the end of the village quickly. Mitchell stopped and looked back from whence they came.

"This is it? This is fucking Karlovy Vary?" Mitchell seemed disgusted. "This city is a nightmare. A joke. There's nothing here!"

She looked around at the scattered citizens dressed in drab, gray clothes among the drab buildings lining the cobblestone streets. She had to agree. Karlovy Vary sucked.

"Okay. Back to the car. We're going to Berlin!" Mitchell spun around and began moving toward the side street where they had parked. So much for their time in that town.

❧

"Mitchell?"

"Yes, beautiful?"

"I'm hungry."

"I am too. We'll be in Berlin soon. We'll be in Berlin soon!" Mitchell glanced over at her. "Look at the map. Where is Berlin?"

"Keep going. We're heading in the right direction."

"Good, so they taught you Berlin at Columbia." He smiled.

"Barnard." She corrected him. And the word "Berlin" was in the biggest, boldest print on the map. It was impossible to miss. Unlike the tiny, crappy city of Karlovy Vary. But she didn't say that.

When they arrived in Berlin, Mitchell rolled down his window and spoke to a passerby in German.

"You speak German?" She was trying to keep a mental tally of all the languages he spoke.

"Enough to ask where the hotel is. We're staying at the Adlon. When in Berlin, it's really the only place to stay."

"Okay. You're the boss."

"I am." Mitchell concurred.

"I know. That's why I said it."

"Don't be obnoxious. I'm the best thing that ever happened to you."

She didn't respond. She just sat quietly in the passenger seat and waited to arrive at the hotel.

They pulled up to a palatial structure that overlooked the footprint of the former Berlin Wall. A majestic crew of doormen greeted them as one held the car door open and escorted her out. He announced their presence in a booming, almost commanding voice. She enjoyed the pageantry but decided that she did not like the sound of spoken German at all.

As they approached the reception desk, Mitchell instructed her to arrange for their room. "I want the best suite they have. And I want to pay the standard room rate. Make it happen."

She looked at him quizzically, but he showed no emotion. They were in public, and Mitchell never tipped his hand in front of people. Especially people in their service. It was clear that this was a test, and she was on her own.

She feigned confidence and strutted up to the reception. "Checking in for Mr. Durman, please."

"Yes. Of course. Do you have a reservation?" The reception manager had a strong accent, but it wasn't German. She wasn't sure what it was. It must have been from having learned English in a non-native English-speaking country. English as a third language. She laughed to herself.

"No. But we don't need one. Correct?"

"Of course, Mrs. Durman. We have a lovely junior suite available for you."

"No."

"No?" The receptionist was confused.

"No." She spoke solidly, with an air that no one could tell was affected.

"I'm so sorry. Of course no. We have deluxe accommodations on the second floor." The receptionist apologized.

"We'll view it. We may not take it. Let's see if we can make Mr. Durman happy," she stated flatly. She was learning to give commands.

"Of course. So sorry for the inconvenience." The man behind the desk seemed sincere and genuinely afraid of her. "Do you know how many nights you'll be staying with us?"

"We'll see."

"Many, I hope?"

"We'll see." There was no melody in her voice. She spoke in a flat, powerful monotone.

A bellman retrieved their luggage, and Mitchell stayed back a few feet to whisper in her ear. "Did you get us the best suite?"

"I think so."

"You *think* so?" Mitchell seemed disgusted by her.

"We're going to see it now."

"Uh-huh. Always a letdown with you, imbecile," Mitchell said under his breath.

On the second floor, they were escorted into a majestic suite. She thought it was spectacular. Mahogany, marble, and brass abounded. Mitchell nodded noncommittally and handed the bellman a twenty-Euro bill.

The bellman left, and Mitchell turned to his companion. "It's . . . okay. It's not their best suite. Take your clothes off."

Mitchell had mastered the monotone better than she, and she knew better than to respond. She certainly wasn't going to question him. She walked into the bedroom and silently removed her clothing. Mitchell opened a bottle of wine from the minibar and watched her silently.

She sat naked on the bed and said nothing as Mitchell poured two glasses of wine and drank half of one of them. He set both glasses on the nightstand and took off his pants and boxers. He never removed his shirt, and judging from his rotundness, she appreciated that.

He pulled her toward him from behind and pressed her body to his in a spoon. She braced herself. He breathed into her ear, and she could smell the wine fermenting on his breath. "You want a cock in your ass, don't you?"

"Yes, Mitchell," she said meekly.

"Good. I know you do. That's what you want. That's what you need."

She took a cue from pornography and said abstractly, "I want your huge cock inside of me."

"Damn it, bitch, why do you give me that bullshit?" Mitchell sounded angry, but he hadn't pulled away from her. His voice boomed into her ear. "I don't have a big cock, and you know that. It's average at best. No need to lie, my dear. It makes you seem. . ." His voice got very small and raspy ". . . pathetic."

He grabbed the packet of lubricant she had remembered to remove from her toiletry kit and place on the nightstand while she had undressed. He applied it liberally to himself and to her, then entered her asshole as they both lay on their sides. He thrust and groaned a bit, and she rolled her eyes and stared across the room at a vase on a table by the wall. Eventually, he climaxed. She had zoned out, so she had no idea how long he had been building up to it.

"There!" Mitchell announced triumphantly. "You have cum in your asshole. You've never had cum in your asshole! Now, you lucky girl, you have my cum in your asshole."

She made an almost inaudible sound.

"What was that? Did you say 'thank you'?"

"Thank you, Mitchell."

"You're welcome, my dear." He kissed her cheek. "Now go take a shower and let the cum drip out of your asshole.

She stood up and walked to the bathroom.

"Soon you'll have some slut to suck the cum out of your asshole. That will be fun, won't it?"

She remained silent and turned on the shower.

As she toweled off and began to redress, Mitchell set down his glass of wine and looked at her with an expression that indicated he had been waiting to speak to her for quite a while. "I've decided. I don't like this room. Call the front desk and let them know. Oh, and send my pants to be cleaned and pressed before dinner."

He was unbelievable, but she knew that he was serious. She called for the cleaning to be retrieved and hung a bag with the pants outside the door on the knob. Then she went back down to the front desk.

"Mr. Durman is not happy with the room. I feel that you've misled us. *That* is not the best room you have."

The manager squirmed a bit and wrung his hands. He might not have known who Mitchell was, but he was afraid of him. "I'm quite sure we have nothing else."

"*No.*"

"Please ma'am, allow me to buy you a drink. Anything you'd like. I'll see what I can do in the meantime." The receptionist was frazzled, trying to accommodate such demanding guests.

It was late afternoon, and the bar was not yet opened. The barkeep was setting up for the evening service and watched her approach.

"Hello, Mrs. Durman. I'm so sorry to hear that you're not pleased with the accommodations here at the Adlon. Please, allow me to pour you a drink at our delight."

She wasn't unhappy with the accommodations. In fact, she thought the suite was magnificent. But for reasons she didn't understand, Mitchell was not pleased. The only thing she was sure of was that she needed a drink.

"I'd like . . . that, please." She pointed to a dusty, gold-plated bottle of scotch displayed predominantly at the center of the liquor cabinet.

"This?" The barkeep cradled the bottle in his palms. "Really?"

"Yes. Thank you."

The barkeep poured a generous fill in a snifter. She noticed that his hands were shaking, as though he had never poured from that bottle and wasn't entirely sure that he was allowed to.

He handed her the snifter. "With our compliments." He bowed his head modestly.

She gripped the stem of the snifter between her middle and ring fingers and cradled the bowl in her palm. She breathed in deeply, and the rich, intoxicating aroma made her smile a little bit. She nodded to the barkeep and turned to walk back toward the reception desk.

"Mrs. Durman, I believe that we have a room that will be satisfactory," the man at the desk told her.

"I hope so." She thought she sounded like a bitch, but she knew that her role was to be Mitchell's henchman. If she wanted to enjoy this lifestyle, she'd have to play the game by Mitchell's rules.

"Are you enjoying your drink?" The man asked.

"Very much. Thank you." She was proud of herself that she was beginning to master the monotone, and she was garnering positive results. Even if it meant that everybody hated her.

She rode the elevator in silence with the manager to the second floor and unlocked the door to the suite she and Mitchell were currently inhabiting. The manager remained in the hallway, his hands linked behind his back. He looked like a soldier. A soldier of hotelery. Maybe she was just losing her mind.

She took a long, slow sip of the scotch and found Mitchell lying on the bed watching television.

"They have Fox News! Marvelous, no?"

"Marvelous, Mitchell." She steered the focus back to her task. "We have a new room."

"The room we should have had from the beginning, you mean?"

"Right. That room." She wondered if she could roll her eyes without him noticing. She decided against it.

"Great! Take me to it." Mitchell popped out of the bed. He still seemed to be manic. She wasn't sure if manic was better or worse than depressive, but so far, his mania extended from effusiveness to hostility. She hadn't seen him depressive; she assumed it was even more unmanageable.

"Yes, Mitchell. The manager's waiting for us in the hall."

"He's scared of you, isn't he?" Mitchell laughed.

"I think so. I was a real bitch."

"Not a bitch. You were in the right. He's nobody. You're somebody, and he's nobody. Remember that."

"Right."

"He bought you a drink." Mitchell motioned toward the glass in her hand.

"Yes. Would you like some?" She held it up for him.

"You didn't leave very much for me."

"Well, I, I guess that. . . ."

"Relax. I just want to smell it. I only drink wine. I don't want to be an alcoholic." He held the snifter to the base of his nose and inhaled. He smiled and turned his attention back to her. "How much did this cost?"

"I don't know. I'll check the list later at the bar."

"My dear, this is a thousand-Euro glass of scotch. You've taken advantage of his generosity." Mitchell winked at her. "Well played." He stood and walked out of the room and into the hallway.

Mitchell acknowledged the manager with a head nod but no eye contact. The manager seemed to shake a bit.

"Sir, we have your pants laundered and waiting in your new suite," the man said, visibly nervous in Mitchell's presence.

Mitchell said nothing, and she realized that it was her job to respond to the help. "Thank you. That'll do." She said it as though it pained her that it had taken so long to clean the pants. But it had only been an hour at most, and quite frankly, she was shocked that they were able to service the laundry that quickly. The hotel staff must have really been afraid of the perceived power couple in residence.

They followed the manager down the hallway to a suite that stood all by itself. The door was already opened, and the shiny brass key was hanging out of the lock. The vestibule was expansive, and on the center table was a large display basket of fruits, nuts, and cheeses set next to a bottle of champagne chilling in a silver bucket of ice.

A bellman scurried past them and hung their coats and other garments in the closet in the front room. When the bellman left, Mitchell turned toward the manager and shot him a look that successfully communicated he had overstayed his welcome. The manager spun on his heels and left.

"This, my dear, this is the room I had wanted." Mitchell smiled broadly. "You, you, my dear, did an excellent job. A wonderful job. I give you praise when you deserve it. You're coming along well." He gestured back toward the vestibule. "Open the champagne. You have earned a glass of champagne." Mitchell gave her a quick squeeze of a hug and walked around the suite.

She poured two full flutes of champagne and walked over toward him. He was standing at the French doors to the balcony, struggling to open them. When he had succeeded, he walked over toward his handbag and removed his professional quality digital camera.

"Stand at the balcony. Hold your champagne. Dangle your shoes from your fingers."

She was happy to have the opportunity to take off her heels, and she quickly obliged. She stood at the balcony, looked through the square to the Brandenburg Gate, and smiled. It was a genuine smile. This was perhaps the most incredible, most expensive place she had ever stood.

Mitchell took her picture and then spent ten minutes telling her what an incredible photographer he was.

"It's about *composition*. Lighting and composition. I understand it inherently. And this, well, this is just an incredible photo."

She looked through the viewer on the camera, and she had to admit that it was perhaps the best picture she had ever seen.

"Now, do you know where you are?"

"You mean Berlin?"

"Don't be stupid. I mean this room. Do you know where you are when you look at the picture of you on the balcony?"

"I guess I don't."

"You, my dear, are on the balcony where Michael Jackson dangled his child over the square. It was this hotel. This room. A dubious honor, but certainly a well-photographed balcony. And now you have a picture of yourself dangling Armani heels and a glass of champagne."

It was definitely a dubious honor, but it did make for an amusing story. She had to admit that Mitchell seemed always to have a game plan and a set objective for the lessons he taught her. She wished that he would tell her his reasoning before making her feel small and unworthy, but she supposed that this was the way in which he operated. It seemed to work out for the best when she just followed his instructions. There was a lot she could learn from Mitchell. At least, that's what he said.

The restaurant in Berlin was sleek and modern, more impressive than any back in New York. They walked through a bubble corridor, with Mitchell leading the way, as he insisted was the norm. They entered a large pod-shaped dining room with electric colors and cool, disorienting low-wattage lighting. Mitchell sat at the banquette, and she paused and looked at him. He caught her eye and looked embarrassed as he motioned for her to sit in the protruding chair and gestured the maître d' away.

He leaned in across the table. "In civilized countries, the man sits at the banquette, not the lady. Look around."

She noticed that all the women in the room were seated in the protruding chairs. In the U.S., it was traditional proper etiquette that the lady of the party sit in the banquette. She looked back at Mitchell and raised an eyebrow.

"You see, my dear, the gentleman sits looking out at the dining room so that he may orchestrate the meal. In America, the lady does. And that is because American men are sissies."

She chuckled.

"It's not funny. This is the downfall of American society. The men are not...
men." He snorted in disgust and turned his attention to the wine list.

She opened the menu. "There are some really interesting dishes on the
menu, Mitchell."

"Close the menu. I'm in charge."

"But, can I tell you what I'd like?" She persisted.

"Close. The. Menu. I swear, I'm going to have to break you of all your disgusting habits." He snarled, without looking up from the wine list, and with
one hand summoned the captain.

"Break me?"

"Like in the army. You have a lot of potential. That's why you're my girl." He
lifted his eyes and gave her a saccharin smile. "But your potential is hidden
under layers of garbage that pussy men you've known in your life have heaped
on you. Stick with me. I'll make you a real lady."

She thought she was a real lady, and she knew that most men desired her.
But none had shown her this glamorous life and handed her the world. So,
she thought it in her best interest to trust Mitchell's judgment and follow
the rules.

Nine

"Wake up."

"Uhhhhhh." She rolled over.

"Wake up."

"Why?"

"Wake up and suck my cock."

She turned her head, and Mitchell was standing next the bed, naked from the waist down.

"I'm sleeping." She buried her head in the pillow. In the brief moment she had looked up, she had noticed that it was still pretty dark outside. It was maybe 5 a.m. at the latest.

"You can sleep after you suck my cock. Come on. Now. It won't take long."

Mitchell was jiggling his stiff dick with one hand and playfully poking her in the rib cage with the other. She was too tired and too hung over not to comply. She sat up in bed, and as she moved over toward him, she briefly thought about the fact that he had not bathed yet in the days they had been traveling. And he hadn't bathed before they left New York. But she didn't have the energy to be disgusted.

She choked against the stench of his festering body odor, which was concentrated by his weight and the tight area of skin around his cock. She hoped that he would cum quickly, but she also knew that she would be reprimanded for rushing.

Mitchell eventually finished, exclaiming, "Here comes your treat!" She rolled over and went back to sleep.

When she woke up at around 9 a.m., Mitchell was passed out on the couch, and there was an empty wine bottle nearby. She called room service and ordered herself a large breakfast. Mitchell never woke up.

As lunchtime approached, and Mitchell remained asleep on the couch, she tried to rouse him. He thrashed, as though he were startled, but it seemed like an act to her. He asked her to order them some lunch and some bottles of wine, and he began to make phone calls from his handheld. Mitchell asked her to leave the room.

She sometimes wondered about his secrecy, but he seemed open about so much else that she shrugged it off as business that was none of her concern. She never asked him what he did for a living, or how his tremendous wealth was acquired. But after his lunch and his phone calls, Mitchell seemed particularly angry. He entered her bedroom, where she was reading some English-language magazines that had been left in the suite.

"Ball gag."

"What?"

"Put in the ball gag. I packed a ball gag. I want you to wear it so I don't have to hear your fucking voice."

"I don't even know what a ball gag is."

"You are an imbecile! I have to do everything. Fine. I'll get the ball gag. You take your clothes off."

Mitchell returned with a pink rubber ball strung onto a black leather strap. He grabbed her violently by the neck and shoved it into her mouth as he tightened it firmly behind her head. Her hair was caught in the buckle, and it hurt. But all she could muster was a yelp.

Mitchell picked her up and flung her onto the bed with such force that she thought her bones would break. She looked at him with tears in her eyes, and he slapped her hard across the face. She began to cry, and he began to masturbate.

He pushed the ball gag further into her mouth, grabbing her hair and pinching her swollen cheeks.

"Your face has a red hand print where I slapped you. You can't be that weak!"

She sobbed, and he picked her up by the hips and threw her onto her side. He entered her asshole, and it hurt this time. He thrust, and she cried. Then he flung her back around, and pulled the ball gag to fall around her neck. He forced himself into her mouth, and she squeezed her eyes closed as tears cascaded down her cheeks. He then put the ball gag back into her mouth and sodomized her again.

The more she cried, the harder he slapped her. She was so thin and so frail, she really thought that he was going to kill her. Maybe accidentally, maybe not.

His hot breath stung her neck as he hissed into her ear, "You're my girl, right? You're my girl."

She sobbed, but mustered "Mmm hmm" through the constricting pink ball in her mouth.

"That's right, imbecile. You're my girl. Turn over."

She rolled onto her back, and he came all over her stomach.

"Don't move."

Mitchell disappeared for a moment, and then returned. Without saying a word, he stood over her on the bed and urinated all over her face. She was ready for him to kill her.

The hot stream of urine burned her through to her core. She was helpless and unable to react. Mitchell then rolled her over onto her stomach, and she lay in the puddle trying to bury her face as far into the pillow as she could. She was exhausted and confused. Her body tried to put her to sleep as a defense.

"Stay there. For an hour. I'm timing you. Stay there with the ball gag in and fuck yourself with this dildo."

Mitchell tossed her a large red rubber cock and left the room. He yelled from beyond the door. "I could come in at any moment. Don't cheat or there's hell to pay. Fuck yourself for one hour. Starting now."

She lay there in the puddle of urine, with the ball gag in her mouth, and tentatively probed herself with the appendage. She felt degraded beyond all measure but was terrified of any further physical violence.

Mitchell reentered. "That's not fucking yourself. Put it all the way in. Now. All the way."

The large red dildo hurt, but she didn't want Mitchell to strike her anymore. She cried, but obliged. Her feet were in the air, and though her legs were trembling, she tried to pretend to look sexy.

"You're pathetic. Forty-five minutes left." Mitchell left the room.

She was miserable and ready to die. Never had she felt such physical pain, and never had it been coupled with such blanket confusion. She was not a God-fearing woman, but she prayed for it to end.

"Beautiful?"

"Mmmm?" She lifted her head while holding the red dildo inside of herself.

"An hour's up. Come, let me care for you."

Mitchell walked over toward her, and she yelped as he reached to touch her. But he was gentle and soft. He removed the ball gag and then cradled her in his arms. He carried her into the master bedroom, where the Jacuzzi was filled with a warm bubble bath. She was shattered and hung limp.

Mitchell delicately placed her in the tub and untiringly began to wash her. She whimpered, and he kissed her tears away from her cheeks.

After he had bathed her, he lifted her from the tub. She tried to stand, but she was unable to bear weight on her trembling legs. He dried her with the towels, swaddled her with the robe, and laid her across the couch.

When another hour had passed, he approached the quivering mass on the couch and kneeled before her.

"You did a very good job. You are a very good girl. I'm going to take you to dinner now. Run of the menu! Get dressed, my love, get dressed."

She was still trembling as they sat in the Biergarten, and she tried and failed to hide her gentle sobbing. She hoped the din of the drunken Germans and tourists would mask her inability to speak. Her jaw still hurt from the strain of the ball gag, and her asshole was sore and throbbing.

Mitchell summoned a waitress and ordered them a round of beers and an assortment of sausages nesting in a bed of sauerkraut inside a metal pail. He wrapped a sausage in a piece of rye bread, applied mustard, and handed it to her on a paper napkin. She chewed slowly and avoided eye contact with him.

"Are you ignoring me?" Mitchell chided her.

"No, Mitchell. I just don't have anything to say."

"You should be saying 'thank you.' Look around you." He leaned in toward her. "You're in heaven. Traveling first class and living like a queen. Don't think you don't have to pay your dues."

"Yes, Mitchell."

"Yes, thank you?" He prompted.

She took her cue. "Thank you for bringing me to Berlin."

"Mmmm. Well, enjoy it. We're leaving Berlin in the morning."

"Where are we going?"

"Don't ask stupid questions. I'm not your tour guide. Just remember that I treat you better than you'd ever treat yourself."

They finished their meal in silence. When they got back to the Adlon, she went into the bathroom, threw up, and cried.

⌒❧

"Wake up! Wake up!" Mitchell was poking her in the back of the neck with his penis. "We have to get an early start to leave Berlin!"

She opened her eyes. She had actually been awake for a while, but she was trying to savor the peace while Mitchell slept. As usual, he had passed out on the couch in the living room; a half glass of white wine had stood on the floor, right beneath his dangling fingers.

But now he was on the bed beside her, playfully goading her into alertness. She felt weak, and her head was swimming. She couldn't tell if she was hung over or just miserable. Mitchell was in a great mood, though, so she opted to enjoy the moment.

She made a feeble attempt to fellate him, and he let her stop early. He moved off the bed, and pulled on his trousers. She wondered if he was ever planning to bathe. But she wouldn't dare mention it. She tried to smile as she dressed. Then she ordered up their breakfast, as Mitchell had requested.

They waited for about fifteen minutes before Mitchell grew impatient. "How long did they say it would be?"

"They said that room service would be up shortly."

"But *how long*?"

"I don't know, Mitchell. They didn't say."

"They didn't say because you didn't ask." Mitchell paused and breathed in deeply. "Honestly, are you that stupid?"

"I'm sorry, Mitchell."

"You will be sorry. Grab your bags. We're leaving now." His tone was harsh, but he somehow still seemed to retain the playful mood in which he had awakened.

"Should I call for the bellman?"

"Did I say that? I said 'grab your bags.' And that's what I meant. Do I ever mince words?"

"No, Mitchell."

"That's right. That's right. Come now."

They walked into the hallway, wheeling their beautiful luggage. As they approached the elevator, they passed the room service waiter who was pushing their breakfast cart into their suite. She thought about how hungry she was and tried to shake the feeling as the elevator door closed behind her.

"You're thinking about the breakfast you're not going to eat. Don't. You, my dear, you are a *consumer*."

They got themselves situated in their comically small car, and Mitchell thrust the map into her lap.

"Find Dresden. We have to go through Dresden. Would you like to see some concentration camps?"

She hadn't thought about it, but now that he mentioned it, she really would. "Yes, please. That would be amazing!"

"Okay." Mitchell smiled at her. He put his hand on her knee and gently squeezed it lovingly. "Please find Dresden, beautiful."

She located Dresden on the map, and the two of them began speeding along toward the border. Snow began to fall as they approached, and the little car was straining to maintain its speed and traction.

"How far?" Mitchell was clearly getting stressed out by the weather, and his demeanor was becoming exasperated.

"I don't know. Maybe thirty kilometers?"

"Are you asking me or telling me?"

"I'm guessing. This map is hard to read."

"Only to you, imbecile. Only to you," Mitchell chortled.

The snow banks along the side of the road were deeper, and the falling snow was dense and driving down against the windshield. The engine groaned against the stress of moving the car through the snowdrift, and Mitchell continuously pumped the gearshift to find the best speed at which to proceed. He turned his head to glare at her, as though the snow were somehow her fault.

"Thanks for directing us into a blizzard, imbecile."

"I didn't plan the snow, Mitchell. I just navigated us toward the border."

"Are you sassing me?"

"What? No. I just—"

"You're sassing me. Stop it." Mitchell flipped his hand and slapped her swiftly.

The slap stung, and she shut her mouth. In the distance, she could see the blinking lights of the border patrol station. But through the snow, the flashes were sporadic, and it was almost impossible to see any vehicles in front of them.

She was tired, and the inside of the car was getting cold. After the slap, however, she had lost any courage to ask Mitchell to raise the temperature of the heat gauge. So she closed her eyes and hoped for the car trip to end swiftly.

"Are your eyes closed? Are your fucking eyes closed?!"

"I'm sorry. I just wanted to be through this storm quickly."

"And I didn't?" Mitchell shook his head vigorously. "I swear, imbecile, you are the worst navigator ever. Ever."

"I'm sorry."

"Don't apologize! Damn it! Don't apologize. Just navigate."

"Mitchell, a blizzard is not on the map."

"You're sassing me! I told you don't sass me! What the hell is the matter with you?"

"I'm sorry."

"Don't say you're sorry. You're not sorry. You're an idiot!"

"Sorry."

Mitchell turned his head to drill his judgmental eyes into the side of her head. She was careful not to turn her head to make eye contact. Just then, the tiny car shook violently, and before either of them realized what was happening, they were overturned in a deep snow bank.

All the windows showed banks of thick dark whiteness. They were buckled in, but their hair hung to the ceiling.

"We are going to die in Dresden because you are an idiot."

She wasn't sure how Mitchell overturning the car in a snow bank was a result of her poor navigation skills, but she didn't want to risk another slap in the face. So she remained silent.

Mitchell breathed heavily and glared at her. She closed her eyes and tried to pretend that they were not upside down.

It seemed like an eternity before they felt a thrust against the side of the car. A German border patrol plow was chugging down the street, uprighting all the overturned vehicles. She smiled quietly to herself as she realized why these small cars had never made it into the American market. They were clearly dangerous. In fact, theirs was one of many stuck in the snow like so many pieces of shrapnel.

After the car was righted, and the street plowed, they joined the line at the border to exit Germany. Their passports were quickly stamped without being examined, and they were waved through. The line at the border was particularly long, probably because of the blizzard, and the border patrol seemed anxious to keep the line moving.

Mitchell seemed in better spirits after they passed through the border. "Let's go to Treblinka."

"The concentration camp?"

"No, the ghetto. Treblinka was a ghetto." Mitchell sighed. "You have a lot to learn about your history as a Jew."

"This is not my history. My family is from Syria."

"Right. Right. *Arab*." Mitchell smiled. He was insulting her, but his tone was playful. "Well, we'll educate you about the *other* Jews."

She wasn't really that upset about the zing. In fact, she had always been curious to visit the historical landmarks of the Holocaust. She put the map away and prayed silently that he wouldn't ask her to be navigator again. The pressure was just too much.

As they approached Treblinka, the snow turned to rain. She thought that it was actually the perfect dreary day to visit a WWII Jewish ghetto. She loved history, and she knew that even though he didn't say it outright, Mitchell had driven out of the way to show her the landmark. He was hard and cold but oddly thoughtful and considerate at the same time. And she—she was just along for the ride.

Mitchell parked the car, and the two of them entered what was now a museum entrance at the main street of the ghetto. He bought one ticket for a tour and handed it to her. She looked at him quizzically.

"I've been here already, my dear. You go ahead. Learn. Enjoy. I'll see you in about an hour. I have some phone calls to make and some business to attend to." Mitchell did not wait for a response from her. Instead he turned around on his heels and sped off.

She presented her ticket and joined the English-speaking tour.

Mitchell seemed upset when she exited at the end of the tour. At least, she thought, his mood had nothing to do with her. She didn't know the content of the phone calls, or to whom they were made, but as long as his anger was directed elsewhere, she really didn't consider it to be her business.

"Did you like Treblinka?"

"Was I supposed to like Treblinka?"

Mitchell laughed. "You're right. You're funny. No one is supposed to like a tour of Treblinka." Mitchell chuckled again to himself.

The two of them got back into the car and began to drive to Prague. She wondered if they were spending the night, or if they were going straight to the airport, but by now, she knew better than to ask.

Thankfully, the highways were better marked, and Mitchell stopped asking her to report based on the hard-to-read map.

It was raining in Prague, and the air was cold and duly humid. She wondered why people thought this was a beautiful city; to her, it seemed wet and gray.

They sped through the puddle-soaked streets and parked the car in the center of the city. She still didn't know what the schedule was, and she was starting to get antsy.

"What are we doing in Prague? How long are we staying?"

"Why are you wasting my time listening to your questions? Why do you expect me to respond? Did I not tell you that I don't play tour guide?"

"I'm sorry."

Mitchell stopped walking.

"Stop. Saying. You're. Sorry." He paused for effect. "You are not sorry. You're stupid."

"I'm sorry I'm stupid."

Mitchell laughed maniacally. "That's even worse! You are more stupid than I had imagined. Ha!"

Mitchell quickened his pace, and with his long legs and imposing height, he quickly gained ground on her. She jogged to keep up. She felt like a puppy following its master. But she dared not linger behind, for fear of worse repercussions to come.

Over the next few hours, they scrambled through the wet streets of Prague. She was still clueless as to the gameplan, and it was clear that Mitchell had no intention of informing her. The afternoon was dragging on, and they had still not stopped to eat.

"Your punishment for getting us almost killed in the blizzard is no food today." Mitchell patted his round belly. "And I am a fat man. I want to eat. So your punishment hurts me too. So I am very displeased with you."

They walked back through the center of town, and Mitchell paused several times to read the menus outside restaurants. She looked on, hoping that he would choose one to enter. But each time, he'd shake his head and keep walking. "I've got to stand my ground. You almost killed us. So we both must be punished."

The smell of cooking food wafted into the cold, damp air, and she longed to taste, well, whatever it was they ate in Prague.

But they never stopped walking. Eventually, they returned to the car, and Mitchell announced that they were pressed for time to make their flight to Paris. They never spent any real time in Prague.

"You'll laugh when you see European business class," Mitchell goaded as they waltzed through security, wheeling their bags behind them and not being asked to use the x-ray. "Air France blocked the center seat out of a few front rows of coach and called it business class. Of course, I'm fat, so I barely fit. But at least they serve foie gras." Mitchell laughed again.

She was starving; she hoped they really did serve foie gras. Or anything, for that matter.

They boarded the plane, and she noticed that Mitchell was absolutely right. The seats were cramped; almost worse than coach seats in the US. But the wine list was admirable, and the food menu was luxurious. She and Mitchell ate and drank their way through the flight to Paris. And Mitchell gave her his foie gras.

Ten

"When I'm in Paris, I like to stay at the airport Marriott. We'll be here maybe a night, maybe two. I have to get my shoes, and then we'll be off." Mitchell looked at her but not in a way that anticipated a response. "I don't know how long we'll stay. Why don't we see if you can produce?"

She looked at him blankly. She noticed that the longer she stayed with him, the harder she was becoming. It wasn't a question of whether she liked herself like that or not. Rather, she was losing all sense of opinion in general. Being with Mitchell was a crazy ride, but she was morbidly curious to see how it would turn out. Plus, she really had nothing else in her life. Mitchell was right—he was the only person on her team. Even if he scared her to death.

They checked into the hotel, and she listened to Mitchell's rant about how much the rates at the airport Marriott at Charles de Gaulle had gone up. He threw money around like refuse, but as they became closer as companions, she realized that he was actually extraordinarily cheap.

They had the bellman bring their bags to their suite, and the duo headed into the hotel restaurant to have dinner. It was late, and they were both tired and in need of something more substantial than airplane food. Even if the airplane food was top-rate Air France cuisine.

"You haven't produced," Mitchell said to her, matter-of-factly, as they perused the menu. "I have been nothing but generous with you, and you've only consumed. In fact, I believe I paid your rent this month."

She had almost forgotten, but he was absolutely right. He had been taking care of everything in her life, and aside from a few blowjobs and a little sodomy, she had not done anything for him in return. They had never even shared a bed. Mitchell always gladly took the couch anywhere they stayed, without any conversation about that arrangement.

"You have done nothing for me, so you are only entitled to whatever prix-fixe menu the chef is offering tonight. You may order from a regular menu when you have actually fulfilled your obligations as my girl." Mitchell leaned in toward her. "You still want to be my girl, right?"

"Yes, please." She didn't, actually. The fun had worn off, and Mitchell was beginning to both irritate and frighten her. But she had nothing else at that point in her life, and this was certainly a lifestyle to which she had quickly become accustomed. She looked down at the mink Piaget watch on her wrist and sighed. She was a sellout. "What do you need me to do?"

"What do I *need* you to do?" Mitchell's voice escalated. "What do I *need* you to do? I need to you to honor your part of our agreement, damn it! You are my girl. My little Jackie O. You think that Jackie O just lived off of Aristotle

Onassis? NO! She did not. She presented him with pussy. She presented him with disposable *pussy*. Find me pussy, O. Find me pussy!" Mitchell laughed a sinister cackle. "It's funny. You look like Jackie O. You act like Jackie O. Strangers respect you like Jackie O. You eat and drink like Jackie O. You even puke like Jackie O." Mitchell glared at her over his menu. "Yes, that's right. I know that you are puking like Jackie O. You think you're fooling me that you ate two portions of foie gras on the plane and you haven't thrown up? Face it—you are the next incarnation of Jackie O! Now be like a good O and find me pussy! The rest is your entitlement if you serve me correctly."

Mitchell was cruel and direct, but convincing. She couldn't expect something for nothing, and she was foolish to think that he would stay with her for her lousy blowjobs and overzealous appetite for consuming everything she could: food, wine, liquor, spa treatments. Mitchell didn't owe her anything. And he made it very clear that in fact she owed him.

"I'll go to the business center after dinner and put up a posting to find pussy when we return to New York."

"Online? What posting? There's a site to find submissive pussy online?"

"Well, there's Craigslist," she began to explain. "It's still pretty new, but there are real people on the site looking for just about anything. And everything."

Mitchell leaned back in his chair and smiled. "Craigslist," he repeated contemplatively. "And on Craigslist you can find me pussy?"

"Maybe instantly. I've only ever put up postings to meet men, but I've gotten hundreds of responses within the first hour. And that's with something as banal as a dinner date. I'm sure there are just as many women ready to respond."

"Craigslist," Mitchell repeated. "Okay, we'll stay in Paris. You find me New York pussy on Craigslist, and we'll fly it out here. Pussy likes to travel to Paris."

Mitchell seemed genuinely intrigued and pleased with her innovation.

"Just for that, I'm going to let you order an extra entrée. I know you're just going to throw it up anyway, but at least you'll enjoy it for a minute."

She couldn't understand why Mitchell seemed to be promoting and encouraging bulimia, but with him, she never knew when her next meal was coming. She learned quickly to indulge in all she could when he offered. And right now he was offering, and he seemed sincerely pleased with her. She was going to take advantage of his momentarily generous spirit.

They finished their dinner, he more quickly than she. Mitchell always ate as though he hadn't eaten in weeks and was afraid the food would disappear before he inhaled it. He watched her closely as she slowly ate her four courses.

"Are you finished? Can we go to the business center now? Can you post to this Craigslist so that girls will see your ad in New York before nighttime sets in?"

She hadn't thought about the time change and cursed herself for mentioning Craigslist. Mitchell was going to keep her up all night waiting for responses from a city that was five time zones behind Paris.

Mitchell paid the dinner tab, and the two of them scurried off to the business center in the hotel. They logged onto the Internet, and she brought up the New York Craigslist page to show him.

"So what do we do?"

"Well, we have to establish an email account, and then the responses to our anonymous posting will forward to the mailbox."

"Okay, okay." Mitchell seemed genuinely excited, and she could tell he was thinking of a screen name alias. "You are elegantdomme."

"Really?" She laughed playfully, and Mitchell squeezed her shoulder tenderly. "Okay, I'll set up a Yahoo account in that name, and then we can begin posting."

Together, they created a posting that read *Elegant, very thin Jackie O lookalike seeks tall, thin, femme sub for generous playtime in Paris.* Mitchell seemed satisfied, and the two of them posted the ad and waited for it to generate responses.

Within the half hour, they had several replies, complete with photos, descriptions, and inquiries. Mitchell read them over and then took over the role of responding to the ones he found most interesting. He wrote the emails as though they came from her, and she was surprised to notice how well he was able to capture her voice. It really did sound as though she had composed the emails. Except, of course, the content was nothing she would ever have imagined writing to an anonymous stranger.

Several emails between the duo and a few girls went back and forth for a couple of hours. She was exhausted, but Mitchell seemed exhilarated. Unfortunately, he was having trouble convincing any of the girls that he truly intended to fly them to Paris on the next flight out of New York. Frustrated, he finally allowed his companion to retire to their suite for a much-deserved night's sleep.

～❧

"I think we have one on the line. Take your breakfast from the buffet and meet me in the business center." Mitchell seemed at once excited and delusional. But at least with his focus on other girls, she felt less pressure in being his sole source of entertainment.

He sat at the keyboard and typed vigorously, and she stood behind him, rocking slightly from one foot to the other. Hours passed, and he seemed to be deep in dialogue with one particular prospect. The girl seemed apprehensive, so Mitchell asked for her phone number.

"Call this fucktoy and make sure you can get her on the evening flight from JFK. I need some fun."

Mitchell had been speaking to the prospect, not she, so before calling, she made sure to read through all the emails to brief herself on the conversations. When she felt confident in having learned the dialogue, she and Mitchell went to find a private telephone.

"I'm going to make sure you don't fuck this up. Just say everything I tell you to. Don't stray from the script. Prove yourself to me, imbecile."

She was tired of the pressure of constantly disappointing Mitchell, and she wasn't happy with the future course of events in importing women to Paris to use them for sex. But she felt trapped in the situation, and Mitchell never allowed her a free moment of thought to conjure up a rational argument for why she wouldn't follow his orders. So she dialed the phone and read and reread the notes that Mitchell scribbled for her on a hotel pad he had placed in front of her.

"Hi, Lauren? This is your elegant domme." She breathed in deeply. "So, are you ready for me to fly you out to Paris today for some playtime?"

The girl seemed excited and surprised that the number in her caller ID was international, substantiating the claim of a trip to Paris.

"So, you'll arrive in the morning, and we'll have some fun with the strap-on. Do you like DP? Will you take the dildo out of your ass and put it in your mouth? Because I'm going to make you." She felt uncomfortable speaking in this way, but she was reading the script Mitchell had written for her, and she didn't want to get in trouble.

Surprisingly, the girl responded favorably. Lauren seemed truly submissive and ready to perform any unsavory sexual acts demanded of her. A look at Mitchell showed that he didn't seem at all surprised that the girl was ready and willing.

"And you have a passport, of course?" She listened to the girl's responses. "Umm hmmm. Uh huh." Mitchell was scribbling on the paper *What is she saying? Repeat it out loud so that I'm not over here, clueless!!!!!* He underlined the exclamation points.

She nodded. "Okay, so you have to work this week? Uh huh. Okay." *Ask her how much she'll make at work.* "So how much will you forfeit if you call in sick? . . . Uh huh . . . five hundred dollars. . . . Right." *Tell her you'll give her two grand.* "What if I were to give you two thousand dollars as soon as you get off the plane? . . . Right. . . .You're sure? . . . No, you won't get fired. . . ." *Don't lose this girl, IMBECILE.* "If you're as fun as you sound, you'll be well taken care of. You won't need that job. . . . Right. . . . You're positive? . . . Okay, well, I'll call you when I return to New York." Mitchell threw down the pen. His face was bright red.

"What the hell was that?! You won't need that job?" Mitchell growled at her through clenched teeth. "You came off as weak! Don't keep making offers. You made one offer. That's all you ever make before hanging up. Damn it! What kind of domme are you? How did you lose that pussy? Damn it!"

Mitchell stood up and paced violently, running his hands roughly through his hair. She just watched him and braced herself for some sort of punishment. She wasn't sure what she could have done differently, and she just had to trust that Mitchell was angrier about having lost the girl on the line than how his companion had failed to reel her in.

"Go upstairs and pack. We're going back to New York." He turned away from her and began muttering to himself. "The idiot can't even get a girl to Paris! She can't even bring in pussy to Paris." He shook his head and skulked off.

Eleven

Back in New York, Mitchell had become obsessed with Craigslist and insisted that she spend hours every day in front of his computer, posting, reposting, and calling girls to follow up. It was labor intensive, made all the worse by the fact that she really didn't believe in what they were doing. She wasn't even curious anymore; she actually dreaded having a girl follow through. The idea of imposing sex on strange girls who would answer her postings was mildly nauseating. In fact, she had been involuntarily vomiting more frequently, and her already slight frame was shrinking. She was losing herself.

"Hello, I'm Mitchell. You must be a beautiful friend of my client's. Don't mind me, I'll just sit here in the living room and allow you two girls to have whatever fun you're going to have." Mitchell smiled at the young woman and took her coat. He then shot his companion a look to make sure that she was ready and confident to see this situation through. She knew that he was at the end of his patience with her and that this girl had better be a great fuck, or there would be hell to pay afterward.

"Would you like a glass of wine?" she offered, and the girl eagerly accepted.

The two girls sat on the couch, and Mitchell sat in his chair. The girl was placed in between them, just as Mitchell had orchestrated and rehearsed with his companion in the morning. Every element of the encounter was orchestrated perfectly down to every detail, in an effort to make it look natural and easy flowing. It seemed to be working so far.

The two girls had met up at a Starbucks around the corner from Mitchell's apartment. She got there fifteen minutes early so that she could quickly whisk the girl out of that environment before actually giving them the chance to sit and drink coffee as though it were a date. It wasn't a date, and she had to keep reminding herself that she was in the driver's seat in this situation, and the girl would only be comfortable if truly sure that the domme knew exactly what she was doing.

She had played the role well, and the girl was easily led to Mitchell's apartment, under the guise that he was a lawyer and family friend there to protect the domme, since all young heiresses must be protected. The girl seemed to trust the situation, and the domme made sure not to act unheiresslike, lest she blow her cover.

The story was believable enough, she supposed. After all, she was taking the playmate to a beautiful Park Avenue apartment, and under her mink coat, she was donning one of her best outfits, which Mitchell had selected. She really did seem to be an heiress looking to indulge in sexual deviance.

And before she knew it, she was sitting on the couch, with the girl lustfully gazing at her. She was disgusted. But Mitchell had the girl talking, and the three of them seemed to be progressing toward bedding quickly.

"I have an Armani shell that would look incredible on your model figure!" Mitchell exclaimed to the lanky plaything. "Would you mind putting it on for me so that I may see how it's supposed to look when truly worn properly?"

The fucktoy blushed and quickly removed her top layer of clothing in anticipation of playing dress-up with clothing she had only fantasized about. Meanwhile, Mitchell's companion laughed in her own mind. That stupid coat seemed to be in his repertoire. She wondered if the reason Mitchell had liked her in the first place was because it hadn't worked as a lure for her that first night. She dismissed the notion and joined Mitchell in admiring the young beauty, who was playfully prancing around the living room.

"You look gorgeous in that. But you'll have to take it off so that we don't mess it up while I'm fucking you." The fucktoy stopped prancing and smiled. Mitchell looked at his companion and winked; he seemed pleased with her having taken control of the situation.

"Remember, the object of the game is to get her to go from being your fucktoy to being our sandwich meat." Mitchell's words resonated in her mind as she watched the girl disrobe and kneel on all fours on the bed. The domme commented on her candy-apple ass and confidently attached her strap-on around her pelvis. Showtime.

She began to fuck the girl from behind, and she slapped the girl's hand away when the girl tried to reach around to touch the domme. She didn't mind fucking a girl as long as the girl didn't touch her. A giant rubber appendage successfully kept intimacy at bay, but if the girl touched her, that crossed a boundary she would not allow.

The girl screamed in pleasure, and she laughed as she got violently slapped on the ass. Mitchell entered the bedroom and sat in his armchair. He and his companion made eye contact, and he smiled. She began slapping the girl's ass in alternating strokes, and Mitchell laughed a deep belly laugh. He seemed genuinely pleased. The girl's pleasure was just incidental.

Mitchell removed his pants and began to stroke his cock. She ordered the girl to the floor and had her kneel without the comfort of a pillow under her knees. Meanwhile, she took a pillow for herself, and as the girl sucked Mitchell's cock, she reentered the girl from behind. She was surprised at how easy that position was to maintain.

The girl climaxed several times, and eventually Mitchell declared, "Get ready to take your gift." He came in the girl's mouth and watched, pleased, as the girl swallowed all of it.

The domme took off her strap-on and put it in the sink under hot water. Then she got dressed, walked into the living room, and took a big swig of wine. She gave the flushed fucktoy a few moments to regain composure and then demanded that the girl dress and leave.

With a smile from ear to ear, the fucktoy put a coat on, took up the purse, and left. After they heard the elevator ping, Mitchell turned to his companion for a debriefing.

"Well, you got some happy sandwich meat. But you made me talk to her for way longer than I wanted." Mitchell sighed. "Don't make me talk to these dirt bags. Don't waste time. Just fuck them."

From the time they had met at Starbucks to the time the girl had left the apartment, only forty-five minutes had elapsed. She didn't have any experience bedding girls, but she was pretty sure that forty-five minutes was an enviably short time. Most men would kill to fuck a girl, kick her out, and not so much as buy her a coffee at the Starbucks where they met.

Even though he was critical, Mitchell seemed pleased too. He appeared to be momentarily content with the notion that his young companion may be a valuable asset to him after all. He hugged her, brought her the Armani coat, and the two of them headed out to a late afternoon lunch.

"Five a week. Just like that. Well, sort of like that. That was a start. The fucktoy could have been thinner." Mitchell gave his rundown of the afternoon's events as he gorged himself on his favorite veal saltimbocca at the elite local cash-and-invite-only Italian restaurant.

"A week?"

"When you get good, and you will soon, you'll be bringing me five a day. Come on, you saw how easy it is."

She didn't think that it had been that easy. Well, the action was easy, but getting herself into the mindset of a domme over a female sub took effort. Mitchell must have known that, right?

"Okay, Mitchell. I'll get to work on lining up lots of fun."

"Very well." Mitchell swallowed his mouthful of veal, swigged his wine, and appeared to be settling into a serious dialogue. "One was easy for you. But that was a test. One is the most difficult, my dear. So, next time you set a date, you invite three or four fucktoys." Mitchell laughed, as though recalling an amusing memory. "And you arrive an hour late. You'll love watching what happens." He stopped for a moment, deep in thought. "Now that I think about it, you'll have to buy more ball gags. A group of pussy tends to get talky. You'll have to plug them up." Mitchell gave her a genuine smile. "My dear, you may be my best girl yet. You're a natural."

She had a date arranged with four girls at 10 the next evening, to be held at a nightclub near her apartment. She went in there at around 8 p.m. to let the owner, Matt, who happened to be a close friend, know what the story was.

"Okay, so, Matt, I'm going to have a group of girls meeting me here. They all know to ask you where I am. I need you to talk me up and keep them here. But I'm going to be late. Keep a tab open and pretend to bill it to me as though I have an ongoing account."

"Ha! You've brought me enough business over the years; you should have an account! And if this pussy is hot, your bill will disappear."

"Really? Because I'm going to be doing this a lot."

"Okay, stop turning me on. Just bring in the pussy. I'll get them hot for you before you get here," Matt said.

She smiled to herself, realizing that even though Mitchell treated her as though she were unlovable by anyone else, there were people in her world who kept an eye out for her and considered her a true friend. She had to remind herself that Matt was one of those guys. In fact, she felt comfortable coming home to her block late at night because she knew that Matt had instructed his bouncers to watch for her. He had never said it outright, but somehow the large suit-clad goons were always at her front door, helping with her keys and groceries, even when there were huge crowds gathering at the velvet ropes.

And once again, Matt was happy to help out.

At the same time, he didn't seem to question anything. Which led her to think again, was she the only one who thought that this lifestyle was a bit off color? She was hoping for Matt to have some sort of reaction; then, maybe she wouldn't feel so crazy.

She sat in her apartment and watched the clock. The girls were going to begin showing up at Matt's bar at 10 p.m.; she planned to arrive at around 10:30. She made a mental list of her plan for the evening. There would be three girls there to meet her, but none of them knew that they were going to be part of a mini competition for her attention.

The plan was to get one or all of them back up to her apartment as quickly as possible. As Mitchell had explained to her, if the girls really thought that they were just having a sexual relationship with her, they'd be far more likely to go to his apartment and fuck him too. It made sense. She resigned to the notion of a sexual bait-and-switch.

When her clock read close to 10:30, she put her strap-on and some dildos into her Burberry purse and went downstairs to the bar. There were three girls sitting at the bar on stools, bickering loudly. They all stopped and turned to her when Matt pointed out that she had just walked in.

Instantly, the girls began to fight for her attention. One girl was a baker and had brought a package of goodies from her shop. Another girl had eaten them, and both were upset and embarrassed. This was going to be even easier than she had thought.

She ordered the girls to stop yelling and to kiss each other, all of them, in front of everyone at the bar. She was secretly hoping for a reaction from the crowd, but when none came, she had to remind herself that this was New York, and nothing surprised anyone.

The girls passionately kissed and fondled each other, and she watched with a blank look of apathy. The girls noticed and tried to grind into each other harder to illicit a signal from her that she was pleased. After several minutes, she ordered the girls to get their coats together and follow her upstairs.

Once inside her apartment, the girls began to talk to her. She quickly realized that they thought this was a date. She had never really been on a date with a girl, let alone three. She pretended to listen for a few minutes. Then she realized why she never dated girls: they were annoying, their stories were boring and long, and they never shut up. She ordered everyone to shut up. Startled, they did.

All three girls sat on the bed as she arranged an assortment of toys and lubrication packets on the nightstand. They seemed to get more excited, so she took a moment to have all of them begin kissing and undressing each other. In a way, she felt bad that she didn't enjoy this, but she just wanted to get it over with so that when she saw Mitchell the next day, she wouldn't have to fabricate a story. Not that she could lie to him. He was such a good interrogator that she was scared to ever veer from the truth.

When all the girls were naked, she had them begin eating each other's pussies. She suddenly realized that they were going to get her quilt all wet, and she made a mental note to lay out towels or a crappy blanket in the future. The girls were moaning and panting, but they were clearly anxious for her to step into the mix.

She put on her strap-on and stood alongside the bed. She had the girls take turns sucking the rubber dick, and then she had them take turns on their knees taking her in from behind. Mitchell had made it clear that she was only supposed to penetrate their assholes. Although she didn't know why, she followed his rules.

The first girl seemed surprised when she entered the asshole, but the girl was much more surprised when she was ordered to clean off the cock with her mouth to make it ready to enter then next girl in line. The girl looked hesitant, as though she were hoping it was just a joke. But when she got nods from her domme and the other two girls, she quickly plunged the purple rubber tube into her mouth and licked and sucked it vigorously.

The second girl realized what was happening when it was her turn and refused to take the strap-on in her mouth after it had been in her asshole. The domme looked at the clock and saw that it was 11:30. She was tired and didn't have the patience for this girl's whining. She grabbed the girl by the hair and forced her face into the cock laden with pieces of her shit. The girl's demeanor changed, and she began talking incessantly and trying to rationalize why she was disobeying.

The domme threw her out, and the other girls laughed.

"That's why you need a ball gag," the baker said.

She felt bad because she realized that in other circumstances, she would actually like the baker and would have enjoyed being friends. But right now, her loyalties were to Mitchell. And so she encouraged the other two girls to laugh at the lost girl's expense.

After about twenty more minutes of fucking and sucking, she sent the other two girls home. She then called Mitchell and reported every detail.

"So, what did you learn from this experience, my dear?"

"I learned that women are talkative cunts, and I need a ball gag to protect my ears."

Mitchell laughed a deep, true laugh. "You're learning quickly! And tomorrow I'll send you out to buy an arsenal of ball gags so that you don't have to listen to any more bitching."

"Amen."

"Amen."

❧

"So, tell me again exactly what happened."

She was tired of repeating the story over and over to Mitchell. But he seemed enthralled by it. So she swallowed the bite of sushi she had in her mouth, took a swig of wine, and told the story again.

Mitchell had a sinister smile as he closed his eyes and pictured the scene with the four naked young women. "Ah yes," he muttered over and over.

She was happy that he was pleased and not actively reprimanding her, so she felt more comfortable that afternoon with Mitchell. He was kind to her.

"And tell me about this Matt? He's okay with the whole situation?"

"Yes, and he's got his employees up to speed, too. It's all worked out. That's our meeting location near my place."

"Good, good." Mitchell thought for a moment. "Put the chopsticks down. Go to the computer and arrange another for tonight. Then go out and buy some ball gags. Here's a few hundies." Mitchell handed her a wad of cash, and she went and returned some emails and set up another posting.

When she was through in the study, she walked back into the living room and picked up her coat and her purse. She looked longingly at her unfinished meal.

"All set?"

"All set."

"Good. You can go home after you stop at the toy store."

That night played out similarly to the night before. She left the three girls waiting, and then appeared after being significantly tardy. This group of girls was gorgeous, but one of them seemed to be on some sort of drug. The girl was rambling, her pupils were dilated, and she seemed agitated and anxious. The domme was trying to figure out which drug caused this erratic behavior, but then she dismissed the notion. After all, who was she to judge?

Just as in the previous night, the girls began to fight. Because one of them seemed so drugged out, the domme opted not to bring them straight up to her apartment. Instead, she ordered them into the ladies' room. *All the play happens in the girls' room*, she heard Mitchell's voice in her head.

She got the girls into the bathroom and affixed a ball gag into each of their mouths to stop the bickering. Two of the girls obliged, but the one on drugs seemed to resent the muzzle. The domme grabbed the girl by the hair and yanked violently.

"I told you to shut up!"

The girl stopped whimpering and fidgeting.

She looked at the three girls on their knees in front of her on the bathroom floor, all of them with ball gags in place, all waiting for her to give her next order. She had to admit, this power was intoxicating.

"Now, if I remove the ball gags, do you all promise to stay shut up?"

"Mmmmm hmmm," they all mumbled in unison.

"Good. You can take the ball gags out of your mouths, and all kiss each other." She realized that she was taking out her anger toward Mitchell on these poor girls. But then she realized that that was probably why Mitchell treated her so badly, to make her yearn for control over someone. He was a brilliant sadist.

The girls began to kiss, and they all began to remove their clothing and suck each others' nipples. One girl moved to another girl's pussy, and the domme looked on as the three girls began to grind on the bathroom floor. She decided to remain standing and drop her slacks to reveal her own perfectly waxed pussy.

The girls wrestled each other for the chance to lick the domme's pussy. Though she was enjoying the moment and the control, she noticed that the drugged-out girl was beginning to act up again. She ordered the ball gag back into her mouth.

"You. Druggy slut. I want you to bend over so I can fuck you in the asshole."

The girl quickly stood and bent over the sink. The girl seemed to enjoy the fucking, but soon began to once again ramble incoherently. The domme demanded that she reinstate the useful ball gag.

The girl took the ball gag, and in her drugged-out sexual ecstasy, she bit through the rubber ball. The other girls laughed, and the domme demanded that she put in one of the ball gags from another girl. One of the other girls fastened it around the back of her head.

Everything seemed to be going smoothly until the drugged-out girl seemed to get more agitated by being put on display in front of the other submissives.

She began to squirm, and the purple cock popped out of her ass. The girl threw on her shirt and her jeans, and with the ball gag still in her mouth, ran out of the ladies' room.

The domme instructed the other girls to get dressed while she went out to perform damage control. When she found the girl on the couches in the back of the bar, she noticed that the ball gag was gone.

"Where is my ball gag?"

"Fuck you and your ball gag. Fuck this bar! Fuck everyone! I need a drink!"

"Why don't we just get you home?"

"I can't remember where I live."

The girl was 5' 10" and blonde, well dressed, well groomed, and drop-dead gorgeous, maybe about twenty-five and definitely a former model. The domme guessed that she had probably screwed up her career with this obvious drug problem, her sexual deviances notwithstanding.

"Okay. Don't make a scene. We'll figure out where you live, and we'll get you home safely." She reverted to her pre-Mitchell state of caring, kindness, and concern. "Come on, just tell me what you took. Do we need to take you to an apartment or a hospital?"

"I don't need a fucking hospital! I don't need a fucking hospital! I just need someone to tell me where I live. I can't remember!"

"Okay, calm down." She looked around and saw the other two girls, their faces still flushed from the joys of sex, standing beside her. She focused her attention on them. "I need you to stay with her and make sure that she's okay. I'm going to make a phone call. Wait here, right?" The girls nodded, and the domme slipped out onto the sidewalk.

"Mitchell?"

"Why are you calling me this late? I only want you to call me when you have pleasant details. But you, you sound stressed."

"I'm sorry. I am a little stressed. One of the girls is on something, and I can't get her under control. The best domme in the world can't overpower crazy drugs."

"Okay, it's fine, my dear. This is not your fault. This happens. Now, what went wrong?"

"Well, she was belligerent and aggressive. I tried fucking her and she broke a ball gag. Then she stole another one."

Mitchell laughed. "She stole your ball gag? Your new ball gags? That bitch! I'll be right over."

She went back into the bar and watched as the gorgeous blonde flared her arms and legs in a drug-induced rage. She had heard of addicts tweaking, but she would have really appreciated it if it hadn't happened in her go-to bar. She didn't want to become persona non grata.

Mitchell arrived almost instantly. In fact, it was almost superhumanly quick. He was wearing a trench coat over his pajamas. His entrance was legendary.

He pushed the bouncer aside and announced with his hands on his hips, "The ball gag patrol has arrived!" Everyone in the bar laughed. She stepped aside and allowed Mitchell to diffuse the situation.

"Okay, ladies. Who lives where?"

One of the girls replied, "I live in Brooklyn."

"Okay, it's really late to get to Brooklyn. Here's three hundred dollars. Will that pay for a taxi?"

The girl looked at the stack of bills, and then looked at the domme. She nodded, dismissing her minion. The girl bowed her head and ran out the door.

"And you, sweetheart? Where do you live?" Mitchell focused on the other girl.

"I live downtown."

"Okay, here's cab fare for you too."

"But I don't want to leave. We haven't finished playing yet."

"Oh, sweetheart, tonight is finished. But your friend will call you tomorrow." He looked over at his companion and mouthed *Get her over to my place tomorrow*. She nodded.

Mitchell then turned his attention to the girl who was now clearly strung out. "And where do you live, sweetheart?"

"I don't remember," the drugged-up girl barely mumbled.

"Well, you're beautiful and well dressed. You must live somewhere!"

"I don't remember."

"Okay. Well, maybe you don't remember that. But do you remember where you hid the ball gag?"

The druggie shook her head.

Mitchell sighed. "Okay, well, we want to get you home. But you've got to help us out."

"Leave me alone!" the girl shrieked. Grabbing a purse, she ran out the door and hailed a cab instantly.

Mitchell turned to his companion. "Well, you didn't get your ball gag back, but she left you a nice coat!" Mitchell handed her an expensive-looking black winter coat, complete with strands of the previous owner's silky blonde hair stuck in the fabric.

She took the coat over one arm and picked up her purse.

"Okay, my dear." Mitchell leaned over and kissed her cheek delicately. "I'm going home. You did a good job tonight. And you were right to call me. Tomorrow, I want the details." He adjusted his top coat and walked down the bar stairs to his car, still idling outside.

As Mitchell settled into the driver's seat, and she exited the bar, he rolled down his window and called out. "I'd have that coat dry cleaned before I'd wear it. No telling where that skank has been." And he drove off.

Coat in hand, and a few ball gags lighter, she walked the few paces back to her front door and trudged up the stairs, exhausted.

❧

"Ball gag patrol." Mitchell laughed. "That was pretty funny, huh?"

"It was hysterical," she replied. "I can't believe you showed up in your pajamas."

"Hey, my girl needed help." Mitchell looked at her warmly. "Come sit next to me."

She snuggled up next to him on the sofa and they lay silent for a moment.

"You know what you earned, my dear?"

She merely glanced up at him and murmured, "Mmmm?"

"We're going to go to Osaka this weekend for the Sumo tournaments. And, if we time everything correctly, we'll catch the cherry blossom festival in Tokyo, too. How does that sound?"

"That sounds wonderful, Mitchell, thank you."

"No, thank you. By the way, I'm sending you out to buy more ball gags. These bitches are fierce."

They both laughed. Then they settled in to absently watch the news ticker on Fox News.

"You know what? I'm going to take you out for lunch. Run of the menu."

She had learned to love that phrase.

Twelve

"We may be gone for a while, so we'll pack our trunks instead of our little bags." Mitchell began to sort and fold his clothes.

She thought it was odd yet strangely comforting that he referred to his home and his trunks as belonging to both of them. But then again, the two of them had settled into a life that seemed to have instantaneously isolated them from the rest of the world. They were somehow each other's family.

Mitchell brought out matching Goyard trunks, one red and one blue. They were beautiful but seemed cumbersome to use; they had but one handle on the top and no wheels or straps. She thought of the Burberry laundry bag with its puny top handles and wondered why Mitchell insisted on owning things that were entirely not user-friendly designs. She supposed it was because the help carried the bags, and people of Mitchell's caste enjoyed watching lesser people struggle with luggage that cost more than a month's pay.

Mitchell assigned her the red trunk and his Louis Vuitton roller bag, and he kept the blue trunk that matched both his Goyard rolling bag and his man purse.

"You know, my dear," Mitchell spoke as he buried his clothes in the trunk, "when you get married, I'm going to give you and your husband matching sets of Goyard luggage. Every new bride needs luggage. Especially you, beautiful, because the man you marry is going to have to bounce around the world with you. The man you marry is going to have this lifestyle and love you as much as I do." Mitchell looked up at her and sneered, "Although, he'll actually be attracted to you and may even want to fuck you. I'll never be that desperate." He laughed.

She couldn't decide if that was an insult veiled as a compliment or a compliment veiled as an insult. But she shrugged it off and focused on their pending flight that afternoon into Osaka. They were going to fly across the Pacific with a stopover in Los Angeles. Then they would fly to Osaka, where they would stay for a few days. After that, she wasn't entirely clear on the plan; her paper ticket had a return flight from Tokyo into Atlanta, via the Atlantic.

"Are you thinking about the trip, my dear?"

"I was just going over the itinerary in my head."

"Did you notice the special treat I managed to book for you? It's a bit of the trip of a lifetime."

"Because we're going over both oceans?"

"Because we're going around the world! We're going around the world!" Mitchell seemed giddy. "I bet you've never flown around the world in one trip."

"No, I haven't."

"It's exciting and special to you, isn't it? Me, I've been everywhere twice. But you! You've never even flown around the world!" Mitchell tapped his forefinger to his cheek to gesture her to give him a small kiss. She gave him a delicate peck, and he blushed. "Don't ever think I don't treat you better than any man you'll ever find."

"I know, Mitchell."

"I know you know. Are you finished packing? It's time to leave."

They arrived in Osaka drunk and exhausted early in the morning. After clearing customs, Mitchell grabbed her by the arm and rushed her into a photo booth to take visa pictures. He explained that it was in the event that they changed their return flight and decided to continue the trip elsewhere. She had always been extremely photogenic, and she was shocked when she saw her roll of photos develop in front of her.

The woman in the photos seemed hollow; the eyes were completely vacant. She looked not only drunk but thoroughly depleted of fight in her soul. She thought for a moment of the stories of vampires appearing soulless in photos and suddenly realized what had happened when she'd agreed to be Mitchell's companion and subsequent pimp. She had joined the ranks of the undead.

"Give me the photos, my dear. I'll put them in my fag bag so that we'll have them safe and at the ready."

She handed him the photos, and he handed her five thousand dollars' worth of traveler's checks to change to yen as he organized their lodging situation. She returned with a large stack of cash in hand. Mitchell grabbed a wad of bills off the top of the pile and handed it to her.

The Japanese taxi had several features she had never seen. For one, there was a three-dimensional GPS unit next to the driver that showed not only the individual buildings as they drove past them, but the relative heights and depths. She was more than a bit intrigued by the technology and continuously looked down at the screen and then over to the buildings that were more than a digital concept. She had been in Japan for only a few minutes and already she was impressed.

They pulled into the St. Regis, and she happened to look at the fare total and was shocked to see that it was more than 300,000 yen. She had just changed the currency at the airport, so she knew full well that that was the equivalent of almost $250. The ride had lasted for less than a half hour, yet it was the most expensive car ride she had ever taken. Knowing that Mitchell had the propensity to be very cheap, she was nervous to witness his breaking point, were it to come.

They settled into a beautiful suite overlooking the factories and commercial buildings that fill Osaka. It seemed to be a cold and sterile place, laden with blue-collar commerce. She thought it odd that such a desolate working-class town would host the Sumo tournaments. Mitchell had already explained to her that tickets cost several thousand dollars, and that people dressed just short of ball gowns to attend. Black tie was encouraged. But somehow, in this city, it just didn't seem to fit.

"Okay, my dear, are you hungry?"

"Always." She smiled at Mitchell. He winked back.

"We'll go out for some kaiseki. Kaiseki originated in Osaka, did you know that?"

"I didn't know where it originated, but I love international tasting menus. Do you know where we can go?"

"My dear, I am not your tour guide. But I do have some ideas. Why don't we go and eat some sushi first? I'm famished. We can figure the rest out from there."

And so, without even so much as washing up or changing clothes after the long travel, the duo headed out in search of a venue for another of their many extravagant meals. After stuffing themselves on sushi, followed by temaki, the most incredible dessert she had ever tasted—a handroll filled with rice, fresh uni, and a raw quail egg on top—they continued on to a restaurant serving real Kobe beef, even though she already felt overstuffed. About halfway through the steak, she excused herself to the ladies' room and barely had time to bend over the toilet before most of the steak and the previous sushi lunch reappeared in a gentle, steady flow. Feeling better, she returned to the table and finished the rest of the steak.

Mitchell summoned the check, and she sneaked a peak. The bill was over 3,000,000 yen. That was more than a couple thousand dollars. Mitchell didn't even blink. For a moment, she was reminded that her new life was that of a hedonistic lady of leisure. And she fit the role very well.

Back at the hotel, Mitchell requested a blowjob. She was still in "training," and as much as she hated taking his foul-smelling cock in her mouth, she did appreciate that he was taking the time to teach her to do it correctly. Mitchell always said that his biggest contribution to her life was going to be her ability to catch and keep a great man. And whether or not she believed him, at the very least, she was grateful for the training. Humiliating as it was.

"Get a pillow for your knees. Your legs are skinny and ugly, so no one will ever see them but me. But still, you don't deserve bruises, my dear."

Mitchell positioned himself in the armchair of the hotel suite, and she physically recited the fellatio strategy that the two had been practicing since they had first met. Mitchell's toes curled and wagged, and he repeated the phrase, "That's it. That's it." It seemed to her that she was finally getting the skills to work for her.

Right before he came, Mitchell muttered, "Get ready for your prize." He groaned and came in her mouth. She took it all and hid it behind her tongue, pretending to swallow. She then went into the bathroom, spit it out, and washed her hands. When she returned to the living room, she realized that in the thirty seconds she had been gone, Mitchell had fallen fast asleep. He was snoring loudly, seated with his pants around his ankles. She wasn't sure if the cause was jet lag, too much alcohol with lunch, or the release of an orgasm. But she was sure that he was out cold. She found a bathrobe in the closet, hung up her clothes, and went under the covers of the bed to take a nap while there was peace.

At 11 p.m., he woke her for yet another meal, this time kaiseki, course after course of incredible food, including innovative versions of whale, blowfish, and horse. Mitchell was the perfect host, and he not only treated her like a queen, but he sent bottles of sake to the other patrons in their enclosures. As other diners filed out, they popped their heads in and nodded *arigato*. It was a perfect evening.

After about five hours, they were sated, drunk, and exhausted. They walked back toward the hotel, navigating their way through the narrow streets and stepping over the drunk men in business suits passed out like so many bodies sprinkling the cobblestones.

"Wake up! Wake up!" She was growing thoroughly tired of being awakened by a manic Mitchell shaking her. "Wake up!"

"What time is it?" Darkness was still seeping in through the blinds.

"It's time to order breakfast—Japanese breakfast, of course—and then I'm going to find the Sumo tickets as you take a day trip to Kyoto!"

"Kyoto?"

"Yes! You'll see Geisha girls and beautiful temples. And best of all, you'll be out of my hair for the whole day."

"What are you talking about?"

"I need you to go to Kyoto to scope it out for yourself. I've been several times, but I need you to see it as it is now." Mitchell's eyes grew foggy as he lapsed into a fond memory. "You see, my dear, I've sent pussy to Kyoto to be dressed as Geisha and have the hair and the makeup and—oh! They eat it up! And they're so grateful afterwards that they'll suck my cock up, down, and sideways. But if you're going to use Kyoto as part of your game, you have to be familiar with it. You can't take a fucktoy there and have her realize that it's your first time, too. So, wake up!"

She pulled herself out of bed. Her head was pounding from a sake hangover, but Mitchell was one step ahead of her; he was already pouring her a glass from a freshly opened bottle of champagne. It was a failsafe plan; alcohol was the only surefire cure for a hangover. That or giving up drinking, which was clearly not going to happen in their world.

She wasn't sure what the Kyoto tour included, but she had a sneaking suspicion that Mitchell was going to make her feel guilty about the cost and would probably not give her any yen. Recently, he had been making more of a show about the prices of things and the amount of money that he gave her. He seemed to think that she was not earning her keep to the extent that he was offering, and she had made it a point never to ask for anything. Mitchell referred to it as "needling" for money, and he chastised her for it.

"Hurry up!"

"What time does the tour leave?"

"Do I look like the fucking tour guide?!" Mitchell raised his voice. "I came up with the idea. I offered the trip. You can do some work, you lazy bitch! Go to the concierge and book your tour." Mitchell slammed his newspaper down and scuffled off into the other room muttering obscenities to himself.

She never understood what caused Mitchell to go from extreme happiness to extreme hostility in an instant. She figured that it had something to do with alcohol, but he seemed to act the same way sober—the few times she had seen him sober. Many new articles had been released on bipolar disease, but even after reading them, she thought Mitchell seemed too extreme to fit the diagnosis. She relinquished herself to the notion that he was just insane, and she resigned herself to relish the good moments and let the painful ones roll off.

She was happy to leave. His mood swings were more than she could process. She gathered some belongings and headed into the lobby to wait for the tour group to retrieve her.

The rest of the group was already waiting on the train platform when the minibus from her hotel arrived to meet them. She took a quick visual survey and determined that she was the only American. Everyone else seemed to be Scandinavian or German, judging by their fair skin and odd apparel. She always thought it odd that she wore European designer brands, but no Europeans seemed to dress as well. She shook off the thought and joined the crowd on the platform.

The train arrived exactly to the second that it was scheduled; to the Japanese, punctuality is paramount. She appreciated the dependability of small graces, and she liked that the Japanese seemed to appreciate pageantry as much as, or more than, she did.

Inside the train, the aisles were clean and the seats were comfortable and spacious. Within an hour, the group arrived in Kyoto, and the guide met them on the platform as they exited.

She smelled something fresh and light in the air and realized that the cherry blossoms had already bloomed in Kyoto. The group boarded a bus, and they drove through the streets as cherry blossoms flew by like snowflakes.

In comparison to the urban wasteland that had consumed Osaka with factories and businesses, Kyoto was a respite of paradise. Time seemed to pass more slowly, and everything seemed to be more beautiful. The group climbed a tall hill strewn with street vendors and shops to reach the temple at the summit. There, they received a lecture, in English, about the history of Kyoto. The group then walked on the bridges over the ponds and lingered in the spiritual chambers. Kyoto was gorgeous. She could see why Mitchell wanted her to bring prospective girls here to wow them.

After they had had a substantial amount of free time, the group reconvened to journey back to the train station. The return trip seemed even shorter, but she glanced at her watch and realized that it was almost 5 p.m. She hoped that Mitchell wouldn't be angry that she had been gone all day.

❧

"No Sumo."

"What?"

"I am very angry with this concierge. He was unable to secure our tickets to the Sumo matches. Look, they're on TV."

"We can't go tomorrow?"

"Imbecile, we can't go at all. This hotel is an aberration! We'll never stay here again!"

She thought that the hotel was lovely, but she knew better than to do anything but agree with Mitchell.

"Kyoto was wonderful."

"Really? Tell me."

"Well, the cherry blossoms were in bloom, and—"

"You saw the cherry blossoms? Damn it! Could this day get any worse? First, I miss the Sumo, which is the only reason we came to this cesspool of a city. Now I've missed the cherry blossoms, too. Damn it!"

"We can see the cherry blossoms tomorrow, if you'd—"

"Tomorrow we go to Tokyo. I've booked our first-class tickets on the bullet train."

"You have to book tickets for the train?"

"Tokyo is on the other side of the country, genius. Taking the train is faster than flying. And the Japanese are so fucking small, I need two first-class train seats to accommodate my fat ass."

"Oh, well—"

"Don't worry. I got you a ticket, too." Mitchell winked at her, sipped a glass of wine, and refocused his attention on the Sumo tournament.

For some reason, Mitchell thought it a good idea to take the subway to the bullet train. So the two of them struggled with the trunks up and down the stairs to the subway. Mitchell seemed not to care that she was in high heels and spent most of the journey yelling at her to keep up. She tried to balance the weights in both arms but failed more often than she succeeded. She hoped that the subway ride did not require any transfers.

When they arrived at the station, Mitchell hired a baggage handler to take the cases, and the two of them found their seats on the train. She thought it odd that Mitchell indulged in luxury, like baggage handlers, only when people of "worth" were looking. He thought nothing of embarrassing both of them in the tunnels of the subway, where the only people who spotted them were common folk. His priorities were clearly unique, but again, she thought nothing of it as she settled into her seat for the three-hour seven hundred-mile train ride.

She napped a bit, but every time she opened her eyes, she watched lush countryside whiz past her. She saw Mt. Fuji in the distance and would have pointed it out to Mitchell, but he was fast asleep in an alcohol-induced haze.

They arrived in Tokyo right on schedule, and Mitchell summoned a baggage handler to bring their belongings to a taxi.

"We're going to stay in Ginza. It's right in the heart of everything. Sure, there are more expensive, fancier hotels, but this hotel is expensive enough, and we can get to wherever we're going."

"Where are we going?"

"Enough with the questions!"

"Sorry."

"Enough with the sorrys!"

"Yes, sir."

Mitchell sighed violently.

He turned to the driver and in broken Japanese asked him to deliver them to the Ginza Nikka Hotel.

"You'll like this hotel. It's simple, very Japanese. And centrally located."

"Okay. Thank you." She knew to thank Mitchell often. It stroked his ego and could temporarily keep his temper at bay.

They pulled up along the sidewalk in front of what looked like a dilapidated old city motel. But Mitchell nodded toward the entrance in recognition, and she realized that this was his desired destination.

There were steps leading up to the lobby from the sidewalk, and there was no valet to assist them. The Nikka was a far cry from the St. Regis Osaka.

She clumsily dragged the bags into the small, narrow, barren lobby as Mitchell rang the desk bell to summon a receptionist. Eventually someone arrived, and Mitchell began to haggle. In the end, he seemed frustrated, and he anxiously grabbed the bags from her hands.

"They want six hundred dollars a night for this hovel. We would have been better off in Osaka. What a scam!"

They pressed the button for the up elevator and then squeezed in to head to their fifth-floor room. She was small, and even she thought that the elevator was not big enough even for one.

They found their room number, and Mitchell unlocked the door to reveal a small, dark, windowless chamber with two small twin beds. "My dear, welcome to Tokyo."

Thirteen

Their first day, they napped, wandered through the streets, ate, ate some more, and napped again. In the pitch black of night, Mitchell shook her violently awake and picked up her shoulders to lift her out of bed. "Hurry up and get dressed, imbecile! We're going to dinner."

"Now? Where?"

"Don't ask. I'm doing something nice for you, and you're needling me. Just get dressed and let's go. Wear a sweater. I think it's cold out."

She dragged herself into the bathroom and gazed into herself in the mirror. There were dark black circles under her eyes, and she looked like she was losing weight. This new lifestyle was aging her quickly.

After a quick taxi ride, they pulled up alongside an insane scene of a seaport. There were tens of thousands of men running as quickly as they were able in their thick rubber boots. Some of the men carried large knives; others were dragging carts overflowing with fish. Men in small forklifts drove erratically between them, like a dangerous game of Frogger.

As they exited the taxi, Mitchell instructed her, "Stay close to me, and move quickly. These people will think nothing of running you down." He began to briskly walk away. As he moved, he called back to her, "By the way, welcome to the Tsukiji fish market."

She had lived in New York City for years and had been to the fish markets. But, short of the similarity in smell, this was nothing like Fulton Street. This marketplace was a hodgepodge of insanity. Everyone seemed to be going through the brisk motions of a daily routine, so she just tried her best to stay out of the way.

Mitchell navigated their way through barrels of fish and puddles of slop until they reached the warehouses at the end of the pier. She noticed that they were the only white people around, and their presence was completely ignored by the natives.

"I want to show you the tuna evaluation area." He motioned for her to walk by his side, and together they entered a massive warehouse brimming with men with large hooks poking at what seemed like a million lifeless carcasses of huge fish. "This is where all the tuna in the world passes through to be priced. Those men are experts at determining the quality and grade of the tuna the ships bring in. After Tsukiji, these fish are put back on ships and in planes and sent either to be canned or sold as real product everywhere else. Do you want to get closer?"

They walked up to the carcasses, trying not to draw attention to themselves. No one seemed to notice them. Mitchell spoke in a whisper, which seemed odd because the space was booming with shouting and forceful voices. But she followed his lead and spoke back in a whisper.

"This is amazing. Some of this fish must be 500 pounds."

"Oh, more than that, I'm sure," Mitchell replied.

"I had no idea tuna fish were so big."

"They're massive. And more expensive than gold. But, now you've seen something few people ever will. And that's why we had to get here so early. The fish come in at 4 a.m. And these men work fast. If we had come any later, we would have missed this. This is one of the truly beautiful sites in the world."

She had to agree. It was an amazing scene to take in. She even forgot about the pungent odor of dead fish and focused on drawing in the scene of what was truly a form of art.

"Thank you, Mitchell."

"Don't thank me. I knew you'd love this. And I bet now you're hungry. So let's carefully exit this area and go get some dinner. Try not to get hit by the men with the forklifts. They're crazy, and they're reckless. They'll mow you down and not even notice. They're Asian drivers." Mitchell laughed.

Sushi bars lined the edges of the market, and men crowded at the countertops of outdoor serving areas rushing through their meals. There were lines waiting at the entrances of some more formal establishments, but Mitchell had no patience to wait.

"We are getting the freshest fish possible. There was a place I liked, but I don't know if I can find it again. And I don't remember what it's called. If it even has a name."

They walked quickly through the huts and restaurants as Mitchell tried to find what was familiar. At about 4:30 a.m. he gave up and found an entrance that he thought appealing.

"The secret in Japan is in the entrances. And this one looks like there's good fish inside."

They moved the canvas overlay aside and crowded into two seats at the sushi bar. Unlike sushi joints in the U.S., these traditional sushi houses do not have table seating. This particular venue had one long bar, and the wall was uncomfortably close to the seats at the bar. It was a tight passage even for the slight Japanese, but Mitchell, at his height and girth, struggled to make his entry.

The waitress brought them sake and beer and a picture menu. Mitchell was offended, as though she thought he didn't speak Japanese and was unable to communicate with the sushi chef! He tossed the menu aside and began to order feverishly in broken Japanese.

The food that arrived was delicate and flavorful. The fish was absolutely perfect. No soy sauce needed, although she did notice that some of the Japanese patrons were dipping the fish into fresh mayonnaise. Mitchell followed her gaze. "You'd love it here. These people love their mayonnaise almost as much as you do."

After they had each eaten a dozen small pieces of assorted sushi, Mitchell patted his belly. "I'm still hungry. Let's get something big."

She couldn't imagine what big item could be served in such a small space, but she could tell that Mitchell was in a good mood, and she was excited to find out.

He looked around the small restaurant pensively. His gaze settled on the fish tank with live fish behind the chef. In broken Japanese, he pointed to the largest fish and inquired the price.

"60,000 yen? Really? A steal! We'd like that, kudosai." Mitchell swiveled on his bar stool and turned back toward her. "All fish in the U.S. is required to be flash frozen. So far, we've had fresh fish that's come in this morning, and that's wonderful. But let's have a live fish, shall we?" He smiled mischievously. She liked him in this mood.

The sushi chef reached a net into the tank and pulled out the fish. As it flopped about in front of him, he deftly stripped it of its scales. Satisfied with its outer cleaning, he grabbed it firmly by the tail and lifted it into the air. The fish flailed about, curving its body every which way. The chef seemed unfazed, and with every downward curve, he nicked the body with his sharp knife. His movements were so quick and precise that she almost thought he missed the fish.

After what seemed like less than a minute, the chef presented a platter before them with the fish jackknifing atop it. There were thin strips of meat just barely clinging to the center of the fish as it flopped on the plate, trying to get away.

"You see that? That's not rigor mortis movement. This fish is alive. I don't think it comes any fresher than this." Mitchell smiled as he jabbed his chopsticks at the fish and plucked out a perfectly sliced piece of living flesh.

She followed suit and waited for a clear moment to get her chopsticks into the fish and pull out a bite for herself. This fish was aggressive but seemed unaware that his body was being eaten from around him. He seemed more concerned with the fact that he was out of the tank than with the fact that he was being eaten alive.

She looked at the fish's eyes as his mouth snapped open and shut, drowning in the air. The eyes were bright and lively; nothing like the glassy-eyed fish she was used to seeing. This fish was fighting to hold onto life as two American gluttons stripped him of his body. But the flavor was fresh and intense. The experience was almost transcendental. And she rationalized it by thinking that in the U.S., this fish would have been frozen and thawed, and much less appreciated. She was having a practically orgasmic experience while eating this life, and she knew that the fish had no nerve endings in its body anyway.

As they flipped the fish to eat the other side, she noticed that it was flailing less aggressively and seemed to be resigning itself to its fate. By the time she and Mitchell had taken their last bites, the fish was bare and motionless on the wooden presentation board.

Mitchell leaned back on the wall behind his stool, with both hands on his belly. "Now *that* was fresh sushi."

"This morning has been amazing. Thank you, Mitchell."

"Hey, it's not morning yet. This was dinner. We'll go back to the hotel and sleep. When we wake up, it will be tomorrow."

They walked out of the sushi bar, and she realized that Mitchell was right. It was still dark out. Tomorrow was a long way away.

Fourteen

Mitchell had a real penchant for airport lounges, and his enthusiasm had begun to rub off on her. Since they always flew first class, the international lounges tended to be beautifully designed and stocked with wonderful food, Internet connections, and top-shelf alcohol. They were flying out in the evening, but Mitchell wanted to get to the airport early to take full advantage of the lounge amenities. More importantly, he wanted to check his email to see if any new young playthings would be waiting for them upon their return to New York.

"Let's see if any pussy has made contact with us. I want to get into the lounge and commandeer a whole computer terminal." Mitchell was practically giddy; it was going to be a day of his favorite activities. They were going to eat, drink, lounge, and search the Internet for eager little fucktoys.

"Relax, Mitchell, we'll be there soon, and we'll have about seven hours to kill." She smiled at him and squeezed his hand in the back of the taxi. He was playful and fun today, and this was the type of mood that made her stick around when he was less than pleasant at other times.

"I know. We just haven't checked email since we left New York, and I want to make sure that we're still in the game."

"Mitchell, we've been gone for four days."

"Five."

"Really? Don't we get one back on the trip home?"

"I don't know. Maybe. It's not like you and I need to be bothered with days of the week." Mitchell chuckled. "It's not as though we have anything to do in our lives except relish hedonism. Well, that and your consumption."

"Hey, be nice."

"I tease out of a place of love."

"I know you do." She wondered if it were possible that Mitchell was drunk. He was so charming and playful that she was reminded of the Mitchell she had first met only a couple of months ago. She mentally pictured her fingers crossing that he would stay in such good spirits.

They arrived at the airport and hired a cart to roll their luggage. Because they were so many hours early, no one waited in line for the first-class check-in. Two Japanese women stood behind the podium.

Together, Mitchell and companion walked toward the podium, but the women, who apparently spoke limited English, gestured for them to split up.

They each held their paper tickets and passports, and the airline representatives began to process their information on the computers. It seemed odd that with two passengers flying under the same reservation confirmation number that the airline would split them up for the check-in process, but there were so many rules and regulations that varied from country to country that neither Mitchell nor she made any indication that they thought this practice was odd.

Mitchell received his boarding pass quickly and walked over to where his companion stood. "What's the holdup? Why am I all set and you're still standing here?" He snarled out of the corner of his mouth. "What did you do wrong?"

"Nothing, Mitchell. Maybe she's a trainee. She's just been holding my passport and staring at the computer screen."

"Well, it's taking too long. I don't like this. Try to speed it up. Just keep smiling." The two of them smiled warmly at the woman in front of them and anxiously anticipated the printing of the boarding pass and the subsequent luggage stickers.

At one point, the woman signaled to her colleague to look at her computer screen. The two women chattered in Japanese, and Mitchell began to grow visibly agitated.

"I don't understand. This other woman is the same one who just assisted me. Why do they need two of them to print your boarding pass when you and I are booked under the same reservation?" Mitchell whispered, but she knew from his tone that he was actually yelling.

Eventually, the two women looked up at them. First at Mitchell, and then at her. Their eyes fixed on her.

"You no fly."

"Excuse me?"

"You. No. Fly."

"Why? I have a ticket. You see my ticket."

Mitchell lightly grabbed her thigh behind the podium and whispered, "Keep your cool. They're in power. Make this work. Or God help me, I'll leave you here."

"Why don't I fly?"

"Ticket no good."

"How is it no good? It flew me here!"

"Um, not ticket." The women looked at each other, searching for the translation of the word they wanted to say. "Um, not ticket. Um, itinerary?" The women nodded, agreeing that that was the word they had been seeking. "Itinerary no good."

"What's wrong with the itinerary?" She was beginning to get overheated, and these women seemed to be on some sort of power trip against her.

One of the airline reps whirled her finger in the air and said, "You go around the world. Cannot go around the world."

"But you ticketed him! We're on the same reservation!"

Mitchell glared at her and muttered, "Don't try to bring me down with you! Be nice."

She took a deep breath. "We're traveling together. Why did you only ticket one of us? It's the same itinerary."

This time, the other representative spoke. Very sternly, she explained. "He is he, and you is you."

"That's your reason? It's because he's a man?"

The woman sighed and repeated. "He is he. You is you."

She turned to Mitchell. "This doesn't make any sense, Mitchell. These women are being ridiculous for no reason!"

"Just keep your cool and keep trying for your boarding pass. I know you're good at needling. You'll get it done." With that said, Mitchell walked away, and she was left on her own to argue, as best as she could, with women who spoke only enough English to be sexist.

For over an hour, the three women debated. The one representative continued to swirl her finger in the air as the other continued to shake her head. The whole process was exhausting the young American traveler, and she was beginning to seriously doubt that she would be boarding that evening's plane.

Mitchell walked up beside her and whispered in her ear, "There is a flight to Seoul we can get on if these bitches don't back down." Then he briskly walked away.

She turned back to the women. "Okay. I called boss in USA. I fly to Korea because Japan has bad system, bad service to customer. Okay?"

The representatives huddled their heads and chattered in Japanese. They were clearly agitated, but also afraid that the American was not bluffing. They did not look back up over the podium, but she heard the soft whir of the printer between them. With no emotion in their faces, and no eye contact, one of the women handed over a boarding pass while the other collected and tagged the luggage.

Triumphant, she proudly strolled over to Mitchell. They began to walk toward the departure area.

"What was that about, Mitchell?"

"My dear, some women look at you, with your gorgeous clothes and your first-class tickets, and they hate you. Or maybe, just maybe, they plain hate you." Mitchell smiled and walked up ahead.

Upon arrival to Atlanta, they had to claim their luggage before clearing customs to catch their connecting flight into LaGuardia. They disembarked the plane ahead of the crowd, since first class had its own jetway into the terminal, and they quickly walked so that they might grab their luggage and beat the rest of the passengers to the customs line.

They arrived at the assigned carousel first and secured prime space from which to collect their bags and move quickly into the next area. The belt began to move, and they carefully watched as the first bags marked "Priority" began to journey past them.

They waited and waited, and soon, business class and then coach class bags began to fill the conveyor belt.

"What is this? We're going to be in a long customs line! Why are our bags taking so long?"

"Who knows, Mitchell? Maybe because we arrived at the airport so early that our bags are buried under everyone else's?"

"Don't make excuses for the airline's incompetence. And by the way, if our bags didn't make the flight at all, I'm blaming you."

She took a breath, and then asked, "Why?"

"Because of the delay in your ticketing. That probably screwed everything up."

"Look, we're not going to argue over this. We had a lovely flight. We're almost home. And the conveyor belt is still moving. Our bags will get here."

"I don't like lines."

"I know, Mitchell." She was trying to reassure him, but she was also reassuring herself. She wasn't entirely convinced that their bags had made the flight. It was hard to believe that the airline representatives could be so catty, but they had no reason for their aggressively bad behavior in the first place.

The deluge of bags being deposited onto the belt thinned into a trickle, and before long, the same bags were continuing to make the circle.

"Our bags are not here."

"Mitchell, the carousel is still moving." She knew that Mitchell would not have an outburst in a customs area, but she was afraid that if their bags did not arrive, his anger would be directed at her later. She really hoped the bags would arrive.

"The carousel is empty, imbecile." Mitchell was snarling at her again.

"But it's still moving."

"It's been. . ." Mitchell paused and looked at his watch. "Forty-five minutes. Forty-five minutes! There are no other passengers here!"

She looked around. They were all alone. And staring at an empty carousel. But it was still moving.

In the distance, she saw something.

"Is that your bag?"

"I think it is! And look, there's yours!"

"See? I knew they made the flight!"

"Well, that's fine. But it took almost an hour to deplane our bags? How is that possible?"

"Just be happy that they're here."

Mitchell grunted, and the bags turned the corner and headed toward them.

He reminded her, "We still have to clear customs and catch our connecting flight."

"We have more than enough time." Mitchell was clearly more intoxicated than she was, but his buzz was beginning to wear off, and she hoped that the process would move quickly. If Mitchell had another glass of wine, he'd relax again.

The bags made it to them, and Mitchell reached out to remove them from the belt.

"What the?"

She looked as he placed them on their Smartcart.

"Look at this! I don't believe it!" Mitchell erupted into laughter.

All of their bags were plastic wrapped and covered with looseleaf paper that bore handwritten signs. On each item was written in thick red marker ink a Japanese character and then the English word "LAST."

"Can they do that?!" She exclaimed.

"I've never seen it before. But apparently they can. And they did." Mitchell laughed, and she couldn't help but join him. The situation was totally bizarre. "Come on. Let's go through customs."

All alone in the arrival space, they wheeled their cart with their ostracized luggage into the customs zone.

"This is one for the record books." Mitchell smiled.

"It's definitely a story."

"Save the signs. I'm reporting them to the airlines. No one will ever believe this."

"I'm here, and I don't believe it."

The customs agents looked at the bags as they passed through.

One agent asked, "Why are your bags tagged like that?"

Mitchell responded, "I know, have you ever seen that?"

"Were they serious?"

"Well, we're the only people here. So I guess so."

"Do you mind if I show my supervisor?"

"Show everybody. Let them see the travesty."

The customs agents gathered around the luggage cart and laughed among themselves.

One agent looked up at her and said, "Someone really hates you in Japan."

She nodded, and she and Mitchell passed the Atlanta terminal, hoping that the rest of the journey would be less eventful. Shame on her for wishful thinking.

They sat in the domestic lounge in small uncomfortable chairs near a bright window. The lounge was crowded and bustling with the tense activity of business travelers anxious to get home at the end of presumably long days working. Neither Mitchell nor she was a member of the lounge, but as first-class international passengers, they had the privilege of entry.

"This lounge is disgusting. These people are disgusting. I can't sit here any longer." It had only been a minute, but Mitchell had already finished one glass of wine and was holding the second. He was visibly antsy and shifting his large body awkwardly in the narrow chair. "Go and ask the staff if there is space on an earlier flight to LaGuardia. I think we have two hours before our flight, and I can't bear the thought of sitting here another moment amongst these. . ." he glanced about the room, ". . . people."

She found it mildly amusing the amount of disdain that Mitchell had for other people. She was beginning not to care much for other people either. Not because they were in a different class, but because after meeting Mitchell and having her way with so many women, she had become jaded at how easily manipulated everyone seemed to be. And she rationalized to herself that if so many people were willing to be objectified, then they rightfully deserved to be. She counted herself among them, as she was beginning to think that she had sold her soul for this lifestyle, but she tried not to dwell on that notion.

The woman at the front desk told her that they were in luck; there were two remaining seats in business class on the earlier flight to New York. Being the first aboard, they watched as the other passengers filed in. The business-class cabin filled quickly, but they noticed that none of the passengers in their cabin seemed particularly well dressed. In fact, they were all in jeans and polo shirts. And they were all men. Considering that most of the patrons of the lounge were in suits, this was a curious anomaly.

The final passenger to board in their cabin was an extremely tall gangly man with bright red hair and a thick wool suit with no tie. He was carrying a large metal suitcase and a black leather satchel. He was assigned the seat right in front of Mitchell, with no one seated next to him.

"That's strange. The agent said that we had the last two seats on the flight, but it looks like the seat next to that guy is empty," she murmured to Mitchell.

"Well, she was an idiot. That's why she has that job. These people have no idea what's going on. We certainly learned that on the flight over here."

The man opened the bin above his seat and placed the metal suitcase with an extraordinary amount of care. He seemed to be a little bit high strung, and his actions were amusing to watch. He then seated himself with enough force to shake the seat back, and both she and Mitchell inaudibly giggled at his bizarre behavior.

After he seemed satisfied in his seat, he took a large set of headphones from his satchel and placed them over his ears with great care. The plane began to taxi, and she and Mitchell settled in for the ride.

Out of nowhere, the man turned and yelled at Mitchell in a thick Irish accent, "Stop kicking my seat!"

Mitchell, being ever gracious, responded, "I was not aware that I kicked your seat, but I apologize."

She looked at Mitchell and the seat back in front of him, and there was a huge amount of space separating his knees from the strange man's seat.

"I don't think you kicked his seat."

"My dear, it's not even possible for me to kick his seat from this distance. But he is clearly disturbed, so let's just hope he focuses on something else."

The man turned his head around again, "Stop kicking my seat!"

"I'm really making an effort not to, sir," Mitchell calmly replied.

The plane took off, and the man stood up and faced Mitchell. "Stop kicking my seat now! Now!"

This time, Mitchell did not respond. Instead, he turned to her. "This man is clearly getting ready to become violent. Switch seats with me. You're so tiny, there is no way for him to accuse you."

She nodded, and the two switched seats. Five minutes later, the man once again turned to Mitchell, who was now in the window seat, and yelled, "Stop kicking my seat!"

Mitchell ignored him and instead turned to her. "Okay, let's look around this cabin. Do you notice anything peculiar?"

She glanced around and saw that the men seated around them had little handheld devices and were using their thumbs to type feverishly.

"Those machines are illegal on airplanes," Mitchell stated.

"I've never even seen them before. What are they?"

"Those are communication devices. Like cell phones but with written words. Like instant email. All of these men are writing to each other. Look again carefully."

She looked at the man who was seated across the aisle in the row in front of the redhead. He was holding a paperback novel, and it was upside down.

"Mitchell, that man is reading a book upside down."

"He's not reading, you imbecile. He has a mirror on the sole of his shoe. Look how he's crossed his legs. He's watching the man in front of you."

She looked again and saw the reflection of light from the man's shoe. "I don't understand."

"You don't need to understand. What you need to do is tell the flight attendant that the man is acting aggressively toward us, and you believe he is a threatening presence to us. That way if he does become violent against us, you have a record of having told the flight crew that you felt unsafe."

"So, what do you want me to do?"

"Pretend to go to the bathroom. When you get to the galley, tell the flight attendant that you're scared. Oh, and ask for some wine."

Mitchell was already very drunk, even by his standards, and she thought that he was being extremely paranoid. He was paranoid in general, but now he seemed much more so. Although she had to admit that there was something strange about the passengers in this cabin. She stood up to pretend to walk to the bathroom.

Mitchell grabbed her arm and pulled her down so that her ear met his lips. "That man with the upside down book is a federal marshal. After you report to the flight attendant, stop by his seat and let him know that you're scared of the man in front of you."

"What? Really? You think I should do that?"

"Don't question me. Obey!"

She was far more afraid of Mitchell than a stranger on an airplane, so she quickly strode to the galley.

The flight attendant was preparing the meals and was surprised to look up and see company in the galley.

"May I help you, ma'am?"

"I'm sorry to disrupt you as you work, but I just wanted to let you know that the gentleman seated in front of me has been threatening violence toward my companion this entire trip."

"Really? How so?" The flight attendant seemed surprised and legitimately concerned.

"Well, he keeps yelling that my companion is kicking his seat. But we switched places a while ago, and he's still insistent that he is being attacked from behind.

The two women looked back at the red-haired man. He was sitting straight up, wearing his enormous headphones, with his eyes closed, tapping his hands rapidly on the armrests.

"Okay, I'm going to tell the pilot."

"Thank you."

"We'll get this sorted out."

She walked back down the aisle as the flight attendant knocked on the cockpit door. She watched the woman slip into the cockpit, and then she continued to stroll casually up to the man with the upside-down book. He didn't even notice her approaching.

"I'm sorry, sir. Excuse me?"

The man appeared startled to find her addressing him. He looked up uncomfortably. "Yes?"

"Are you a federal marshal?"

"What?" he exclaimed. "What?"

"Well, it's just that the man in front of me has been acting aggressively, and it seems that you've noticed him too. Are you a federal marshal?"

The man averted his eyes, and his manner of speaking completely changed. "Go back to your seat, ma'am."

"But—"

"The situation's under control."

She was now really confused, but the man had clearly confirmed Mitchell's assessment. Maybe Mitchell wasn't as paranoid as she had thought.

"Well?" Mitchell asked as she returned to her seat.

"The flight attendant is alerting the captain. And that man said, and I quote, 'the situation's under control.'"

"God, the standards of this country's intelligence agents are going to shit. Look how obvious they are! It's an embarrassment!"

"Oh." She sat quietly pondering for a moment. "Wait, why do you care?"

Mitchell took a deep breath. "I'm going to tell you some things you must never repeat." Although his speech was slurred, she could tell that he was being honest with her. She prepared herself for the intake of some heavy information. "I used to be in the CIA. During the Gulf War. I was, well, forced to resign. The bastards." Mitchell sighed deeply. "They said that I used gratuitous cruelty to extract information." He took a gulp of the wine, then looked at the near empty glass. "Is she bringing wine?"

"I asked her to. Go on."

"That's it. That's all you need to know. But I was a professional. These morons are a joke." A tear streamed down his face.

She had never seen Mitchell cry, and she assumed that he was upset at being forced to recall some horrific memory. "Why are you crying?"

"I love you. I really love you. I don't love people. Well, except my son. But I really love you." Mitchell embraced her tightly and wept.

She had no idea how to deal with Mitchell on an emotional level, and though he had been drunk in her presence many times, she had never seen him cry. As she held him, the flight attendant appeared with a bottle of wine. The attendant was clearly uncomfortable with interrupting the moment but wanted to pass on some information from the pilot.

"I spoke with the men in the cockpit. They said that you have nothing to worry about. Do you know what's going on?"

Mitchell waved her away without looking up. He was sobbing near the point of convulsing.

The flight attendant seemed like she was going to inquire into Mitchell's state, but then thought better. Instead, she refilled their wine glasses and quickly walked away.

Mitchell eventually stopped crying, and neither of them spoke. The plane finally landed at LaGuardia. She thought how strange it was that this short hop from Atlanta seemed a much longer trip than their earlier flight from Tokyo.

As the plane taxied to the gate, the flight attendant reappeared. "I'm sorry to bother you folks, but I've been asked to keep you aboard until everyone has deplaned."

Mitchell turned to his companion, "First our luggage is last, and now we can't even get off the plane."

She could tell that he was tired and wanted to go home, but she heard his heavy breathing, and she knew that he was regaining his stern composure. Oddly, she felt safe as long as he was there beside her.

As the passengers left the plane, the business-class section emptied last. Normally, being seated in the front of the plane nearest the door brought the privilege of early deplaning, but instead, the red-haired man exited, and every other man remained seated. They all moved their thumbs quickly on their strange machines, and after the coach section was empty, the men in business class finally stood. She and Mitchell stayed obediently confined to their seats.

"Watch this." Mitchell nodded at the man across the aisle and in the row in front of them. He had left his large duffle bag under the seat in front of him. "He's getting off without his carryon."

The man directly across the aisle seemed to go out of his way to appear nonchalant as he put on his coat and picked up his briefcase. Then, in a bizarre move, he quickly grabbed the duffle bag belonging to the man who had been in front of him. Neither man had acknowledged each other in transit, which made this act even more noteworthy.

"Mitchell, that man just took the other man's luggage!"

"Shhhh," Mitchell hissed, trying to calm her but clearly getting worked up himself. "Just do what they say and hopefully we'll get out of here soon."

Finally, the pilot himself came to escort them out of the empty plane.

"Sorry for the delay, folks. Welcome home."

"How did he know we live here?"

Mitchell waved her silent. "Don't say another word unless directly asked."

She was beginning to get extremely nervous. As they walked the jetway, she noticed that she was sweating heavily, and her heart felt ready to burst out of her chest.

When they emerged into the terminal, no fewer than thirty men stood at the gate. All the men from the cabin were there, as well as several in official jackets bearing the letters FBI whom she did not recognize from the flight.

The man to whom she had spoken in flight was the first to approach them. He was now wearing an FBI jacket. "Mind if I have a word with you two? We just have a couple of questions."

She was nervous, but Mitchell was standing stiff as a board. He seemed cool, confident, and collected. She took her cue from him, inhaled deeply, and pretended that it was normal to be met by the U.S. government at the end of every flight.

"May I see your passports?"

They both handed the men the documents.

"And may I have your social security numbers and full names for the record?"

She gave hers first, and the man typed it into his machine with his thumbs. He nodded and returned her passport.

"And you, sir?"

Mitchell quickly gave a name and a social security number. She couldn't hear him clearly, but she was positive that she did not hear the name Mitchell Durman.

"Sir, are you aware that your social security number does not exist prior to 1992?"

"Yes, I am, sir," Mitchell stated coolly. "That is the new number I was issued for my safety."

The agent turned his attention to her. "Ma'am, you IDed me as a federal agent. Why did you ask me that?"

Quickly she responded, "He told me to." She glanced at Mitchell.

"Ma'am, are you aware that we were tracking the man in the seat in front of you?"

"Ummm—"

The agent didn't wait for her reply. "That man had a supersonic hearing device. He was able to hear every conversation aboard that aircraft. We have been tracking him for a while, waiting for him to make a move." The agent paused for effect. "Ma'am, your question intercepted a terrorist heist and cost the United States millions of dollars."

She stared at him with her eyes open wide, her jaw agape. She had no idea how to respond.

The agent nodded at one of his cronies, and she was approached by five agents.

"Ma'am, we'd like you to come with us."

She followed them dutifully and heard Mitchell's voice behind her. "If anyone calls you tomorrow, have them contact my lawyer!"

The agents escorted her through the exit. One of them leaned into her and said, "Go home."

She got into a taxi alone, without her luggage, and gave the driver her address. She had no idea what had just happened, and she had no idea who Mitchell Durman was. Considering all that she had had to drink, she sat in the back of the taxi and prayed that it was all a strange dream.

Fifteen

"Did anyone call you?"

She hadn't heard from Mitchell in over three days, and his voice on the other end of the phone startled her.

"No. I haven't heard anything. Why? What was that all about?"

"Nothing. Never mind. Come over and bring me the *New York Times*. Thank you. That is all." Mitchell abruptly ended the conversation.

It seemed that they were going right back into their old routine, and Mitchell had no intention of acknowledging the strange events that had transpired only a few days before.

Shaking off the confusion, she pulled herself out of bed and got dressed. It had been refreshing not having heard from Mitchell in a few days; she had actually worn jeans and comfortable shoes. But now she was putting on her ankle-breaking heels and well-starched slacks in preparation for another one of many days sitting in Mitchell's apartment, binge drinking and looking for pussy. Just another day in April.

"I'm thinking we should go to Tino's. You like Tino's, and you can have run of the menu." As she let herself into his apartment, Mitchell was smiling cheerfully as he looked up at her from his reclined position on the sofa. "But first, I have to punish you. You know I hate to punish you, but you keep forcing me to do it. Silly imbecile."

"Why am I being punished?"

Mitchell groaned like a man much older than his years as he righted himself on the sofa and hauled himself to his feet. "My dear, you sold me out."

"What? When?" she asked.

"'He told me to.' *He told me to.*" Mitchell sneered at her. "Sound familiar? The feds asked you why you spoke to the marshal, and you said, and I quote, *He told me to.*" Mitchell lifted his foot and slammed it on the hardwood floor. "Are you stupid? Are you a moron? Do you want me to squash you like a bug?" He breathed in deeply. "We are a team. A team! And at your first opportunity, you sold me down the river like a stranger. It's you and me against the world. It's you and me against the world!"

"I'm sorry, Mitchell, it's just—"

"Sorry? You're *sorry*? Your sorries are useless. Meaningless! What were you thinking? Were you even thinking? Damn it! You idiot!"

"I was asked a direct question, and I gave a direct answer. I really am sor—" She caught herself mid-word. "I was cooperating with the authorities. I didn't mean for anyone to get in trouble."

"The authorities? Those government assholes are not authorities. I am your authority! Do you understand?"

"Yes." She looked at her feet.

"Do you understand?" His voiced boomed menacingly.

"Yes. I understand." She mustered conviction.

"Good." The deep red color began to drain from Mitchell's cheeks, and he seemed to be calming down. "The second order of business is important: Did you hear me give my real name?"

"What?"

"When questioned, before you and I were separated, they asked me my real name, and I gave it. Did you hear it?"

"No, I—"

"Good. Maybe you're lying. I don't care. Just erase it from your memory. It's not relevant. Got it?"

"Yeah, sure, I—"

"Stop talking. Come and receive your punishment."

She hadn't thought it possible for her to get more confused with the whole situation, and yet now she was. This was just too complicated for her brain to process. She put her head down and followed Mitchell into the bathroom.

"Take off your clothes and get into the bathtub."

She didn't question him; she knew better. Silently, she stripped and stepped into the cold porcelain tub.

"Kneel."

She carefully lowered herself to her knees.

"Take a deep breath, open your mouth, and close your eyes."

She shook a bit but did as she was ordered. A few moments passed, and then she felt the hot stream of his urine strike her face and settle in her mouth. Her first reaction was to snap her jaw shut, but he warned her not to, so instead she began to cry.

The punishment was a torture that seemed to last forever, but it did eventually end. Mitchell silently turned on the water to the shower and knelt beside the tub. Her eyes were still closed, and she was shaking violently. Tenderly, Mitchell washed and caressed her with a soapy washcloth. Delicately, he kissed and tasted her tears. When he was satisfied with her degree of cleanliness, he lifted her to her feet and draped her in a huge bath sheet. He pressed her swaddled body against his and hugged her dry.

Carrying her like a child, he placed her on his bed and whispered into her ear, "When you're feeling the shame and sadness passing, get dressed and I'll take you to lunch." He kissed her lightly on the cheek and retreated to the living room. Her eyes were still closed.

❧

They sat at their favorite table in the small Italian restaurant around the corner from Mitchell's building. The table was at the very back of the tiny restaurant and had a clear sightline to both the kitchen and the front entrance. It was a table reserved for people of status, and those who were "friends" of Tino's. For most patrons, Tino's was cash only. But for certain customers, Tino kept a ledger. Mitchell had recently earned himself a page.

Their favorite waiter, a Frenchman named Claude, sauntered over to their table with a graceful, yet forceful, presence that was a rarity in New York. He snapped his fingers toward a runner, and a bottle of Mitchell's favorite Chianti and glasses of sparkling water instantly appeared. Claude stood back as a basket of bread appeared by another runner, and then when the access to the couple was clear, Claude cleared his throat and began to speak. His eyes remained fixed firmly ahead, careful not to make eye contact with his esteemed customers.

As he recited the specials of the day, she took inventory of the waiter standing before her. Claude wore a perfectly pressed tuxedo, clinched with an impeccably tied bowtie at the neck. A pressed linen napkin was draped over his forearm, and his hands never moved. His shoes were recently polished and spotlessly sparkling, and his thick head of silver hair belied his youthful skin. The steely blue eyes that stared at nothing in particular suggested that Claude himself was a force—a man to be taken very seriously and with much reverence.

His thick French accent was usually difficult to understand, but he was making an effort as he spoke toward her to make sure she understood what special concoction he was instructing the chef to make especially for her.

She was about to have a wonderful lunch. In the days since the LaGuardia incident, she hadn't eaten very much; she was a little afraid of spooks arriving at her door, and she had avoided making her presence known. But now, she was starving. And Claude had designed the perfect feast to fill her body with relief. She looked about her and quickly realized that Claude had not even given them menus. She was impressed with his confidence, and with his true ability to gauge the desires of his customers.

Claude walked away, and she braced herself for the parade of courses that was to come. She tried to focus on the food and wipe away the memory of the horrifying punishment that she had just survived less than an hour ago. She hoped that Mitchell would avoid it as a conversation topic as well. But Mitchell was not one to engage in either omission or commission, and without being prompted, he quickly tackled the subject.

"You hated that punishment, didn't you? You hated it when I pissed in your mouth?"

"Well, I—"

"Don't answer. I'm telling you. You hated it. It was a horrible, demeaning punishment. You hated every moment of it, and you hated me for it. You hate me now!" Mitchell threw his arms up in exclamation of his point. "And

I hated doing it. But I had to. You had to learn, and I had to teach you. But think of this: there are women out there who will do whatever you tell them. You are a strong, beautiful, dominant woman! Not over me, of course, but over everybody else. And those women will do anything for you. The next bitch who crosses you will get the piss treatment. But worse!" Mitchell's lips curled into a devious grin. She was unsettled. "The pussy you think deserves that treatment will have her mouth clamped around my dick so hard that the piss will come out of her nose. Have you seen that? Can you imagine? I can piss so hard that it comes out of the fucktoy's nose. And I will. And now..." Mitchell leaned in toward her across the table. "And now you know how it feels on the receiving side. So you will be that much better on the dominant side. Those women will deserve it, and know it. And you will understand the true impact of the moment."

She said nothing. Instead, she stared blankly at Mitchell and prayed that their food would come. But it didn't, and she was forced into this corner where she had to either lie or acknowledge the direct question.

"I wouldn't wish that on anyone."

"Ahhh, my dear. But you would!" Mitchell's eyes danced feverishly. "Of course you would. You know it's a survivable punishment, and you know how awful it is. And the first sub to piss you off is going to be ordered to be pissed in and on. Because, my dear, that's how this world works. And to be a successful domme, you have to have been a successful sub. After all, how can you administer discipline if you don't fundamentally understand the intricacies of the operation?"

"Well, I..." She was hoping to stall her response, and luckily, the first course arrived before she could finish her sentence. Quickly, she changed the subject. "These brains look delicious!"

Mitchell looked down at his prosciutto and melon and mumbled, "Only to you, my dear. Only to you."

In a pregnant silence, they devoured their first course.

When the meal had ended, Mitchell reclined leisurely in the chair that seemed almost too small to support his mammoth frame. He inhaled a pregnant breath, then switched his demeanor into business mode.

"Why is it, my dear, that we are sitting here just the two of us? Why do we not have a beautiful and vulnerable fucktoy sandwiched between us? Why do you leave me so frustrated with your incompetence at performing the only task for which you are qualified in this relationship?" He leaned in toward her. "You can't suck cock worth shit. You're funny looking. You're stupid. And I'm pretty sure you're insane. Totally mentally ill." He smiled. "But I love you, baby."

She had no idea what response he was trying to illicit from her. So she remained silent.

"You see, my dear little imbecile, you have power over women. And you learn quickly. Now, that punishment you took before lunch—you hated it, right? It was humiliating and horrifying and emotionally painful, right?"

"Right. . . ."

"But you took your punishment so willingly. There was no back sass. No resistance. Because you are strong, and brave, and powerful. Only truly great characters can accept a fate with such conviction. I respect you for that." Mitchell smiled broadly. "But I would respect you even more if it were another girl you had ordered into the bathtub. I'd love to piss into her mouth and watch it drain out of her nose. And you'd like that, too, wouldn't you?"

"I wouldn't like it. But I'd do it to please you."

"Bullshit. You're sick and twisted and demented. You'd love it. You'd love to save yourself by changing the balance of power. You'd love it. I love you because you'd love it."

She really hoped she wouldn't love it. But she had had a lot to drink by that point, and she was feeling increasingly distanced from her emotions. She had no idea what she felt anymore. So she trusted that Mitchell knew better than she. At least, that was the last bit of hope she could muster.

The moment they entered Mitchell's apartment, she walked right into the study and turned on the computer. Mitchell wanted to see that she was making a real effort to find sex for him, and at the very least, she was going to make a strong, and visible, attempt.

She put up a fresh posting on an online sex bulletin board, and she began to check email responses from previous postings. Her tactic was pretty standard; she could easily weed through the notes and determine who was serious about meeting and fucking. From there, she would request a phone number, and she would call from her personal cell phone to determine if the voice on the other belonged to the photo she had received online. To her surprise, most of the responses tended to be from real and eager young women who craved being dominated and fucked by another.

She was beginning to have an ever-increasing contempt for other women, and people in general. The fact that a stranger would give her control instantly made her question the worth of such a weak soul. But perhaps this disdain for other people was exactly why they were so quick to give her submission. Maybe they had something to prove. Maybe they just wanted to be close to her, as though that signified earning her respect. She knew that this notion was totally counter-intuitive; the more they submitted, the more she despised them.

And at the heart of this was Mitchell. The puppet master who kept her dancing with strings that the fucktoys never saw. He was the truly sick element in the equation. She was nothing more than another trick pony in a long succession of castoffs.

"How's it going in there?" Mitchell called from the living room, yelling over the blaring television. "Any good ones?"

"Some," she called back. "I'm weeding through and following up. When there are some solid leads, I'll run them by you."

"Okay." Mitchell paused and then added, "By the way, major points for you for just walking into the office and getting to work. That tenacity makes me happy. Good job."

"Okay, Mitchell. But don't praise me yet. Let's see what I produce."

"That's it! That's the perfect attitude!" She heard Mitchell get up from the couch, and she looked up as he entered the room.

Mitchell walked right over to her and planted a wet, sloppy kiss on her cheek. "Maybe there's hope for you yet." He walked out of the room.

She looked over at the computer screen, which was studded with photos of naked women, exposing themselves in gestures that showed them hoping to receive her aggressive fucking. *No*, she thought, *There's no hope for you left.*

Sixteen

So, you like to be fucked in the asshole?" She was on the phone with one of the prospective fucktoys. Standing in Mitchell's presence, she drove the conversation as he had trained her. "And if I take the strap-on out of your ass, you'll lick it clean? . . . Ummm. . . . And you're very submissive? . . . Well, is there anything else I should know? . . . So, I'm going to take you to lunch tomorrow? . . . Hmmm? . . . What?"

Mitchell looked at her expressively, trying to get her to give clues through her end of the dialogue. She was trying, but the conversation was a little tough to convey.

"What? What's that? Oh. . . . Okay, asshole. Goodbye."

"Well? *Well?*" Mitchell wanted details and fast.

"It was a man."

"What?! You idiot. You just wasted twenty minutes on the phone with a *man*?! And you couldn't tell?" Mitchell spat on the floor. "You disgust me. Get out of my house. *Get out!*"

She didn't want to be there anymore than he wanted her there, so she quickly put on her shoes, grabbed her handbag, and left.

She was about two blocks away when her cell phone rang. Mitchell's name appeared in the caller ID.

"Come back."

"Are you sure?"

"Come back. I don't want a beautiful day to end with such anger. Let's talk it out before we go to bed. I need to understand what went wrong."

She pivoted on her heels and walked back to Mitchell's building. He seemed pleasant enough on the phone, but that meant nothing with regard to his demeanor when she saw him in person. She was nervous, but she was so tired, she really just hoped that the tirade (which she knew would ensue) would be over quickly so that she could get home and have dinner before collapsing into bed.

Hesitantly, she opened the door to Mitchell's apartment. He wasted no time in interrogating her.

"So, you called up this 'thing' thinking it was a potential fucktoy. You spent a large amount of time talking to it, which, by the way, you know is the kiss of death—if a fucktoy keeps you on the phone, there's no chance of meeting. That's the angle. But regardless. Fine. You call. You chat. And you're so stupid that you can't tell that it's a man? Seriously?"

"I don't know. It seemed convincing enough."

"Fine. Convincing. Whatever. You should have known when it kept you on the line that it was playing a game with you. Right?"

"I guess."

"I said, *right?*"

"No, no, Mitchell. You're right. I screwed up. I'm sorry."

"You know what I think? I think that this freak show thought that you were a gay man. So he was pretending to be a woman to a gay man."

"I don't think that that's what—"

"Don't speak. I'm telling you. You are like a skinny little gay man. I'm changing your name. From now on, you will be addressed as Eugene. A nebbish, pathetic little gay man." Mitchell turned his attention back to the television. "That's it. Go home, Eugene. Goodbye."

"Goodbye, Mitchell."

"Goodbye, Eugene."

She walked to the subway, drained from the day. Tomorrow would be awful. Mitchell was not going to let this accidental gender misidentification go easily. She sighed. This life—the privileged life—was a lot more work than people perceived.

Massive translucent trash bags lined the sidewalk, and a closer inspection revealed that they were filled with prepared foods from the display cases at one of the neighborhood deli-cafes—wraps, panini, pizza, heros, all in their original packaging. She looked around the deserted street, then at herself in her Armani heels and Joseph suit, and chuckled. Then she grabbed one of the trash bags and headed to the subway. At this point, she really just didn't care anymore. For all she knew, Mitchell would kill her the next day. She might as well binge now.

Since it was New York, the other passengers in the subway didn't even seem to notice the juxtaposition of the incredibly well-dressed woman with her bag of restaurant trash. And if they did notice, nobody seemed to care. There was something to be said for being anonymous in a crowd.

She trudged through the streets with her bag of goodies and up the four flights of stairs to her apartment, then stripped naked, opened a bottle of wine, and sat on her bed surrounded by the food. A nondescript documentary was playing on her small television, and she absently began to fill herself. She really hoped tomorrow wouldn't come.

❦

"Eugene! Get your faggot ass over here. You've got work to do."

With a heavy heart, she threw on the same clothes she had worn the day before. There was no point in wasting the energy looking for a different outfit to wear. She was probably going to be held captive in Mitchell's apartment all day anyway.

She stopped off at the newsstand near her building on the way to the subway and bought Mitchell his copy of the *New York Times*. She didn't bother to even glimpse at the headlines. There was too much misery in her life for her to concern herself with that of others. At this point, she was just surprised that her body still woke up every morning. Her weight had been steadily decreasing, and her spirit was completely broken. She in no way wanted to die, but Mitchell had made it pretty clear that she should be prepared for it.

The subway ride was quick, almost too quick. Mitchell was going to be unbearable, and she just didn't have the stomach for it anymore. She hoped the train would get stuck in the tunnel. Or maybe that she would be hit by a car crossing Park Avenue. But she arrived at Mitchell's place unscathed.

"Hello, Eugene." Mitchell had an unfortunate ability to throw his voice like the Hannibal Lecter character in *Silence of the Lambs*. It was seriously disturbing.

"Hello, Mitchell." She acknowledged the reclining mass beached on the couch. "I brought you the paper."

"Good. Good boy. And I didn't even have to ask. You're getting good at this, Eugene. You can be my manservant." Mitchell laughed.

She said nothing. Instead, she placed the newspaper on the coffee table in front of Mitchell and stood alongside the couch.

"Oh, don't be like that, Eugene. Come. Sit. Have some wine." Mitchell was now smiling broadly. He clearly found his behavior entertaining.

She sat and looked blankly in the direction of the television.

"Oh, Eugene. You hate it when I call you Eugene, don't you? You really, truly hate it, huh?" Mitchell almost seemed like he was going to apologize and stop calling her by that horrible name. But she knew better than to expect even remotely civil behavior from Mitchell. And she was right; he instantly turned into a monster. His face turned beet red, and he began to shout. "You are a disaster! You are a huge disappointment! You are a mess! Your family hates you. You can't get pussy. I'm the only one in your life. And you keep letting me down. You take and take and take and take!" Mitchell spat. "And what's in it for me, Eugene! What's in it for *me*?"

She continued to look straight ahead, avoiding eye contact with Mitchell. "Nothing." She spoke in a soft voice, only barely audible.

"Nothing? Nothing? You had better hope it's not nothing! I'm not wasting my time anymore, Eugene." Mitchell took a deep breath. "Now, get in the study, and *find me pussy!*"

His voice boomed, and she scrambled to her feet and into the other room.

"By the way, Eugene." Mitchell's voiced drifted in from the living room. "Your mother emailed you at your personal email address. I emailed back, in your writing style, and told her she needed a good dildo-fucking up the ass."

She shivered as she waited for the laptop to boot. She hoped he was just making a cruel joke.

"Oh, and there's no point in you trying to check if I'm telling you the truth or not. I've reset your passwords so that you no longer have access to your accounts. You're a failure at communicating anyway, are you not? So, I'll be taking over."

She said nothing.

"Did you hear me?"

"Yes, Mitchell."

"Good. Now, bring me some pussy!"

She checked the email account to which potential fucktoys could respond to her anonymous Internet postings. There were several emails that she knew would result in dead ends. But one looked a little different. The email handle was *GreenwichMommy*, and the photos attached were of a strikingly beautiful young blonde-haired, blue-eyed WASP. The photos were of her surrounded by other similarly dressed and statuesque women with their faces scrambled out, set against a golf-course background.

"Mitchell?" She tried to get his attention without leaving her post, as though if she moved, this perfect woman's profile might just disappear off the computer. "Mitchell, I think you should come see this."

"You want me to get up? This had better be good."

She heard the grunts and groans of Mitchell lifting himself from the sofa. He made a show of how much effort was required for him to travel to the other room.

She could feel his presence hovering over her, but she didn't dare lift her gaze from the computer screen. Mitchell was obviously reading the email over her shoulder, because he quickly shoved her out of the chair and demanded that she move to grant him access to the computer.

He was quiet for a while, reading and rereading the email. Then, slowly, he swiveled the desk chair to face her. "This bitch. This WASPy princess. She wants to meet you *today*. She's in the city, out of Connecticut, and she wants to meet you *today*." Mitchell smiled maniacally. "Here's what you do: Take her to that kaiseki restaurant on Madison Avenue. Buy her champagne, sake, and the full-shebang lunch. Talk her up. Charm her. Take control. Then bring her here. And fuck the shit out of her." Mitchell raised an eyebrow. "Got it, imbecile?"

At least she was no longer Eugene. "Got it, Mitchell."

"Good. Email her back. Get her on board. This bitch is yours to lose. Please, please don't fuck it up."

She emailed the woman and heard back immediately. They would meet in front of the restaurant at 12:30. That gave her just about an hour to prepare, and she correctly assumed that Mitchell wanted to coach her.

"Remember: Seem interested in her, but not sincerely. Take control of the situation. Make her feel comfortable with you, but inexplicably insecure. That's your power, remember." Mitchell thought for a minute. "Oh yes, do not mention me. Let her know that there will be a man in the apartment, but don't let her know that she'll be sucking my cock until you already have your cock in her asshole. Got it?"

"Yes." He was right, if this woman was who and what she claimed, then this situation was ideal, and almost foolproof. But she was nervous too; if this woman was not who she claimed, and for some reason was not suitable to be delivered to Mitchell, then he would most certainly shift the blame. And she did not want to go back to being Eugene.

"Good. Get my ATM card out of my fag bag. Take out a thousand dollars. If you're good, you can keep the change."

That almost sounded like a good deal, but Mitchell had also picked an outrageously expensive restaurant, and there might not be any change.

"Oh, and do something about that hair. You look like a homeless lady."

She tried to remember the last time she had showered. She tried to remember the last time Mitchell had showered. She drew a blank on both. Fixing her hair might be a wasted effort. Nonetheless, she went into the bathroom and fiddled a bit in a weak attempt to make herself presentable. Eventually satisfied, she put on her heels and left to walk to the bank, allowing enough time to be on time for her "date."

The beautiful blonde woman wore a powder-blue spring coat over a powder-blue mini-skirt business suit. The two women shook hands and kissed on the cheek.

"I'm sorry I'm so stodgily dressed. I had to let my husband believe I was coming into the city for a business interview." The woman flashed a huge white-toothed smile. "I'm Betty, by the way."

"Hi, Betty." She nodded towards the stairs leading into the restaurant. "Shall we?"

"We shall!" Betty exclaimed.

"*Let's shall.*" The alpha female corrected.

"Really? I always thought it was 'we shall.'"

"Many people do. But many people are stupid. It's 'let's shall.'"

"You are incredibly sexy. I'm already learning from you. I'm going to like being your bitch." Betty flashed a wicked smile and ascended the stairs.

Holy shit, the domme thought. This girl just might be the one!

The two women sat shoulder to shoulder at the kaiseki bar as the meticulous Japanese chefs worked in front of them, preparing their multi-course meal in prodigious stages. Neither one of them actually watched the chefs work; they were far more enamored with each other. The culinary display was more of a background distraction than a source of entertainment.

Betty seemed to be drawn to the raw power her lunch companion exuded. The alpha female was drawn to Betty's poise, intelligence, and outrageously perfect physique. Mitchell was going to be thrilled.

"So, I guess I'm about ten or fifteen years older than you." Betty was trying to draw a linear connection between them.

"Really? You don't look it." She wasn't trying to flatter Betty; she really meant it.

"Thanks. But I'm old. With two kids. And a boring husband. And my life is just golf and country club lunches and stupid, stupid, stupid!"

"Well, isn't that what you wanted?"

"Can I level with you?" Betty leaned in closely. "I married money. I was a middle-class girl from the Midwest. I got a big endorsement contract modeling for a clothing company campaign when I was in college. A trust-fund baby found me, married me, and moved me to Greenwich. And I've been miserable ever since." Betty seductively put her hand between her companion's legs and winked. "That's where you come in."

The domme grunted, feigned disinterest, aggressively grabbed Betty's wrist, and threw her hand out from inside her inner thigh. The hand was flung with such force that it hit the edge of Betty's chair and made a dull clunk. Betty didn't even wince. She seemed eager to be abused.

"Anyway, my husband is dull. And mildly retarded, I think."

"Really?"

Betty sighed. "No, not really. But it would be easier to justify if he were. It's embarrassing to be married to him. Not to the family, mind you. But to be married to him is torture." Betty took a gulp of wine. "We live with his parents. Isn't that pathetic?"

Something clicked in the domme's brain, and she realized to whom Betty was married. She had never been enticed by the prospect of fucking another woman until now. She really wanted to fuck this guy's wife. His last name was plastered on the sides of trucks, loomed overhead on billboards, and was even on some of her most prized childhood toys. Oh yes, this fucktoy was one hot conquest.

"You know what? You look like you'd like my entrée too. Would you?" Betty pushed her meal toward her new friend. The key to the domme's heart at this point was through food. Betty was offering up her meal, and the duo locked in their friendship.

"Actually, let's just get to the end. I'll grab the check," She waved a finger in the air. "And we'll go back to my place for some wine."

"Do we have to have wine?" Betty breathed against her neck. "I was hoping we could just fuck." Betty adjusted herself in her seat. "Actually, I just want you to fuck me."

"Check, please!"

They burst through Mitchell's front door in so much frenetic energy.

"Who is your friend?" Mitchell was sitting in his armchair in one of his best suits and Frette slippers. He was clearly trying to look like this was how he reclined all the time, and she just found it refreshing to see him in something other than dirty boxer shorts and a stained Brunelli shirt, opened at the collar.

She smiled back. "This is Betty. Betty ___"

"Ahh? ____, as in the wealthy oil barons?"

"Well, as in my husband's family. I'm more as in the legs of the ____ campaign."

"Really?" Mitchell seemed genuinely interested. "Well, if you'd like to show me your legs, I'll let you know if I recognize them."

Betty looked over at her domme for affirmation that Mitchell was part of the equation. The domme gave no emotion and beckoned for Betty to disrobe and sit down.

Betty took off her Wall Street attire and revealed a leather corset underneath. She had come ready to play. The reveal of a corset from under a suit turned on both the domme and Mitchell, and Mitchell was already sitting in his armchair with his pants around his ankles, stroking his cock.

Betty grabbed her domme to kiss her but was instead fended off with a swift and firm smack across the face. Betty smiled and fell to her knees. The domme grabbed her by her hair and dragged her violently to the bedroom. Betty squealed in both pain and ecstasy. Mitchell pulled his pants up above his knees and shimmied himself into the bedroom after them. His hand never left his cock.

Once in the bedroom, the domme opened the closet door that concealed her arsenal of sex toys and paraphernalia. She dropped her pants and underwear and pulled on her purple strap-on dildo. She said nothing to Betty as she gestured for her to take to her hands and knees on the bed in front of the them. Mitchell shimmied over to his armchair and groaned in a creepy yet genuine way.

Betty presented her asshole and yelped while receiving her fucking. The domme slapped her ass until it was red and swollen, alternating sides in an aggressively, comically apathetic way. Mitchell laughed and stroked himself harder.

"Now drop to the floor and suck his cock while I pile this into your asshole."

Betty quickly dropped to the hardwood floor and put Mitchell's cock down her throat. Her body trembled and swayed as she was fucked from behind by the large purple rubber dildo. Betty came; Mitchell came; Betty came again. Both girls stood and walked into the master bathroom together to shower. Everyone was sweaty and sticky from wayward flying lubricant. Mitchell sat in his armchair and struggled to catch his breath.

She liked Betty, which surprised her. Betty was submissive, but with an edge. Almost like the domme had to constantly stay on top of things to maintain dominance. And that was appealing in a masochistically dominating way.

In the shower, Betty whispered in her ear, "I'm going to have my husband pick me up. That loser SOB. He's so weak, he'd pick me up from the home where I cheat on him and act out lesbian fantasies. And he'd do it happily. I'm so glad I met you. I love you." Betty kissed her tenderly on the cheek. It was a lover's kiss, but there was something maternal and nurturing about it, too. The domme hadn't felt nurtured in a long time.

Seventeen

"I want to see some tigers. Do you want to see some tigers?"

Mitchell was already into his third bottle of wine, and their sushi lunch had not even arrived. She had no idea what he was talking about. "What tigers? Where?"

"In India, Eugene! We'll go see some tigers in India!"

"When do you want to go to India?"

"Next week. We'll fly Singapore, play for a while in Bangkok. Did I ever tell you about the time I rented a brothel in Bangkok for a night?"

His non sequiturs were confusing, but she was trying to keep up and put the puzzle pieces together to figure what exactly he was planning.

"I had this fucktoy, and she had some friends. And they were in my home in Malibu one night, and they wouldn't fuck me. So I told them I'd take them anywhere the next day if they'd fuck me when we got there. I mean, Eugene, these pussies were 10s. 10s! You're only a 6, and men find you attractive. Loser men, but I digress. These were 10s I was going to fuck!" Mitchell took a gulp of wine. "So, I said I'd take them anywhere, and this one bitch says 'Bangkok.' So, I booked the four of us on a flight the next day to Bangkok. Do you know about Bangkok?"

"You mean, do I know where it is?"

"Imbecile, you are an Ivy League graduate. I know that you know where Bangkok is. I'm asking if you *know* about Bangkok?"

"I don't understand the question."

"Fair enough. I'll explain." Mitchell took another swig of wine and beckoned for her to refill his glass to the top. "In Bangkok, these asshole parents sell their daughters to the sex industry when they're very young. They work in brothels and are trained to have incredible skills doing acrobatics with their pussies."

"Acrobatics?"

"Acrobatics. Like opening a champagne cork or a bottle of beer."

Her genitals ached just hearing about it. "Really?"

"And shooting darts! My lord, can those little girls shoot darts!"

This all sounded bizarre. Mitchell didn't seem drunk enough to be fabricating the story.

"This girl gets into position like this." Mitchell slunk down in his armchair to demonstrate. "And she cocks back one leg." He brought a knee up toward his chest. "And she snaps it and the dart shoots out of her pussy. And a bull's-eye every time!"

"A bull's-eye?"

"A bull's-eye! With her pussy! A bull's-eye! If you're nice, I'll take you to a show." Mitchell looked back toward the television. He seemed to have forgotten that he was telling a story.

"Mitchell?" She coaxed. "Bangkok?"

"Yes! Bangkok. Worst traffic in the world. Really awful."

"Um, we weren't talking about traffic. You had just brought three 10s to Bangkok?"

"Yes! The brothel! So, I told them about these sex slaves, and their skills, and these bitches don't believe me. So we go to my favorite brothel in Bangkok, and I give the owner two hundred dollars, and the place is ours for the night. We bought all of the girls!"

"You bought a brothel for the night?"

"My dear, you know that I don't pay for sex," Mitchell answered the question she hadn't yet asked. "I rented them for a private show!"

"A show?"

"A pussy show!" Mitchell seemed far away, lost in the memory. "Ahhh, the private pussy show."

"So you want to go to Bangkok for the pussy show?"

"No, imbecile! I want to go to India to see tigers. But the visas are going to take a while. That's why we're going to Singapore. If we got our visas in New York, they'd take forever. But in Singapore, they'll issue them in a week. We'll go to Bangkok while we're waiting."

All of a sudden, his Bangkok stopover made sense.

"We won't stay in Bangkok. We'll go to Phuket or Phi Phi Island. The traffic in Bangkok is awful."

"You mentioned that."

"You only fly into Bangkok to get out as fast as you can."

"Right. Okay. So what happened with these girls?" She tried to bring him back to the story.

"The fucktoys. Right." Mitchell sighed. "They were lousy fucks—10s always are. One of them went home the next day. The other two spent the week with me."

"She went home?"

"And I learned my lesson!" Mitchell began to get worked up again and visibly agitated. "She met some billionaire asshole on the plane and married him!"

"And that's bad?"

"I *do not* fly bitches first class so that they can pick up some other asshole on my dime." Mitchell shook his head strongly. "From then on, bitches are coach if they're not flying with me. What a user!"

"So that's the end of the story?"

"What, you want more? They were bad fucks. Game over. Goodbye."

"Oh."

"So, we'll go to Bangkok. Or, at least, through Bangkok."

"Okay."

"Yes. Okay. Now earn it. Suck my cock."

❧

"Good morning, Eugene."

"Good morning, Mitchell." She responded into the phone.

"I've been thinking."

"About?"

"Well, that I want to not feel like you're dependent on me. I mean, we're going to India to see the tigers, but I think I'd feel more comfortable if you had your own money."

"My own money?"

"Sure, I'll pay travel expenses, but you never know what else could add up. So I'd like you to go the bank and get some money."

"But I don't have any money."

"Oh, sure you do. What's in your savings account? Like forty thousand dollars?"

"No, like twelve thousand." She caught herself. "But I have to pay my rent! And I have no income!"

"Oh, link. The missing link between the apes and humans. Hairy Eugene. Link, you mooch off of me. I pay for everything."

"Look, Link. I'm not going to pay for your existence if you're not bringing me an endless supply of pussy." Mitchell paused for effect. "I don't want your money. I don't need your money. I just want to know that you actually *have* your money. Okay?"

"How much?"

"How much for what?"

"To go to India?" She knew that a trip of the caliber that they were going to take would cost well over sixty thousand dollars, and she'd be stupid not to pony up a fraction for a once-in-a-lifetime opportunity. After all, unless she died with Mitchell, she certainly wasn't spending the rest of her life with him. Plus, as much as she was wary of his antics, she also knew that he would not outright take her money. He was unscrupulous, but not with ethics. If that were at all possible.

"Ten thousand dollars."

"Ten thousand dollars?!" She choked on the words. "How am I going to get ten thousand dollars?"

"If you were serious, you'd find a way. Go to the bank. Like a normal person, Link. Get the money. Meet me at JFK at 6 p.m. And don't bother showing up without the money. Goodbye." Mitchell hung up.

She was in shock. He wanted her to liquidate her savings account and carry cash to God-knows-where in the world? He couldn't be serious!

But she knew Mitchell. And when he issued an edict, it was to be executed. She knew that if she showed up at the airport with even a penny short of ten thousand dollars, he would publicly destroy her. So, she prepared her luggage for a trip of an unknown length, grabbed several forms of ID, and went to the bank.

Withdrawing the money was much more involved than she was led to believe, but she managed and showed up at the airport, where he confirmed that she had it. Eventually, he transferred it to his man purse.

They flew to Singapore and quickly transferred to a flight to Bangkok. The next day, they continued on to Phuket, which was far more impoverished than Bangkok had seemed. Shanties lined the dirt streets. The extreme arid heat only amplified their struggle with congested breaths of dust-filled air.

"I don't like Phuket."

"Mitchell, we've just arrived!"

"It's a cesspool. We'll leave tomorrow."

"We always do," she replied matter-of-factly.

Mitchell stared at her, then chuckled. He reached a hand over to ruffle her hair. "You're right. We always do."

At the drab hotel, Mitchell plopped himself on the couch. "They have Fox News! I like Phuket now!"

She stood awkwardly for a moment, not sure what to do with herself.

Without looking at her, Mitchell said, "Pass me my fag bag. I'm giving you a thousand baat to get the hell out of here and leave me alone for a while. But it's not to be used for food. Buy something I can see."

"Mitchell, it's a thousand degrees out there! You want me to wander the streets in this heat?"

Slowly and powerfully, Mitchell pivoted his head so that his eyes could pierce hers. "Are you complaining?" he roared.

"No! No! I'll go! I'm going! Look, I'm leaving!"

"You ungrateful troll!" Mitchell's voiced boomed so loudly that she could swear she saw the walls shake. "I bring you around the world. You see things that others could never dream of. You live a life that women would beg and kill for. And you! You complain about the heat! *Get out!*"

Mitchell threw money at her, and she ran out of the room. She waited until she was in the hallway before she allowed the first tear to fall down her cheek.

Was this really a life that other women desired? She lived in fear every day; she knew that Mitchell could easily kill her. Perhaps accidentally. Perhaps intentionally. How could anyone wish for this life, this uncertainty of being? She belonged nowhere, she rationalized. She might as well belong with him. She had become a mercenary slave to all that she thought she *should* want. Money was not the root of all evil. The fact that self-loathing sadists like Mitchell possessed most of it was.

It was surprisingly peaceful to walk the quiet streets of Phuket alone. The heat was oppressive, but it was dry. Her skin itched from lack of moisture, but the climate was tolerable once she acclimated.

There wasn't much to see near the hotel, but one of the dirt roads nearby seemed to be more bustling than the others. She had always been blessed with a great sense of direction, and she knew that as long as she made a mental note of from whence she came, she would not get disoriented.

Many of the shops were filled with beautiful garments hanging from cords across the ceilings. Some had prices written in bold marker on index cards affixed to them, so she was able to get an idea of the value of the merchandise as she wandered. It occurred to her that a new dress, or Thai outfit, would be the perfect thing to bring back to show Mitchell. If she found one compelling enough, she could lie about the price and pocket the change. At this point, even a few spare baat were priceless to her.

Many of the clothes were beautiful, but few looked well made and expensive enough for her to convince Mitchell that she had spent all the money. She walked for a few hours, enjoying the solitude, and feeling at ease, alone with the poor Thai merchants.

It was getting late. She had no idea if Mitchell was aware of the time, but she wanted to return at exactly the right moment. Too early would incite rage; too late would be worse.

She had almost given up on finding the perfect outfit when she saw a bit of fabric peeking out from behind a mass of dresses. It was grey silk, interwoven in spun gold in the shape of tiny elephants. The fabric looked amazing. It was delicate, yet indulgent, and clearly well made.

Pointing to the mass of dresses, she used sign language to have the woman working in the shop take notice. The shopkeeper took a long pole with a fork on one end, reminiscent of a western boat hook, and pried the hanger out of the bunch.

The outfit was a small, tailored, short-sleeve shirt with a separate wraparound skirt designed to be worn underneath. It was tiny, and she could see that it would fit her ever-shrinking frame. She negotiated with the shopkeeper, bringing the price to seventy baat. The outfit was folded and carefully placed in a black plastic shopping bag. She hid the change in the sole of her sneaker.

"Mitchell?" she gently called out as she opened the door to the hotel room.

"Come in, Link. Did you scare the people of Phuket with your funny looks?"

"Um, I hope not."

"Because you are funny looking. You know that, right? Like a circus freak." Mitchell shook his head for effect.

"I guess so." She quickly changed the subject. "But I got a great new Thai dress. I think you'll like it."

"*You* think I'll like it? That's dubious praise if ever I've heard it." Mitchell looked up at her from the couch and wagged his hand, indicating for her to open the plastic bag. "Let's see what you've done with my money, Link."

My money, she thought. Silently, and a bit apprehensively, she pulled out the clothes.

"You picked this out? You found *this* in the cesspool of Phuket?" Mitchell asked incredulously.

"Um, yes?" She had no idea how to read him and feared the worst.

"This is gorgeous! Let me see!" Mitchell reached out for the garment, and she released a sigh of relief. "Really, Link, this is incredible!"

"You like it?"

"I love it. No, I *love* it!" Mitchell fondled the fabric. "Is this gold?"

"Yes, spun gold in grey silk."

He held it up. "And it looks like it's your size!"

"I think so."

"Link, you have surprised me. You have impressed me. Maybe my good sense has actually rubbed off on you after all." He handed the clothes back to her. "Go on, put it on. You might look so good that I just may join you for dinner."

She smiled radiantly and raced into the bedroom to change. Maybe Thailand would be a pleasant leg of this trip after all.

They each filled their first plates and returned to the dingy yet well-set white-clothed table. Mitchell quickly chugged a beer. She sipped hers cautiously and picked up her fork and spoon. In Thailand, they had apparently never incorporated knives into the routine. But she did know that chopsticks were taboo in that country, despite the misguided notions of Americans back home.

"You look amazing in that outfit. All eyes are on you. They think you're somebody." Mitchell drank a long swig of his second beer and continued, "By the way, you're only filling three plates. That's it. I'm not sitting here all night."

She was tired of his mandating her food intake, but the food was so repulsive that she didn't mind. She was surprised to realize that Thai food in New York was far superior to Thai food in Thailand. There were a million stations at the buffet, but all the dishes tasted the same. Maybe quality ingredients were a struggle to source.

"That's fine, Mitchell." She took a bite. "I'm exhausted anyway."

"Don't speak with your mouth full, O," Mitchell admonished.

She was momentarily embarrassed by her lack of manners but was happy that Mitchell was once again calling her "O" and not "Link."

She swallowed. "A million apologies. But I am starving."

"And you look it! Have you been losing weight?"

"Not intentionally."

"If you're trying to blame me for you wasting away, stop it. The fact that your body consumes itself when you're mentally ill is not my fault. Finish your meal and let's head back to the suite so that you can suck my cock while wearing that outfit."

In a perverse way, she was flattered that he found her attractive again. They had still never had "sex," and it seemed as though that was not desirable to Mitchell at all. She was pretty sure he no longer viewed her as a sexual object; he treated her as a liability and an annoying dependent. Except, of course, when she functioned well as his madam. But she was his companion, after all, and not his girlfriend. And there was a strong distinction between the two roles.

The next day, after a failed attempt to take a boat to Phi Phi Islands, they returned to Bangkok late in the afternoon. Once checked into their suite, Mitchell said, "I don't feel well."

He rarely complained as a normal person, and she was concerned. "What's wrong, Mitchell?"

"I think I'm sick."

His speaking manner was so nonchalant that she quickly dismissed his gripes. But she played along. "Okay, we'll get you into bed, you can rest, and we'll have dinner. Okay?"

"No, stay with me."

"Seriously? You want to camp out in the room?"

"I told you. I'm sick."

Mitchell looked fine, if a little hung over. "I really want to go to dinner."

"You're going to leave me here? In this suite alone?"

So she stayed. Mitchell silently watched the television, while she watched the clock. After an hour of dead air, she let him know, "Mitchell, I'm tired and exhausted. I'm going down to dinner. Are you sure that you don't want to join me?"

"Go, go. I'm fine"

"Okay. Let me know if you need anything."

"Uh huh."

She knew that he didn't want her to leave, but it didn't seem like he wanted her to stick around either. She drew him a bath, complete with bubbles, and left the suite to dine by herself.

When she returned from dinner, there was a doctor in the room examining Mitchell. In broken English, the doctor let her know that her friend was very ill and that they would be advised to spend as much time in Bangkok to recuperate as possible. The doctor then quickly exited the suite, and Mitchell lay in bed, glaring at her.

"I was sick, and you left me."

"I didn't know you were that sick."

"It doesn't matter. You left me."

"I'm sorry."

"You're always sorry."

"So what do you want me to do, Mitchell?"

"Nothing. Just go to sleep and ignore me, as always." He paused for effect. "I hope you enjoyed your dinner."

They awoke in the morning and headed to breakfast in the hotel together. It was a buffet, and she and Mitchell filled their plates before retiring to their table.

"Eat quickly. I think we'll go to Bali now."

"Now, Mitchell?"

"Well, we have nothing to do before our visas to India come through. We might as well kill some time in Indonesia. I figured we'd go to the airport, stop by the Cathay Pacific desk, and book some tickets."

"Great! Let's go."

"You're paying for your flight, though."

"Right." Her voice dropped, but she tried to act casual in light of this new financial burden. "I know."

"That's your last plate of food. No more times to the buffet."

She looked at the spread laid out along the walls of the hotel restaurant, and then looked down at her nearly empty plate. "But, Mitchell, I'm starving. And we don't know when we'll get to Bali."

"Fine. But I'm leaving now." Mitchell stood, grabbed his luggage, and walked away.

She figured he was making a point and would soon return. Silently, she sipped her orange juice and stared at the restaurant entrance. When five minutes had passed, she collected her luggage and walked into the hotel lobby.

When she realized that Mitchell was not there, she walked over to the reception desk to see if he had retrieved the keys to go back up to their room.

"Mr. Durman hired a car to take him to the airport."

She stared incredulously at the man behind the reception desk. "But he has all of my money! And my passport!"

The man shrugged. "He left a message that you should meet him at the airport. He said you'd know where to find him."

"How can I find him? There's no way to call him, and I have no idea where he'll be!" She was beginning to get hysterical, and the receptionist could see that she was about to burst into tears.

"I will give you the money to hire a car to go to the airport. You will find Mr. Durman there."

She couldn't imagine that Mitchell had abandoned her in Thailand with no money and no passport. Was he playing a game with her? A knot began to tighten in her stomach as she sat in the Bangkok traffic en route to the airport.

Once she arrived, she ran through the terminal toward the ticketing office for Cathay Pacific. Out of breath, she panted, "I need a ticket to Bali. My gentleman companion has my money and my passport. Has he purchased a ticket?" She gave Mitchell's name to the ticketing agent.

"Yes, madam. Your friend purchased a ticket to Bali. But I'm afraid that flight is closed, and there are no more today."

"Has it taken off? Do you know where Mr. Durman is?"

"Madam, he may be in the first-class lounge, but he is probably boarding the plane."

"Where is the lounge? Can I look for him there?"

"It's on the other side of security. You'd have to have a ticket."

"But he has my money! And my *passport*!"

"I'm sorry, madam, but I cannot help you. Perhaps your friend will come see you when he returns." The agent spoke robotically.

"Do you know when he's going to return?" She was struggling to keep from crying. Was Mitchell leaving her in Thailand to die? How sick in the mind was he?

"Madam, he only purchased a one-way ticket. I'm sorry that I cannot help you anymore." The agent looked behind her and flatly called out, "Next!"

Confused and scared, she collected her thoughts. Mitchell wouldn't really abandon her, would he? And would he really steal her passport? She could imagine him stealing her money, but she also couldn't imagine him leaving her with no identification. Quickly, her mood went from scared to vindictive. She saw a police officer in uniform, and she changed her mindset entirely.

It was easy to find the police station in the airport, and she marched in, determined to file a report against Mitchell. Hopefully, the Thai police could intercept the Bali-bound flight before it left the ground.

"My passport and money have been stolen by a passenger on one of your outbound flights." She spoke authoritatively, in a manner that years living in New York City earns. "I'd like to file a report and recover my belongings."

The Thai police seemed disinterested. She repeated her plea to one of the policewomen, hoping that their gender bond would incite some compassion. It was a fruitless venture.

In broken English, the policewoman asked her to identify herself, then nodded at the response and stated, "Your friend left your passport with us. You may have it."

She was shocked. She held her passport in her hand and just stared at it for a few moments. She looked up with her mouth agape. "He left my passport here? Really?" Pausing to collect her thoughts, she asked, "Did he leave my money?"

"Only the passport, madam." The officer stared at her, emotionless.

"Is this a joke? I have no money! Can't you arrest him? He clearly stole my passport!"

The police officer shrugged and walked away.

She stood in the middle of the police station and cried. She was hurt, angry, and confused. Clearly, she had to reconnect with Mitchell in order to get home, but he was obviously playing a cruel game with her. The knot in her stomach tightened, and she quickly ran to the bathroom to throw up.

Why is Mitchell doing this? Does he really want me to die in Thailand? Is this a test? How did I ever let myself get into this situation? Is Mitchell insane, or am I?

When she had calmed herself down, she took a cold, hard look at reality and contemplated her next move. Though Mitchell had her money, she still had her plane tickets. The next leg of their journey was to Singapore, and then on to India. She decided that she would go to India and then back to New York the same day. She was still a beautiful young girl and determined that she'd be able to wing the details and figure the rest out later. There was no way to call Mitchell, and they were on the other side of the world anyway. Maybe this is where their joint journey was destined to end.

Eighteen

She booked herself a first-class seat on the next flight to Singapore. She knew that the people and the culture there were safe, and Changi Airport was one of the best in the world. If nothing else, she'd have a nice dinner in the first-class lounge while awaiting her departure on the flight into Delhi.

When she arrived at Changi, she went straight to the first-class ticketing office to plan her exit to India. The ticketing agent looked at her flight bookings and her passport carefully. "I'm sorry, madam, but you do not have your visa for entry into India."

"But I just want to fly through, on my way home."

"Yes, madam, I understand that. But you still have to go through immigration. If you do not have a visa, this airline will be heavily fined," the agent explained.

"But I don't want to go to India! I have to, . . . to catch my next flight back to New York. That's how my itinerary is ticketed."

"Yes, madam, I see that. But I cannot put you on a flight to India until you have your visa. I am sorry."

"So, I have to spend the night in Singapore?"

"Yes, madam. I think so." The agent actually seemed sympathetic. Mitchell's former companion still was lost, a nomad bound for nowhere, but at least this agent seemed to understand that without immediately dismissing her.

"Okay. Where can I find a taxi?" She knew where Mitchell had been planning to stay in Singapore that night, and she hoped that maybe, just maybe, he had returned from Bali and made his way to Singapore a few days ahead of schedule. It seemed like the responsible thing to do, everything else excluded.

She found a taxi and instructed him which hotel was the destination. He nodded, and they sped off, hopefully in pursuit of Mitchell. And more importantly, her money. She had no way to pay this taxi driver.

When they arrived at the hotel, she explained to the driver that the friend she was meeting had her money and that she would pay him promptly, if he didn't mind waiting. The driver nodded and pulled over to the side of the entranceway with his hazard lights on.

She ran to the reception desk. "Is Mitchell Durman here?"

"I'm sorry, madam. We have a Mitchell Durman booked, but not until Thursday. It's only Tuesday. Would you like to leave a message for him when he arrives?"

"Yes, please. Give him my name and let him know that I will be finding my way back to New York."

"Yes, madam."

She returned to find her cab driver leaning on the hood, smoking a cigarette.

"I'm sorry. My friend's not here. I can't pay you. I'm sorry."

"Your friend's not here?"

"No. I'm sorry."

"What will you do? It's ten o'clock at night." The driver seemed genuinely concerned.

"I don't know. I'm sorry."

"Get back in the car."

"Excuse me?"

"Get back in the car. My workday is over. You look like you'd enjoy some dinner. Let me help you."

"You don't have to do that."

"I know. But I want to. Let me call my wife and tell her I'll be late." He extinguished his cigarette and extended his hand. "My name is Johnny."

"Wow, Johnny, thank you. . . ." Her voice cracked, and she was unable to say any more.

"It's an honor and a privilege to help someone as beautiful as you." Johnny opened the door to the cab.

In normal circumstances, she would have been suspicious of Johnny's motives. But he really did seem sincere, and for some reason, she blindly trusted him. She had a feeling that there was no malice in Johnny's open kindness.

"Okay. Thank you, Johnny." She got into the car, and the two of them began to chat.

"Have you been to Singapore before?" Johnny asked.

"I have. It seems lovely. And the people are wonderful." She intended it as a compliment to Johnny, and he processed it as such.

"But have you really seen Singapore?" Johnny made eye contact with her through the rearview mirror. "Have you been to our red light district?"

She had no idea that Singapore even had a red light district; it seemed so antiseptic. "No! Is there one?"

"It's small. But it's alive at night. And we can get some good local food at this time of night."

They had a wonderful dialogue all the way to their destination, and she had a sudden recall of what it felt like to be in the presence of a man who actually treated her well and was a decent human being. She had become so anesthetized with Mitchell and their fucktoys that she had forgotten what it was like to be with a nice person. Just a nice person.

Johnny parked the cab, and the two of them exited onto a street laden with drunken revelers. She took in the sights, and the smells, and the crowds, and she knew that this was the heart of Singapore.

"It's so alive!" she exclaimed. "I had no idea that this even existed here."

"It's a secret. For the natives." Johnny laughed. She laughed too. It was the first time she had felt at ease in months. With Johnny, she could just be. He interrupted her reverie, "We'll find a good place for dinner. Have you had boiled frog? Or oyster pancakes?"

"No." She laughed. "But I'd love to try!"

"Okay. I know a good place for frogs up the street." Johnny extended his arm, not his hand, and she took it. She was in the presence of a true gentleman, and she relished it. For the first time in recent memory, she smiled. A real, authentic, happy smile.

They walked through the throngs of prostitutes and drug dealers and stepped into a narrow opening lined with tiny tables. A large terrarium filled with live frogs was at the entrance. They sat at a tiny table for two, and a waiter came by to take their order. Johnny ordered two beers and two frogs. The waiter wrote down the order and walked away.

"Go pick out the frogs."

"What?" She had no idea what Johnny was saying.

"Go to the tank and pick out our two frogs. The waiter is waiting."

She had never eaten live frog before and had no idea how to select one. It's not like squeezing a melon in the produce aisle.

Johnny sensed her trepidation. "Just pick any two frogs. They're all the same. It's just for show that you point to them in the tank."

She collected her spirit and followed the waiter to the tank of frogs. Confidently, she pointed to two of them and watched as the waiter scooped them up with a net and put them in a bag. She tried to pay no mind to the image of the frogs with their arms and legs splayed wide open as the waiter retrieved them and instead focused on how excited she was to eat this unique Singapore dish.

"Did you find good frogs for us?" Johnny asked facetiously.

"I think so. I guess we'll find out." They each took a big swig of beer and smiled.

In a matter of minutes, two large bowls filled with a boiling white porridge were presented in front of them. Johnny looked pleased; she looked confused.

"What is this? Did we order this?"

Johnny laughed. "This is the frogs!"

"These are the frogs? It's just a bowl of white creaminess."

Johnny laughed again. "They kill the frogs by putting them into the boiling porridge. Your frog is in there. Trust me."

"Really? Okay." She shoved her spoon into the mixture and hit a bone. She smiled at Johnny and pulled up a chunk of fresh frog meat.

"Welcome to Singapore." Johnny raised his bottle in a toast.

"To Singapore." They clinked bottles and relaxed in the midst of the bustle of the middle of Singapore.

They were having such a good time that they had no idea how much time had passed. Johnny looked at his watch and informed her that it was nearly two in the morning.

"You don't have a place to stay tonight, do you?" He seemed genuinely concerned.

She was embarrassed. She had been enjoying herself so much in his company that she had almost completely forgotten that she was alone and penniless, with no real plan for what was to come. "No. You completely took my mind off that."

"Good." Johnny took her hand, and they rose from the table. "We'll find you something."

They walked back to the taxi, and she sat in the front seat next to Johnny. They drove for a few minutes, and Johnny pulled the car alongside a dilapidated building with a neon sign blinking *otel*. She looked apprehensively at Johnny, and he caught her gaze. Silently, he nodded in a way that said, *You're safe here.*

There was a man standing behind a small desk, wearing a white tank top, precariously balancing a lit cigarette out of the corner of his mouth. Johnny and the man mumbled a few words to each other, and then she saw the man hand Johnny a key as Johnny slipped him cash.

"Did you just pay for my room?" She was shocked and embarrassed.

"Shhh, don't worry about that," Johnny cut her off as she tried to thank him. "I spoke with the man, and he understands your situation. You'll be fine here. He's watching out for you."

"Thank you, Johnny," she whispered.

"Enough with the thank yous." Johnny began ascending a narrow winding staircase. "Let's just find your room and get you some sleep."

She nodded and followed him up to the third floor of the concrete building. This hotel was worlds away from where she had gotten used to staying with Mitchell, but then she shook off the notion. Any place looked fit for a pauper compared to hotels in her life with Mitchell. The one overriding appeal of this hotel was the fact that Mitchell was not there.

Johnny opened the door to a tiny little room. It had all the creature comforts and nothing else. There was a short, narrow bed, a small refrigerator, a bathroom with a standing shower unit, "And a phone," Johnny pointed out. "I'm going to leave you my phone number. If you need anything, even just to say goodbye, please call me."

"You're leaving?" It suddenly occurred to her that she had just naturally assumed that Johnny was being nice to her because he had been planning to make a sexual advance. In all honesty, she had become so emotionally distant from her carnal pursuits that she really didn't think much of whether or not she was desired. She tried to think if she would have slept with Johnny if he had asked her to. She thought she might have.

"No, it's gotten really late, and I want to get back to my wife and children." Johnny paused, "I think you'd like my wife. If you're ever back in Singapore, I'm sure she'd love to have you for dinner."

She was unable to speak.

"Hey, I never showed you a photo of my children. Would you like to see them?"

"I would love that. Please."

Johnny reached into his back pocket and opened his wallet to reveal a picture of a beautiful young woman with three babies of different ages perched on her lap. "This is my wife, my two sons, and the baby is my little girl."

She was a little surprised that he had such a large family and was no older than she. "They're beautiful. You're very lucky."

"You can be very lucky too." Johnny slipped a wad of cash onto the refrigerator, next to the telephone.

"No, Johnny. . . . Don't." She couldn't bear accepting money from a cab driver when she lived such a life of privilege.

"Right now you need it more than I do." Johnny leaned in toward her and kissed her lightly on the cheek. "Good luck. Be safe." And with that, Johnny closed the door behind him.

❧

When a ray of sunshine seeped in through the barred window, she pulled herself out of bed. Her agenda for the day bore one mission: She had to go to the Indian consulate and secure a visa for entry. Her return to New York was routed through India, and she had no choice but to comply with the immigration laws. The itinerary actually called for her to fly into Delhi and out from Mumbai, but she resolved to deal with that caveat when the time presented itself.

There was a different old man sitting at the desk in the hotel entryway, and she asked him if he could provide her with a map. She knew that Singapore was a small island, and she was determined to budget her money as best as she could and walk as far as her feet could take her. The man at the desk pointed her toward a nearby 7-Eleven to purchase a map, and she promptly left the hotel.

There were several 7-Elevens on the horizon as she looked down the road from her hotel. She chuckled lightly to herself at such an amusing sight. She entered the first one she saw and purchased a road map and a Slurpee. She was hungry, but she decided to bribe herself with a good meal after the important task of procuring a visa was completed.

After about three hours of walking, she ascended the hill that led to the gates of the Indian consulate. She casually sauntered past the military guards with their machine guns and found the door marked *Immigration*.

The small, crowded room was hot and humid from human perspiration. The air smelled of curry and body odor. She tried to take the shallowest breaths her body would allow. Most of the people milling about were clutching papers with numbers on them, so she immediately sought to find a number for herself. The setup looked like an even more miserable version of the American DMV. She signed in and took her number.

"Passport." The agent behind the window extended a hand without looking up.

"I need an entry visa to India."

"Uh huh. Passport."

She handed the agent a passport and watched as documents were attached to it with a paperclip. The agent handed her a slip of paper that seemed to be a claim ticket.

"Do I leave my passport with you?" The last time her passport had been out of her hands, she had almost freaked out. This situation did not seem comfortable.

"Surrender your passport. You may pick up your visa at noon tomorrow. Next!"

"Okay, thank you."

"Next!"

On her way back, she stopped at a Mongolian buffet restaurant. There were oysters, and shrimp, and huge cuts of meat. And best of all, there was no Mitchell hovering over her, monitoring her intake. She ate solidly for two hours, until she felt like her stomach would burst. She then summoned for the check, which was surprisingly less than she had anticipated, left the cash, and began to leave. Walking past the host's desk and toward the stairs that would lead her back down to street level, she saw the ladies' room. She walked in, sat to pee, and then quickly turned to throw up.

She wasn't sure if she had gotten sick because she had eaten too much, or if she had gotten sick because Mitchell had been exercising control over her by limiting her intake. Perhaps her stomach just couldn't digest anymore? Maybe she was so angry that her system was failing.

She rose early the next day and left her luggage with the clerk in the entryway, promising to pay for her second night when she returned for her bag. She hoped that the collateral would be enough to keep her belongings safe.

When she arrived at the consulate, the waiting room was even more full than she had remembered, and it smelled even worse. Not being able to find a seat, she leaned on her elbows against a long table that people used to sign forms and absently watched the numbers tick across the board.

"Hello, Eugene." A voice behind her shook her core.

Nineteen

She spun around quickly on her heels and found herself eye to eye with Mitchell. Her throat closed, her mouth went dry, and the best she could muster was a feeble "hi."

Mitchell was grinning his classic plastic smile, but his eyes looked angry and menacing. "It's nice to see you here, Eugene. Are you enjoying Singapore?"

She choked on her words, and none came out.

"It's a shame you couldn't make it to Bali." Mitchell dramatically threw his head back. "Ah! You would have loved it! And the flight! Ah! The service, the wine, it really would have blown you away. Yes, yes, it's really too bad you couldn't make it."

"Couldn't make it?" She finally found her voice. "You abandoned me in Thailand!"

"Abandoned? Such a strong word!" Mitchell's voice softened. "Come now, wasn't it you who abandoned me?" He giggled a fake laugh. "I left you because I thought that's what you wanted."

"You thought that I wanted to be left alone with no money and no passport in the middle of Bangkok?"

Mitchell leaned down and gripped his fingers around her upper arm so hard that she really thought her elbow would pop right off her body. He maintained his plastic smile but hissed his words through his teeth. "You reported me to the Thai police."

"You left my passport there. You knew that I would."

"Of course I knew! I know how stupid you are!" Spit flicked from his words onto her face, and she blinked. Would he hit her here? "Imbecile! Do you know what could happen if you file a police report in Thailand?" Mitchell was furious.

"You stole my money and my passport. They would apprehend you."

"No, you idiot. They would apprehend *you*." Mitchell let go of his grasp on her, and she felt the blood rush back to her arm, forming a bruise. "You moron! You should know by now that I'm more powerful than you realize. C'mon, the Thai police held your passport, for God's sake! Do you think they do that for everyone?"

"You mean that—"

"It doesn't matter what I mean. What I'm saying is that you are crazy, and they know that. Everyone knows that." Mitchell flailed his arms about to express the magnitude of his point. "They look at how skinny you are. You show up with no passport, no money, no visa. You look crazy! You are crazy! Only I am on your side. Remember that."

Her number came up at the same time Mitchell's did. Had he followed her here? She tried not to dwell on the whys and wherefores and instead followed Mitchell up to the window.

He turned to her and said, "I will pay for your visa. I promised to cover basic travel expenses."

"Thank you, Mitchell," she mumbled.

"By the way, how stupid are you trying to talk the Air Singapore representatives into giving you a boarding pass without a visa?"

She couldn't imagine how he knew that.

"Oh, and how dare you expect the hotel concierge to pay for your ride to the airport? You, Eugene, are a disgrace."

Mitchell knew too much, and she knew too little. Clearly, everything had been orchestrated from the get-go. She was a pawn in a psycho game of power. It was better not to inquire, and even more important, not to protest.

"I am a disgrace," she droned flatly.

"Good." Mitchell patted her patronizingly on the head. "I'm glad you see that now."

"I have a driver. Come, I'll give you a ride." Mitchell led her through the courtyard and out toward a line of idling black Mercedes. The one that he had hired was closest to the entrance, and the driver quickly exited the vehicle and ran around the back of it to open the rear passenger side door for her. This was a far cry from the life she had been living the last few days. This felt normal again.

"I'll let the driver know where my hotel is. We can pick up my bags."

"And then go to Changi." Mitchell finished her thought.

"Right. I'm assuming there's a flight tonight?"

"*I'm assuming there's a flight tonight,*" Mitchell mimicked her. "Imbecile, why would I know whether or not there is a flight tonight? Am I a travel agent? Did you check to see if there was a flight tonight?"

"No, I'm sorry, Mitchell."

"*I'm sorry, Mitchell.* ENOUGH!" Mitchell roared. And then his voice promptly softened. "Yes, my dear, there is a flight tonight. And we are on it."

"Oh." She really had no idea how to respond to Mitchell. It seemed that everything she said was wrong. She thought it was best to say nothing, but even her silence agitated him. She kept her eyes on the road and directed the driver.

"You stayed here?" Mitchell scoffed as they pulled up. "I won't even get out of the car here. What a fleabag! You should be embarrassed."

"I am, Mitchell," she droned apathetically.

"Good. Go get your bag and settle up your tab."

"Umm, Mitchell? You have my money."

"I most certainly do not!"

"Yes, you do, in your fag bag."

"Are you accusing me of stealing?" Mitchell feigned shock.

She tried to play his game. "No, you were kind enough to hold it for me to keep it safe. And now I need some of it to pay for my hotel. Thank you for holding it for me."

Mitchell smiled; she had done well. "Okay, my dear, I will give you some money from my fag bag. But I am certain that money is not yours, nor was it ever." He reached into his man purse and handed her some cash. "Here you are, dear."

"Thank you, Mitchell."

"Keep the change!" He called as she ran upstairs to the hotel.

She did not respond.

They went straight from her hotel to Changi Airport and deposited themselves at the computers in the first-class lounge, where they checked on the latest responses and photos from women and sent an email to arrange to meet one of them when they got back to New York. The flight to India was relatively quick and uneventful. They disembarked the plane and walked through the barebones terminal to find a taxi.

"I know where I'm staying. Where are you staying, Eugene?"

"We're not staying together?" She was tired and confused.

"Well, I really don't think you've earned that privilege, do you?"

"What do you mean?"

"You sicced the Thai police on me. I'm thinking you're on your own tonight."

She tried to convince herself that he was kidding, but just in case, she stayed close on his heels and didn't let him out of her sight as he wheeled his way outside the terminal.

Mitchell walked up to one taxi driver, spoke to the man briefly, and then approached another. Then he walked back toward her.

"Okay, that man is taking you somewhere. It's not my business where. Try to make sure he doesn't rape you. I'm going to a nice hotel. I'll see you in the morning!" With that, Mitchell hopped into the taxi and sped off.

She couldn't believe that he was doing this to her again! It was already late at night, and she had no idea what was in store. With her fingers crossed, she got into the cab and hoped with all her might that she would be safe.

"Where are we going?" She had seen Mitchell speaking with the cab driver and had assumed that the two men had made a plan for her destination.

"Your friend goes to very nice hotel tonight. Too bad you don't join him." The cab driver didn't answer her question.

"But where are we going?"

"I haven't decided yet. First, we go and speak to my cousin. I think you may be very valuable to my family."

Now she was terrified. Was she being abducted? Was this another one of Mitchell's tests of her character?

"But my friend spoke with you. Where did you tell him we were going?"

"Your friend believes my family owns a small hotel in the middle of the city. We'll go to my house. I'll arrange with your friend a way to retrieve you when I've had a chance to speak with my cousin."

She could not believe that Mitchell had allowed her to be kidnapped for a ransom in the middle of Delhi. This was just plain cruel.

The cab driver turned around to make eye contact with her. "You look scared. Don't be scared. You will be safe. No rape, no death."

Was this supposed to reassure her? Would anyone even believe this story? It was official: her life was now entirely out of her control.

Twenty

They pulled up in front of a huge white stucco building with a crumbling façade.

"I didn't exactly lie to your friend. This did used to be a hotel in fact." The cab driver seemed genuinely concerned with calming her nerves, and he spoke in a paternal voice.

She considered her options for the evening. Mitchell still had all her money, but at least now she had her passport. It was too late to call the U.S. embassy for help. And, she had to admit, it didn't appear that she was in any imminent danger. She decided to just keep an open mind and try to make it through the night safely.

The cab driver shook hands with several of the men gathered around the foyer of the old building. He then turned to her and signaled with his head that she should follow him. He led her into a large room on the ground floor. There was a queen-sized bed made up with dirty and tattered sheets, a small vanity, and an attached bathroom. There was a bolt lock on the inside of the door. There was also a bolt lock on the outside.

"You are comfortable here?"

She set down her belongings near the vanity and took a moment to assess the situation. "Yes, I am comfortable here."

"Good. Would you like anything? Are you hungry?"

She wasn't hungry, but she let him know that she was thirsty.

"I will bring you a lassi. Do you like lassi?"

She did like lassis, but she had to first consider whether this man would poison her, or slip anything dangerous into her drink. She looked him up and down. He seemed harmless. "Yes, thank you. A lassi would be lovely."

"Right back." The driver walked out of the room and shut the door behind him. She heard the deadbolt slam shut on the other side. She may have been safe, but she was most certainly a prisoner.

She sat on the bed with her hands folded tightly in her lap. There was a light rapping on the door to the room. This was odd, because the door was locked from the outside, and she would have been unable to open it to the visitor. It was strange that people who would lock her in a room would also follow basic patterns of etiquette and respect her privacy. Nevertheless, she called out, "Come in!"

An elderly woman carrying a tray with a glass of the yogurt drink entered. She deposited the glass on the vanity and scurried away without having said a word. The door remained open, and once again the driver appeared.

"Do you like the lassi?"

"I haven't tried it yet." She paused to look up at him from her perch on the side of the bed. "Was that your wife?"

"Don't worry about who that was." The driver's eyes were heavier and narrower than when she had last seen him. It was clear that he was high. "We are having fun out there. Would you like me to bring you some fun also?"

It was one thing for her to have accepted a beverage from this man, but there was no way she was going to accept drugs from him. Politely, she declined.

He shrugged his shoulders and left the room. She heard the door lock, and she stood to lock it from her side as well. She went into the bathroom to freshen up, and then turned out the light and threw herself into bed.

⁓❧

"Miss! Miss!" Someone banged on the door. "Your friend is on the phone!"

She rubbed the sleep out of her eyes and stood to unlock the door. How was it possible that Mitchell was on the phone?

Beneath the large wrought iron and cement staircase that spiraled up to the next floor, she saw a tiny telephone table with a receiver dangling off the hook. Barefoot and only wearing a T-shirt and underwear, she walked over to the small space beneath the stairwell and put the phone to her ear. "Mitchell?"

"Good morning, Eugene." Mitchell began to speak quickly and didactically. "Imbecile, you have done it again. You have managed to get yourself kidnapped. And all because you angered me and I didn't baby you. I leave you on your own, and you make my life miserable. So, now, how do you propose that you will get yourself out of this predicament?"

"Uh."

"Uh? *Uh* is not a word. Speak to me."

"Well, Mitchell, I don't know. I'm not really sure what's happening."

"You're not really sure? You're not really sure?" Mitchell was getting the boom in his voice again. "I'll tell you what's happening! What's happening is that you are an imbecile. You make my life unbearable by your very presence. And then when I get rid of you, you find a way to get back into my life and ruin it again. So, now I have crazy Indians calling me at my hotel in the morning, negotiating with me to figure out an exchange to get you back. And I don't even want you back!"

She looked at the harmless group of men who had assembled to oversee her phone call. She didn't really believe Mitchell, but she had no other information.

Mitchell continued his tirade, "So if I leave you there, you're what, a white slave? They'll rape you, and beat you, and have you lick their dirty Indian assholes for fun. I can't have that on my conscience, now can I? So, now you ruin my day of going to see the tigers because now I have to go and rescue you from sociopath kidnappers who steal pathetic little white girls from airports. How can you be so inconsiderate?"

It was a rhetorical question, but Mitchell paused as though awaiting her response. "Uhhh—"

"Enough with the *uh*s." Mitchell took a deep breath. "Here's what's going to happen. I'm going to leave my beautiful hotel, figure out how to get to the cesspool where you are, and deal with these terrorists who have stolen you. In the meantime, you stay there and try not to get raped and killed. Okay?"

"Okay, Mitchell." It wasn't really okay. She was completely confused. But as usual, she had no choice but to play along. Mitchell was very skilled in denying her any options but his.

She sat alone in the bedroom with the door opened, waiting for Mitchell's arrival. She wasn't looking forward to seeing him; in fact, she was a little nervous. It was ironic that she felt safer in the ward of kidnappers than with the person to whom she was closest in the world. She sighed and stared down at her feet, wringing her hands in her lap restlessly.

Soon, she heard the authoritative boom of Mitchell's voice, and the subsequent chatter of the Indian men. They were having a conversation but were too far away for her to make out the content of the dialogue. Within moments, one of the Indian men came to retrieve her from the room, and she followed him out into the foyer.

She could see Mitchell through the open door to the street and watched as he slipped American bills into the hands of the various Indian men milling about. Mitchell didn't look up to see her, and she knew not to interrupt whatever transaction was taking place. She stood silently in the foyer.

Eventually, Mitchell waved a hand to dismiss the men surrounding him.

"Let's go, my dear!" Mitchell used a friendly word and a kind tone toward her, not for her benefit, but for the show he was putting on for the Indian men. "You're free! Come, come!"

She smiled a big, phony smile to fulfill her role in the charade. "Mitchell! Thank you for coming for me! It is so wonderful to see you!"

"Yes, yes. But I'm sure you had a lovely evening?"

"Oh, my hosts were very charming and kind toward me." She motioned her head back toward the building to acknowledge them. "Very nice people!"

"Superb!" Mitchell opened the passenger door to the car he had driven. He helped her inside, and then walked around to take the driver seat.

As soon as the car was moving, his demeanor changed entirely. "You little bitch! Do you know how much it cost me to buy you back? No, scratch that. It cost *you*. You paid for your release. It is not my responsibility to cover your ransom when you are stupid enough to get abducted!"

She tried to change the subject. "When did you rent a car?"

"When did I rent a car? That's what you have to say? You're talking about the *car*?" Mitchell laughed in feigned exasperation. "Imbecile, I rented this car when I thought that we were going to see the tigers. You know, before you were your typical all-consuming self and threw a wrench in my plans."

"So, we're not going to see the tigers?"

"Well, how could you, anyway? You've spent all of your money on your insanities!"

She could say nothing further, so she sat in silence and watched the ugly Indian cityscape go by through the windshield.

Mitchell returned the rental car and left her standing with the luggage near the entrance to the New Delhi Airport. They were at the domestic terminal and were the only non-Indians in sight. The terminal had no outside walls, and though she was on the sidewalk, she could see Mitchell sitting at the booking desk for Jet Airways, a local carrier. The agent handed Mitchell two tickets, and he walked back toward his waiting companion.

"We are going to Goa. Grab your things." Mitchell picked up the handle to his bag and walked away. She picked up her luggage and followed suit.

They strolled through security, and Mitchell made his way toward the first-class lounge. He stopped at the entrance. "You have to wait here. You don't have a first-class ticket. I'll see you in two hours." Mitchell disappeared behind the wooden door.

She stood for a moment under the driving breeze from a ceiling fan and stared at the closed wooden door. After about five minutes, she decided that this arrangement did not work for her, and she opened the door and walked through.

"I'm not flying first class, but my companion is. May I sit with him?" she asked the desk agent.

"Which gentleman?" the agent inquired.

"Him. Over there." She pointed toward Mitchell, who was reclined and chugging a large lowball glass filled with wine.

"Oh. Mr. Durman? Of course you may accompany him!"

"Thank you."

Without looking up, Mitchell muttered, "What are you doing here? Are they letting in all the riff-raff now?"

"Sorry to intrude, Mitchell. But I didn't want to be kidnapped again." She was only being half facetious.

"Fine. Sit. Don't embarrass me." Mitchell stared into his glass of wine.

"When does our flight leave exactly, Mitchell?"

"My dear, if I were you, I would not be too eager to leave this lounge to board that plane. I can guarantee you that you are far more comfortable in here than you will possibly be in flight."

"Are the domestic flights really that bad?"

Mitchell smiled broadly, recalling a bad memory. "Just you wait and see."

They boarded at the same time, but through different jetways. She had to assume that his was far nicer than hers; the din of the raucous crowd as everyone shoved and elbowed to enter through the small door almost deafened her. It was as though she had joined a wild herd of beasts, all fighting for one carcass. She had no idea how long the flight would last, but she knew that even ten minutes with these out-of-control passengers would be too many.

She found her seat and wedged herself into the space between an obese man in filthy clothing and portly middle-aged women sweating through a traditional sari. The man's horrible body odor was actually overpowered by the woman's pervasive smell of strong, spicy metabolized curry. For a moment, she thought she might actually expire from olfactory overload.

There were more people in the plane than there were seats, and after several minutes of screaming at the crowd to sit down, the flight attendant gave up and closed the door. The plane began to taxi with its aisles filled with passengers.

She had flown a lot in her life, but this sight was a first. The plane was actually going to take off with people standing, jammed into one another, as though this were just a public bus! She was happy that she was protected in her position in the middle seat; hopefully no wayward passengers would fall on her. Maybe this airline made it a practice to take a literal interpretation of the term *standby*.

After the plane had been in the air for a little while and had begun leveling out, half a dozen soccer balls began flying overhead. A young man was sliding through the rows on his belly, as though he were crowd surfing over the seatbacks. His sweaty chest and stomach stuck to her hair and pulled it slightly as he made his way from her seatback to the back of the seat in front of her.

The stench and discomfort no longer bothered her. At this point, she was only concerned with the captain landing this flying circus safely.

When it was time to begin the descent, the flight attendants once again yelled futilely for order, then gave up and strapped themselves into their jumpseats. The landing was bumpy, and a stray soccer ball hit her in the side of the head. The crowd cheered and applauded as the flaps slowed the plane to a halt on the runway.

The first class was deplaned immediately, and she battled the crowds to find Mitchell standing at the gate looking bored in wait. "That, my dear, was an *awful* flight."

"Mitchell, I'm not complaining, but you have no idea."

"I heard the commotion. I don't think you could possibly complain enough."

"Thank you, Mitchell." She appreciated that he understood her misery and had almost expressed compassion for her.

Mitchell rubbed her hair into her head playfully. "My dear, I think that you and I are going to a resort. We both deserve it."

They smiled and made their way to the taxi line at the Goa Airport.

The trip to Goa was short and uneventful. But, by this time in her life, uneventful was preferable. After a night there, they went on to Mumbai, where Mitchell decided to abort their stay at the hotel and continue home. She had never been so happy to be en route to JFK.

Twenty-One

"That girl is coming over today."

"*That girl*," Mitchell sneered. "What girl? Speak like a normal human being. Use complete sentences. Put that Ivy League degree to some use!"

"Sorry. I meant the girl that we agreed upon in the airport lounge."

Mitchell perked up. "Ah. And you spoke with this girl?"

"Yes." She was limiting her dialogue with Mitchell to avoid giving him any ammunition to launch a tirade.

"And you really voice confirmed? You asked all the questions?"

"Yes."

"Submissive? Anal? DP?"

"Yes to everything."

"Good. When are you meeting her?"

"After work. Like 5:30. She's coming here."

"Good. Good." Mitchell stared at Fox News. "It's almost 5:00 now. Don't you think you should get ready?"

She nodded in apathetic agreement and went into the bathroom to put on a little makeup and perfume. She ran her fingers through her greasy hair. Mitchell's poor hygiene habits were now fully her own.

She took as long as she could in the bathroom, knowing that Mitchell would leave her alone if he thought she were busy beautifying herself. In reality, she was staring into the mirror, catching her own gaze with her dead eyes. She wasn't surprised to see her glazed look. She wasn't even saddened by it anymore. Taking a deep breath, she returned to the living room, ready to earn her keep.

Her cell phone rang at exactly 5:35.

"Hi!" A cheerful voice greeted her. "It's Felicia. I'm crossing the street now. What name should I give the doorman?"

"You're crossing the street?" she repeated aloud, for Mitchell's benefit. "Tell the doorman you're going to Mr. Durman's. The elevator man will bring you up."

Mitchell was already pressing his face up to the living room window that overlooked Park Avenue.

"I think I see her!" Mitchell exclaimed, with the enthusiasm of a young boy. "She looks great!"

"You see her?"

Mitchell beckoned her to join him at the window. "Look. See the beautiful piece of pussy in the blue dress in the middle of the street? Walking alone? See her?" He pointed.

"Yes. She looks great from here. But we're eighteen stories up."

"Exactly! She looks great from eighteen stories! She'll be a 9 in person. Watch!"

With that, Mitchell ran into the bedroom. She could hear him opening and closing the wardrobe doors and rifling through drawers in his closet. Without looking, she knew that he was setting up the bed with a fresh sheet and towels and laying out the necessary toys for a session of devious fucking.

Mitchell reentered the living room wearing slacks. They were filthy, but at least he realized that it was inappropriate to greet their guest in his boxer shorts. He was fiddling with his sleeves as he seated himself in the living room armchair.

"Do my cufflinks, please."

She walked over to him and helped fix his French cuffs. He tousled his hair with his fingers and straightened his collar.

"How do I look?"

"Very handsome." She leaned over and gave him a kiss on the cheek, noting how pathetic and fragile he seemed at the bait of sex. She tried not to smirk.

Felicia was about her height, but with a much healthier figure. The two girls kissed hello with a mutual peck on the lips.

"Mitchell, this is the friend I was telling you about. Felicia."

Mitchell rose from his armchair and extended his hand to shake Felicia's. "Hello, Felicia. I'm Mitchell Durman. We seem to have a mutual friend. I'm glad she brought you here."

"Thank you." Felicia seemed oddly comfortable in the situation and took a seat on the couch without being prompted. Mitchell seated himself in the chair, and the domme sat on the far side of Felicia. It was refreshing that Felicia had immediately taken her position without instruction.

"So, Felicia is an interesting name." Mitchell smiled at the guest broadly. "What's your background?"

"I'm half Puerto Rican and half French."

"Fascinating combination!" Mitchell exclaimed.

"Would you like a glass of wine?" The domme tried to move the situation along, to avoid Mitchell yelling at her later for delaying the play.

"Sure. Just a bit." Felicia took the glass of wine in one hand, sipped lightly, and placed it on the coffee table. "So, can we fuck now?"

She was taken aback by Felicia's forward approach, but nothing surprised her anymore. This girl had come on a mission, and fucking was her target. "I'll tell you when we fuck." She took charge. Then she smiled at both of them, and said, "We fuck now. Take off your clothes, Felicia."

Obediently, Felicia disrobed. Mitchell took off his pants and shorts, and his companion took off all her clothes and went into the bedroom to retrieve the strap-on. She marched back into the living room with her giant affixed appendage on display.

Mitchell laughed. "Doesn't she look gorgeous?"

Felicia salivated a bit and uttered a soft, "Uh huh."

"Okay. Enough talking," the domme commanded. "I'm going to fuck you in the asshole while you suck his cock."

"Lying on the couch, or on the floor on my knees?" Felicia was making this very easy.

Taking a cue from eye contact with Mitchell, she said, "Lying on your back on the couch."

Felicia quickly positioned herself and waited with her legs spread and her mouth opened wide. The domme filled her asshole with the purple rubber dong, and Mitchell walked over to the edge of the couch and filled Felicia's mouth with his cock.

The position looked awkward, but Felicia didn't seem to mind. She was moaning and thrusting and soon orgasmed in harmony with Mitchell. Without even batting an eye, she swallowed Mitchell's cum.

Everyone reclined on the furniture in exhaustion, and then Felicia stood and began to dress herself.

"Are you leaving?" Mitchell asked Felicia.

"I have dinner plans. But this was fun!" Felicia turned to her hostess. "Please call me?"

It seemed to be an eager, and sincere, plea. The domme was almost taken aback. Coolly she replied, "We'll see."

"Let me give you some cab fare to get to dinner." Mitchell thrust a stack of fifty-dollar bills into Felicia's palm.

Disgusted, Felicia dropped the cash on the floor, without even wrapping her fingers around it. "I have cab fare. Thank you."

Felicia turned to her hostess as they walked to the door, and they tongue-kissed goodbye. "Thank you," Felicia said, breathily, while turning to walk away.

As the door closed, she exhaled. Turning to Mitchell, she prompted, "Well?"

"I like that one." Mitchell threw himself forcefully into his chair, picked up the television remote, and repeated, "I like that one."

"Felicia smelled like body odor. Like I was back in India." She knew that Mitchell wanted her to rip Felicia apart and point out the flaws. And Felicia really did smell like bad sweat.

"Yeah, well, Felicia was hairy too." Mitchell didn't let his gaze leave the television. "You tell her to take care of all that hair before she comes back here. I'm not sticking my cock in that forest. Got it?"

"Done." She was about to sit down on the couch but then thought twice about it. "Can I go?"

Mitchell laughed. "Yes, imbecile. Get out of here. Take some cab fare out of my fag bag and go." He chuckled again and raised the volume on the news.

Silently, she palmed a wad of fifties and walked out of the apartment.

Twenty-Two

Mitchell left on a mysterious weekend trip. She thought that this would allow her a little time to herself, but Mitchell had other plans. He called her from the airport before his flight out of New York boarded to give her instructions for the weekend.

"My dear, my son's mother is coming to the city this afternoon and spending the night. I believe she has some doctor's appointment or whatnot to take care of." Mitchell paused, as though waiting for a response.

"Okay, so why do I need to know this?" She was actually curious to find out what her assignment would be.

"Well, Pamela, my son's mother, will be staying in my apartment. For some reason, she seems to think that in bearing me a child, she has the right to live off me forever." She could tell that Mitchell was about to digress into a tangent, so she tried to reel him back in.

"So, you want me to stop in at your apartment to monitor Pamela?" she asked.

"No! No. Nothing like that." Mitchell inhaled deeply. "Pamela doesn't need a babysitter. Pamela needs a girlfriend; someone to pal around the city with."

"You want me to befriend Pamela? Really?" She was honestly shocked that he would want to create a potential powder keg situation.

"You see, my dear." The fact that he called her 'my dear' indicated to her that this was a genuine favor he was requesting. "Pamela on her own will spend lots of my money. She'll buy shoes, and couture clothing, and other silly things she doesn't need. Women dress like shit in San Fran-sissy-co, and there is no reason for Pamela to buy more designer clothing to sit in her many closets."

"So you want me to distract Pamela so that she doesn't spend your money?"

Mitchell laughed. "Oh no, my dear. Pamela is going to spend my money with or without you. So, I'd prefer that it's with you."

"Oh. Okay. So, what's my role?"

"Pamela will call you tonight. You will offer to treat her to dinner."

"You want me to buy her dinner?"

"Let me finish speaking before you begin a barrage of questions." Mitchell paused. "Yes. You will buy her dinner. This will both shock and please her. In doing so, she is going to feel ingratiated toward you. Pamela will call me to tell me how nice you were to take her to dinner in my absence. I'll then insist that she take you to a spa and dinner tomorrow. You will make reservations at one of those amazing restaurants you always want me to bring you to. And Pamela, or should I say I, will foot the bill."

"That's going to be a several thousand dollar day, Mitchell."

"It's a fraction of what she'd spend at a store. And this way, my best girl gets to benefit from it." Mitchell coughed into the receiver. "Those are your instructions. I will be home Sunday night, just after Pamela leaves. Do you have any questions?"

"Just one. Where are you going?"

"Goodbye." The receiver clicked, and she regretted asking something that was clearly not her business. She settled into her couch and waited for a phone call from Pamela.

"Hi, this is Pamela. Mitchell said that you'd be expecting a call from me."

"Yes! Pamela, hi. How was your flight in?" She tried to be polite.

"Fine, I suppose. I'm just planning on a nice quiet night to relax after a travel day and a doctor's appointment."

She purposely didn't inquire about the appointment. "Great!" She paused before asking to indicate that the idea had just popped into her head: "May I take you to dinner tonight?"

"Really?" Pamela seemed surprised. "You don't have to do that!"

"It would be my honor. I'd hate to think of you all alone in Mitchell's apartment."

Pamela was silent for a little while, probably weighing the pros and cons of this situation. Eventually, she said, "I'd love to join you for dinner. Just let me know when and where."

"I'll pick you up from Mitchell's at 8 p.m."

"Okay! I'll see you then. Do I need to let them know downstairs that I'm expecting you?"

"No, the doormen know me."

"Of course they do," Pamela said dryly. "I'll see you soon."

She was nervous about having dinner with Pamela, and she had the feeling that Pamela was also apprehensive. But she was sure that Pamela was now on the phone with Mitchell and would soon enough realize that neither woman had any say in the matter.

She decided that they would go to a trendy local bar and restaurant near her apartment so that there was no awkward parting of ways after the quick meal was over. She would merely tell Pamela that she lived nearby and was ready for bed. The stores would be closed by then, and she would have completed her task.

Just as Mitchell had planned, Pamela called her early Saturday morning. Even though the women had filled the previous night's dialogue with trivial small talk, they both shared the unspoken element of a life wrought with Mitchell.

"I've booked us mani-pedis, massages, and haircuts. I'm getting a color, too. You don't color your hair, do you? You can get a facial while I get my color," Pamela informed her by phone.

"So, I'll meet you at the spa?"

"Ten a.m."

"See you soon."

She hung up the phone, and then realized that the responsibility of a dinner reservation probably lay with her. She thought for a moment of the recently opened restaurants that Mitchell had promised to try with her but never would. She settled on Masa in the brand new Time Warner Center and secured a chef's viewing table for two at 6 p.m. If the spa treatments took as long as she imagined, they would make their reservation just in time. Dinner would be finished by nine, and once again, the stores would be closed, and she would have fulfilled her purpose of keeping Pamela from shopping. Plus, she really wanted to dine at Masa.

Pamela was waiting for her at the entrance to Fekkai, and the two kissed hello on the cheek as though they were old friends. Their brief dinner the night before had proven to both that they were able to carry on small talk without mentioning their respective connections to Mitchell at all. They were now much more comfortable with spending a day together, bizarre as it was.

Their treatments began with their pedicures, and when Pamela sat in her massage chair without picking up a magazine, her companion took her cue and sat down in the adjacent chair, also without reading material. She assumed this meant that they were going to talk, but she made a mental note to leave it to Pamela to take the lead.

There were several minutes of silence before Pamela broke through it.

"You know, you don't have to call me Pamela. You can call me Pammy," Pamela said as she sorted through the polish colors. "Only Mitchell calls me Pamela. And it makes me uncomfortable."

"Okay, I'll call you Pammy. But if it's okay with you, I'll continue to refer to you as Pamela in Mitchell's presence."

"Of course! That's a given."

"Does he ever refer to me as Eugene when he speaks to you?"

Pamela looked at her new friend, eyes ripe with confusion. "No! Why?"

"No reason. Just curious." She changed the subject. "Do you like the polish color I've selected?"

"It will look great on you. Why?"

"No reason. Just don't know how to paint my toes."

Pamela stared at her hard. "This isn't your first pedicure, is it?"

"No! Of course not!" She tried to sound offended, but then confessed, "It's my second."

"Well," Pamela eased back further into her chair. "Enjoy it while you still can."

"What?"

Pamela realized that the words had come too soon, and she tried to cover up. "Nothing! No. I meant nothing. Just . . ." Pamela cleared her throat. "Just don't let Mitchell drink too much."

She didn't like the idea of bringing up the Pandora's Box that was Mitchell. And she certainly didn't want to do it during a supposed day of relaxation. She pretended that she hadn't heard the comment and instead focused her attention on playing with the controls of the massage mechanism built into her chair.

"Good chair, right?" she tried endlessly to steer the conversation away from Mitchell.

Pamela took the cue, and the women finished their spa treatments in abject silence.

They arrived at the restaurant just in time. The spa treatment had lasted just up until the last few seconds in which they could still make their reservation at Masa. It was the hottest, newest restaurant in the city. But because it was also the most expensive, they were still able to get two seats in front of the sushi master himself.

When the wine list was presented, Pamela casually mentioned that she didn't drink. "But you go ahead!"

"You don't drink, Pammy?"

"Not anymore." Pamela turned her attention back to the sushi chef. "So, this is chef's choice, correct?"

"Yes. It's a set price. We just watch, eat, and enjoy."

She and Pamela were seated side-by-side, staring at the sushi master, Masa himself. This was the perfect seating for the two to enjoy an evening together without being forced into awkward conversation. Instead, the evening was filled with comments like *What is he making now?* and *Is he kidding me with these tiny portions?*

In the end, they both agreed that the meal was a major disappointment, especially at five hundred dollars a head, before tax, gratuity, and alcohol. She was glad that she had not convinced Mitchell to take her; he would have been miserable, and she never would have heard the end of it.

The two parted ways in front of the Time Warner Center, both agreeing that they would probably go to their respective apartments and order a pizza. Masa had left them hungry.

They hugged goodbye and walked off in separate directions. It had been a good day.

Twenty-Three

The days in early June became repetitive. Mitchell left his apartment less and less while drinking more and more. They ordered sushi from the same place most afternoons. If Mitchell was feeling generous, they ordered expensive Italian food from a local restaurant that actually delivered. They hadn't gone to Tino's in weeks. Her world consisted of purchasing a *New York Times* on the way from her house in the morning, then retrieving Mitchell's ATM card from his apartment and withdrawing one thousand dollars. She would then walk to the discount wine dealer (they no longer drank the good stuff) and buy a case of wine. Upon return, she'd tell Mitchell that the bottles cost twenty dollars when they really cost ten. She'd pocket the change. She knew he knew, but he was too drunk to care.

He'd yell and roar from his chair, demanding that she bring him girls. When she didn't, he'd think of creative ways to punish her.

Sometimes he would demand a blowjob while he was sitting on the toilet. She hated this punishment because there was always a little bit of pissing awaiting her open mouth.

He demanded that she lick his asshole clean after he'd taken a shit and hadn't wiped. He insisted that his ex-girlfriend had loved it and that his current imbecile was clearly a prude. He grabbed her hair once and shoved her head between his legs, but even he couldn't stand to hear her crying, and he let her go after just a few pathetic flicks of the tongue.

And sometimes she found girls for him. She no longer took them to fancy restaurants; now she met them at a Starbucks around the corner from Mitchell's apartment.

All the girls were eager to fuck—she had made sure of that with a phone call before each rendezvous. But she was increasingly selective in which girls she actually brought back to Mitchell. He was becoming more demanding and picky; fickle even. And when he was drunk, he would force her to insult a girl he didn't like and forcibly remove the girl from his apartment.

And then he would beat her.

The more she cried, the more he flung her about like a rag doll. She was usually convinced that each beating would bring her death. But a little inkling inside made her believe that Mitchell's strategy was to bring her to the brink of death but not actually go all the way.

When they had first met, Mitchell had ruled her with kindness and generosity. Now Mitchell ruled her with fear and force. Either way, she accepted that she was now Mitchell's puppet.

Sometimes, Betty would come by. Betty liked the idea of desecrating her Greenwich housewife image with the torrid lesbian affair. The domme had to believe that on some level, Betty cared about her, but she had learned that everyone in her life had self-serving motives. Even she.

Felicia came by on several occasions, too, and even looked for pussy together. Felicia accepted domination and obediently waxed her body hair. She seemed generally concerned as her domme continued to lose weight. Mitchell seemed enthused by it. Once, he had Felicia and her go into his bedroom to take photos of her skeletal frame. "Just as a record of how mentally ill you are," Mitchell mused to his companion.

Betty seemed concerned too. But Betty and Mitchell had a strange connection. Mitchell treated Betty badly, but Betty never forfeited her will entirely. She was the only playmate that Mitchell fucked in the pussy. What made Betty different? Maybe it was the global power of her husband's family. Mitchell's companion didn't waste too much time figuring it all out. It didn't matter anymore. Nothing mattered to her anymore except daily survival—and even that was growing less and less important.

She barely slept anymore. Her mind alternately raced and ran blank. She was always hungry. But she was so embarrassed by her appearance that she dared not enter a store. Sometimes she took garbage bags home from the deli, shamefully eating the contents of that day's display case alone on her bed. Usually, she ate so much that she got sick. It was hard for her to keep anything down anymore. Even her own body was rejecting her.

Her parents no longer returned her phone calls, and she had lost touch with all her friends. Mitchell had driven away those who remained. She was dependent on Mitchell for companionship and sustenance, but every glass of wine he gave her was laced with poison.

She tried to think that Felicia and Betty were her friends, but that notion was difficult to believe. After all, how could their friendship be real if it was based on her ordering them to suck Mitchell's cock as she fucked them in the asshole? She was certain that domination was not a foundation for true friendship. Her relationship with Mitchell had taught her that.

Every night, she dozed off certain that she would not wake up. And each morning when she did awaken, she tried to decide whether her survival was a blessing or a curse.

One day, she was able to schedule Felicia to come over to Mitchell's apartment to play with two new fucktoys she was introducing into the mix. In his anxious anticipation, Mitchell insisted that she first acquire several new strap-ons and ball gags in case the girls decided to fuck each other. With one thousand dollars in her pocket, she made her way west on Fifty-Seventh Street to a secluded sex shop on a high floor in an inconspicuous Midtown office building. It was starting to rain a bit, and she hoped that the inclement weather would keep people off the streets so that she could carry her bag of toys unnoticed. Or, at the very least, others' umbrellas would keep them looking at their feet and not at her.

She was beginning to feel like a monster. Or a predator. Although the stream of girls that she had brought in the past few weeks had all been eager and willing to play, because she was so miserable, it was inconceivable to her that they were truly enjoying themselves. She had no idea what these girls could possibly tolerate, let alone like, about the situation. Who could possibly want to be sodomized by a drunken skeleton?

There were several other passengers in the elevator that brought her to the floor location of the sex shop, but she was the only one who exited at that level. She wondered if the people who worked in the building knew what was hidden on the floor. Surely, they must. But, this being New York, no one even looked up as she walked out of the elevator car and turned down the hall.

She was happy to see that she was the only customer in the store at the moment. The salesgirl behind the counter was fiddling with the register and merely muttered a greeting without looking up. The customer hoped that she was free to shop in peace.

As she browsed the strap-on section, she heard the friendly salesgirl's voice behind her. "Can I help you find anything? Need any suggestions?"

Startled, she spun around. "Nope, thanks. Just here to grab a few strap-ons and some ball gags."

"A few? Nice!" The salesgirl giggled. "Having a party?"

"Sure, sort of."

"Can I come?"

She looked the salesgirl up and down. The full-sleeve tattoos and facial piercings were a turnoff. And the pink hair and heavy waistline were just not going to go over well with Mitchell. She sneered at the salesgirl. "Nope."

With three new purple strap-ons and two new ball gags in her arms, she walked over to the checkout counter. The salesgirl's face was tomato red from embarrassment at having been rejected, and the girl didn't look up from the countertop. Silently, the money and the receipt were exchanged, and the tools were loaded into a nondescript purple paper sack. She turned and walked out of the store with her errand accomplished.

She was alone in the elevator on the ride down, and she momentarily questioned her own shocking degree of bitchiness in dismissing the salesgirl's request for sex. Her contempt toward other people, and women specifically, was growing exponentially daily. She contemplated feeling regretful of her behavior, but it was difficult for her to really feel anything.

The receipt was still in her free hand, and she uncrumpled it to put it in the bag with the newly acquired apparatuses so that Mitchell couldn't accuse her of inflating the price. The salesgirls' cell phone number was scrawled on the bag of the small piece of paper, with a name, and the single word *please*.

What the fuck was the matter with these girls?

"Did you get everything?"

"Yep."

"*Yep?*" Mitchell chastised. "English, please."

She wasn't sure if Mitchell was in one of his moods, or if he was just nervous and excited by the sex romp that lay ahead. "Of course. Sorry, Mitchell." She held up the bag. "Lots of brand new toys."

"Good!" Mitchell clapped his hands together like a giddy child. "New toys for our new toys!"

She couldn't help but laugh. Mitchell's behavior and emotions were so erratic that he was almost amusing. When he wasn't frightening.

~❧

Charlotte and Kate arrived separately but at the same time, meeting in the elevator on the way up to Mitchell's apartment. Felicia showed up next, and Jamie came through the door about five minutes later. All the girls were on time.

She poured everyone a glass of champagne, but heeding Mitchell's warning, she offered no seconds. He was very clear in relaying his understanding of the law, and he wanted no potential liability from a girl claiming inebriation and the resultant forfeiture of free will. Play was play, and there was no room for drama.

The girls mingled about the living room making introductions, but the dialogue was not heartfelt, and the conversation was superficial. They all knew their purpose for being there, and though the orgy was a surprise to all, they were eager to commence the festivities.

She brought them all into Mitchell's bedroom and instructed them to disrobe and fondle each other on the bed. As they did so, she, too, took off her clothes and put on her trusty strap-on. She hadn't bothered to deal with the thick packaging of the new strap-ons, and her old one was sized to fit anyway. Also, she thought that with this many girls, breaking in new dildos would probably add to their level of comfort in an otherwise unorthodox situation.

As two of the girls began to lick the pussies of the others, she entered one of them from behind. When she was bored with that asshole, she instructed the girl to lick it clean before she entered the other pussy eater.

At some point, Mitchell entered the room and dropped his pants to his ankles as he planted himself firmly in his armchair. Happy that she finally had her intended audience, she began to perform the ass-slapping dance that had amused him so much in the past. She flailed her arms wildly and flipped her hair from side to side as she made forceful, and loud, contact with the strangers' ass cheeks.

After about three minutes of the ass-slap dance, she grew tired and bored. She got off the bed and retrieved the new strap-ons. She opted not to introduce the ball gags since the girls all seemed happy to eat each other's pussies and were relatively nonchatty as a result.

She threw the strap-ons, still in their packaging, onto the bed and said nothing. Excited, Charlotte and Jamie grabbed them and tore through the thick plastic cases. They each put on a harness with a dildo and then looked at her to orchestrate their next moves.

She knew that this was the moment at which she could prove herself worthy of Mitchell's esteem, and so she choreographed a chain, all leading to Felicia sucking Mitchell's cock. Mitchell seemed overcome with pride. Or pleasure. Or something.

Now that she had effectively taken herself out of the equation, she refilled her glass of champagne and stood in the bedroom doorway.

She was quite a sight to behold: naked, wearing a harness with a large protruding purple cock, while holding a glass of champagne and barking sex orders at a group of veritable strangers.

Charlotte seemed particularly adept at working the strap-on. Though she claimed to be a novice, her moves were pure genius and came from a place of visceral pleasure. The domme had never enjoyed the act of fucking another girl, but she did enjoy Mitchell's response. Charlotte, on the other hand, was seemingly oblivious to the presence of the other attendees of the orgy and instead had transcended into a hedonistic trance.

For more than an hour, the domme stood in the doorway shouting instructions and gauging Mitchell's response. Eventually, he came powerfully in Felicia's asshole. Anticipating his fantasy, she instructed Jamie to lick out and swallow the cum as it dripped from Felicia.

When Mitchell was finished, it meant that everyone was finished, and she instructed the girls to clean themselves up and leave the apartment. Charlotte protested and begged to stay the night. The domme firmly denied the request, and all the girls left at once. Their cheeks were flushed and blotched with red patches, and she wondered how they all truly enjoyed an act that left her feeling empty except her contempt for the sluts.

Twenty-Four

"Come over quickly! I have a reward for you!"

She had figured that her production the night before would warrant a prize, but she had no idea what it would be. It certainly hadn't been financial. Mitchell hadn't taken care of her in that way before she'd left his apartment the previous evening. But with Mitchell, surprises were never small.

Though she was no longer emotionally attached enough to her life to be excited, she was genuinely curious to know what Mitchell had in store.

She took the subway to the stop nearest his apartment, bought the *Times*, and headed up the elevator to see him.

She opened the door to find him feverishly typing on his computer at the desk in his office.

Without looking up, Mitchell said, "Guess what? That cunt Charlotte sent you an email claiming that you abused her and took advantage of her last night. She says her boyfriend is pissed and coming after you."

It was too early in the morning to process Mitchell's rants. She tried to slow him to a pace she could understand.

"What are you talking about? Which one was Charlotte?"

"Charlotte was the one who really loved giving the fuckings. The one who wanted to spend the night." Mitchell looked up at her. "You really have to start paying attention to these girls and their names. I know you don't give a fuck, but when emails like this arrive, you should at least know who sent them." Mitchell turned his attention back to the computer screen and chuckled to himself. "You really despise these bitches, don't you? You can't even be bothered to retain their names for 24 hours!"

"That's not fair to say, Mitchell," she said flatly. "I didn't know their names last night, either."

Mitchell laughed loudly and deeply. "That, my dear, is why I love you. Because you really do hate these girls you bring to me. And they know it. That's why they love you."

"Anyway. . ." She tried to subtly divert the conversation back to the surprise he had mentioned on the phone that morning.

"There is no anyway." He paused for a moment. "Before I forget, here's forty dollars for your taxi." Mitchell threw her a ball of cash. She knew when he preemptively gave her money that something big was coming.

"Thanks."

"Don't thank me yet." Mitchell closed the lid to his computer and looked at her sternly. "This bitch is claiming abuse. Drugging. Malfeasance. This cunt can make life miserable for you. Well, for me through you."

"What are you saying, Mitchell?"

"I'm saying that this Charlotte cunt seems to have a boyfriend whom she confessed to. It looks like he's pissed. And he's threatening you."

"He's threatening me?"

"Okay, he's writing from Charlotte's email account pretending to be Charlotte writing to you. I'm pretending to be you writing back."

"I'm confused."

"You always are." Mitchell chided.

"And?" She had no idea where Mitchell was going with this lecture.

"And now we have to leave."

"Leave New York?" She was almost excited; they hadn't traveled in almost a month.

"We're leaving the country until this Charlotte whore cools down. You haven't read these emails. This is a serious situation."

"But she seemed to have such a great time."

"Well, she has regrets after the fact. And I have no energy to spend destroying a fucked-up twenty-year-old girl. So we're leaving."

"Okay. I trust you." She did trust him. Charlotte had seemed to have a great time at the orgy, but she knew that eventually one of the girls they fucked with would become vindictive in a hindsight revision of a playdate. "So, what now?"

"We leave tomorrow for San Fran-sissy-co. We'll stay with my son and his mother, and then you and I will go to Fiji. And then Australia. And then South Africa. How's that?"

"Sounds like a good itinerary."

"Yes." Mitchell curled up his lip in an intimidation strategy. "It's a very good itinerary. Don't make me regret rescuing you from Charlotte."

Rescuing me *from Charlotte*? She couldn't believe how severely Mitchell had subverted the entire situation. But she chose to ignore the comment and focus on the trip ahead.

"That sounds great, Mitchell." Her speaking voice was flat. "I can't wait to go to South Africa."

"Fiji and Australia first, Eugene." Mitchell got nasty again for no reason. "This trip is for me to bring my son. The world does not revolve around you."

She bit her tongue. Mitchell was clearly upset by the email he had received from Charlotte—or whoever was writing on Charlotte's behalf—and his erratic emotions had taken hold. She tried to focus on the benefits for her.

"Thank you for taking me to those places, Mitchell. I can't wait."

"I'm not taking you. You go home and book the trips. I'm thinking Air Pacific through Fiji. First class for me. Coach for you."

"Coach?"

"Yes. That's your punishment for sticking me with this Charlotte bullshit. You should have prequalified the pussy better."

"But she had a great time! You thought so too!"

"Are you sassing me?" Mitchell squinted his eyes angrily.

"No, sir."

"Good. Because one more sass and you're flying steerage."

She took the wadded-up forty-dollar cab fare and walked to the subway to go home.

∽

"I have a mission for you."

"What's the mission, Mitchell?"

"What's your mission always?"

"To find pussy."

"That's right. But this is special. I'm saying goodbye to you today."

"Forever?"

"*Forever?*" Mitchell mimicked her. "No, imbecile. I'm leaving for San Fransissy-co this evening to see my son. You're going to meet me there as soon as complete your mission."

"So, what's special about this particular mission?"

"I'm glad you asked." Mitchell paused dramatically for effect. "We are going on safari, and we are bringing a fucktoy with us. You are to find and interview potential travel mates, and when you've found your selection, you will meet me on the west coast. We'll then fly to LA, and then take Air Pacific to Fiji. We'll spend a few days in Fiji, and then fly on to Melbourne. You and I will then drive to Sydney, where we will meet up with my son and his mother. They'll go on to New Zealand, because my son loves New Zealand, and I will fly to Tanzania to take care of some business I have there."

"And me?"

"And you. It's always about you." Mitchell sighed audibly.

"Sorry, I was just—"

"You will fly back to New York and pick up our fucktoy. The two of you will then fly to meet me in Jo'burg, and we'll take it from there. Get it?"

"Yes, Mitchell."

"You realize, of course, that if you fail to provide passable pussy, your part of the trip is off. I will go alone. Correct?"

"Yes, Mitchell."

"Good. You know what you need to do. Goodbye."

"Good—" She heard the telephone click.

The Internet posting she listed seemed over the top, and when she hadn't received any responses in the first couple of hours, she reconsidered the wording. It was hard for any prospective girl to believe that someone was actually offering a first-class trip to Africa in two weeks. Her second posting merely requested a travel companion/fucktoy and highlighted "all expenses paid." Slowly responses began to trickle into her inbox.

Most of the replies seemed to be from girls who were clearly more curious than committed to the notion, so she spent a lot of time deleting useless emails. But one girl seemed a little lost in New York and truly eager to explore the world with a domme friend.

The girl had sent a few photos in the response, and the thin body and flowing blonde hair seemed promising. Clearly, this girl was some Midwestern transplant who had come to New York to chase a dream but had failed. She was the perfect mix of vulnerable, desperate, and open to anything.

The girl gave the name Laura and was willing to meet that afternoon at a coffee shop on the Upper East Side. She was perfect and passed every test to "prequalify" her, as Mitchell would say. The two girls went out into the sunlight, and the domme took several pictures of Laura against the backdrop of a brick wall. She also took some photos with her head next to Laura's so that Mitchell would know the pictures were taken that day.

After the mini photoshoot, she grabbed Laura and kissed her firmly on the mouth, making sure to bite down firmly on Laura's bottom lip. Laura trembled in arousal, so she then took a hand to Laura's shoulder and pushed her away violently. Without looking back, she said, "Maybe I'll call you."

Mitchell's response to her email containing Laura's photos came immediately. He must have been waiting by his computer for the update on the interview.

If Laura's real, prequalified, and up for anything. . . . you, my dear, have earned yourself a trip to Fiji and Australia. And Africa. You bitch. You won. You came through. . . . When you really work, you can produce. Let's not be a consumer so much in the future. . . . You've proven you're far more valuable than you often lead me to believe. xxx Mitchell

She smiled when she read Mitchell's email. It was immediately followed by an eticket confirmation number for her departure from JFK to San Francisco the next morning. It was a coach seat, but Mitchell had already warned her of her downgrade status. She knew the trip to Africa would be first class, and Mitchell was just trying to force an exercise in humility on her.

It wasn't working. She was very proud of herself for finding Laura and really hoped that Laura was the real deal. All indications suggested that this was going to work out.

Twenty-Five

Mitchell was waiting for her at the terminal. As they drove, in his semi-drunken state, he began to debrief her. "We're going to my son's house. Do not be the imbecile that you and I know that you are. Be a small presence. Don't scare my son."

She had been a nanny in college and knew that children loved her. In fact, Mitchell's son loved her, even though it pissed Mitchell off to acknowledge it. So she ignored Mitchell's snide remark.

They pulled into the narrow garage at Pamela's house, and he quickly ushered her in. "Come now, little imbecile. Don't make me wait for you. I want to see my son!" Mitchell held the door to the house open and widely gestured his arms in exasperation.

She left her bag in the garage, not wanting to assume that she would be staying the night there. Mitchell didn't acknowledge it, so she figured that he wasn't sure where she would be sleeping, either.

Mitchell's son, Adam, was in the middle of a piano lesson in the living room, so she and Mitchell sat in the kitchen with Pamela.

She wasn't sure how to behave in front of Pamela. Certainly, they were friends of sorts, but for them to show each other any familiarity or affection would have infuriated Mitchell. And all three knew it.

Mitchell broke the silence. "So, I'm paying for Adam to take piano lessons now, am I?"

Pamela ignored the jab. "He's coming along really well, and he enjoys music."

"Good, good." Mitchell reclined in his chair. "Pamela, do you have any of my wine in the fridge?"

Pamela didn't verbally respond to the attack on her sobriety but stood up and removed two glasses from a cupboard. "What would you and our guest like, Mitchell?"

"Our guest?" Mitchell scoffed, "Come now, the missing link is not *our guest*. She is a festering lesion that I have burdened myself with and must now care for." Mitchell smirked at Pamela. "Surely you know the type?"

Both women exchanged a brief glance of commiseration. Whether they had spoken it or not, they were both marionettes in this puppet show.

That evening, she, Pamela, Mitchell, Adam, and a random Russian model dined at a local restaurant near the house in San Francisco. No one ever explained to her who the tall, thin young girl across the table was, but she had learned a long time ago not to ask questions. Past or future fucktoy brought by Pamela? It didn't really matter anymore.

The model ordered fish-and-chips and then passed the rest of the food on the plate to Mitchell's companion. Even an anorexic model wanted to fatten her up.

Adam colored on his paper placemat and seemed totally oblivious to the bizarre hodgepodge of adults surrounding him. To Adam, insanity must have been normal. This was the Durman family status quo.

The next morning, she awakened in one of the guest rooms on the top floor of the tall house. Mitchell was still asleep and snoring in an adjacent room.

When she descended the many flights of stairs, she found Adam and Pamela in the kitchen. Adam was eating microwaved waffles, and Pamela was at the stove cooking eggs.

"Good! You're down. Just in time! I started your omelette when I heard the shower turn off." Pamela seemed cheerful and bubbly in the morning. She liked that. "Sit, sit!"

She sat at the kitchen table across from Adam and waited for her breakfast. Adam was an adorable, if spoiled, little boy. His heart was genuinely filled with love and compassion, and she wondered how he could possibly be kin to Mitchell. If he hadn't looked so much like Mitchell, she would have questioned the paternity altogether.

"Is your breakfast good?"

"Umm hmm." Adam had his mouth full. "Are you daddy's girlfriend?"

She loved how direct children were, but this was a question that even she couldn't answer. "I'm your daddy's companion."

"Oh." The answer seemed to satisfy Adam's curiosity, and she breathed a quick sigh of relief. He was a smart boy, and she knew that a wrong answer could incite a barrage of impossible questions.

Pamela set a beautiful breakfast plate in front of her, and she realized in looking at the food how intensely hungry she was.

Halfway through her breakfast, Mitchell appeared. He was unshaven and unshowered and aggressively flung open the swinging door to the kitchen.

"That's it! Stop eating! Get your things and get out of my son's house!" Mitchell boomed.

She was startled, and Adam started to cry.

"Look! You bitch!" Mitchell continued to scream. "You've made my son cry! You horrible person! You come into his home! You eat his food! And you terrorize him!"

She was shocked and confused by what was transpiring. She and Adam had been having a pleasant little conversation. She and Pamela got along well. As far as she could tell, the discomfort was all a delusion of Mitchell's.

"Get up! Get out!"

She was scared of Mitchell, and Pamela apparently was too. She ran over to the table, scooped up Adam, and dragged him to safety in another part of the house.

"Look what you've done!" Mitchell yelled. "My son couldn't even finish his breakfast because of you!"

The moment felt surreal. She couldn't figure out what she could have possibly done wrong except that she had ingratiated herself into his family, and that scared him.

"Mitchell, we were just eating breakfast, and—"

"And that is my son's food!" Mitchell's face was a violet shade of red. "You cozy up in a house that doesn't belong to you! You speak to people whom I've told to hate you! And they do! And yet, you put yourself in their world! You sit at their kitchen table! You eat with them! What must my son think?"

Adam must think, *My daddy is insane,* but she had no idea what previous companions had dealt with, so she remained silent. She hoped the attack would end.

Instead, Mitchell continued. He grabbed a tuft of her hair and thrust her face into the wooden table. He repeated the motion several times, like a WWF wrestler.

When her nose began to bleed, Mitchell became irate. "Are you bleeding on the table where my son takes his meals?!" Mitchell's snorting sounded like a bull ready to attack. "Are you intentionally trying to kill him with your horrendous missing link blood?"

Tears were streaming down her face. She couldn't catch her breath long enough to respond. She hoped that the presence of Adam would prevent Mitchell from outright killing her, but she wasn't so sure.

"Stop sobbing! You goddamned fucking freak! Get your bag and get out of my son's house!" Mitchell was serious, and she was scared.

The blood from her nose dripped onto her pants, and she debated the consequences of removing one of the linen table napkins to sop up the flow. With her lip quivering, and her vision blurred, she left the kitchen table and began to ascend the flights of stairs to her guest bedroom.

She stopped off at the bathroom as her body convulsed. She threw up both violently and weakly and tried not to look in the mirror as she splashed her face with cold water from the tap.

She tried to clean the blood from her pants but quickly realized the effort was futile. She heard Mitchell pacing several floors below, and she knew that she had only a few minutes before he would come up to drag her down the stairs.

She zipped up her small suitcase, took a deep breath, and returned to the firestorm.

As she passed Pamela on the way down the stairs, Pamela reached out to her and gave her a few pairs of pants and a sweater. "You have blood on your clothes. These should fit you. They fit me when I was with Mitchell."

She didn't question the comment but was taken aback. *Was this how he treated all his companions?* Pamela hadn't seemed at all surprised, or even all that concerned.

She looked at the tags on the pairs of pants Pamela had given her. They were children's size 14. She couldn't believe she had physically deteriorated into children's sizes. And she couldn't believe the now seemingly well-adjusted Pamela had been there too. Mitchell was a sick fuck.

Cautiously, she entered the garage. She had already put the newly appropriated clothing into her luggage so that Mitchell wouldn't attack Pamela for helping her as well.

He already had the car running and the garage door opened. As soon as she had thrown her bag under the hood and taken her seat on the passenger's side, Mitchell sped off.

They zipped along in silence for a while, but eventually she said, "I thought we were going to Fiji and Australia?"

Mitchell kept his eyes focused on the road. "We were. Until you sabotaged our plans by forcing my son to speak to you!"

Mitchell jerked the car into the parking lot of a Safeway supermarket. The Porsche had barely slowed moving as he threw it into park.

"Out!"

"Here?"

"OUUUUT!"

She scrambled to find the door handle and practically tumbled out of the car. She picked herself up from the asphalt and was surprised to see Mitchell get out of the car, too.

"Are we going to the supermarket?"

Mitchell backhanded her across the face. "Don't ask questions. Follow me."

She held the swollen side of her face and obediently followed Mitchell into the supermarket. He moved quickly. He threw several large hoagies into the cart and a large bucket of fried chicken. Then he turned to her.

"Think that'll hold you?"

"Hold me?"

"Yes. You are now a homeless person in San Fran-sissy-co. Do you think this is enough food to get you by for the week?"

"I'm a homeless person?"

"Well, you have no place to go, no ticket home, no family to speak of, and no money in your possession." One side of Mitchell's grin curled. "That's homeless!"

The reality of the situation began to sink in. "Wait, you're leaving me here?" Her bottom lip began to quiver, but she knew that crying would only make Mitchell angrier.

"No! Here?" Mitchell laughed. "I wouldn't leave you in a supermarket parking lot!"

"Oh!" She exhaled.

"No! I'm leaving you with all the other homeless people in the park across the street."

Mitchell seemed serious. As much as she wanted to believe that he was playing with her, this situation seemed real.

Without looking back toward her, Mitchell made his way back to the parked car. She was hoping that this was all a joke, but when Mitchell pulled her suitcase out of the hood, she knew he was serious.

He handed her the luggage and the bag of food, aggressively kissed her on the cheek, and said, "Goodbye. The homeless park is across the street." He pointed with one finger. "Don't get hit by a car when you walk over there. Oh, and try not to get raped." Mitchell licked his palm and ran it through her hair. "You look like a bag lady."

She stood looking at Mitchell in shock. He wouldn't really leave her standing there in the Safeway supermarket parking lot alone, would he?

She watched with her mouth agape as Mitchell started the car. She ran around to the passenger side and tried the handle, but it was locked. She watched as Mitchell put the gear into reverse, and thinking quickly, she ran behind the car and stood firmly where Mitchell could see her in the rearview window.

He lowered the window and roared, "I swear, imbecile, I will run you over if you don't move! I'll tell the police that you were a homeless woman who attacked me, and they'll let me off. And if I don't kill you, and you're able to speak, who do you think they'll believe? You? Or me?"

A single tear rolled down her face.

"*Move!*"

She dropped her eyes to the ground, and her shoulders slumped forward. Mitchell was serious.

Dragging her feet, she walked away from the car toward her luggage and grocery bags. She heard Mitchell's car peel out of the parking space, but she didn't turn back to watch.

She was crying heavily now, overwhelmed by her feeling of helplessness. Through her tears, she saw Mitchell's car at a traffic light, and she watched in angst as the light turned green and he drove out of sight.

For a few moments, she stood in a near catatonic state. Then she picked up her belongings and crossed the street to the park.

She sat on a park bench next to a homeless man, taking care to keep her distance and not impinge on his territory. She stared blankly into the distance. She couldn't even cry anymore. Her transformation into a zombie was complete. She was now an empty shell, and she didn't care if she lived or died.

Twenty-Six

The sun was beginning to set over the water, and she hadn't moved from the park bench. The homeless man had left a while ago, and she assumed he had gone to a local shelter for dinner. She, unlike the homeless man, had nowhere to go.

Her eyes hadn't left the horizon in hours, and her jaw was still slack from shock. Her mouth was dry, and she had the chills, even though she was wearing a sweater in eighty-degree weather. She had no feeling in her hands or feet, and her back hurt from her slouched posture. But she couldn't move.

"Get off the bench."

Mitchell's shadow against the setting sun was enormous, eclipsing her small frame.

She didn't look up.

"I said, get off the bench." Mitchell's tone was flat; neither angry nor apologetic. His voice was authoritative yet not aggressive.

She said nothing. She was unable to respond. Her ability for rational, cognitive thought and basic internal dialogue had retreated, and she couldn't even process the moment.

"Imbecile? Helloooooo." Mitchell waved his hand in her line of sight to try to get her attention. "Eugene? Are you in there?"

Mitchell walked over toward her and grabbed her firmly by the hair. He pulled her painfully to her feet and smacked her hard across the face.

She looked up at him, completely pathetic. She was like a puppy in a cage at the pound.

Mitchell chuckled maniacally. "Did you enjoy your day at the park?"

Her mouth opened, but no sound came out.

"Oh, come on, imbecile. It was a gorgeous day in San Fran-sissy-co." Mitchell motioned toward the water. "This is a beautiful bench to sit to watch the day go by. And you had a nice lunch, right? I took care of you and bought you a nice lunch, right?"

Still, she said nothing.

"Okay, you've obviously experienced some sort of trauma that has paralyzed your already small brain. Did a homeless person rape you?" Mitchell pretended to look her over. "No, you look just as bad as you did when I left you, but no worse." Mitchell paused. "Are you going to speak?"

Mitchell waited a few moments for a response, but she was still lost in a gaze at the colors of the sunset on the horizon.

"Okay, clearly you are too mentally ill to speak right now. That's fine." Mitchell gestured toward her belongings. "Gather your things. We have a flight to Fiji to make out of LA tonight."

Silently, and almost robotically, she picked up her bags and followed

Mitchell to a waiting taxi. Mitchell's luggage was already in the trunk, and the driver ran around the car to add her bags to the pile.

She sat next to Mitchell, behind the driver, as was Mitchell's rule, and she gazed passively out the window. She couldn't bear to look at Mitchell.

He broke the silence. "You know why I had to get you out of that house, right?" Mitchell poked her with a finger to get her attention. "You scared my son."

She said nothing.

"Poor little Adam. Subjected to seeing a crazy woman, a homeless-looking schlub, in his nice and proper home. Really, imbecile, a travesty."

Silence.

"I just want you to understand that you traumatized my son." Mitchell poked her again, hard. "You may think that Adam likes you, but that's only because he's been well trained to be polite."

Mitchell's words didn't even hurt her anymore. There was no point in trying to analyze or even acknowledge his hostile statements.

There were low-flying planes overhead, and she knew that they were getting close to the airport.

"Two different airlines, please, sir." Mitchell gave the driver the names of the respective airlines.

She looked at Mitchell quizzically.

"Ah, you're wondering why we're flying from different airlines? The answer is simple: I'm flying in style, and you're flying steerage, or some other bullshit comparable class."

Still, she said nothing. Silence was more potent than words.

❧

They arrived in Fiji in the daylight, and she ran to find Mitchell in the customs line. She said nothing as she cut the line to stand next to him.

"How was your flight in the poor people section?"

She had gotten some sleep on the plane and was excited to be in Fiji, so she was able to respond. "I sat on the butt pillow in a bulkhead seat. It was just like first class."

"My dear, it was nothing like first class," Mitchell scoffed. "Anyway, we have to decide what we'd like to do in our time in Fiji."

Her favorite childhood movie was *Blue Lagoon*, so she knew that she wanted to get out to the small surrounding islands. But she didn't say that to Mitchell. Instead, very diplomatically, she said, "Whatever would please you, Mitchell."

Mitchell laughed. "Very good. But first," he held up his boarding pass for their continuing flight to Australia, "we have to get out of this flight. You will go to the ticketing counter and tell them that you're having stomach trouble. They'll reticket us for a later date, when you're 'feeling better.'"

She did as she was told, and their layover in Fiji was made to be indefinite.

They found a booth filled with brochures, and as they skimmed them, Mitchell found a little getaway that struck his fancy. It was accessible only by boat, and there was airport pickup available.

They called the resort and then waited outside for their escort.

"You know, imbecile, you haven't said 'thank you' in a while." Mitchell pinched her arm. "You haven't said much at all, actually. Not that I'm complaining. I like you when you don't speak."

She looked ahead at nothing in particular.

"Most women would kill to be taken to Fiji. You, my dear, have become a spoiled ingrate."

She still didn't respond.

"Jackie O was grateful. When Aristotle wanted her to find pussy and fuck him with her asshole, you had better believe she did it. With gusto!"

Mitchell seemed to think he knew a whole lot about the sex life of the upper class. She decided that he might be far more delusional than she had even imagined. She remained silent and stood rigid as they waited for their ride.

After about an hour, they gave up on the hope of an airport pickup. Mitchell left her with the luggage as he went to find a car rental, coming back with a cherry red SUV.

The resort was easy to find, but when they arrived at the parking lot, they realized that it was accessible only by boat. So once again, they were left waiting for an escort.

They were the only couple that had arrived at that time, so they had plenty of room for themselves and their luggage on the quick ride to the resort island.

The sun had already set, so all they could see of the resort grounds were the areas lit by tiki torches and Christmas lights. The edge of many buildings came right to the waterfront, so the lights reflected back up in the water. It looked magical.

In the back of her mind, she made a note to return to Fiji in the future. When she had someone whose company she'd actually like to keep.

Because they had the rental car, Mitchell had the idea to drive all the way around the island to have lunch in Sudi. He estimated that the drive from Nadi, where they currently were, would take about two hours.

He appointed her navigator, as always. But this route was easy to navigate because there was really only one road around the perimeter of Fiji.

They started off making good time, but then a torrential downpour began. Mitchell tried to adjust the headlights, but only one was working. He squinted in the darkness and slowed down. They were pretty much the only people on the road at the time, so they didn't really fear hitting another vehicle. They did, however, have reason to fear veering off the road.

Mitchell was doing well driving safely as she looked for traces of a town. Hopefully, they would find a suitable area to pull over and wait out the storm.

Mitchell swore and pounded the dashboard.

"Is everything okay, Mitchell?"

"Fuck, fuck, fuck! Not only do the headlights not work, but now the windshield wiper is gone! Fuck!"

"Gone?"

"Gone. Ripped right off the car in the force of this rain. Damn it!"

"So you can't see?"

"I can't see!"

"Can we pull over?"

"I can't even see that much!"

Her heart began to pound. Every time she got in a car with Mitchell, there was life-threatening drama. Every goddamn time.

She saw a building, and then another, and then one more.

"Mitchell, I think we're entering a town. We can stop the car!"

"Thank you, God," Mitchell prayed and lifted his gaze upward. "Thank you, God!"

They stopped the car and ran out into the driving rain to hide under an overhang and plan their next move.

She turned around and was pleasantly surprised by what she saw.

"Mitchell, we're standing in the vestibule of an auto body repair shop!"

"That, my dear, is the power of prayer."

Mitchell spoke to the men who were sitting around and drinking in the garage. He found one who was willing to brave the storm outside and replace the missing windshield wiper. In the meantime, she found the bathroom. She didn't have to go, but she wanted to make herself scarce. When bad things happened to them, Mitchell always found an excuse to take out his frustration on her.

The repair didn't take that long, and the storm seemed to be letting up too. It was still mid-morning, so they were on schedule.

They made it to Sudi at exactly noon and were pretty disappointed in the environs.

"The women here are actually uglier than the women in Nadi!" Mitchell spat in disgust.

Normally, she thought that Mitchell's assessment of women was a little harsh. But looking around, she had to concur that Fijian women were most definitely the ugliest women on Earth. Freakishly and universally ugly.

"We are not staying here for lunch!" Mitchell exclaimed. "I cannot look at these people any longer. We'll finish our circumnavigation of the island and eat back at the resort."

She couldn't object to his plan. No restaurant in Sudi looked to merit a visit.

They got back into the car and exited through the other side of the city from whence they came. They drove about twenty minutes before one of the ugly local women stopped their car. She waved her hands frantically, and Mitchell hit the brakes.

"Is there something wrong?" Mitchell asked.

The woman replied, "I am a traffic officer, and it is my duty to inform you that this road is closed due to landslide."

"You mean a landslide from today?"

"No. There was a landslide six months ago."

Mitchell laughed in disbelief. "You mean, ma'am, that this road has been closed for six months, and no one thought to tell us until now? Now?!"

"This road is closed, sir. Go back to Sudi."

"I want to go to Nadi!"

"You have to go back through Sudi. That's the only way."

Mitchell rolled up his window and once again pounded his fist on the dashboard. "Fiji sucks! What a fucking cesspool. And filled with incompetent, ugly morons running the show!"

As they drove back toward Sudi, the rain began again. And the new windshield wiper broke in mid-swipe.

"Are you fucking kidding me? Are you fucking kidding me?!" Mitchell rolled down his window and leaned forward so that his arm could extend to move the broken wiper.

She said nothing. But the situation was mildly amusing. It would have been outright funny if she hadn't feared death by vehicular failure.

When they arrived back in Sudi, Mitchell announced, "Out of the car. We're leaving the vehicle."

She was confused. "What are we going to tell the rental car company?"

"Fuck them. They gave us this piece of shit. And a map that doesn't show closed roads. Fuck them. It's their problem now."

"So how are we getting back to Nadi?" She knew the Mitchell had a plan, but she had no idea what it was.

"Boat or plane? You choose." Mitchell ruffled her hair playfully.

"Plane."

"Okay, let's go charter a plane."

They left the car on the side of the road and found a small travel agency, where they negotiated a plane charter.

The airport was a short cab ride away, and they arrived at the small open-air airport in less than ten minutes.

The storm had now passed, and the skies were crystal clear blue. But their charter plane was not there.

Mitchell seemed to be managing his anger well, and they sat at a table in the food stand area and ordered a meal. It was already getting close to dinnertime, and she was hoping that their plane would arrive before the sunset. She really wanted to see Fiji by air in the daylight. She knew that Mitchell did too.

They drank some beers and ate the forgettable mush of food. Both she and Mitchell were drenched in sweat; the storm had brought a hot and humid front with it. The beers and spicy food helped cool them, but not much.

As the evening settled in, their plane finally arrived. They entered the plane by climbing onto the wing and crawling through a small door. Mitchell took up most of their seat with his overweight figure and broad shoulders. Even though she was squished by him, she knew that he was more uncomfortable than she. His head was pressed against the ceiling.

The plane took off as dusk approached, and the view of Fiji from the air was mesmerizing. Each had a nose pressed against their respective windows, and other than a few *ooooh*s and *aaaah*s, neither said anything.

The center of the main island of Fiji was rolling hills covered in lush jungle. Judging by how green the landscape was, she assumed that the storm they had just weathered was typical.

The flight to Nadi was only about fifteen minutes, and they had no wait to find landing space on the runway.

In the airport, Mitchell made a detour to inform the rental car company that they had left the "piece of shit" on the other side of the island. He demanded his money back, and he got it.

They hailed a taxi, and made it back to the resort in time for dinner.

She woke up the next morning and found Mitchell snoring loudly on the couch in the living room. The empty bottle of wine next to him told her that he had continued last night's party a little later than she had.

Silently, she showered and dressed, then sneaked out of the room to breakfast.

It was a pleasure to have breakfast without Mitchell; she could eat slowly and relax, and her every move wasn't met with criticism.

After breakfast, she walked through the lobby and collected a few brochures. Mitchell liked it when she came up with her own activities, and certainly, in this case, she was happy to do so.

She found some pamphlets for local scuba operations. She had been diving since she was ten years old, and even though she was older and much more frail, her athletic appetite was still there, though quelled.

But as appealing as the diving advertisements were, what really struck her was a brochure for a barbecue lunch cruise that ended with an overnight on a private island with a private chef, manservant, and maid.

She knew instantly that this was the Fijian moment for her and Mitchell. In fact, this wasn't even a sell to him; he would laud her for her excellent sleuthing abilities in finding fabulous moments in a world of hedonism.

When she arrived back at the room, Mitchell was already fiddling with his European laptop, trying to get it to link up with the hotel broadband line. Frustrated, he slammed it shut.

"I'm going to the fucking business center!"

She stood silent with a hand holding the brochure extended.

"What?!" he snarled before looking at the pamphlet. Upon reading it quickly, his facial expression changed. "Ah. You found us a private island for tonight? You really do have a *Blue Lagoon* fantasy, don't you?"

"How did you know that?" She had never mentioned it and was truly surprised that Mitchell was so inquisitive.

"Oh, please! All of you bitches from the late 70s, early 80s, have a *Blue Lagoon* fetish. That and *Pretty Woman*." Mitchell giggled for a minute. "And I'm not sure if you're pathetic because you fell into it, or if I'm pathetic because here I am financing your private trip to an island outside of Fiji."

She resented the statement, but Mitchell made a good point. They were in the middle of every little girl's fantasy. *My god*, she thought, *if little girls only knew how fucked up their fantasies are!*

❧

They met the boat at about 10 a.m. near their resort. Theoretically, the cruise served brunch, but she had already had breakfast a few hours before, and Mitchell was too hung over to eat. Instead of joining the other passengers in the hold, they stayed up top and watched the archipelago of Fiji go by.

As the boat slowed to reach its destination, the captain pointed out the islands on which *Blue Lagoon* had been filmed. As excited as she was, there was a little anger in her heart that she was sharing something so special with Mitchell.

She was genuinely excited as they passed the *Blue Lagoon* islands, and even Mitchell perceived it.

"Sit there, Eugene." Mitchell searched her purse for his camera. "I'll take your picture." Mitchell paused and said warmly, "I've never seen you so genuinely excited." Then he killed the warmth by adding, "I just wish you could get as excited by finding pussy as you do in finding islands."

He sighed more for affect than for genuine disillusion, then took a few photos of her on the top deck of the boat. Years later, those photos would haunt her: Pictures of European tourists poorly dressed in jeans and sneakers flanking her. Her in a gold, hand-stitched summer gown.

If only she felt as valuable as the clothes she wore.

Even though other people were on the boat that left them off at the private island, at four p.m., after the barbecue, the island belonged only to her and Mitchell.

There was one small cottage with an outhouse and mosquito netting, but on this abandoned island off the coast of Fiji, it was a palace. And it was only theirs. As usual, they were the envy of the people surrounding them.

They were the only passengers who had boarded the boat with luggage, and the looks from the others made it clear that no one understood how they could have had the foresight and the ability to rent the island for the evening. She was actually a little surprised herself, but Mitchell had an uncanny talent for making magic happen.

The boat was anchored as close to the shore as the captain would allow, and a dinghy was lowered to shuttle passengers to the beach. Workers were going to shuttle the luggage and the food for the lunch barbecue after all the passengers had disembarked.

She and Mitchell were in the first shuttle run. As they got closer to the beach, she became increasingly more giddy, but Mitchell firmly squeezed her thigh in an indication that she needed to stifle her excitement; this sort of adventure was normal to them, after all. At least, that's what their fellow passengers had to believe.

The dinghy pulled into knee-deep water, as that was the closest the outboard motor would allow. She got out of the dinghy first, and holding her skirt up out of the water, she waded to shore.

Standing on the sand, she watched as Mitchell plunged his large body out of the dinghy and braced the cuffs in his slacks to walk the ten feet to where she stood.

Suddenly, and without warning, Mitchell, who was so consciously avoiding getting his pants wet, fell backward into the water. He lay underwater for a moment, with just his belly peeking through the surface. She felt paralyzed as she waited for him to right himself; she knew that the backlash would be insurmountable, and that fickle Mitchell would now be incorrigible.

In a burst of water, Mitchell thrust himself back to his feet. He looked at her and snarled, and then ungracefully walked onto the beach.

"I cannot believe these bastards let me fall in the water. What kind of service is this?" Mitchell spat in frustration.

"Mitchell, it wasn't their fault that you fell."

"Not their fault? Whose side are you on?" His eyes were bloodshot and filled with contempt.

"I'm on your side. Are you okay?"

"Of course I'm not okay! I'm salty, wet, and I hurt my back."

"I'm sorry."

"You're not sorry!" Mitchell looked down. "Great. Fuck. My foot is bleeding."

She looked down at the slow, red stream that led from the top of his foot into a little puddle in the sand.

"Can I get you anything for the cut?"

"How about a tetanus shot?" Mitchell barked. Then he inhaled deeply. "All I want is for you to get me off this island."

"But we're here for the evening."

"Not anymore. Tell them to hold our luggage on the boat. I'll not die on an abandoned Fijian island from a fatal foot wound!"

Mitchell was acting like a child, and she was hoping that this flood of anger would pass quickly.

"You don't really want to leave, do you?"

"What did I just say, imbecile? Are you not listening?" Mitchell seemed like he was simultaneously going to burst into tears and beat her to a bloody pulp.

"Okay, I'll take care of it."

"Good. Because we were only going to stay here for you. I wanted to do something nice for you. And this!" Mitchell looked again at his bloody foot. "This is how you repay me!"

For the life of her, she couldn't imagine how she was responsible for Mitchell falling in the water, but she knew better than to dispute his claim.

"Okay. I'll let them know." She began to walk away through the sand, and then turned back again to address Mitchell. "We still won't be able to leave here until the boat with everyone else turns back."

"I know. I know. I'm doing this for you!" Then, at no one in particular, Mitchell exclaimed, "All of this pain, just trying to be nice to a fucking imbecile."

With her head hanging low in disappointment, she found the head of the barbecue tour group and let him know that she and Mitchell would not be staying on the island for the night.

The tour guide seemed confused, but because she wasn't really sure why Mitchell getting wet equaled them having to return either, she just repeated her statement of intent. The guide nodded in mock understanding and then quickly auctioned off the night on the island to the other couples who had sailed over on the boat.

It broke her heart that she couldn't stay on the island in Fiji, and it upset her even more that it was so easy for them to find another couple to take her and Mitchell's place. She felt enormous resentment toward Mitchell. More than that, she feared his wrath.

The tour operator let the group know that they had a couple of hours to tour the island before the lunch barbecue would be ready. She asked Mitchell to join her for a walk, but he was intent on staying where they had landed and sulking until it was time to leave the island.

Dejected, but determined to enjoy Fiji, she asked the guide if she would have time to circumnavigate the entire island and was assured that she could. She began walking counter-clockwise around the island, hugging the water's edge as closely as she could.

From the shore, she could still see the islands from the *Blue Lagoon*, and she wished that her life were that charmed. The characters in that movie may have been abandoned, but at least they were content—a feeling of happiness she had long since given up.

The water was clear blue, and the sand was a powdery white. She walked as best she could in her Thai evening gown and tried to appreciate the moment of solitude.

She decided to return here some day to spend the night with someone whose company would actually be enriching. That is, if she ever lived to experience a positive relationship.

Near the campsite, she passed several other couples. Some were frolicking in the water, and some were merely lounging in the sand. But as she walked farther toward the backside of the island, she became less aware of her loneliness and more aware of her solace.

As she turned at the opposite end of the island, she could see the smoke from the campsite and approached it with dread. Mitchell's anger and resentment had had the last two hours to condense.

She took a few snapshots of herself, her face framed against the backdrop of some of the most beautiful pristine water she had ever seen. She smiled in the photos. In paradise, one always tries to feign happiness.

She found Mitchell sitting alone in a wooden chair drinking a beer. He had obviously already had a few, and his demeanor was much more settling.

She decided to try again to see if he was amenable to spending the night.

"Are you feeling better? Are you sure you want to leave?"

"Imbecile, I never wanted to stay in the first place. But I make sacrifices for you." Mitchell looked at his foot, which was now, melodramatically, wrapped in gauze. "And I always seem to regret it."

The barbecue meal was unmemorable, but she and Mitchell ate and drank well. They left on the return boat ride with all the other passengers, and she tried to pretend that she didn't notice that they were all gossiping about Mitchell and her.

She wasn't sure where they were going to sleep that night. The resort still had the bulk of their luggage in storage, but they had obviously not reserved a room for that evening. She didn't verbalize her concerns; she would just follow Mitchell's needs.

They were able to procure a small junior suite for the night, and Mitchell, who was drunk by the time they reached their room, was asleep on the couch in moments.

She took herself to the buffet dinner, but the knot in her stomach was so tight that she could barely eat. She just sat alone at a large table and drank several island cocktails until the dinner service was broken down and she had no choice but to return to the room.

She slept fitfully but still managed to get some rest. At around 4:30 in the morning, she was shaken awake by Mitchell.

"Get up, suck my cock, get dressed." Mitchell clapped his hands to try to get her moving. "We have a flight to Australia in a few hours! No time for breakfast! Chop, chop!"

Mitchell must have awakened in the middle of the night and made some calls to address their onward travel plans; she chose not to inquire further.

Obliged, she followed his orders. His cock tasted salty, and she realized that he still hadn't bathed to get the salt water off his body. But it didn't matter. She had mastered the rhythmic technique that worked for him, and he came quickly. This meant that she was off the hook for the rest of the day, and that at least offered her some respite.

They continued on to Australia, where Mitchell insisted she get a full-body waxing at salon in the airport. He even forced her to wax her forehead, explaining that with her low hairline, she only exacerbated her strong resemblance to the penultimate missing link.

After the humiliation and pain of another full body and facial waxing, Mitchell drove his three passengers into the city. He then deserted her across the street from a youth hostel while he, Pamela, and Adam stayed at a glorious three-bedroom condo.

But the hostel had not been what she, or Mitchell, expected. Recently built, the lobby was like that of a four-star hotel. She stayed in the newly opened women's wing, with brand new linens and a down comforter. She took her dinners at the hostel buffet, and was delighted by the included free European breakfast.

She spent her first day at the Good Food and Wine Show at the convention center only a short walk away, where she made lunch and dinner out of the samples on the show floor for only an eight-Australian-dollar entry fee. On her second day, she went on a winery tour and took in the sights of the countryside.

When she returned to the hostel after the tour of the vineyards, there was a note waiting for her. It informed her that Mitchell had called earlier in the day, and that he would pick her up at around 5 p.m. It was clearly stated that she should check out before his arrival.

As she waited for Mitchell, lots of happy travelers passed her. Some were coming in, some were going, all were smiling. She used to think that her first-class lifestyle was more favorable than the life of a backpacker, but she knew better now. Besides, here she was at a hostel just as they were. Except that her backpack was an expensive Louis Vuitton roller bag.

At exactly 5 p.m., Mitchell walked through the front door of the hostel. She could tell by his posture that he was readying himself to express his nausea at her dire accommodations. She laughed to herself as she watched his predetermined look of disdain turn to one of shock and bitterness.

"This is a *hostel*?" Mitchell spat incredulously as he picked up her luggage.

"This?! This place is amazing. Like a nightclub! Here I thought you were roughing it. Rotting away in some armpit fleabag." Mitchell snarled at her. "I'm only here because Pamela felt bad for you. Little did she know!"

She said nothing and just followed Mitchell to the car. He had left it idling, presumably because he had anticipated a quick getaway from hostel filth.

They drove to Mitchell's deluxe high-rise accommodations and left the car with the valet.

The penthouse had floor-to-ceiling windows looking out over the Opera House, but Adam seemed oblivious as he sat and played with some plastic toy soldiers at the table in front of the view. He did, however, notice her walk in and immediately jumped up and ran over to her.

"Do you get to stay with us now?!" the exuberant little boy asked as he threw his arms up to hug her.

She reached down to his level for the hug, but Mitchell stepped in between.

"Don't touch her, my son! She's just come from a . . ." Mitchell choked on the word, "hostel."

Adam had no idea what a hostel was, but the way his father said it, the boy quickly put down his arms.

Mitchell admonished her, "Stop trying to scare my son. And don't infect him with your hostel filth." He pointed toward one of the closed doors. "Go shower and rinse the dirt off yourself. We're going to dinner."

She and Adam exchanged a somber look, and she went into the bathroom to bathe.

The foursome drove to a nearby restaurant and took a table with a view of the water. She sat next to Pamela and listened with interest to her stories of the trip to New Zealand that mother and son had taken en route to Australia.

"It was amazing!" Pamela gushed while flipping through photograph after photograph of bright blue water and a smiling little boy. "I think Adam and I will go back. Maybe the day after tomorrow."

Mitchell spoke very little as he pounded through two bottles of wine. He poured generously for her as well. When Pamela saw that the two were getting tipsy, mother and son left Mitchell and his companion to finish their lamb and kangaroo.

"I'll take the car, if that's all right," Pamela said with a palm outstretched to take the keys from Mitchell.

"Fine, fine. Go, go." Mitchell didn't even look up at Pamela as he handed over the keys.

After Pamela and Adam were gone, Mitchell decided to let his companion know of the tentative itinerary for the upcoming days.

"So I'm thinking that we'll go to the zoo tomorrow. You can see the koalas." Mitchell smiled genuinely. "They're funny looking, just like you."

"The zoo sounds great, Mitchell. I'm assuming that Adam is coming with us?"

"Don't assume." Mitchell's admonishment seemed playful. The wine was working positively. "But yes, of course Adam and Pamela are coming to the zoo. I wouldn't make a special trip for you, now would I?" Mitchell pinched her cheek hard.

"Ouch!" She yelped and put her hand to her face. She didn't mean to let him know that he hurt her, and she immediately regretted it and braced herself for the backlash.

But none came. Instead, Mitchell chided, "Come now, that didn't hurt. Get some resilience, damn it!" He then went back to describing the itinerary. "There is a route called the Coastal Highway that reaches from Sydney to Melbourne. I'm thinking that you and I will drive through the night tomorrow and see what's going on up there."

"And Adam and Pamela?"

"You heard Pamela. They want to go back to New Zealand. They have a flight to Christchurch tomorrow evening."

"Adam is a very lucky boy." She wondered how long Adam could live this lifestyle with childlike innocence before becoming as jaded as his father.

"That marvelous little boy deserves nothing but the best. He is a prince among children. And one day he'll be an international playboy like his father."

She thought that Mitchell was being facetious, but he spoke with a straight face.

"Pamela doesn't want him to grow up like me." Mitchell must have read her mind. He continued, "But worse things could happen, right?"

She couldn't think of any, but she forced a slight grin of confirmation. Mitchell didn't press any further. He looked at their empty plates and signaled the waiter for the check.

All four of them had a great day at the zoo. Mitchell was happy that he got to see the black swans, she had fun with the koalas and the sloths, and Adam cooed all the way through the tram ride.

She watched in awe of the way Mitchell deferred to Pamela. It almost seemed that he feared Pamela. But she knew that it hadn't always been that way. Adam must have been the variable that turned the tables of power in their situation.

She liked Pamela, but she found it hard to believe that a woman could be so mercenary as to technically pimp a child for personal financial gain. But then again, who was she to judge?

After Pamela and Adam left for the airport, she and Mitchell loaded their bags into the car and prepared for the all-afternoon and evening drive to Melbourne.

Mitchell had a map, but it looked like a pretty straight journey, and she knew they wouldn't need it. Plus, Mitchell was so aggressive when she played navigator that she really hoped there wouldn't be any reason for him to attack.

The trip began peacefully enough, although they couldn't see the water. It seemed that "Coastal Highway" was a misnomer. Mitchell complained as they drove through forests and not past beaches, but he focused most of his complaints on Pamela.

"Can you believe that monster?"

"Which monster?"

"Pamela, the mother of my son. Aren't you paying attention?"

"Pamela is a monster?"

"Have you ever seen me alone with Adam?"

Now that she thought about it, no, she hadn't. "No. Why is that?"

"Court mandate. That bitch told the courts that I sexually abused my son. My own son! Now that, that is a monster."

Pamela seemed so genuine, the most mentally well member of that family. Mitchell's companion found it hard to believe that she would have made such vulgar claims against Mitchell. He was a malfeasant, of that there was no doubt. But Mitchell was certainly not a pedophile.

"I'm sorry you had to go through that, Mitchell. It must have been very painful."

"All Pamela seeks to do is bring me pain. Oh, and spend my money. Bitch."

She said nothing and continued to stare at the road ahead. There was nothing to see, really. Australia seemed to be a lot of boring land.

Mitchell broke the silence. "Did you like Sydney, my dear?"

She was surprised that Mitchell was back to calling her "my dear," but perhaps contempt for Pamela had stifled his contempt for her. "It was all right, thank you."

"Yes, it was just all right. That's the right word." Mitchell agreed with her. "Of course, you realize that your flight back is from Sydney, so at some point you'll have to return."

"My flight back? You're not flying with me?"

"Pamela and Adam and I are flying to Tanzania. From there, they will go to the Mauritius for a vacation, and I will fly to South Africa."

"I'm not going to Africa with you?"

"Pay attention. Where is your brain, silly? You have to return to New York to pick up our new fucktoy you found. The two of you will meet me in Jo'burg."

"Got it."

"Sound like a good plan?"

"Sounds excellent."

"Good. Now, where the fuck is the coast? Goddamn Aussies can't even name a highway correctly."

They both laughed, and kept driving.

❧

The sun set as they pulled into a McDonald's drive thru.

"I've never seen you eat McDonald's, Mitchell."

"Well, it's the only option out here in the middle of nowhere, and we skipped lunch, remember?"

She thought about it and realized that they hadn't eaten at the zoo. Her stomach was growling.

Mitchell ordered them each two Oz burgers, which were like Big Macs except they included a fried egg and a slice of red beet. They parked in the lot and ate silently as the dusk turned into black.

Back on the road, they once again found themselves driving through the forest. They had been driving for almost five hours and had yet to see the coast. According to the map, they should have been able to see water from the right side of the vehicle, but the woods were so dense that all they saw was a never-ending sea of trees.

They had been the only car on the road for quite some time. It was strange that there was no oncoming traffic this entire journey. Did people from Melbourne not drive to Sydney? This was a two-way highway after all.

Because they had gotten used to not seeing any light up ahead, they were both surprised when they saw a glow in the forest in front of them. They determined that it wasn't headlights, but they couldn't figure out what it was. Perhaps a town up ahead? No, the color was too orange. In fact, it glowed like a sunset.

They kept driving toward the light, thinking not much of it. The Oz burgers had made her sleepy, and she found herself drifting off.

"Holy fuck! Fuck, fuck, fuck!" Mitchell screamed like a woman as he slammed on the brakes.

She was frighteningly jostled awake as the car skidded sideways off the road.

A giant, fiery tree limb had slammed against the windshield and stuck to the hood.

"Mitchell!" She looked outside. They were surrounded by fire.

"Get out of the car! Get out of the car!" Mitchell screamed. "The car is on fire! Grab whatever bags you can and run!"

She couldn't imagine that running into the blaze was a better option than staying in the car, but she knew that the car was very likely to explode. A few burns from outside were probably a better choice than absolute death inside the vehicle.

She had no time to process. She grabbed her bag from the backseat and jumped into the street.

Fiery branches were whizzing past her head, and she ran with one arm covering her eyes.

The heat was persistent and penetrating, but the fierce wind kept anything from actually landing on her.

It was as though they were trying to run between flaming raindrops. This was certainly a losing proposition.

They were about one hundred yards from the car when they heard a huge explosion. She turned her head just enough to see the fireball in her peripheral vision. She saw tears streaming down Mitchell's soot-covered cheeks. He may have been more scared than she was. She had already prepared for death, but Mitchell had not yet made peace with his mortality as she had.

A million thoughts passed through her head as they ran through the inferno. But the one that kept persisting was that she had acquiesced to the notion of dying at Mitchell's hands, or dying from her fragile weight, or dying from sheer unhealthful exhaustion, or simply dying from lack of will to live. It had never occurred to her that she could die at the mercy of nature.

Her clothing clung to her with sweat and soot, but she kept running. Mitchell labored behind her, but he was still marginally keeping up with her pace. Terror can overcome even the worst athletic aptitude.

She ran down a steep incline and found herself waist deep in running water. She had no idea if this was a stream or a river, or if it was going to get deeper at some point and pull them under.

Through the thick, smoky haze, she could make out the other bank. It wasn't that far, and she continued to trudge through, pulling her bag behind her.

She heard Mitchell splashing behind her as she reached the other side. It must have been a swift-moving steam, since it never submerged her deeper than her waist.

Mitchell reached the other bank a few moments after she did, and they pulled themselves up the steep, muddy incline. At the top, through the smoke, they saw a multistory building with lights on in the windows. She pointed toward it, but was unable to speak from all the soot in her lungs. Mitchell nodded, and through the crackle of the fire behind them, she could hear him panting heavily.

There was no fire on this side of the stream, and they slowed their pace to a brisk walk as they ascended the hill toward the building.

The front door was locked, but they pounded on it, hoping that someone would open it.

"The restaurant is closed," a muffled male voice yelled through the door.

"Please! Let us in!" she beseeched the stranger.

A moment passed, and then the door opened slowly.

The man in the vestibule looked them up and down. He said in a thick accent, "We closed the restaurant early because of the firestorm." He looked at their dirty black faces and singed clothes and said, "But I guess I don't need to tell you about the firestorm." He stepped back from the doorway and invited them in. "The cook's still here. We'll get you some supper."

She and Mitchell followed the man into a large dining room and opted for a table farthest from the windows with an open view of the blaze.

When the man returned with menus, she asked, "What was that? A forest fire?"

"First time in Australia, no?" The man chuckled. "That was a firestorm. They're pretty common around these parts. Not too many people drive this way because of that. Guess no one warned you."

"No." Mitchell sounded bitter. "No one warned us."

"Is your car in the lot?" the man asked them.

"Our car was a casualty. It caught fire and exploded," Mitchell stated matter-of-factly.

The man laughed. She was shocked that he could take their disaster so lightly. But then Mitchell laughed too, a deep belly laugh. It was infectious, and soon all three were laughing hysterically.

She hadn't really processed the event yet; she was still in shock. Instead she looked out the window that faced the uncharred side of the forest and sighed pregnantly.

Mitchell poured her an overflowing glass of wine from the bottle he had ordered. They each took a large gulp.

The man returned in a moment with some complimentary appetizers. "I've checked with the innkeepers, and I have good news: there is a room available in the inn upstairs."

Mitchell turned to her. "I guess we're not making it to Melbourne tonight, my dear."

She laughed. "You realize, Mitchell, that this was the second rental car we've abandoned in a week."

Mitchell became playful. "You know what this means, my dear?"

"What?"

"I don't think anyone's going to rent us a car for a while."

"You know what I think, Mitchell?"

"Tell me?"

"I think we're flying back to Sydney in the morning."

"My dear, sometimes I think you're a genius."

The two of them clinked glasses and laughed. They laughed and laughed and laughed. Not even a sweeping wind carrying a blazing inferno could maim the devil himself. Nor the woman who had sold him her soul.

Twenty-Seven

They flew back to Sydney, and the next day, he met Pamela and Adam coming back from New Zealand while she departed for home, with a layover in Fiji. She paid cash to upgrade herself to first class and ended up with a free night and a full day on her own. When she finally landed in LAX, it was the morning of the day before she had left Fiji. She found it exciting to get a day back when circumnavigating the globe. And because she landed in California, she not only got a day back, but she got an additional three hours to the time she normally got when landing on the East Coast.

She wandered aimlessly through LAX trying to plan her strategy for returning to New York. Mitchell was somewhere en route to the bowels of Africa, so calling him for help would be futile. She had several thousand dollars in cash on her person, hidden in the soles of her sneakers, but that was her emergency escape from Mitchell fund, and she didn't want to touch it for something as banal as a domestic flight.

Attempting to turn on her cell phone, she quickly realized that she had not only forgotten to charge it before leaving the States, but she had neglected to pack the charger. It was dead. Frustrated, she threw it to the bottom of her Burberry sack purse.

She ran her fingers manically through her greasy hair as she sat on a cold metal bench in the middle of the airport. An hour had already been wasted without action, and angry with herself for such poor planning, she clenched her temples and let out a guttural groan of disappointment in herself.

Sitting on the bench alone was not going to make a ticket home appear, so she jumped to her feet and began to walk briskly through the airport, keeping her eyes peeled for answers, or at least inspiration.

There was a large open space filled with little computer terminals to access email, and travelers from all over the world were typing frantically at the individual stations. For a moment, she thought it would be a good idea for someone to invent a way to beam Internet access to people's personal computers so that these kiosks would be unnecessary, but she dismissed the idea and waited for an Internet terminal to become available.

When one did, she wheeled her luggage over and took a seat. She pulled out her rarely used credit card and crossed her fingers that it still worked. It did.

She looked at ticket prices from LAX to the New York airports that day and was disgusted at the high fares for last-minute booking. If only Mitchell had booked her first class, the domestic leg of her trip would have been covered. She wondered if this was an oversight, or if Mitchell had orchestrated this situation to test her resolve and independence. Mitchell never did anything without foresight, so she determined that this was a test.

She logged off the computer and found a nearby payphone. Throwing in a few quarters, she called the man of last resort: Dad.

Her father never took her phone calls, and she half-expected him to hang up on her now. Surprisingly, he didn't. In fact, he seemed happy to hear from her.

"Dad?"

"Hi, sweetie!"

"You're taking my call?"

"Your mother's out of town for the week. We can talk."

"Okay." She took a deep breath. "You have a lot of free tickets and spare miles right?"

There was a brief pause. "Yes?"

"I'm in LA. But I forgot to book a ticket home."

"You got a one-way ticket to LA?"

"No, I'm just back from Fiji and Australia. I just totally forgot to plan this leg of the trip."

"Where's Mitchell?" Her father knew about Mitchell, and though the two had never met, it was obvious that they hated each other.

"He's in Africa."

"Mitchell abandoned you in Los Angeles."

"No, he left me in Australia." She realized that her father was going to get heated, so she explained, "That was the plan, though. I have to . . . um . . . pick something up in New York and then meet him in Africa."

Silence on the other end of the phone.

"Dad?"

"So, you just flew back from Australia this morning?"

"Well, I stopped in Fiji first."

There was a long drawn-out sigh. Her father, a nice Jewish boy from Queens, could not even fathom the information she was giving him. But this was his daughter, and without his nay-saying wife dictating his actions, he could actually act like a father.

"I have lots of free domestic tickets on Southwest. I'll put one in your name and call you back."

"Southwest gets into Long Island, not New York. Won't Mom be mad if you pick me up?"

Another deep sigh. "Obviously, we won't tell your mother." Her father paused, and she heard him rifling through papers, presumably looking for a Southwest coupon. "Okay, I'll call them and then call you back."

"Oh, Dad!" She caught him before he hung up. "I have to call you. You can't call me. My cell phone's dead."

"You just came home from Fiji . . . first class?"

"Yes." Her voice betrayed her and added an element of shame.

"And you're calling from a payphone."

"Right."

"Right." Her father agreed. "You've got some life. Call me back in twenty minutes."

She took a seat on yet another metal bench and watched the minute hand tick on a large wall clock. She waited twenty-five minutes, knowing that her father always underestimated the amount of time anything took, and then returned to the payphone.

"Dad?"

"Well, the good news is, I got you a free one-way ticket."

"Great!"

"The bad news is that it's for tomorrow."

"Okay."

"Okay?"

"Okay."

"So, you're going to spend the night in LA? No problem, just *okay*?"

"I've got it from here."

"Oh, sweetie?"

"Yes, Dad?"

"Don't call me like this again."

"Well, thank y—" She heard the phone click. Her father was angry. But at least she had her free ticket home.

Her next mission was to find a place to spend the night in LA. Before she had met Mitchell, she'd had true friends all over the world. Mitchell was not the only wealthy man with whom she had been associated; he was just the meanest.

She raced through her mental rolodex. A year ago, she had been walking down the street in midtown Manhattan when a handsome, well-dressed man had approached her on the street. It was the eve of Internet dating, and people had still met each other the old-fashioned way. She lamented that it didn't seem they did that anymore. Then again, she no longer looked healthy, vibrant, or approachable.

She had had a quick, passionate, fun affair with Craig, and she knew that he lived in Santa Monica. Taking a chance, she called information and was pleasantly surprised to catch him at home.

"Hi, Craig! It's your friend from New York!"

"Hey, babe! Haven't heard from you in a while. What's up?" Craig seemed genuinely excited to hear from her.

"I'm at LAX, figuring out a way to kill a night before flying back to New York tomorrow. What are you up to?"

"Where are you staying, babe?"

"That's in the works." She knew this was working perfectly, and she was really looking forward to a friendly face.

"No longer in the works. Take down my address. Grab a cab. It's on me."

Problem solved. Sometimes her life seemed too easy. Or at least it wasn't as hard as it could have been.

The cab pulled up in the driveway of Craig's Santa Monica beach house, and he came out as he heard the sound of the engine. The driver rolled down the window, and Craig stuck a one hundred dollar bill through the opening. Then he came around, opened her door, and scooped her out.

"Damn, you got thin!"

"It's been a strange few months."

"Strange in that you lost twenty pounds?"

"That's just a symptom of the strangeness."

Craig grabbed her luggage and led her up the front steps. "Well, come in. Sit down. Relax. Tell me about it. Or don't!"

They walked into Craig's spacious bachelor pad-condo and she took a seat on the balcony as he opened the fridge and found a bottle of champagne. As he opened it, she found her camera in her purse.

"Can you do me a favor, Craig?"

"Anything!" Craig responded enthusiastically as he handed her a glass.

"Can you take a picture of me with the beach in the background? This may sound silly, but I have a photo of myself that I took at this exact same time today in Fiji."

Craig laughed hysterically. "So you're in two places at once?"

"Pretty fucking crazy, right?" She laughed with him.

"Not to someone who knows you." They clinked champagne flutes, and Craig took her camera from her hands and snapped a photo of her with the beach in the near distance. He showed her the photo on the display screen.

"God, am I that thin?"

"You hadn't noticed?"

"I've stopped looking in the mirror. It's depressing."

"So you didn't do this on purpose?"

"Craig, you know me. Remember when I was obsessed with competing for Miss Fitness USA?"

"Yeah, you were drinking those nasty weight gain shakes and eating your body weight in sushi."

She chuckled. "Exactly. Is that someone who intentionally gets this thin?"

"Do you want to talk about it?"

"Let's just say that it's really nice to finally be in the presence of a good guy for a change."

She stood up, and Craig picked her up in a bear hug. It was a true embrace of friendship. She hadn't felt that in a while.

She and Craig took a shower together, and he helped scrub the travel funk off her. His touch was tender and caring, and not the evil, powerful grabbing to which she had recently become accustomed.

Craig dropped to his knees on the standing-shower floor and delicately began to kiss her tenderly, up one thigh and down the other. When his tongue made contact with her clit, she felt her knees begin to tremble and give out. Sensing that she was about to fall, Craig cradled her in his arms and carried her into the master bedroom.

Both of them soaking wet, they tumbled around on the bed and spent nearly an hour just exchanging the pleasures of each other's mouths. The one thing she had learned from Mitchell was how to suck a cock. And it was so much more enjoyable when the cock belonged to someone who actually mattered to her.

When they had both cum, they lay panting side by side on the wet duvet. She got up to retrieve the champagne and the glasses. When she returned, she sat at the edge of the bed watching Craig's chest rise and fall as his relaxed body tried to regain its composure.

"Well, babe," Craig panted, "You got skinny, but you're still just as sexy as I remember. And talented!"

She sighed a bit, and Craig heard.

Craig sat up. "What is it?"

"No, nothing. I just haven't been feeling very sexy for a while."

"You're telling me that there's no lucky man back in New York telling you every day how sexy you are?"

"Let's not talk about it, Craig. Can we just enjoy this moment?"

"I think you deserve a moment to enjoy." Craig delicately kissed her neck. It wasn't an action of foreplay; it was a genuine expression of compassion.

A single tear ran down her face. This. This was the closeness she was meant to feel. Mitchell was driving into her a distance. But she was a good person. Not the monster Mitchell was creating in his image. What a fool!

She hoped that Craig hadn't noticed the tear, or that at least, he had no idea the pain that it represented. She sniffled a bit and looked into Craig's eyes. "Thank you."

Twenty-Eight

Her father was waiting for her in the baggage claim at Long Island MacArthur Airport. They exchanged an awkward half-hug and made a kissing sound without actually touching.

After three straight days of air travel, she was physically exhausted. She fell asleep in the car for the duration of the fifteen-minute drive back to her childhood home.

Her father gently nudged her awake, and he carried her luggage into the vestibule of the back door. He explained that there was no bedroom for her; her brother had reappropriated her old room, and her brother's old room was an unmitigated sty. So her father offered her his bed, and he conceded to navigate the squalor of one of her brother's two filthy bedrooms.

She was hungry, but she was too tired to eat. She dragged herself up the stairs to the master bedroom, threw on one of her mother's nightshirts, and instantly fell asleep.

Her father awakened her in the morning with a large bottle of Ensure with a straw sticking out of the mouth. He explained that a doctor friend of his had suggested that she drink it to combat her rapid weight loss. She was surprised to hear that her father had been discussing her current state with anyone; her parents had been feigning disobservance so well that she had believed it. Maybe her father was more aware than he let on.

She propped herself up in the bed and turned on the television. It was a beautiful summer day, but she had no energy to go out and about. At least she was able to charge her phone. She spent the day sipping the Ensure through the straw and absently surfing the cable channels.

Now that she finally had a moment to herself, she was able to feel her body's presence around her mind. Previously, she had been oblivious to her physical discomfort. It was as though her mind had amputated her physical being, and her spirit had disconnected from her mind.

The fragments were now beginning to reestablish themselves, and she realized how run down and sickly she felt. As though she were a real-life Dorian Gray, she had aged an eternity in only five months.

Her father popped his head in the room occasionally to check on her. Even though he was fidgety and uneasy, she somehow felt nurtured by him in a way that she never had before.

Together, they drove to a local supermarket and picked up some sundries for dinner that night. Because it was a beautiful summer's evening, her father suggested they grill shishkebabs outside.

For a fleeting moment, she wondered why he was being such a gracious host. Her plan was to head back to the city to retrieve the fucktoy and fly out to meet Mitchell. Spending a minivacation with the father who had ignored her for so many years had never even entered into her realm of possible realities. But perhaps in her mother's absence, her father was actually able to express the basic human kindness in the parental connection he had with her. Regardless, she was so overcome with the pipedream that her father truly loved her as kin that she foolishly chose not to analyze it, let alone challenge it.

Together, they marinated the meat, chopped vegetables, and crafted a beautiful summer dinner. She was so overcome with a false sense of security that she almost didn't think it odd that a distant family acquaintance happened to "stop by."

Jinny was a friendly neighbor who moonlighted as a prominent pediatrician. Jinny's family and hers were close enough to extend party invitations to each other, but neither family was close enough to the other to just show up unannounced. It seemed that there was something premeditated in the works, but she really hoped that she was just being paranoid and that her father was truly surprised by Jinny's appearance.

She was blessed and cursed by a keen sense of observation, and it didn't escape her that her father was beginning to sweat as his voice markedly changed timbre. Jinny didn't even pretend to make small talk. Instead, she walked right up to her and asked to speak with her privately in the house.

Jinny had her lie on the couch and have her pulse timed, then asked her to stand up to check the pulse change. Apparently, according to Jinny's professional opinion, the huge difference in pulse rate indicated imminent distress.

"You're going to die. I'm going to tell your father that you need to be taken to the emergency room," Jinny stated matter-of-factly. She showed not an ounce of compassion, but perhaps fear was part of the premeditated strategy to hospitalize her.

"You want me to go to the hospital?" She wasn't really surprised. Since her flight home from Fiji, she had felt sickly and anemic. Her energy levels were negligible, and even breathing had become arduous. "I'll need to think about it."

"You have no time to think. You need to take care of this before you die." Jinny looked her straight in the eyes. "You may not have until tomorrow."

"There are other factors at play. I need to think about it."

The "other factors" keeping her from checking into a hospital were just as black and white as her possible life or death. Her maternal grandmother had passed away several years ago and left the bulk of her sizable estate to her only granddaughter. Because her grandmother truly, fundamentally hated her mother, she had named her mother as executor of the will. It was essentially a thumb of the nose, a posthumous *fuck you* gesture.

Her mother, in a desperate act of greed and fear, had forged both her own mother's signature to a revised will and her daughter's signature to a document agreeing to the new distribution of assets.

Her mother had sent her the consent form no fewer than twenty-five times without her even acknowledging receipt. Her mother's lawyer explained the pressure of time in executing the will, and her mother had conceded to her the forgery. In the small safe in the daughter's apartment, she had a note written in her mother's handwriting:

Couldn't wait any longer for you to sign the release. Forged your signature. (Illegal, but okay.) Mommy

She had to assume that her mother's lawyer had not been aware of the forgery at the time it was done, but after the fact, her mother had told the attorney and was told that the only way she would be unable to contest the distribution of the estate would be if her daughter were declared mentally unfit to inherit. If her mother failed to achieve such a verdict, not only would her daughter stand to be awarded the estate, but her mother, as acting executor, would be charged with felony fraud and perjury in mental health court.

In New York State, HIPAA laws clearly cite a concession of autonomy when a patient voluntarily signs into a facility, even if it be for just an hour for stitches in the ER. In her current physical condition, it would be difficult to prove mental competence, no matter how strong her mind.

Her mother was an unmedicated victim of borderline personality disorder. This diagnosis of trace schizophrenia would most certainly squash her mother's case against her. But then again, she weighed only seventy-some-odd pounds. Perhaps both mother and daughter were out of their minds. And her younger brother was probably the most unstable of the bunch. Her brother had inherited her uncle's narcissistic insanity. Her uncle had died in his early forties of poor judgment.

If this battle went to court, it would certainly be a loony tunes trial at best.

The paramount fact remained that she really didn't want to die. She had made peace with it, and Mitchell had made sure to remind her every day that death was imminent, but her spirit wasn't as easily clouded as her insight had been.

She had no reason not to trust Jinny's medical opinion, but she had every reason to distrust Jinny's motives. Her mother had almost no friends. In fact, Jinny was probably the only friend her mother had.

On the flip side, her father seemed truly concerned for her welfare. Even though her father was scared of her mother, and always took his wife's side in the interest of preserving the peace in his household, her mother was out of town now.

She asked Jinny how long her stay in the hospital would be, and Jinny assured her that with a little intravenous fluid treatment, she would probably be in and out of the emergency room in one afternoon.

Stupidly, and in a pathetic attempt to fight for her life, she trusted Jinny.

The next morning, she told her father that she was willing to go to the emergency room on the explicit and sacred agreement that her mother not be informed. Her father gave her his word, and he truly appeared sincere.

Twenty-Nine

There were several hospitals within a ten-mile radius of the family home, so she had reason to be concerned when her father entered the highway on-ramp.

"Dad, where are you taking me?"

"We have a great hospital for you. Jinny is going to get you into North Shore Jewish Hospital, which is her professional affiliation. You're very lucky."

"You're taking me into another county? Jinny said I'd be in and out in a single day."

"Well, sure, but you've never been to an emergency room. You don't know how this works."

"I have been to an emergency room. You've taken me several times." She was referring to multiple visits throughout her young life when she had suffered blows to the head at the hands of her mother, and two visits from violent attacks from her strong younger brother. He had once punched her in the temple and concussed her, and on Christmas day, when she was eighteen and he fourteen, her brother had broken her foot by snapping it with both hands as she lay on the floor.

"Those visits were not serious. This is serious."

"I came home on crutches on Christmas."

"Come on, you were milking that one."

She had crawled on her hands and knees through the snow. A neighbor, who happened to be a psychiatrist, had rushed her to the emergency room in her pajamas on Christmas day. Events like that are hard to milk. Those neighbors, who had previously been friends of her family's, moved away shortly after, leaving no forwarding address. The psychiatrist had told her that she had a case against her family to have her mother and brother incarcerated in mental health facilities, but had also alluded to the repercussions of that action. She preferred to inflict as little drama on others as possible, in a hope that they would return the favor.

"I couldn't milk a broken foot, Dad."

"Okay, let's not talk about your broken foot."

"Mom verbally attacked me when I returned home on crutches. Mom called me a little bitch and accused me of faking. I ate Christmas dinner alone in the guest bedroom, where Mom banished me."

"Your mother was scared. Let's not talk about that. Let's just get you healthy now, okay?"

Her father was like an ostrich with his head the sand. The power of denial was incredibly strong. She may have been in a bad situation with Mitchell, but she never denied it.

"You promise you won't tell Mom."

"I promise."

"I don't believe you."

"I wouldn't lie to you."

"You have many, many times." Her father was the king of broken promises, both big and small.

"Well, you have my word now."

"I'm trusting you."

"You can."

She said nothing but just stared at the cement highway ahead. Mitchell never lied to her; he just flat out let her know his intentions of malfeasance. With Mitchell, there was a fear of the known, not the unknown. Her parents were more deceptively and uncreatively sneaky. There was no place in this world where she felt safe.

They arrived at the emergency room, and sat together in the waiting area. She was nervous. Her father's tension was even more palpable. She was not going to gain strength from him. Of that, she could be certain. Everything else was blind faith.

It was a long time before her name was finally called by one of the ER nurses, and she followed the nurse into a giant warehouse-like room filled with beds holding patients in various degrees of pain, agony, and certain dismemberment.

Her father stood next to her bedside as they drew blood and charted other vital signs. An intravenous needle was stuck into the crook of her elbow but was capped off without being attached to anything. This seemed to be more of a formality or a precautionary measure than anything else.

The staff spoke to her father as though she weren't in the room, and she had to speak up to remind the doctors that she was of majority age and capable of managing her own healthcare.

The doctors apologized and informed her that they would be admitting her into the hospital to replenish fluids. She was told that she would be released in the morning.

Her father interjected. He explained that it had been prearranged that she would be treated in Schneider's Children's Hospital, adjacent to the adult-intake building.

The doctors seemed confused, and she was too. She was twenty-three years old, obviously long past the age at which a children's hospital would admit her. But her father gave the staff Jinny's name and number, and after a few phone calls and due diligence, it was decided that she would be placed overnight in the children's ward.

She questioned her father, and he assured her that an overnight in the children's hospital would be far more pleasant that an overnight in the adult ER.

"There are clowns and balloons, and the nursing staff is much nicer."

"But I'm a grown woman."

"I understand that, sweetie, but I promise that you'll like this better."

"Dad, you've never been in a hospital."

"I was in a hospital when you were born." Her father was failing at his attempt at humor.

"Well, I've outgrown the nursery."

"Just go with it. Please?" Her father really did seem sincere, and she did want to feel better. If one overnight in a hospital could get her feeling lively again, then she was willing to go along with it. She needed to rest up before her flight to South Africa anyway.

"You'll drive me back to the city tomorrow?"

"Promise."

She was given a private room in the children's hospital. Her father tried to make it seem more appealing than it was and tried to convince her that it was because of Jinny's connections.

"Dad, I have a private room because it would creep parents out if their child was roomed with a grown adult."

Her father thought for a moment. "Okay, that's probably true. But still, it's not a bad room, right?"

"It's a hospital room, Dad. It feels like a hospital room. What do you want me to say?"

A couple of nurses entered the room, and one of them hooked her IV up to a drip bag above her bed.

"We're just giving you some salt, honey," the nurse tried to reassure her. "Just so you know, this is KCl, and it's going to burn."

Obviously a salt IV would burn. That's why there was the expression *pouring salt in a wound* in the lexicon of pain.

"But other things hurt too, right?" She was hoping for some reassurance.

The nurse paused, trying to find a way to skirt the truth. "Well, actually, KCl is the most painful intravenous therapy there is."

"Really?" Surely the nurse was toying with her.

"Sorry." The nurse straightened the lines for the drip and quickly walked out of the room.

Immediately, she felt a stabbing burning sensation shoot into her left arm. She grimaced, and a single tear rolled out of the corner of her left eye and moistened her hair against the pillow.

Her father stood awkwardly, shifting his weight from one foot to the other. His eyes darted around the room, pretending to find something to look at. His hands alternated from plunging into his pockets to resting in his armpits with his forearms crossed.

"Do you want to go, Dad?" She wasn't a sadist, and it was overwhelmingly obvious that her father was miserable. He was just waiting for his cue to be dismissed.

"No. I, uh, I promised I'd stay here with you. I want to be here." His voice cracked into falsetto as he lied. He tried to change the subject, then reached into his pocket for his phone. "I'm going to call Jinny to let her know that you're all settled." He dialed Jinny's number and left a message on the machine.

Her father put his phone back into his pocket and stared at the wall.

"Dad, you look really uncomfortable."

"Well, I mean, I have to let the dog out. . . But . . ."

"You can go, Dad."

"I mean, I'm just going to have some dinner, and then . . ."

"Go home, Dad."

"I'll come back tomorrow."

"Early?"

"As early as they'll let me. Do you need anything?"

"Well, I'm lying here in jeans. So, I guess a sweatsuit would be more comfortable."

"Do you have anything in your luggage?"

She had just come from an international trip with Mitchell. She would never have been allowed to pack anything remotely resembling a sweatsuit.

"No. Do you mind buying one?"

"Like, um, a sweatshirt?"

She motioned her head toward her left side, signaling to her immobilized arm with the IV protruding from it. "Something with a zipper."

"Right." He couldn't even look at her. He didn't want to see the IV. "Okay. Well." Her father fumbled about, looking for his jacket.

"Dad? Are you looking for your coat?"

"Yes, have you seen it?" He still didn't look in her direction.

"Dad, it's the last week in June. You don't have one."

"Oh. Right. Okay, bye." The word *bye* was muffled as her father scurried out of the room.

She tried to turn on the television, but the access had not been registered for her stay. She thought about asking for a book to read, but being unable to move her left arm, there was no way she'd be able to hold a page open.

She wanted to toss and turn to get comfortable, but she was in jeans, and her entire left side now felt as though it were on fire. Comfort was not going to happen. She pushed the call button with her right thumb. A nurse nonchalantly sauntered into the room.

The nurse said nothing but raised an eyebrow signaling for her to make her request known.

"I have a prescription for Ambien. May I please have one?"

"Yes, I see that noted on your chart." The nurse acknowledged the request but made no signs of moving to retrieve the medicine.

"May I please have a sleeping pill?" She asked again, too weak to argue this point but in desperate need of respite.

"Miss, this is a children's hospital. We don't stock Ambien. *Children* don't take sleeping pills."

The nurse was clearly irked by the presence of a grown woman on the floor. She wished that she could let the nurse know that she was just as irked to be there herself.

"Okay. Sorry." She plunged her head backward, deeper into the pillow, and began to sob softly.

The nurse pulled out a walkie-talkie and gently said, "I'll see what I can do."

She was given twice the amount of Ambien than she was prescribed, but even though she slept soundly, she awoke at dawn.

Her left arm was stiff and sore, and the circumference of her elbow had nearly quadrupled. She had a Popeye forearm. It was as though her hand had swallowed a football. She didn't want to see it, so she quickly averted her eyes to the ceiling.

There was a knock at the door, and her father entered. She realized that one of the benefits of being in a children's hospital was that normal visiting hour rules were not enforced for parents.

"Hi, Dad." She was surprised at how weak her voice sounded when she heard it.

"Hi, sweetie." Her father walked over to the window and stared outside. He wouldn't look at her. "How are you feeling?"

"I'm okay. Ready to get out of here."

"I know. Have the doctors come to see you yet?"

"No, not yet. They haven't even brought breakfast."

"Okay. Well, we'll see what they say when the doctors check you out."

"They said I could leave today. *You* said I could leave today."

"Sweetie, let's just wait to speak to the doctors, okay?"

She had no energy to fight. She said nothing. The two of them spent a half hour in silence. Her father's eyes never diverted from the window.

After a blood technician came to draw a sample, a food tray was delivered to her. It contained a hard roll in plastic casing and a 4-ounce plastic cup of milk with a foil lid.

She stared at the tray. Her father stared at the tray. She was starving, but there wasn't even enough fluid to drink to choke down the stale roll.

"They're going to make you eat that." Her father anticipated her insolence.

"Can I pour the milk into the roll?"

"Is it really that stale?" Her father didn't wait for an answer. He picked up the roll and tried in vain to split it. "Oh." He let it fall back onto the tray with a thud.

"I'll have breakfast when they release me."

"Please try to eat the roll." Her father sounded earnest.

With her one good arm, she tried to split open the roll. When that didn't work, she tried to open the container of milk. She couldn't do that either.

"I can't even access the food." She tried to laugh. If she tried any harder with the milk, the best-case scenario would be that the container would explode all over her when she punctured the foil.

Her father inadvertently caught a glimpse of her swollen arm. He quickly reclaimed his post at the window.

Eventually, a doctor came into her room and looked at the uneaten meal. "Not eating?"

"Not for lack of trying. I can't move my left arm, and this meal has been child-proof sealed." She tried to make light of a serious moment.

The doctor continued, "But you would eat the meal if you could access it?"

"Dad, back me up."

Her father turned toward the doctor. "She tried to open the food. It was hard for me to watch her struggle." His eyes looked down toward the floor. "I should have offered to help her with the packaging, but I just didn't want to get any closer to the hospital bed." Her dad actually looked ashamed.

The doctor changed the subject. "Well, your blood test results came back. Everything's normal."

"Great, so I can leave now?"

"Well. . . ." The doctor looked over toward her father.

"Don't look at him. I'm twenty-three years old. He's my visitor, not my custodian."

The doctor ignored her.

"Did you hear me?"

"I heard you. I just would want to keep you here for more testing before we release you." The doctor seemed focused on an agenda.

"But, you said that my blood tests were normal. What about my other vitals? Are they abnormal?"

"No, everything is normal. But that's not the point."

"I think that is the point. I'd like to go home now. I'm hungry for breakfast."

"You have breakfast. We'll remove your IV, and your arm should feel better the instant the potassium stops flowing."

"And then I can go home?"

"No, then you can open your breakfast." The doctor looked back toward her father, who was so close to the window now that it looked like he was about to jump out. "I'd like to have a word with your father in the hallway."

"You may not. It is against HIPAA law for you to discuss my situation with an unauthorized party outside my earshot."

The doctor sighed. Because this was a children's hospital, these issues were not usually challenged by patients.

But she had rights, and she knew them. And the doctor would have to comply with the laws of New York State, regardless of whether it was a children's hospital. The bottom line was that she was not a minor, and her medical affairs were not privy to her father without her permission.

The doctor looked pissed. "Okay, here's the thing. There's something going on with you. You wouldn't have come here if you didn't feel sick. So you tell me, why were you so weak when you checked in yesterday?"

"Well, in the past week, I flew from New York to San Francisco, San Francisco to Los Angeles, Los Angeles to Fiji, Fiji to Sydney, then Melbourne to Sydney, then Sydney to Fiji, Fiji to Los Angeles, and then back here to Long Island. That's a lot of time in the air! Wouldn't you be exhausted?"

The doctor stared at her expressionless. "Yes, I would be tired if I flew that much in one week, too. But we're addressing reality, not fiction. Are you're here because you starve yourself?"

"You're telling me that you don't believe me?"

"I believe that you are very sick."

She sat up in the hospital bed. "Look, I have a flight to Johannesburg on Thursday night, and I still have to get back to the city to get some things in order first."

"You're going to South Africa?" The doctor's eyes rolled. "It's Tuesday now. So you're going to South Africa the day after tomorrow?"

"Shit, I didn't realize it was so soon. I have to pick up my paper tickets from South African Airways in the satellite office near Grand Central today." She pointed toward the IV. "Can you please disconnect this? I'm running way behind schedule."

The doctor replied, "Look, you weren't in Fiji or Australia or wherever you dreamed up. And you're not going to South Africa tomorrow!"

"Thursday."

"Whatever! You're obviously delusional from anorexia, and we're here to help you get your mind back." The doctor leaned in toward her face. "You're in *Long Island*. Do you think you're in Fiji now?"

"Um, what the hell are you talking about?"

"What are *you* talking about?" This doctor was becoming confrontational.

"Look, you told me that my tests were normal, right?"

"Your tests are normal as of this morning. That is correct."

"So, then I can check myself out, right?"

"Not if you're mentally ill. You just told me that you were in Fiji twice in the past week!"

She turned toward her father. "Dad?"

Her father looked at the doctor. "I don't know where she has or hasn't been."

"Dad! You picked me up from the airport!"

The doctor looked at her. "You're obviously getting upset. We'll leave you to rest."

The doctor and her father exited the room together. This was not good.

The little hospital phone on her bedside rang. She picked it up. Through a scratchy connection, she heard Mitchell's voice.

"Where are you?"

"You called me! How did you know where I was?"

"I know everything. Don't you know that by now?" Mitchell sounded at once concerned and seriously irritated. "Why the fuck fuck fuck are you in Schneider's Children's Hospital?"

"I don't know! It happened so fast. They said I would die!"

"Idiot! You let your parents play you. What did the doctor say?"

"The doctor said my tests were normal."

Mitchell sighed pleasantly. "Good, then pack your things and go."

"They won't let me go."

"What do you mean, they won't let you go?"

"I asked to leave, and the doctor ignored me."

"My dear, they have to let you go."

"Mitchell, they said no. Please tell me what to do!"

Mitchell breathed heavily into the phone. "I cannot believe that I have to waste my time calling from Tanzania to get you out of another jam. I leave you alone for a couple of days, and your parents have already incarcerated you."

"I'm not incarcerated."

"Can you walk out?"

"Um, no."

"Earth to imbecile. They're trying to lock you up and throw away the key. AND THROW AWAY THE KEY!" Mitchell shouted for emphasis. Then he sighed deeply. "I'll make some calls. We'll get you out." As he hung up, just before the click, she heard him repeat in the background, "and throw away the key."

The phone rang again only a few minutes later. It was Mitchell's friend Jack. Though she had met him casually several times, she was unclear about the two men's background as friends and had decided that she didn't care enough to pry.

"Mitchell just called me. How do you get yourself locked in a children's hospital on Long Island?"

"I don't think I'm *locked* in, Jack."

"Can you leave?"

"No."

"Are your tests normal?"

"Yes."

"Sorry to say this, but you're locked in. We have to get you out before they implement a mandate to hold you."

"Hold me? For how long?" She was getting scared now. The hospital was supposed to be a safe place. She thought Mitchell was just paranoid, but she actually trusted Jack's opinion to be the truth.

"For as long as they like. Maybe forever. This happens more than you'd imagine. People spend the rest of their lives institutionalized for bullshit like this." Jack paused for a minute. "I'll have to call you back. This is Mitchell on the other line."

She sat at the foot of the bed and stared at the wall. The throbbing pain in her left arm didn't even bother her anymore. Now, all she could focus on was her rapidly increasing heart rate and the sweat percolating on her brow. Her mind was racing. Could this really become a catastrophic situation?

Her mother! She could not allow her mother to know that she was here. Her father had promised not to say anything, but he was weak. *And Jinny!* An obvious player in this game too. Fuck, fuck, fuck, fuck!

The phone rang again. She didn't recognize the voice.

"This is Bob. We haven't met, but I'm the head of Mitchell's international legal team. I'm calling from Paris, but I've put in a phone call to Stuart in the New York office. You'll be hearing from him shortly."

"Hi, Bob." Her voice was barely audible.

Bob didn't acknowledge her salutation but continued his speech. "Look, I've seen this happen before. The moment you are told that you are well, but that you cannot leave of your own volition, it's a slippery slope to institutionalization."

"Is this a joke?" This information was just too much to process.

"The U.S. has crappy healthcare. They'd rather lock you up than have something happen to you after release."

"Something happen to me?"

"Look, they can't figure you out. You don't conveniently fit into their 'typical patient' box. So, they're going to hold you for 'observation' for who knows how long. Like an animal at the zoo."

"They're going to observe me?"

"No, they're not even going to look at you. They're just going to say they're observing you. They're going to let you rot."

She repeated Mitchell's words. "So, they're really going to lock me up and throw away the key?"

"No. We're not going to let that happen." Bob paused for a breath. "Didn't you think it was strange that you were put in a private room in a *children's* hospital?"

"Well, sure that's strange. But you're saying that's part of a strategy?"

"Walk outside your room. What do you notice about the front doors of your ward versus normal hospital wards?"

She rested the phone receiver on the bed, walked out of her room, and looked down the hall. She saw a physician type a security code to open the doors to *get out*. Her face grew hot with rage. She shut her door and picked up the phone.

"Bob, the doors lock from the outside!"

"Exactly. You were put in the children's ward because it's the only part of the hospital where the patients are locked *in*."

"As opposed to visitors being locked out." Her voice trailed off at the end of the sentence. Everything was beginning to make sense, in a disgusting, perverted way. She was a fool to trust a family that had historically betrayed her. They had stolen her entitled fortune, and now they were stealing her autonomy. Where was her father? He had left with the doctor. She didn't see them outside the room.

"Now, think carefully. Is there anyone who could have facilitated gaining you entry into the children's hospital?"

"My father said he pulled strings." She then tried to jump to her father's defense. "But he said that staying in the children's ward was nicer than being lumped in with adults!"

"I'm sorry to say, you were duped." Bob paused. "I'll have to call you back. This is Mitchell on the other line."

"Hello?"

Another unfamiliar voice: "Hi, this is Stuart, calling from Mitchell Durman's New York legal team."

"Right. Bob told me to expect your call."

"Well, I have some news."

"Good news?" She really needed to hear something positive.

"Well. . ." Stuart hesitated. "Revealing news."

"Revealing what?"

"Apparently there was a transfer plan in place for you."

"They already made a transfer plan? They're moving me? I haven't even been examined by an actual doctor yet!"

"Well. . . ." Stuart hesitated too often. "That's the revealing part. This transfer plan was in place long before you checked into the hospital."

"What does that mean?!"

"Ummm. . . ." Another Stuart pause. "Is there anyone who may benefit from your institutionalization?"

"Fuck."

"Excuse me?"

She took a deep breath and tried to collect herself. This only happened in bad horror movies, right? This couldn't actually be happening to her. And who was in on it? Her mother? Jinny? Her father? The doctor? *Mitchell?* No, not Mitchell. He did a lot of bad things, but he was always up front about them.

"So, Stuart, this is really happening? Someone's trying to put me away?"

"I have a feeling that there is a much bigger machine behind this than you realize, I'm sorry to say." Stuart sounded genuinely compassionate. "Big money breeds contempt."

That much she knew was true. She had seen how money had destroyed Mitchell. Now she was seeing that money could make a mother turn on her child.

"Stuart? I'm going to hang up now to leave the line open for Mitchell."

"You can't use your cell phone?"

"They took it. They said that it interfered with heart machines."

"So they confiscated your father's too?"

Fuck, fuck, fuck, fuck. She really was an imbecile.

The phone rang again. This time it was Mitchell.

"Your lawyers called me."

"Say thank you." Mitchell's voice was calm and collected.

"Thank you?! Mitchell, what's going on?!" She tried not to sound as frazzled as she felt.

"My dear, how many times have I told you that the only person in this world you can trust is me?"

"I know, Mitchell. But my parents?"

"Your mother is motivated by greed. Greed and hate. She hates that her mother hated her and loved you. And she's going to try to punish you for it." Mitchell may have been speaking the truth.

"But my father said he wasn't even going to tell my mother that I was here! He promised! He told me that I was physically sick!"

"Come now. Is there any time at which you are *not* an imbecile?"

"How do you mean, Mitchell?"

"Your father is a pussy. This is not news. Your father has no free will. He is a puppet to your mother. Think about it, my dear. Who is pulling these strings?"

She had a flashback to a song she had written about her mother when she was in her third year of college. It was called *Puppet Master.* The chorus was:

Manipulate me until
I can't remember what I came for
And break me until
I finally become a slave
For you

Crap. Talk about ignoring her own foresight. She had written that song almost five years ago, and now the lyrics haunted her.

"My mother's a puppet master."

"No kidding." Mitchell's voice softened. "Don't worry. I'll take care of this. Just don't speak to anyone."

"Okay."

"My dear, have you already spoken to someone?"

"What do you mean?"

"Have you told anyone that you have to leave for South Africa?"

"Well, yes! I told the doctor this morning that I had to leave to pick up my ticket."

"Oh, my poor, naïve, beautiful imbecile. Now they think you're crazy."

"But, Mitchell, let's get back to basics. I *do* have to pick up the tickets. Both mine and Laura's. This is really affecting my time management."

"Don't worry. I have very good, very *expensive* lawyers. You'll be on that flight."

"Okay, Mitchell." She really wanted to believe him.

"Hey, imbecile?"

"Yes, Mitchell?"

"I'm on *your* side. Remember that."

"Okay."

"I love you." Mitchell hung up before she could respond.

Her father entered the room without knocking.

"Where have you been, Dad?"

"I had an errand to run."

Her lunch and dinner were sitting untouched on the tray at the foot of the bed. If that had been an errand, it had taken ten hours.

"What errand?"

"Nothing." Her father searched for a lie. "I work. I have a job. I can't stay here all day."

"What errand?"

Her father shifted subjects. "I think it would be really nice if you called your mother."

"She doesn't know I'm here, does she?" She knew that her mother did, but she needed to see her father crack.

"Just call her and tell her you're all right." Her father handed her his cell phone.

"I'm not all right! It's been a full day here. No doctors have come to see me. The only human connection I've had is with lawyers." Oops. She had revealed too much information.

"Lawyers?"

"Nothing, Dad. Don't worry about it."

Her father desperately tried to pretend that he knew nothing about either side of this battle. "Please call your mother."

"And say what?"

"Tell her you want to see her. Make her feel needed, like a mother."

"But I can't see her. She's in New Hampshire for the week, right?"

Her father's eyes dropped to the floor. "She's back now."

"Was that your errand?!" She was livid. "You drove to pick her up from New Hampshire?"

"No." Her father's voice adopted the all-too-familiar wussy falsetto. He shifted back and forth on his feet. "I picked her up in New Jersey."

"You said she was in New Hampshire!"

"She was. But, um. . . ." He searched for words to bolster his lie. "She got a ride to New Jersey. I picked her up there."

"Dad, is anything you've said to me true?"

"Um. . . ." Her father's forehead dripped sweat, even though the room was overly air-conditioned. "I love you?"

"Is that a goddamn question?!" Her voice was booming. And she had no patience to interpret her father's pussy footing.

"Please call your mother."

"And say what? You piece of shit excuse for a father." She was practically foaming at the sides of her mouth. "And say *what?!*"

"Please don't yell at me." He was on the brink of tears. But she knew it was from her confronting his shame and not her yelling. "Just ask your mother for something. Make an excuse for her to have to come see you here."

"Why? You can't stand to stay here with me alone?"

"Please, please call your mother." Her father was pathetic. He may have been just as trapped in this situation as she was. But he didn't deserve the benefit of the doubt.

"Okay." She extended her hand. "Give me your phone."

Her father dialed the number and passed her the phone. She noticed that the number ringing was to her family home. Had her mother been in the area the whole time?

"Hello!"

"Hi, Mom."

"Oh." Her mother's voice dropped to a tone of disdain. She had obviously noticed the number in the caller ID and had assumed that it was her father calling.

"I'm calling from the hospital."

"Oh, you're in the hospital?" Her mother was a shamefully bad actress.

She looked up at her father. He mouthed to her, *make her feel needed.* "Mom? It's heavily air-conditioned here. Will you please come and bring me a blanket?"

Without missing a beat, and just before hanging up, her mother delivered a line that she knew would haunt her for the rest of her life:

"You're just going to die anyway. Who gives a fuck if you're cold?"

Thirty

Another morning began at Schneider's Children's Hospital. Another stale roll was delivered with a small container of milk. It seemed as though they were trying to make her *lose* weight.

Still no doctors had examined her. It was going to become increasingly difficult for them to try to convince her that they were trying to help get her well if no doctors ever came to see her. This whole situation reeked of a scam.

A group leader entered her room and asked if she'd like to take her breakfast to eat in the rec room with the other girls in the eating disorder program. Staring at the wall had become boring. She might as well eat in company.

Walking into the rec room, she was instantly disheartened. She saw a group of about a dozen girls in their teens pushing Cheerios around their trays without putting any into their mouths.

She wanted to ask if she could have their cereal. She was starving. But she thought that would be in poor taste. And she was nothing if not mannered.

Several of the girls had tubes taped over their ears and stuck up their noses. Large drip sacks hung from rods on wheels behind them. These girls were being forcefed. The nose tubes were inserted all the way into their stomachs. She couldn't look.

She was twice the age of some of the girls, and not even as thin. These girls were starving themselves for body image purposes; she was praying for someone to feed her! This was not the right place for her, but it was better than sitting in her room.

She poured her milk over her stale roll to help soften it. A nurse, not even older than she, yelled at her. "You can't have weird food behavior in here!"

"I can't eat a hockey puck," she replied flatly.

"Then you won't eat. And that's going on your chart."

"What chart?! I haven't even been seen by a doctor yet, and I've been here for two days!"

The nurse looked as though she were about to throw her out of the room when they were both saved by the sound of the phone ringing in her room.

"Still locked up, huh, my dear?"

"Yes, Mitchell. I'm still here. With no sign of reprieve."

"I can't let you out of my sight for a moment, can I?" Mitchell was only half kidding.

"I'm sorry."

"Don't be sorry. Just make sure that you make your flight tomorrow evening with your fucktoy in tow. What was her name again?"

"Laura."

"Laura," Mitchell repeated. "Well, make sure that you call Laura to let her know that she should have her bags packed and ready to go."

"Will I be out of here by then, Mitchell?"

"My dear, for the amount that I am paying my lawyers, you will own the hospital when you walk out this afternoon."

She tried to convince herself that this was true, but her doubts were running high.

The phone in her room was not set up for outgoing calls, so she asked a staff member if she could use the phone in the nurses' station.

"Who are you calling?" she was asked.

"A friend. It's a local call."

The hospital employee looked at her sternly then passed a phone unit over the top of the desk.

Laura picked up on the first ring. She had probably been waiting for her call. After not hearing from her for so long, Laura might have thought that the entire trip scenario was an elaborate ruse.

"Laura, I'm calling about our travel plans for tomorrow."

"Are you canceling on me?" Laura had clearly been sitting alone with doubts for too long.

"No! No, of course not. But I'm a little, uh. . . ." She looked at the nurse who was eyeing her strangely. "I'm a little tied up at the moment. I'm going to need you to go to the South African Airways satellite office near Grand Central to pick up the tickets. Can you do that?"

"Yes! Of course. Do you want me to bring them over to you when I have them?" Laura sounded relieved to know that soon there would be physical proof of the trip.

"No, I'm not, um, at home at the moment. I'll have to meet you at the airport tomorrow."

"Okay. Is there anything else I can do? Should I call you when I have the tickets?"

"Um, no. I've, um. . . ." She glared at the nurse. "I've lost my cell phone. It may have been stolen."

"Oh no! Should I get you a new one?" Laura really was eager to please.

"No, but thank you for offering. I actually know where mine is. I just can't get it at the moment." Her eyes never left the nurse. She was trying not to express as much hate as she felt. "I have to go now. I'll see you at JFK tomorrow." She hung up the phone.

The nurse chuckled. "You're really working this imaginary trip to South Africa, aren't you?"

"I'm booked on a flight tomorrow," she replied dryly.

The nurse's hands went into the air. "Hey, that just may be true! But let's see if you make that flight."

She said nothing and spun around to walk back into the privacy of her room. As she crossed the floor, she saw movement behind the translucent glass doors at the entrance to the children's ward. She recognized the voices and strained her eyes to identify the shadowy figures.

She was able to make out the form of her mother, her father, and several bodies in white doctors' coats. This was bad. This was really, really bad.

She was immobilized where she stood, watching her mother's arms flail in the dramatic display her mother often employed. She had no idea what was being said, but from the rapid flapping of her mother's arms, she knew that something big was about to happen.

The sound of the phone ringing in her room snapped her back into the moment.

"Mitchell?"

"Who but?" Mitchell chuckled.

"Mitchell, this is not good. My mother's here."

"Well, that's nice that your mother came to visit you in the hospital."

"No, Mitchell." Her voice was getting raspy and agitated. "She doesn't know that I know she's here. She's with doctors behind closed doors."

"But that's illegal! You're an adult!" Mitchell began to sound upset as well. The fear was contagious.

"I know, but that door is locked. I can't get to them!"

"Okay." Mitchell took an audibly deep breath. "Let's calm down. I'll let the attorneys know what's happening, and we'll shut this crazy train down."

"Oh, I spoke to Laura, by the way."

"And?"

"All systems are a go."

"Good work. Now let me get on the phone with the legal team."

"Mitchell?"

"Yes, my dear?"

"Thank you." She was sincere. Mitchell was her only hope now.

After dinner, two doctors came into her room and asked to speak with her.

"Are you here to examine me? No one has actually examined me yet."

The doctors exchanged a tired glance. One of them pointed to the chair in the corner of her room. "Sit down."

"You're not doctors, are you?" This was scary. A late-night visit from mysterious doctors.

"We're psychiatrists sent to evaluate you."

She knew she had to play the game. She made a mental note to avoid being combative. Even though these doctors were asking for it. "Evaluate me for what?"

The doctor continued the line of questioning. "Do you really think that you were out of the country last week?"

"Do I think? I don't understand—"

"Do you think that you are going to South Africa tomorrow?"

"Well, I have someone picking up the tick—"

Again, the doctor cut her off. "Are you currently employed?"

"No, I—"

"Just a 'no' is fine. Do you live alone?"

"Yes. I have an apartment on the Upper East Side."

Both doctors raised an eyebrow in unison. One asked, "Who pays your rent?"

"I do."

"Are you homeless?"

"I have an apartment."

"You said that already." The doctors were scribbling down notes. "Why are you here?"

"I was told I was sick."

"Do you think you're sick?"

"I think my last trip left me run down." The dim light was hurting her eyes, but she didn't ask to turn on the main light in the room. She didn't want to wake the children in the other rooms.

"Uh huh." The doctors continued to take notes. "Your trip to Fiji, right?"

"Right." She was just going to answer questions directly. It was best not to elaborate.

"Alone?"

"The second time alone. The first time with my gentleman companion."

"So, you think that you were in Fiji twice last week?"

"I think? I had a layover in both directions for a trip to Australia."

"Okay." The two doctors stood.

"That's it?"

"That's all." One of the doctors went into the hall and returned with a hospital gown. "Please put this on."

"You want me to get out of my clothes?"

"You may be a flight risk. Put on the gown and get into bed."

She did as she was instructed. The two doctors left, and she heard voices outside her door. She pulled the covers up over her nose all the way to her eyes. If this was a nightmare, it was the worst ever.

A tall, obese black man wearing scrubs entered her room and seated himself on the chair in the corner.

"Who are you?"

"Go to sleep," the man said. He didn't even look at her.

"Are you a doctor?"

"I'm a bodyguard. Go to sleep. Don't try to leave."

Her body shook as she began to cry. She pulled the blankets up all the way over her head. She prayed to no one in particular that this would all end.

Her crying drained her of the last of her energy, and she began to doze off. Just as she was about to achieve slumber, the door to her room was flung open. Several men in uniform entered. They grabbed her belongings, and one of them shook her in her bed.

"Get up. We're moving you."

"Moving me?" Her voice cracked. "Moving me where?"

No one answered her. Instead, one of the men barked the order, "Up. Now. Let's go."

She did as she was told and got out of the bed. Her hospital gown was open in the back, revealing her small, pale ass. Her body was shaking.

A man on each side took her arms and led her into the hallway. As she passed the nurses' station, she asked the onlookers, "Where am I going?"

Most of the nurses looked down at the desk. But one answered, "Hillside."

"Hillside? Is that part of this hospital?"

The same nurse explained, "Hillside is the state psychiatric ward. You've been 2PCed."

"2PCed?"

"Two Physician Certificate. Two psychiatrists agreed that you should be institutionalized."

Her body fell limp, and the men dragged her off the ward. Her feet barely touched the floor. She couldn't believe it, but Mitchell was right. She was about to be locked up. Now, all she could do was hope that no one had thrown away the key.

Thirty-One

Hillside wasn't located too far from North Shore Jewish. The ride was short enough that she wasn't able to dwell on her fear of her impending fate.

She sat in the backseat of the security minivan next to one of the guards and peered out the window to try to get a feel for the Hillside campus. This was a heavily gated area, and she half expected to see crazy people wandering about in the dark. Instead, she saw a series of rundown and vacated government buildings lost in a tangle of overgrowth and refuse.

She didn't know what she thought a state psychiatric facility would look like, but she was surprised at how much it looked like an abandoned military base from a wartime.

The minivan stopped in front of the administration building, and one of the guards walked her into intake while the other followed behind with her belongings.

She was downright shocked to see her childhood friend Samantha sitting on one of the metal chairs in the waiting room. Her mouth opened to speak a greeting, but no words came out.

She hadn't seen her in the two years, since she had been a bridesmaid at Samantha's wedding. Samantha hadn't spoken to her since the bridesmaid had accidentally run over the groom's best man in the parking lot after the rehearsal dinner. Her former friend had made it known to everyone that she had ruined the wedding. The bridesmaid thought that the poor choice in a ne'er-do-well groom had ruined the wedding, but that was a totally different issue. To say that this encounter at Hillside was entirely out of context was a vast understatement.

Samantha looked up from a magazine and jumped up to hug her old friend. She only half-hugged Samantha back. This was too weird.

Samantha spoke first. "When I heard you were being committed, I rushed over here to make sure that you wouldn't go through the process alone. Plus, you'll need someone to safeguard the belongings you don't want stolen."

"You *heard* I was here? It's one in the morning! Was it broadcast on the radio?"

Samantha laughed as though this sort of reunion of old friends were commonplace. "No, silly. Your mom told me."

"My mother told you I was being committed to Hillside? My mother called you?"

"No. I called her. We speak at least once a week." Samantha said this as though it were no big deal.

She decided not to overanalyze this piece of news but to instead appreciate the fact that she had a friendly face in a very unfriendly situation. "Okay. Well, thanks for coming."

"Hey, it's going to be a while. Want to go out for a cigarette?"

"I don't smoke," she responded.

"That's okay. Let's go outside now. You're going to be inside a lot for a while." Samantha seemed to know a lot about the process of committal.

"Aren't we locked in here? I don't think they'll let me go back outside." She motioned her thumb in the direction of the security guard who stood in front of the door through which she had just entered.

"No, silly. There's a gated smoking area right through that door over there." Samantha walked toward a metal door at the far side of the room.

She followed Samantha out the door, and the two girls took a seat on the steps next to the fence that was keeping them in.

Samantha took long, deep drags from her cigarette and watched the smoke clouds rise into the summer night air.

"Sam, how do you know so much about all this?"

"You mean the loony bin?" Samantha smiled. "You remember, don't you? I was committed twice into South Oaks during the year you were abroad in high school. South Oaks is like the Hillside for Suffolk County."

This was all too much for her to process. She wished she did smoke; now would be a good time for that. She went back to Samantha's story. "So, because you were committed, you thought that you would drive all the way out here just to keep me company during my intake? It's the middle of the night! Don't you have a kid?"

"Yes. And I also have a husband. The two of them are asleep at home." Samantha took one last long drag on her cigarette before putting it out on the concrete steps. "Anyway, I wish that I had had someone to stand by me when I was put away."

"Why were you in South Oaks?" She knew that Samantha had been through some trying times, but she didn't realize that those times included two involuntary committals.

"Suicide," Samantha answered casually, then qualified the statement by saying, "but I don't try to kill myself anymore." She smiled broadly. "See, the system works! I didn't kill myself, so a stay at one of these places can work."

"Okay, two things. First, you said you were committed twice. So, I'm not so sure that the system worked if you tried to kill yourself after you were released—"

Samantha interjected, "I didn't try to kill myself again until *much* later."

"Right. Good. Not the point, Sam." She continued with her statement. "The second thing is that you weren't an adult at the time."

"What do you mean? My mother had me committed. Same thing."

She raised an eyebrow at Samantha. How did Sam know that her mother had had her committed? She tried to just keep the conversation flowing naturally. "My point is that you were a minor at the time. Your mother could have just as easily grounded you, or taken away privileges, or whatever. Do you see what I mean?"

"So what got you committed, then?" Samantha was beginning to see that there was more to the story.

"Insolence. I played the game badly. Or at least my attorneys played the game badly. The hospital felt threatened. With good reason, too, because I think that a suit was cited. So I'm out of their hands, but not on the street, which could be grounds for another suit." She looked solidly at Samantha. "This is much bigger than my mother."

"You mean that your mother's not in control here. The State of New York is." Bingo. Samantha was smarter than she appeared.

"Exactly."

"I hadn't thought of that. You're right." Samantha reached for another cigarette. "That's heavy."

"Heavy."

The two old friends sat out on the smoking stairs until an intake officer opened the door and announced that it was time to do the deed.

She was put in the back of another minivan, and after asking nicely, Samantha was allowed to come along. The CB radio on the dash was chirping in and out, but she was able to make out through the static that she was going to unit 6B. Whatever the hell that was.

"Oh, 6B. That's a nice one!" Samantha chimed in.

She looked at Samantha incredulously. "How the hell would you know?"

Samantha's eyes dropped, with voice timbre following. "I don't know. I'm just trying to make you less scared."

Samantha and she moved closer to each other to meet in the center of the backseat and hugged each other tightly.

The guard driving looked at them in the rearview mirror and barked, "No touching!"

The two girls released each other from the embrace. She had the sneaking suspicion that a state mental health institution was sort of like jail, but with fewer rights.

They entered one of the unmarked beige buildings and took an elevator to the second floor. The guard unlocked a series of thick doors and prison-style sliding-bar gates. This was a full lockdown facility.

One last giant door was opened, and they entered into a narrow cinder-block corridor. It was the middle of the night, so all the doors along the corridor were locked, and none of the "patients" was out in the common area. She noticed that the light switches were lock-switches located outside the rooms.

She took a deep breath and kept walking. Samantha placed a hand lightly on the small of her back. At first she interpreted it as an act meant to comfort, but then she remembered that she was wearing a hospital gown and her ass was sticking out. Samantha was attempting to give her a little dignity. Like that made a difference at this time.

They were led up to the staff station. It was exactly the opposite of the nurses' station at Schneider's. The nurses there wore colorful scrubs and big smiles. These employees wore ill-fitting jeans and surly expressions. Oh, and they sat behind a thick layer of bulletproof glass laced with wire to prevent potential shattering.

One of the nurses came out from a door in the back of the nurses' station and very slowly, seemingly disinterested, sauntered a large fat body over toward them. She carried a few plastic trash bags.

Trying to calm herself, the new ward made light of the situation in her head. She had known Samantha since they were in the sixth grade together. She loved Samantha as a person, but she also knew that Samantha really *was* crazy. Samantha had been heavily medicated by a variety of psychotropics for the duration of her friendship, and when a cocktail of meds went awry, she had seen Samantha have truly frightening psychotic episodes. Yet, here *she* was in a hospital gown in a narrow fluorescent-lit hall being led into a cell. Not because she was crazy, but because state mental health laws said that the accused was guilty until proven innocent. This was going to be an interesting night.

They followed the obese nurse down the corridor, and after the correct key was found on the enormous keyring, the new ward was led into a tiny little room.

There was a figure asleep on one of the two plywood platforms, and a bright light streamed through the tall, thin window against the far wall. The bars on the window were almost thicker than the window itself.

"Your roommate's had her meds tonight, so you don't have to worry about waking her up," the nurse informed her.

"You mean she's been sedated."

"Everyone's sedated, girl. That's how we keep the peace." The nurse motioned toward her luggage. "Put it on the bed. I've got to inspect everything. Whatever you don't want me to see, you can send home with your friend here. Whatever I confiscate goes into these trash bags. If you get out, you get your shit back. If no one steals it."

All of a sudden, she realized that she had tons of sexual paraphernalia in her luggage. Luckily, it was all in one big Givenchy sack with a drawstring closing, so she quickly snatched it out of her open suitcase and handed it to Samantha.

She whispered into Samantha's ear, "Don't open this bag." All she needed

was for Samantha to find a sack filled with strap-ons, vibrating dildos, assorted sized butt plugs, and several ball gags.

Besides the toys, she gave Samantha her cell phone, her laptop, and all her
jewelry.

"Give your friend your belts and shoelaces, too. Oh, and your shaving ra-
zors and tweezers," the nurse snapped.

"Really?"

"Really. And don't make me put you on suicide watch." The nurse wasn't
joking around.

In the end, she was left with a single pair of jeans, two pairs of underwear,
sneakers that wouldn't stay on her feet without laces, and the sweater that
Pamela had given her two weeks before. She also held on to one of her nicer
outfits and fancy shoes, hoping that the other prisoners wouldn't realize the
value of the clothing. She had the feeling that there was a court appearance in
her very near future.

She also made sure that Samantha had the pair of shoes with all her money
in it and hoped that Samantha wouldn't aggressively search her belongings.
Last, she handed Samantha her passport with the strictest instructions to
guard it as though it were a brick of bullion. She didn't particularly trust her
friend with such an important document, but she certainly didn't trust Nurse
Ratched.

Her suitcase was placed into one of the trash bags. Her remaining few items
fit into the sliding drawer beneath her bed.

The nurse escorted Samantha out of the room, and the door was locked
and the lights turned out behind them.

In the glow of the security light that beamed through the window, she got
under the single sheet that covered the bed and shivered against the hard plywood bench that would be her new sliver of home for the foreseeable future.

Thirty-Two

All the doors in the corridor were electronically opened at the same time, and a voice over the loudspeaker yelled *Smoke break at 6:30. Meds at 7 a.m. Breakfast at 7:30. Shower towels are gone; no showers this morning. Mooooove, people.*

She rubbed her eyes and tried to sit directly up. The plank under her one-inch mat hurt the bones at the base of her back, and she realized that she had to roll to her side to get upright. Her roommate was already awake and reading.

"Hi. Good morning."

Her roommate didn't respond.

"What are you reading?"

"The Old Testament. I'm getting back to my faith." This was followed by voices in different tones, "Don't talk to her! Don't tell her what you're doing! You don't know her!" followed by the original voice yelling, "Shut up! Shut up! I'm reading. Leave me alone with the bible!"

She sat looking slack jawed at this otherwise beautiful young woman. She had no idea how to handle this fight her roommate was battling internally.

Her roommate grabbed fistfuls of blonde hair and screamed, then turned to her and apologized. "I'm sorry. I'm Rachel. I'm a multiple personality schizophrenic. I can't control it. My sister put me here."

It was a lot of information to pack into one sentence.

"It's nice to meet you, Rachel. I hope I didn't wake you up when I moved in last night."

Rachel screamed again, "Shut up, shut up, shut up! Don't talk to her! She's new! You can't trust her!"

Okay. Time to leave this room. She liked Rachel, but the other personalities seemed a bit hostile.

The hallway was filled with slowly moving people in various stages of undress. All dragged their feet, but that may have been because no one had any shoelaces more than anything else.

There was a line outside the nurses' station, and she assumed that that's where people were given their meds. She had no idea if she was on anything, so she thought it best to line up with everyone else and ask the nurse. She had nothing better to do anyway.

She had a patient number on her wristband, and she showed it to the meds nurse. Flipping through a binder, the meds nurse informed her that she had no morning meds. "But you don't eat breakfast with the others."

"Where do I eat breakfast?" What was going on?

"Well, you eat in the common room with everyone else, but your breakfast is being sent over by the nutritionist from Schneider's."

"Really?" This was the first act of compassion she had experienced. As long as it didn't mean she'd be given more stale bread while everyone else ate eggs and juice.

"Yes. You apparently made quite a good impression on the folks there." The nurse looked up at her with one eye above the level of the glasses. "Welcome to Hillside." Then, looking past her, the nurse chortled, "Next! Meds!"

In the common room, most of her fellow prisoners were milling about, waiting for breakfast. Some were sitting and drooling on themselves on the hard plastic couches. Some were standing in groups and shouting incoherently. Some were looking blankly at the single TV mounted from the ceiling in one corner.

She sat down on a hard wooden bench and sized up the demographic of 6B. Most were black—some with Caribbean accents and some African American. The remaining population was mostly Hispanic. There were enough white people to count on only one hand. That her roommate was white was probably no accident. The staff probably had some racially motivated reasons to segregate the sleeping quarters.

The breakfast bell rang, and everyone raced to get in line in front of the massive steam troughs. She held back, awaiting instruction.

A male attendant approached her with a tray covered in cellophane. "You the new ward?"

"Yes, sir."

He handed her the tray and dryly stated, "Breakfast."

She opened the cellophane and was pleased to see that her meals sent here were far better than the meals she had been given at Schneider's. She couldn't remember having met the nutritionist, but she had a sneaking suspicion that the staff at Schneider's was afraid she would certainly perish at Hillside, and they were doing what they could to keep up her energy.

She had a bowl of fruit, some cereal, a cup of yogurt, and a plate with a fried egg, a single sausage link, and a piece of buttered toast. There was also a handwritten note with a smiley face instructing her to ask the servers at Hillside to provide her with milk and juice.

She took the note up to the staff serving the food, and she was given a carton of milk and a plastic cup of grape juice.

When she returned to her tray, her sausage link and her cup of yogurt were missing. She pretended not to notice and sat down.

She heard a loud, middle-aged black woman's voice yell, "See! White girl's skinny! We gotta take care of her, not steal her food! You an asshole, Tyrone! You an asshole!" The woman then slid a banana down to her. "Here you go, baby girl. Don't worry. I ain't gonna let no one else take food from yo' mouth."

Tyrone, an overweight black man, looked ashamed. Without looking up, he said, "I'm sorry I stole your food. I'll hook you up at lunch. I promise."

She wasn't really sure how to read this situation. On the one hand, these people were stealing her food. On the other hand, they also seemed eager to care for her. She was going to have to learn the code of honor in the psych ward, and fast.

After breakfast, most of the residents of 6B went outside for a smoke break. She stayed in the common room and looked around.

She took in the beige walls and the narrow spaces. She processed the bulletproof nurses' station and the drooling bodies on the couches. She looked at the single, tiny TV dangling from the ceiling. It was straight out of *One Flew Over the Cuckoo's Nest*. Except the space of this ward was smaller, the nurses were meaner, and the wards slept on wooden planks instead of beds. Who knew that the movie was actually more glamorous than the reality? The movie had been pretty bad.

Lost in thought, she almost didn't hear someone in the distance calling her name. She followed the sound and saw a payphone hanging off the hook in the rear of the corridor. A small Hispanic woman was standing nearby, pointing toward the swaying receiver. "It for you."

She picked up the phone and was not surprised to hear Mitchell's voice on the other end. "Convinced yet? Are you sufficiently locked up enough now to know not to trust your parents?"

"I fucked up, Mitchell."

"Yeah, you fucked up. And now this bitch Laura is coming to South Africa to see me without you." Mitchell groaned. "Thanks a lot."

"You wanted me there?"

"I need you for one thing and that's to control these fucktoys. Without you, I have to deal with them. And I hate them. I need you." Mitchell paused. "Plus, I love you, gorgeous. You know that."

"I'm not feeling a lot of love in here, that's for sure."

"Hillside's bad, huh?"

She laughed a pretend laugh. "My roommate's a goddamned multiple personality nut job."

"Are any of the personalities fuckable?" Mitchell was trying to lighten the mood.

"Not for any amount of time to get the job done!"

They both laughed.

Then Mitchell got serious again. "Look. You're now going to have to go to court to get out. No big deal. You're not crazy, and no judge is going to waste taxpayers' dollars keeping you in there. I'm going to make some calls and get you the best mental health lawyer there is, okay?"

"Okay."

"You'll be fine. I promise. I have to go now though. Have to fly to Jo'burg to meet this bitch Lisa."

"Laura, Mitchell."

"Whatever. You behave. Keep your head up. I'll try to send you some surprises."

Surprises? In Hillside? She had the feeling nothing could surprise her anymore.

Lunch was delivered to the ward, and it was mildly amusing that her meal was an entire layer cake, frosting and all. She looked incredulously at the nursing staff. It wasn't possible that she was expected to devour an entire cake as her lunch. That couldn't be nutritionally balanced!

She didn't want to make waves, so she didn't say anything about the fact that she hated sweets. She knew that the delivery of a layer cake to her was more about the basic caloric statistics than nutritional guidelines. She poked around at the cake for a few minutes, and then asked if she might be allowed to have a ham sandwich, like all of her floormates, instead.

"Are you refusing to eat?" the staff member asked accusatorily.

"No! No! I want to eat! I really want to eat!" She looked down at the cake. "And I'm happy that they sent me cake. Very happy! I'm just wondering, um, if I can have something a little less sweet?" She looked directly at the nurse, who looked clueless. "I'm just thinking that eating an entire cake for lunch is going to give me a sugar crash."

"So, what are you saying?" The attendant was obviously clueless.

"I'm saying that I want to eat the cake. But from a nutritional standpoint, I want to eat it after I've eaten something veggie and protein laden. Is that an unreasonable request?"

"Eat. Your. Fucking. Cake." The attendant stormed out of the common area.

Lunch sucked.

She sat alone, pushing her crappy cakey lunch around her plate when she heard her name called. She looked up with low expectations and was surprised to see Felicia standing in the common room.

"You have a visitor!" Felicia ran over to her and gave her a long kiss on the mouth in front of the entire group.

Embarrassed, she stepped back and brought the back of her hand to her mouth. Muffled, she said, "Let's go to my room."

She led Felicia down the long narrow corridor and into her small box of a bedroom. Rachel was standing on one bed having a fight with another personality. Felicia watched Rachel and stared, not daring to enter the room.

Catching Felicia's eye, Rachel's roommate said, "Are you going to come in?"

Felicia pointed at Rachel. "Is that okay?"

"They're having a fight. They'll work it out. Ignore it." She sat on her bed and motioned for Felicia to join her.

"*They?*" Felicia sat but never stopped staring at Rachel.

"Yes. There are apparently a few people in there, and they don't get along very well."

"Is that normal?"

"No, it's not fucking normal, Felicia! We're in a fucking mental hospital. No one here is fucking normal."

"You're normal." Felicia kissed her cheek and caressed her hair.

She didn't resist the affection, but she did say, "No, Felicia. I'm not normal."

Felicia laughed. "Okay. You're not normal. But you're not insane."

"No kidding. But I still managed to get locked up."

"Hey, it could be worse."

"Worse than this? Really? *Worse* than Hillside?"

"No, not worse *than* Hillside. Worse *at* Hillside."

She realized that Felicia had seen much more of Hillside than she had. Felicia had actually arrived during daylight hours and had been treated as a visitor and not a resident.

"Really?"

"When I told them that I was visiting you, they told me that 6B was the minimal security unit." Felicia was serious. "You're with the nonviolent crowd. Nice and safe."

"Nonviolent?" Rachel was now pounding the wall with one fist and pulling out a clump of hair with another.

"Well, not violent to other people, at least." Felicia paused. "Well, other people outside their heads."

"Great. I'm with the least crazy people in the mental hospital. Yea me!" Both girls laughed.

When they had collected themselves, they both exhaled and settled in to have an actual conversation. She realized that she and Felicia had never had a real conversation. She was always the domme to Felicia's submissive. But here, locked in Hillside, she was certainly not in control.

"So, how did you know I was here?"

"Mitchell called me. Did you know that he's in South Africa?"

"Yeah, I'm supposed to be there with him."

"Oh. Sorry." Felicia looked around and asked, "So, seriously, what happened?"

"I'm not sure. No one's really told me anything. The best that I can figure out is that my parents orchestrated some sort of hospitalization to keep me from suing my mom or something—"

"You were trying to sue your mom?" Felicia interjected.

"No! No! I would never sue my mom. My mother stole some money from me, but I'd never reduce myself to her level of deception and thievery."

"Good." Felicia thought for a moment. "But don't you want your entitled possessions?"

Felicia's friend didn't want to sound macabre, but she figured that she may as well tell Felicia what she honestly believed. "Look, my mother's father died young, her brother died young, and her mother died young. I'm not exactly spinning the roulette wheel when I bet that I'll be inheriting sooner rather than later."

"You think your mom's going to *die*?" Felicia sounded shocked.

"Hey!" She needed to nip this in the bud. "I don't want my mother to die! That's sick! I hope she lives a long, healthy life. I hope she even finds happiness. But the odds on her longevity? Not good. That's not me talking. That's nature and common sense."

"Okay. So, you're not going to sue your mother?"

"No."

"But she thinks you are, so she had you locked up?"

"No, she thinks I *could*, so she had me locked up."

"And Mitchell?"

"Mitchell and his team of attorneys got into a pissing match with the hospital's attorneys. So that expedited the whole process."

"And now you're in a bad scene from *One Flew over the Cuckoo's Nest*."

Great minds think alike. "So, it's not just me? You get that too?" She laughed.

"Honey, it's exactly like the movie. If Nurse Ratched had been short, fat, and Dominican." Felicia hammed up her Puerto Rican accent.

After they finished another round of laughter, she said, "Felicia, I'm really glad you're here."

"Yeah, Mitchell wanted me to bring a bunch of the girls, but I thought that for a first visit, it was probably best if I came alone. Plus, those other girls are sluts."

She didn't see how Felicia could call fellow fucktoys sluts, but she had always noticed something different and special about Felicia, so she let the comment slide. She went back to trying to understand the situation. "So really, Felicia, why are you here?"

"I came to support you."

She found it hard to believe that Felicia would journey all the way out from Manhattan to Nassau County on public transportation just to support her. They weren't really close friends. They might have been, had they met in different circumstances, but the fact remained that they weren't.

"Seriously. You came just to see me? Not because you were curious to check out the loony bin?"

"Okay, at first I was curious," Felicia admitted. "But after three subway transfers and an hour-long ride on a Nassau County bus, I was coming just to see you. Getting here was a nightmare."

"Being here is a nightmare." She looked deep into Felicia's eyes. "Thank you for coming."

"They told me I only have an hour for a visit. So they're going to be kicking me out soon. I'll come back tomorrow. What's the currency here?"

"What do you mean by currency?"

"You know. Like in jail, people exchange cigarettes, or phone cards, or blowjobs. I don't know. But there has to be a currency here."

She thought for a minute. There were payphones in the hall. "A phone card would be good. But that would be for me. Hmmm." She thought about currency. All of the other wards of the floor got really excited at meal times. Food was probably good. "I think that doughnuts and candy bars are probably good. I'd say cigarettes, but the smokers here all seem to be hooked up."

"Okay, doughnuts and candy bars it is." Felicia stood to leave. "Oh, I actually already bought you a phone card." Felicia handed her a cellophane-wrapped piece of plastic. "So you can call me if you think of anything else for me to bring."

The two girls embraced tightly. Felicia was maybe a real friend after all.

Thirty-Three

S he was sitting on her bed reading a book she had found in the common area when one of her fellow patients told her that she had a phone call. She went into the hall and picked up the swinging receiver.

"Did you like your surprise?"

"Thank you for sending Felicia, Mitchell."

"She wanted to come. That bitch is a true sub. You've done a good job. Even in the psych ward, Felicia looks up to you." Mitchell was serious. He was probably right.

"It was a great break. There's nothing else to do here. And she's coming back tomorrow."

"As she should. Felicia is a good one." Mitchell shifted topics with no segue. "I have some contacts for you. Write this down—"

She interrupted him. "Hold on, I have to get a pen and paper."

"Hey, genius. From now on, always come to the phone with a notebook ready to get information. Got it?" Mitchell sounded exasperated. In fairness, there were probably better ways for him to spend his vacation than on the phone with a ward of the state.

She returned with a notebook and a pen. "Okay, shoot."

"*Shoot*?" Mitchell hated colloquialisms. "A day in the nuthouse and you're already ceasing to be a *lady*?"

"Sorry, Mitchell. You're right. Please continue."

"Okay, I've spoken with the director of the organization of public mental health defenders in New York State to find you the best publicly appointed attorney they have."

"Publicly appointed?" Why couldn't one of the Durman lawyers who got her into this mess get her out?

"Yes. In New York State, the only attorney who can work with a committed psychiatric patient is a public defender."

"Got it. Okay. So what did the director say?"

"Well, I told him your story. I explained the situation in its entirety." Mitchell paused for dramatic effect. "And he's flying down from Albany to represent you himself."

"That's great! So, I'm getting out today?"

"No. Think for a minute, you imbecile. What's this weekend?"

"The Fourth of July."

"The Fourth of July," Mitchell repeated. "The first court date they could get you is Tuesday."

"Damn it! Do you think my parents picked this weekend to commit me on purpose?"

"What do you think?"

"Well, one of my cousins is getting married on the Fourth of July. So not only would my parents be able to hold me in Hillside for longer because of the holiday weekend and the delay of the court date, but they get the added benefit of telling my entire extended family that I'm crazy and locked away in the mental hospital."

Mitchell sighed audibly. "Finally! You're ceasing to be a naïve imbecile and finally thinking like the evildoers who are out to get you are."

"You think my parents are out to get me?"

"You're in the fucking cuckoo's nest!" Mitchell yelled into the phone. "Have they visited you?!"

"No."

"And they won't! They think that they've locked you up and thrown away the key!" Mitchell's voice was shaking. "But they haven't. They are crazy to think that they can break you. Don't let them break you!"

She was surprised to realize that Mitchell was as upset as she now saw. "I won't let them break me. I promise."

"Look, my dear." His voice returned to a normal decibel level. "You have five days in the nuthouse. You cannot, I repeat *cannot,* let the craziness penetrate you before your day in court. Got it?"

"Got it."

"Good. Be like Teflon to the crazies."

"Teflon to the crazies," she affirmed.

"I'll call you tomorrow."

Dinner that night was another fucking cake. She carried her tray to the nurses' station and asked to speak with the head nurse.

"I understand that you're trying to fatten me up. But I'm hoping that before the holiday weekend, I can meet with a nutritionist." She was respectful but firm.

The head nurse, an elderly black woman with eyeglasses perched on the tip of her nose, looked back and forth between the cake and the patient holding it. "Okay. I agree. Giving you a big cake for dinner is probably not nutritionally sound. Would you like a *Boost* shake to drink with it?"

"No, but thank you. I can't handle any more sweets. May I please meet with a nutritionist?"

The nurse looked her up and down. "Mmm hmm. I'll make the call. Now go eat your cake."

She ate her cake in the common room and tried to explain the situation to the onlookers sharing her table. "They're making me eat cake. They're trying to fatten me up."

"For the slaughter?" one of the older women at the table asked. "Ooooh, baby, that ain't healthy. Would you like some of my chicken?" The woman slid a tray toward her.

"I'd love some, but I can't. They're watching." She nodded toward the staff. "They'll say I'm sneaking food. Or something. I'll have to wait till tomorrow for a real meal."

"What's tomorrow?" A man asked.

"They're sending me a nutritionist."

Everyone at the table laughed.

"That's funny?"

"Good luck getting a doctor down here!" The generous elderly woman chortled. "They don't send doctors 'round here! Not to us crazy folks!" Everyone laughed again.

She finished as much of the cake as she could possibly stomach before getting a piercing sugar headache. When no one was looking, she threw the last few bits in the trash and went back to her room.

Lights out was at 8 p.m. Lying face up in the dark, it occurred to her that right now, in a parallel space and time, she'd be sitting in a first-class sky suite on her way to South Africa.

Fate was cruel.

❧

She was awakened at 6 a.m., before the wakeup call, to meet with the nutritionist who was waiting for her in the common room. She was told to come out in her pajamas, because the doctor wanted to meet with her as quickly as possible so that she could leave the floor before the other patients woke up.

The nutritionist was a doctor she recognized from her brief stay at Schneider's. She was surprised to realize how happy she was to see a familiar face from what she had then thought was a nightmare situation. Little had she known how bad the situation could get.

"So, we're here to discuss your meals." The nutritionist began speaking before she had even taken a seat.

"Yes. My last two meals have been cake."

"Is that a euphemism? Like *easy as cake*?"

"No, I have actually been given cake. Like whole birthday cakes."

The nutritionist laughed.

"It's not funny. They're making me eat cake!" When she said it out loud, it did sound a little funny.

"I'm sorry I'm laughing. It's just that I'm looking at your chart. I had prescribed for you a 10,000-calorie-a-day diet. I fought with the staff at Schneider's because they had you on the malnutrition diet." The doctor explained further, "You know, dry rolls, measured fluids, et cetera. They thought your body couldn't handle more, like you were anorexic. But I knew better. So when they sent you here, I prescribed the diet I actually thought you should be on, based on your resting heart rate and all."

"You're losing me." She was getting a lot of information at once, early in the morning.

"What I'm saying is that given your past history as a competitive light-weight body builder—"

"You know about that?" she interrupted.

"We have your file." The nutritionist continued, "Given your past as a high-performance athlete, coupled with your rapid heartbeat at night, you have a fast-burning metabolism."

"Okay—"

"But you are *way* too thin."

"No kidding. I'm like bones with skin."

"A far cry from your muscular body during competition, huh?"

"An eternity. My former personal-training clients would die of shock."

"A lot of people would." This nutritionist was warm and personable; a trustworthy-seeming physician. "Anyway, I put you on a high-calorie diet. Clearly, the kitchen here at Hillside is cutting corners. I say 10,000 calories a day, so they give you two cakes. What you need are large balanced meals, several times a day."

"I agree."

"You agree? You know about nutrition?"

"I'm embarrassed to admit that I'm a licensed nutritionist. Well, I was licensed." She felt silly admitting this. "I don't know if the license expires. But I know that my insurance has expired."

"You were licensed and insured as a nutritionist?" The doctor looked at once both shocked and intrigued. "And you ended up here?"

"It's crazy, I know."

The doctor tried to shrug it off. "Anyway, obviously the kitchen at Hillside is not cooperating with the program to address your needs. So, I'm going to send over your meals from the kitchen at Schneider's."

"Thank you."

"Let me finish." The doctor handed her a piece of paper with her meal schedule. "You will be getting six balanced meals a day. I will also send over a half-dozen protein corn muffins every day. You will eat a protein muffin every hour, on the hour, between each of your meals."

"Muffins?"

"It says on your chart that you specifically stated that you hate *Boost* and *Ensure* shakes. Is that wrong?"

"No! No, I *hate* those chemical shakes. They make me gassy, and I burp up the artificial flavorings for hours after I drink them!"

"Right. So muffins, then."

"Muffins."

The nutritionist began to put the files back into an attaché. "Okay, so beginning with lunch, you'll get your new meals. You're going to have to eat another cake for breakfast though."

She laughed.

The nutritionist was serious. "I'm not kidding. They'll probably give you a cake for breakfast. Eat it. The guards are watching. Don't give them any reason to think you belong here."

"Eating an entire cake for breakfast isn't a red flag for craziness?"

The nutritionist laughed. "Good point." Putting a hand on her shoulder and squeezing lightly, the doctor said, "Just play the game so that you can get out."

She thought about going back into her room, but she figured that Rachel would be fighting with a few personalities right about now. She'd probably get the most peace and quiet waiting in the common room. Sitting, waiting for cake.

Thirty-Four

At 1 p.m., as instructed, she went over to the nursing station to request her post-lunch muffin.

"We don't have any muffins for you. Drink a *Boost*." A nurse placed a warm can on the counter.

"I'm not supposed to drink a *Boost*. I'm supposed to eat a muffin."

"Well, we ain't got no muffins for you," the nurse said dismissively.

"Look, when my lunch was brought over from Schneider's, I saw them deliver a bag of muffins." She was trying not to be combative, but this nurse was a bitch.

"Oh, those was your muffins?"

"My name was on the bag."

"Oh, those muffins is et."

"Those muffins is et?" She didn't even know what the nurse was saying. "Is that English?"

"I be saying that those muffins was brought over here, and the nurses be eating them."

"So, you ate my medically prescribed protein muffins?"

"Heck, I ate *one*." The nurse cocked her head. "Those was *healthy* muffins? No wonder they tasted like ass." The nurse turned and walked away from the window.

"Hello? Hello!" She was beginning to see that the staff at Hillside was a joke. "Hello!" She called out to no one in particular.

Great, here she was, practically on her deathbed from Mitchell-induced starvation, and the staff at this facility was stealing her food. What a system. What a great fucking system.

Life in the psych ward was pretty dull. The other patients basically waited for mealtime, med time, and smoke breaks. That was it. It was a gorgeous summer outside the concrete walls, so she began to look forward to smoke breaks, too.

When she would go outside, she made it a point to only look straight up at the sky. The small outdoor space was enclosed by a forty-foot-high fence with barbed wire at the top. It made her feel like a caged animal at the zoo, and, not surprisingly, she found it depressing.

The sound of Rachel fighting with invisible people made it difficult to read in her room. And there were too many people in the common area to read there. So, she tried to be sociable and get to know the other crazies.

She developed a friendship with a petite young black gay man who was in the terminal stages of AIDS. His name was Isaac, and he had a large bodyguard following him at all times. Isaac was one of the several patients on the

floor who had a mandatory round-the-clock suicide watch. He wasn't allowed
to go out for smoke breaks.

When she was outside, she spent time talking with a tall, thin white man in
his early thirties. His name was Bill. Years of hard drinking and chain smoking had given Bill leathery skin and sunken eyes. He had been committed for
almost killing his wife. Twice. He was happy to be at Hillside because he had
no money and nowhere else to go.

The rest of her time was spent fielding phone calls from Mitchell and the
attorney she would meet on Tuesday. And with visits from Felicia. She realized that she was the only resident of 6B who ever had anyone come to visit.
Everyone else had been abandoned.

Her parents didn't call. Samantha didn't call. Only Mitchell and Felicia
seemed to make any effort at all. Maybe she had been abandoned too.

Sunday was Independence Day, and 6B had a barbecue lunch/dinner out
on the smoking deck. A grill was brought in, and a festive tablecloth was laid
out on one of the picnic tables and covered with trays of coleslaw and potato
salad and corn-on-the-cob. Hamburgers and hotdogs were grilled up by the
nursing staff and security guards.

She wasn't allowed to eat any communal food. The kitchen staff at Schneider's must have had the holiday off, because she, once again, was given a
cake. At least this cake had a colorful American flag drawn in the icing. The
irony wasn't even funny.

Her tray also had a plate with little compartment sections. There was baked
ziti, mashed potatoes, rice, and macaroni and cheese. This meal made no
sense. She must have been given a meal of leftovers calculated to meet her
calorie requirements.

Since the staff was busy cooking, she wasn't being watched as carefully as she usually was. She gave away slices of cake to her new friends,
who sneaked her their food under the picnic table. She didn't even have to
ask. Turns out, she was popular even in the mental hospital. Crazy people
seemed to like her.

She had finished off two hotdogs and an ear of corn before she was caught
eating a hamburger and yelled at by Nurse Ratched. The nurse claimed to
be writing some sort of violation down on her chart, as though that were a
big threat. What could they possibly do to punish her when she was already
locked up by the state? Lock her up more? What was downhill from Hillside?
There's no backsliding when you're already at the bottom.

The Fourth of July party was fun. At least, as fun as can be had with heavily
armed guards standing around the perimeter of the twenty-by-twenty-foot
chain-linked fence holding in the prisoners. And Nurse Ratched confiscating
her hamburger.

Since she had not seen any doctors on the floor of 6B, and she had her doubts that any of the nursing staff were actual RNs, she stopped thinking of herself and her fellow floormates as patients. They were clearly prisoners. And they were genuinely sweet, kind, considerate nut jobs. Good hearts, broken brains. Maybe she was in the right place.

She tried not to think about the wedding she had missed. It would have made for a much better excuse to have said she was in South Africa and couldn't attend. But, instead, her parents would have the extreme pleasure of telling all her extended family that she was twenty miles away, locked in the loony bin. Her mother would probably make it sound like she was in a straitjacket in a padded room with a ball gag in her mouth to keep her from swallowing her tongue.

"Mitchell, I've discovered the origin of ball gags."

"Really? What's that?"

"Ball gags come from the loony bin. It's all the rage in fashion here."

"Well, I'm glad they took yours off for long enough for you to take a phone call from me." Mitchell laughed.

"Oh, no! They wouldn't give me a ball gag. They're theoretically trying to fatten me up."

"Theoretically?"

"I'm supposedly on an elaborate meal plan."

"But?"

"But the staff keeps stealing my food. And they can't even claim ignorance. They can't say 'we didn't see your name on it' because it all has my fucking name on it."

Mitchell laughed uproariously. "That, you have to admit, is funny."

"It is funny. But not in a good way. It's funny like, how fucked up is this?"

"You're swearing a lot more now."

"It's the language of the nuthouse."

"Well, don't get too used to it. Your court date is tomorrow, right?" Mitchell sounded almost as excited as she was.

"Yes. I have no idea how I'm supposed to get there or anything. I guess I should speak to one of the food thieves and arrange for some transportation."

"Well, you'll get out, go home, and relax. Lesson learned."

"Lesson learned?"

"Sure. Now you know the motives of your parents. And you know how bad it can be without me on your side."

"It's pretty bad."

"And lonely, I'll bet, too." Mitchell was reading her mind. "Has anyone but me called you?"

"No." The reality was enough to make her cry.

"And has anyone but the fucktoy *I* called come to visit?"

"No."

"There you go. So now you'll trust me when I tell you that those monsters are out to get you."

She really didn't want to believe that there were people who really wanted to ruin her life. But then again, there she stood. In the narrow concrete hallway of a psych ward, talking on a payphone, wearing sneakers with no laces, hair matted to her head, unbathed for a week, preparing to go to court to prove her sanity.

Thirty-Five

There were still no shower towels Tuesday morning, and she tried to convince herself it was because the laundry delivery hadn't come during the holiday weekend. But she had the feeling that there were never any shower towels. The well-being and hygiene of the residents at Hillside didn't seem to be a priority. It was becoming apparent that this was just a holding facility. As long as very few people died inside the gates, the staff had done its job. Period.

While the rest of the group was eating breakfast, one of the guards came over to let her know that her ride to the courthouse was waiting. She abandoned her tray and went into her room to change out of her pajamas and into her fitted slacks and blouse, and her Armani shoes.

Her shoes had sharp pointy heels, and she was surprised they were not confiscated at intake. She thought of the scene from *Single White Female* where the crazy stalker plunges a high heel into a man's head and kills him. Maybe the staff at Hillside hadn't seen that movie.

She did the best she could with her greasy hair and hoped that her body odor wouldn't overwhelm the breathing air in the courtroom.

She was escorted to the idling minivan and locked into the backseat. She asked the driver where they were going.

"Creedmore. Courthouse is at Creedmore," the driver told her dryly. He obviously wasn't in the mood for conversation. But she was curious.

"What's Creedmore?" She didn't even like the sound of the word. It sounded scary and evil.

"Like Hillside. Only older. And maximum security."

"Maximum? Hillside's not maximum security?"

"You see," the driver made eye contact with her through the rearview mirror, "when you go to Hillside, maybe one day you get out. When you go to Creedmore, ain't nowhere else to go." He made a gesture with his head as they passed through the gates at Creedmore. "You'll see, Creedmore be a lot more run down than Hillside."

"Why is that? Aren't they both state facilities?" She looked at the grounds and was shocked to see that it looked like a fallout scene in a bad Vietnam movie.

"See, the thing is, if you at Hillside, maybe you have visitors. You know, your kids, your parents, they visit you at Hillside. Ain't no one visits the people at Creedmore. This is they last stop."

The court was conveniently located on Creedmore's campus, presumably so that the serious offenders of the mental health trials wouldn't have far to travel. This was one place where you didn't want to be held in contempt of court.

The minivan stopped and parked in a gravel driveway that was sprouting tall weeds, verging on bushes. It looked like the back entrance to maybe a grungy nightclub in a bad neighborhood in Queens. This couldn't be the courthouse. There was an overflowing dumpster at the side of the unmarked steel door.

"Where are we?" She hoped that the driver would just say that he had stopped to pee.

"This is the court. Creedmore. We here." The driver opened his door. "Wait here. I'll get your security escort."

She didn't even want to get out of the van. The weeds in the parking area were so high that she thought she might get Lyme disease from a Long Island tick.

A security guard opened the van door to the backseat from the outside, and she was led into the dilapidated building through the massive metal door. The guard made a grunt when he pulled it, so she knew that it was even heavier than she thought.

"Is this really the front door to the courthouse?"

The guard didn't answer her. Instead, he led her into a cavernous room furnished with decomposing metal and plastic furniture from the 1960s. Everything was in shades of burnt orange and puke green. There was a broken glass window letting a crooked stream of light into the waiting area.

No one was there except Felicia. And it was really nice to see a friendly face. The two girls embraced with a solid, strong hug. The guard left the area.

"This place is *scary!*"

"Thanks, Felicia."

"No, I mean, it's really scary!"

"This isn't anything like what I pictured a courthouse to be."

"You've never been in a courthouse?"

"No, have you?"

"A speeding ticket and a dismissed shoplifting charge, both in college." She looked at a bucket in the corner that was collecting water from a leak in the roof. "But no. Real courthouses in New York don't look like this. I feel like I'm in a bad movie."

"Hey, this is actually my life!" She couldn't even believe she was acknowledging it out loud. "This bad movie is my *life.*"

"Creepy."

"Creedmore."

The two girls sat in the forty-year-old chairs and tried to pretend to laugh. But Creedmore was definitely not funny.

Eventually, a middle-aged man in a rumpled suit walked past the waiting area and asked if his client was in there.

"I think I'm your client." She stood up. "Are you here to get me out of Hillside?"

"I am." The two exchanged a handshake, and her attorney led her into what looked like a closet. Aside from the dingy wooden desk inside, she was pretty sure that it was, in fact, a closet. "This is the attorneys' office. Sorry there are no chairs."

"I guess there's just not enough tax money for chairs."

"Don't get me started—"

"Sorry. I didn't mean to touch a nerve." She shifted topics. "Thank you so much for coming all the way from Albany to represent me."

"Don't mention it. When I heard about your case, I was happy to represent someone interesting."

"Interesting?"

"I mean, and as a lawyer I shouldn't say this, but I represent a lot of people who really do need help." The lawyer was trying to carefully choose his words. "I mean, they need help, but the state mental health system is not where they're going to get it. You understand?"

"And that's relevant to me because—"

"Oh, because you don't even need help. They're saying you're delusional, thinking you're jet setting around the world. This is a fun case to represent."

"Fun?"

"Fun because I can't wait to see the prosecutors' faces when we present your passport. Case closed." The attorney chuckled a bit. "I bet their expert medical witnesses haven't even examined you, have they?"

"What do you mean?"

"Well, have any doctors met with you?"

"No."

"Well, they'll have doctors on the witness stand. You can believe that."

"Doctors who have never met me?! Is that legal?" She found this entire system to be shady.

"This is not normal court, I'm sorry to say. This is mental health court. Defendants' rights do not apply."

"Wow. No kidding, wow."

He rifled through his paperwork. "You have your passport, right?"

"My friend Samantha's bringing it. I didn't want to keep it at Hillside, in case it got lost."

"Stolen," he corrected.

"I'm going to give the staff at Hillside the benefit of the doubt and say lost."

"Good for you. Is your friend Samantha here?"

"She's coming." She really hoped Samantha wouldn't let her down.

Back in the waiting area, she found Samantha talking with Felicia. She was relieved that Samantha had showed up; she hadn't doubted her loyalty until the attorney had freaked her out.

She and Samantha exchanged greeting kisses, and then all three girls sat to wait.

"So, what time is the trial?" Samantha asked.

"No idea," she responded. "They just told me 'morning.'"

"Cryptic." Felicia was trying to lighten up the mood.

"Yep. Crazy people can't tell time."

"And even if they can, the intake guards take their watches anyway," Samantha said.

"Good point." She had to give credit to Samantha for making her smile.

She looked at the light refracting from the shattered glass of the window, watching its crooked shadow dance on the peeling paint of the cinder block wall. If she lost this trial, the consequences would certainly be devastating.

When a guard came to get the girls out of the waiting area, the gravity of the situation seemed to hit all of them at once. They silently followed him into the courtroom. All three dragged their feet, and the slurred sound of their steps, coupled with the rattling of the guard's keys, was maddening.

She composed herself by taking a deep breath before entering the courtroom. She was half expecting to see her parents there and had mixed emotions about their absence. If they were there, it would have confirmed Mitchell's allegations about their evil doings. But the fact that they weren't just confirmed her suspicions of their blatant apathy regarding her fate and well-being.

Based on her experience of other New York State courtrooms, she expected to see lots of defendants and attorneys waiting on the benches in the back, like a perverse congregation of the DMV. But she was surprised that she recognized everyone she saw.

The two psychiatrists who had 2PCed her were there. There was also the doctor she had met the first morning at Schneider's. Her nutritionist was also there. And sitting in the back was Nurse Ratched from Hillside. It was like a sick episode of *This Is Your Life*.

One of the psychiatrists was called to the stand first. He testified to her delusions of travel and cited her low body weight as an indicator of further mental distress.

The second psychiatrist made the same claims. They had obviously rehearsed their testimony in anticipation of the trial.

The doctor from Schneider's testified that she had tried to check out of the hospital before further tests could be administered.

And Nurse Ratched was called to the stand to report on her behavior at Hillside. Shockingly, she stated that she was a model patient, popular among the other inmates, and nondisruptive. The nurse did mention the stolen hamburger at the Fourth of July barbecue, but this was presented as a minor issue.

Finally, the defendant was called to the stand.

The judge asked her how she felt about her weight.

She was honest. "I feel like a skeleton. I'm uncomfortable and rickety. I'm looking forward to the opportunity to nurture and nourish myself back to a healthy weight."

"So, you don't think you're fat?" The judge looked straight at her with one eyebrow raised.

"How could I think I'm fat?!" She was truly surprised by the question. "I can't even find clothes small enough to fit me! I think I'm vastly underweight."

The judge responded to her honesty. "Based on the testimony of the defendant, and the evidence of travel documents, I rule that this woman is mentally competent." The judge banged his gavel and then looked at her directly. "But I do think that she is too thin."

There was a rush of murmurs through the courtroom.

"Quiet! Everyone, quiet!" The judge banged his gavel again. "I can see that my ruling is unpopular. But I cannot in good conscience rule that a psychologically stable woman be held as a ward of the state." The judge stood from his seat. "That is all."

Felicia grabbed her by the arm and squeezed. "That's it, baby! You're free!"

"I can go." It was just as much a question as it was a statement.

"You can go!" Felicia affirmed. "Let's get out of here!"

Samantha said nothing as the three rose to leave the courthouse.

The recently released young woman followed her friends through the building and out the exit door. There was a nice little landscaped area and a circular drive. *This* was the front entrance. She knew she had come in the back. There was no way that the dumpster area was the front of the courthouse.

Once in the driveway, Samantha lit a cigarette and drew heavily from it.

"Are you going to get your car?" she asked Samantha.

"I'm not sure what I'm supposed to do now," Samantha answered.

"What you're supposed to do? You're supposed to celebrate with me. Give me back my stuff. Maybe even drive me into the city."

"Yeah." Samantha stubbed out the cigarette. "I guess." Samantha palmed the car keys and shuffled away toward the parking lot.

"I don't know your story with that girl, but I don't think she's happy you were released." Felicia sounded concerned.

"I know. It's weird, right? Like she was secretly rooting for the other team."

"Not so secretly," Felicia replied.

Samantha pulled up in her teal Saturn and left the car idling while stepping out of the driver's side door.

"So, I guess I have to take you to Hillside to get your stuff?" Samantha lit another cigarette.

"That would be nice." She was trying to analyze Samantha's odd behavior. "Yes, please. Will you drive me into the city? Will you take me home?"

"I'll take you somewhere. Just get in the fucking car."

She didn't want to get in Samantha's car, but she also didn't want to stand in the middle of Creedmore with the possibility that the judge could change his mind and keep her here. Not that it could happen, but everything else this week was so weird, why not?

She got into the passenger's seat and looked at Felicia. "Are you getting in?"

Felicia looked freaked out. "No. I'm not getting in the middle of whatever fucked-up shit is about to go down. I'm taking the bus back to the city." Felicia walked over to the car and gave her a kiss on the mouth. "You call me if you make it home."

"*When* I make it home."

"Right." Felicia glared at Samantha. "When you make it home."

She and Samantha packed up her belongings at Hillside. She said goodbye to Rachel and all her other "friends" and left the floor.

Samantha was quiet as they drove along the Long Island Expressway. Samantha actually seemed angry with her. She didn't know why; her "friend" had come to the courthouse to support her, right?

"So, we'll pick up my stuff and then you can help me get back to the city?" She tried to break the silence. Plus, she really wanted to know the itinerary.

"I can't drive you to the city."

"The train station then?"

"We'll see." Samantha dismissed her question and lit another cigarette. "First, I have to pick up my daughter from daycare."

"Great! I haven't seen her since the wedding! How is Jean?"

"Jane."

"Sorry."

"Well, she still makes me play that CD for her. You know, the song you wrote to her on the day she was born." Samantha seemed to be warming up again.

"You still have that CD?" She was flattered.

"I had to make copies of it. So I'd have one in the house, one in the car. Jane loves the song." Samantha turned to her. "It's a beautiful lullaby. Why did you stop writing?"

"I ran out of words."

She hated when people questioned her writing cessation. She hated writing. It was solitary and isolating. And she felt manic when she entrenched in the process. She was glad that people still listened to her music, but she was more glad that after several years, people had finally stopped asking her to write more.

Samantha pulled into a strip mall parking lot. "Hungry? It's lunchtime. You must be hungry."

She couldn't tell if it was a question or an order. But she said, "You have my wallet."

"I know. Lunch is on me."

"I appreciate that you're offering, but aren't you strapped for cash? I really wouldn't feel comfortable letting—"

Samantha cut her off. "I came into a little extra cash recently."

She knew that Samantha wouldn't steal from her money shoe, and Samantha's husband was a pothead who lay like a beached whale on the couch all day. Where did Samantha get extra money? For a fleeting moment, she felt a little paranoia. Was she being set up again?

The two girls ordered matching lunches of chicken salad sandwiches and fruit smoothies. They shared a diet soda.

They drove while they ate, and the food provided a barrier to possible conversation. That was probably Samantha's plan, to facilitate silence. Samantha seemed to be trying hard to keep a secret from her, but a slip would come soon.

She sat in the car while Samantha ran into the daycare building to retrieve Jane. After Jane was strapped into the carseat in the rear, she had someone to focus on other than Samantha.

"Hi, Jane! Do you remember me? I was at the hospital the day you were born!"

Jane covered her face with her hands in a dramatic display of shyness.

"Of course you don't remember that. You're such a big girl now, and that was when you were a little baby!" She was able to flip her demeanor back to her nannying days quickly.

Jane giggled.

"I knew it! I knew you remembered your auntie! I knew it!"

"Jane, this is the auntie who wrote you your lullaby," Samantha chimed in. "Do you love your lullaby?"

Jane nodded vigorously. She didn't seem to speak much. Maybe that would be a good thing, if she could maintain it through the teenage years. The way Samantha and Jane's father fought, though, she doubted that Jane would grow up to be any more well adjusted than the knocked-up young Samantha or the just-released-from-the-psych-ward aunt. Good luck, Jane.

Samantha's family of three occupied a tiny one-bedroom apartment above a garage in the next town over from where the two girls had grown up. Samantha hadn't gone very far, geographically speaking.

The apartment was strewn with toys and beer cans. There was a bong sitting on the coffee table in front of the ratty old couch.

"He's still getting high?" She really was concerned for Samantha's well-being in this toxic marriage.

"He says he's going to get a job." Samantha was good at making excuses. "But his back hurts, and he has a heart condition."

"Isn't he twenty-one? He's younger than we are!"

Samantha changed the subject. "Anyway, I have to start getting dinner ready, and we have to find your stuff—"

"You're going to start dinner? Sam, I have to go home! I need to get back to the city."

"I know, I know." Samantha was hiding something from her. "We'll get you home. No sweat. I just have some wife and mother duties."

She raised an eyebrow and stared at Samantha, who avoided eye contact. "Uh huh. So, where's my stuff?"

"I'll get it soon." Samantha was beginning to sweat. "Hey, you play with Jane."

At least when she was a prisoner at Hillside, she knew the drill. Here at Samantha's house, she was also stuck but now clueless too.

Samantha made a superficial attempt to remove the top layer of filth from the house. She wasn't really cleaning; it was more of a delay tactic. Samantha was burning time. Something was up.

She sat on the floor and played dolls with Jane. Samantha was bumbling around in the kitchen pretending to cook.

"Sam?" She looked at the clock on the microwave. "It's, like, after 5 o'clock. If I'm going to take a train, I think it's time to start moving."

"Wow! It's that late?" Samantha was a lousy actress. "Are you hungry? Do you want something to eat before you go? I have some of my mother's eggplant parmesan left over in the fridge. You always loved my mother's eggplant parmesan."

"Sam, I have to go home. Please. Where's my stuff?"

Defeated, Samantha opened a small cabinet storage space in the corner of the living room. Out came the laptop, the cell phone, everything.

Samantha handed her the Givenchy sack last of all.

"Did you look inside?" She knew Samantha had to have gone through everything.

Samantha blushed a deep fuchsia. "No?"

"Is that a question?" She laughed at Samantha's embarrassment.

Samantha said nothing but palmed the car keys, took Jane by the hand, and walked to the front door.

"So, we're leaving?" She was excited to get home.

"You wanted to leave, so we're leaving."

"Yea! Back to the city. Finally, a night in my own bed. It's been three weeks since I've slept in my own bed." She was surprised when she said the number out loud. It seemed like an eternity since she had left to meet Mitchell in San Francisco.

"Let's get in the car." Samantha was being creepily dismissive.

When Samantha began to drive east, she became really concerned.

"Sam, where are you going?"

"I can't take you to the city. I can't, I can't, I can't." Samantha's eyes began to well up with tears.

"Is this because you're worried about me? Don't worry! The doctors said I was healthy, and hey, I managed to survive the loony bin without losing my mind, right!"

"I'm not worried about your health." Samantha was beginning to confess.

"Then what the hell is this all about? Why won't you let me go home?"

"I need the money."

"What money?" All the bad things in her life seemed to be rooted in money.

"Your mother was going to pay me to keep you in Hillside." Samantha was hyperventilating. "I'm sorry, I'm sorry, I'm sorry."

"You sold me out? You're my oldest and best friend!" She really was shocked to the core of her being. "You were going to offer up my freedom for your wallet?"

"You don't understand. There's no money. It's just so . . . hard." Samantha was sniffling so loudly it was difficult to hear. "And it's so much money! And your mother said you were sick anyway. And you ruined my wedding. . . ."

"Oh. My. God." This wasn't compassion at all. Was this some sick game of revenge? She was getting scared. "Where are you taking me?"

"To your parents' house."

"To my parents' house?! Are you insane? They'll rip me to shreds!" She tried to remain calm. "Please, just leave me at the train station."

"I'm taking you to your parents' house. I'm sorry. But I need the money."

"What, I'm some fucking bounty to you?" She looked toward the backseat. "Sorry, Jane, bad language."

"Jane's used to bad language." What a sad sentiment.

"So you're really, honest to God, taking me to my parents' house."

"Yes."

"After they had me committed."

"Yes."

"Because I 'ruined' your wedding?"

"Yes. And the money too."

"I hope it's a lot of money, Sam. I hope it's a lot of fucking money. 'Cause it was the price of your soul."

They drove through the center of town, and Samantha pulled off to drive through a side street. This old town had been designed with service roads leading to all the houses, presumably to keep the help out of sight. Now it just meant that the residents didn't have to watch the garbage trucks in *front* of their houses.

The service road held many good memories for Samantha and her. It was where they used to keep the kegs and other banned substances when they had parties at her house in high school. Her parents never minded; as long as contraband wasn't technically on their property, they turned a blind eye. She used to think they were cool.

But now the service road was scary. Samantha drove up behind the fence and put the car into park.

"You're not pulling into the driveway?" She was shocked that Samantha was such a traitor. And a wimpy one at that.

"I don't want your parents to know I brought you here."

"So take me to the train station!"

"I can't. I made a deal."

"They don't even know that I'm out of Hillside. You can get your blood money, I can go home, everyone wins."

"I'm sorry. This is the last stop. Get out of my car." Samantha couldn't even look at her.

"You're really doing this? You're really leaving me here?"

"Get out." Samantha popped the trunk.

She got out of the car and took her luggage out of the back. Samantha revved the engine and peeled off on the unpaved service road before her betrayed friend had even shut the trunk.

Out of the frying pan, back into the fire.

Thirty-Six

She left her luggage in the driveway and let herself in through the unlocked back door to her parents' house. No one was inside, but she heard voices coming from the porch off the kitchen.

She opened the sliding door and found her parents having cocktails around the glass dining table. The grill was smoking, and she could see that they were getting ready for dinner.

Her mother looked up first. "What the *fuck* is she doing here?"

"They declared me mentally competent. I'm sane."

Her mother turned to her father. "They let her out! You said they wouldn't let her out! How the fuck. . . ." Her mother's voice trailed off in rage. "Why the fuck would they let her out?!"

"The judge ruled that I was mentally fit for discharge."

"Is this a fucking joke?" Her mother was shrieking at her father. "Say something! Is this a joke? Can they do this?"

Her father sat silent, almost paralyzed by the information he was processing. And her mother's screaming wasn't helping him think.

Her mother turned to her. "Get out of my house before I call the police! Get out, get out, get out!"

"You're throwing me out? You haven't seen me in almost a year! You're just going to throw me out?"

"You're not going to die on my property. Get out!" Her mother's eyes were bright red. There was a flash of evil in them.

"Why do you think I'm going to die? The doctor's don't think I'm going to die. The judge doesn't think I'm going to die. Why do you keep saying that?" It was best not to argue with her mother, but this whole situation seemed a bit *Twilight Zone*-ish.

"You're going to die because if you don't get off my property, I'm going to kill you!" Her mother reached for one of the kitchen knives they had been using to prep dinner for the grill.

Her father finally stepped in. "Put down the knife," he said to his irate wife, his voice calm. To his daughter, he said, "We need you to leave now."

"You need me to leave? A week ago, you were begging me to stay! Now you want me to leave?"

"A week ago was different. We didn't know you'd be able to get out of the—"

"So it was all planned. All premeditated. You were trying to lock me up. What, for the money?"

"It wasn't all planned!" Her father was earnest. "We didn't think you'd go to Hillside!"

"Really, you tell the State that your twenty-three-year-old daughter is insane, and you're surprised that she gets sent to a mental hospital?"

"You were supposed to stay in the children's hospital. Just until the paperwork went through." Her father really thought this was a legitimate defense. "But then your friend Mitchell stepped in with his attorneys, and they bullied the hospital. The hospital got scared. They had to transfer you."

"Don't blame this on Mitchell! You had a carefully conceived plan, and now you're surprised because it didn't work out as you had envisioned."

"You need to leave now."

"And go where?"

"Anywhere but here. Get off our property." Her puppet father mimicked his wife's orders.

"Okay. I'm leaving. Enjoy your dinner."

She went back into the driveway and sat down with her luggage. Her mother appeared moments later.

"The driveway is my property. Get off."

"You want me to sit out in the street?"

"I don't care where you go, as long as it's not here."

She picked up her bags and repositioned herself in the grass surrounding the public pond across the street from her parents' house. She dug around for her cell phone and called the local cab company to get her to the train station.

The receptionist for the cab company informed her that the last cab had stopped operating, and the last train to the city had left for the evening. She arranged for transportation home the next day, to pick her up at 6 a.m.

She hung up the phone and watched as the lights went out in her parents' windows. She actually found herself missing the shelter of Hillside.

She slept fitfully on her luggage in the dew-laden grass. She woke up tired and wet and a little bit cold. Even though it was summer, sleeping outside could chill a person to the core.

The honking geese around the pond awakened her as the sun rose. It was a beautiful morning.

She thought about going into her parents' house to pee, but then she realized that she didn't have to pee. She hadn't eaten or drunk anything the evening before. She was hungry and dehydrated, but she didn't have to go to the bathroom.

She watched the sun rise and tried to feign nonchalance as she waved to the early morning joggers. Seeing a well-dressed woman with expensive luggage camped out on the grass was probably a curious sight for passersby.

She was hoping that her cab would come before her parents came down the driveway to retrieve the morning paper. Unfortunately, she had no such luck.

Her father, fully dressed and ready for work, sauntered down the driveway, clutching a mug of coffee in one hand. As he reached for the rolled up newspapers, he pretended not to notice her.

A few minutes later, her mother came down the driveway in her bathrobe and slippers, with hair disheveled and wearing a pair of glasses. When had her mother started wearing glasses? Her parents were getting old.

Her mother walked right to the foot of the driveway and tried to make small talk across the street.

"So, you're going back to the city now?"

She said nothing.

"Are you waiting for a cab?"

Did her mother really expect her to answer?

"Oh, you're playing catatonic, huh?"

She kept her eyes fixed on the horizon.

As though her prayers had been answered, her cab drove up at just that minute. The driver loaded her bags into the trunk, and she made her way to the backseat.

While she was trying to shut the door, her mother sprinted across the street and tried to grab her head in a physically aggressive way.

"Come on, give me a hug." Her mother manhandled her head painfully. "I want a hug. Or a kiss!"

Was her mother serious? Could any human being be as mentally ill as her mother? Even Rachel from Hillside seemed sane compared to this bizarre display.

She shook her head free from her mother's tight grasp, reached for the door handle, and tried to pull the cab door closed.

"Oh, come on! You're not going to stay longer? You're going to leave like this? Catatonic?"

She was pretty sure that her mother was misusing the word catatonic. Catatonic people are not blatantly ignoring other people. She was too shocked to speak. That's not catatonia. That's common logic.

She finally got the door closed, and her mother banged the window with both fists, shouting, "I love you! Get home safely! I love you!"

She realized that Mitchell, crazy and mean and unpredictable as he was, was the only stable figure in her life. That was not a settling sentiment. Maybe she should have stayed at Hillside.

Thirty-Seven

Her apartment was hot, and the air was stale. The windows had been closed in her absence for nearly the entire month of June. She peeled off her clothing and opened all the windows.

She took a long, cool shower, and then spent a while staring at her own eyes in the mirror as she struggled to focus on brushing her hair. She had always had a strong and fervent internal dialogue flowing through her mind. But as she looked into her own eyes, she saw only emptiness. There was nothing beyond the pupils.

Naked, she walked into her bedroom and sat at the foot of her bed. She decided that this was a good time to cry. She prepared for the tears, but none came. This was it. She was finally empty. She felt nothing.

It almost seemed that she had left her body long ago. Her abused and labored mind had conceded to merely observing her life as though it were a movie being shown in a theater with no exit.

She lay back on her bed and stretched out her arms above her head. She let out a long yawn. It wasn't from tiredness, or stress, or even apathy. She yawned from what was now clearly a pervasive state of ennui.

Nothing could shock her anymore. There was no one to trust, nothing to love, no reason to wake up in the morning. Except for the fear that she wouldn't.

She wasn't afraid to die; enough people had told her in the past month that her mortality was imminent. She was more afraid that she was missing something.

It's hard to complain of first-class international travel and couture fashion extending all the way to one's luggage. And it's hard to complain of an abusive companion when one voluntarily returns to his home daily. It's even hard to complain of a surplus of female lovers and acolytes who will follow you, in one case, all the way to the psych ward. On paper, she lived a charmed life of sorts.

But her head pounded.

It pounded with self-loathing. It pounded with contempt for Mitchell. It pounded with disgust for the women who so willingly offered her their bodies. It pounded with sadness for a family who had never loved her and were now trying to erase her from the family tree. It pounded for the friends who could be bought for treason. It pounded for the pain that her bony body felt every time it came in contact with anything outside her own skin.

And it pounded because she had no reason to go to sleep tonight, and no reason to wake up in the morning.

She tasted blood and jumped off her bed to look in the mirror. She was sickened to see blood caking in the right corner of her mouth. There was a huge open sore where her lips met. It throbbed, it hurt, and it bled.

She considered calling her primary care physician, but just one day out of Hillside, she thought that a medical emergency was best dealt with privately.

But she had no one else to call.

On the Internet, she researched bleeding lips and massive oral sores. They were signs of fatal malnutrition, most often seen in starvation victims in Africa.

How ironic that her hospital stay had made her sicker than she had been when she had first admitted herself to the emergency room.

She put Vaseline on her sore and wore big sunglasses as she walked to her neighborhood pharmacy. She bought two cases of Ensure and returned directly home.

She sat upright under the covers of her bed and sipped bottle after bottle of Ensure through a straw. She made a half-assed attempt to watch television. But really, she just dozed in and out of consciousness.

The next few days were unmemorable and isolated. As each day passed, she was surprised that she was alive for every sunrise.

Her sore did not get better, and another one appeared on the left side of her mouth. She was at a loss for what to do.

She visited her home psychiatrist. Her visit was to serve two purposes: she wanted to deliver the paperwork from Schneider's and Hillside, and she wanted to find answers for her current state of nothingness.

Her psychiatrist was a beautiful, Nordic, blonde septuagenarian who specialized in body issues, mania, and apathy. The doctor had a very matter-of-fact, no-nonsense approach to medicine, and the patient responded to that.

Looking over the paperwork, the doctor said, in a thick accent, "Oh no, no. They put you in a psychiatric hospital, but you are not crazy! That is not the place for you."

"But I feel so sick! And my mouth is bleeding. Don't I have an eating disorder?"

"No, no. You do not have an eating disorder. Your body is fighting your mind, and the two are trying to destroy each other! You need balance, structure, order. Not a facility."

"Balance? Structure? Order?" She tried to process this. "Should I get a job?"

"No. You cannot hold a job. You can barely hold up your own head!" The doctor leaned against the side of the giant desk in the office. "But you do need a reason to wake up every morning. You have an active mind, and an active lifestyle, and the two are in conflict. You need a lifestyle that nurtures your mind. Then your mind will stop cannibalizing your body."

"My mind is killing me?" She was trying to process the doctor's theories, but she was having difficulty with the practical application.

"You have no reason to live, and your mind is angry. So it is punishing you." The doctor walked behind the desk and rifled through the papers. "But it will not kill you."

"My mind is pushing me to the brink of death?" She thought she must be misunderstanding.

"Your mind will push you close, but you won't fall all the way." The doctor picked up one of Schneider's medical forms. "Your pulse races when you sleep."

"They told me that."

"Do you wake up wet?"

"Like, sweaty?"

"Yes, are you wet when you wake up?"

"I'm soaked."

"Your mind is racing at night. It is eating at your body. We need to slow your mind and strengthen your body."

"You mean medication?"

"Wait here." The doctor left the room.

Several minutes later, she returned with a veritable gift bag of prescription cocktails.

"So, you want me to be drugged?"

The doctor ignored the question and instead looked closely at her face. "Those sores— they're new?"

"Yes, they came from Hillside." She looked at the ground. This was a humiliating doctor's appointment, but at least this doctor was the first one to actually communicate with her.

"You have hypomania. You will always be stable until there is a drastic change in your surroundings. To your mind and body, Hillside equaled death. Pay at the reception. I want to see you in two weeks."

"That's it? I'm through?"

"Take the medicine. Feel good. Get up with the sun. Walk a dog."

"I don't have a dog."

"Get a dog." The doctor shuffled her out of the office.

In a trance, she walked back to her apartment. At any other point in her life, she would have thought that that was a strange doctor's visit. But after the past month, it was one of the most normal interpersonal exchanges of dialogue she'd experienced.

Thirty-Eight

"I'm home! Come over. We need to talk!" Mitchell was practically shouting into the phone.

"You're back?" She responded groggily. Her new medicine made her sleepy all the time. But, on the plus side, she had gained weight, and her mouth sores were healing.

"I'm back. Oh, and Laura gives terrible blowjobs. I thought she was prequalified?"

"Do you want to continue this in person?" she asked.

"Yes. In person. Come over." Mitchell stopped for a moment. "What's wrong with your voice? Are you high?"

"I think I'm on psychotropics."

"Oh!" This didn't faze Mitchell a bit. "Good. See you in twenty minutes. Wear heels! I need beauty!"

She hated herself for going over to Mitchell's even though she knew he was not a positive presence in her life. But she had nothing else to do. And she had no intention of getting a dog.

As she walked to the subway, she was proud of herself for having remembered to send out, and pick up, her dry cleaning. Mitchell would be happy to see her clean and pressed.

"What the hell happened to your mouth?" Mitchell stared at her face as she entered his apartment.

This was not the happy reunion she had anticipated. "I acquired some sores during my tenure at Hillside."

"Well, after Laura's terrible blowjobs, I was looking forward to some of your skillful efforts." Mitchell squinted to examine her sores. "But looking at that!" Mitchell gasped dramatically. "I don't want some flesh-eating virus to devour my penis."

She had to laugh. "I don't think it's a flesh-eating virus, Mitchell." Although she was relieved to be excused from blowjob duty.

"How do you know? Have you seen a doctor?" He was legitimately concerned, but he was also hamming it up for dramatic effect.

"Actually, yes. Remember my Norwegian or Swedish or whatever the hell she is psychiatrist? Dr. Kaala?"

"Yes! Dr. Kaala!" Mitchell was really overacting his enthusiasm. But it was amusing. "How is our friend Dr. Kaala? How did she feel about Hillside?"

"Well, she thought the whole thing was mishandled." She chose her words wisely. "At least, for me."

"For you?"

"Because she doesn't think I have an eating disorder."

"Praise God!" Mitchell had a real tear streaming down his face as he extended his hands. Sometimes she forgot that he had been raised an Orthodox Jew. But every once in a while, he behaved in such a way as to remind her. "Thanks, God!" Mitchell was sincere.

"Anyway, she said that my mind is cannibalizing my body because I have hypomania and an unstructured life."

Mitchell nodded as though he understood this information. But he didn't. "So what does that mean?"

"Well, Dr. Kaala gave me one idea, other than some drugs."

"Great! And?"

"She said I should get a dog."

"And eat it?"

"Fuck you."

Thirty-Nine

The usual cast of fucktoys filtered in and out of the apartment. She and Mitchell were not as focused on finding new pussy as perfecting the old. Betty was driving Mitchell's BMW out to the house in San Francisco in exchange for ten thousand dollars. Mitchell's companion didn't really understand how that transaction had been arranged, but she didn't ask. She did know, however, that Mitchell had been seriously pissed off while driving the 911 during their recent trip to San Francisco, so his sending another car out west did not surprise her.

Felicia hadn't contacted her since the uncomfortable moment in the Creedmore parking lot. And she certainly wasn't going to contact Felicia.

Other girls came and went. The fucked, they sucked, they left.

Mitchell was still nervous about her mouth sores. He was convinced that they were contagious lesions, and she didn't really care to correct him. It gave her a bit of respite, anyway.

Instead, she ruled over the drones of pussy who walked in and out of the door. Ass in the air, ready to take her dildo in the ass and Mitchell's cock in their mouths. Sluts.

Their days rolled into each other. Mitchell would send her out for wine, they'd order sushi from the same delivery restaurant, he would pass out. Sometimes Mitchell would awaken with a craving for Kit Kats, and she'd run to the drugstore to buy a fun-size sack. Mitchell would eat the whole bag and fall back asleep.

They never went out anymore. If she ever met new pussy prospects, she just met up with them at the Starbucks and determined quickly if there was even a point in moving forward.

Life at Mitchell's apartment was just as boring as life at Hillside. And, she admitted to herself, it was just as confining.

"I'm bored." Mitchell was lying across the arms of his black leather chair in his boxers.

"You had good sex yesterday."

"Yes. What was her name?"

"Why would I know?"

"I love that you hate the bitches." Mitchell laughed, and repeated, "I love that you hate the bitches." Then he sat up. "Hey, do I have anymore Kit Kats?"

"No. Do you want me to get some?"

Mitchell thought for a moment. "No. Let's go to Tokyo tomorrow."

"Okay." A change of scenery was exactly what they needed.

"Great. You book it. I have a headache." Mitchell lay back down across the chair. He didn't have a headache; he had a hangover. But at least it mellowed him out.

"Okay. I'll get on that now. Did you want to take any pussy with us?"

Mitchell thought for a moment. "No." He laughed. "Did I tell you what that crazy bitch Laura asked me when we were on safari?"

He had told her this story several times, but she decided that it was always better to act surprised. "No, what?"

"That stupid bitch was cold the first night, so she asked me, 'Does this tent have heat?'" Mitchell's laugh boomed. *"Does this tent have heat?!* Can you believe it?"

"So, no girls on the trip, then?"

"What, so some other crazy bitch can ask if the sushi is cooked? Or if the Kobe beef is vegetarian?" Mitchell was really amusing himself. "No, thanks. No more travel bitches."

"Okay."

"Just you."

"Just me what?"

"You're my only travel bitch." Mitchell's voice softened. "You're my only friend." His eyes closed, and he passed out.

She left the room and went into the office to make the travel arrangements. She wrote everything down for Mitchell and left a note on the glass coffee table near his chair.

She took forty dollars out of his fag bag and wrote that down on the note as well. Then she went home to pack.

It was late summer now, so she remembered to bring heavier clothing than she had brought on their previous trip to Japan. She even brought one of her mink coats, just to make Mitchell happy, even though she knew she most certainly would not need it.

They arrived at Narita at noon, so they had plenty of time to figure out their plans once inside Tokyo. After customs, Mitchell found an Internet hub and logged into his email account. He handed her two thousand U.S. dollars and asked her to buy yen.

She returned with a stack of bills, and Mitchell barely eyed it to make sure it was the right amount. She was actually more trustworthy than she liked to admit. It was often easy to steal from Mitchell but never wise. Plus, she just had no desire to incur any more bad karma in her life.

Mitchell eventually logged off of his account, seemingly dissatisfied with whatever he had, or had not, received in his inbox. He wheeled his luggage off and exited through one of the doors in the airport. She followed.

Then Mitchell wheeled his belongings back in through the adjacent entrance door in the same spot. She was confused, but she followed.

He walked through the terminal to the next exit and repeated the same pattern. Again, she followed.

He picked up his pace. She quickened hers.

This went on for about a half hour, and they exited and entered no fewer than twenty doors. Both were out of breath, and now both were irritable.

Mitchell glared at her. "Why are you following me?"

"What do you mean, *following you*? We just got off a plane together. I'm not following you. I'm *with* you." She had no idea what game Mitchell was trying to play.

"I'm sorry. I have no idea who you are. Shall I get the police?"

"Mitchell! What's going on? What are you doing?" She struggled to catch her breath.

"How do you know my name? Who are you? Why are you following me?"

"Mitchell, seriously. This isn't funny. Come on. Are we taking a taxi into Tokyo or not?"

Mitchell looked at her dead in the face. He really seemed to have no idea who she was. This was creepy.

The two of them maintained the deadlock face to face until Mitchell broke the silence. "I think we'll take the train." And he wheeled off as though nothing had happened.

They were in Tokyo for four days, but Mitchell never left the hotel room. Then he decided they would return home.

"I thought Tokyo would be good for me, but I think it's only making me worse."

"Making you worse?" She wasn't sure what Mitchell was trying to say.

"I hate my life. I hate myself. I can't see my son. I have no purpose. And I drink too much. And I'm no better halfway around the world than I am in my own apartment back in New York. So, it's time to go home." Mitchell poured himself a tall helping of sochu and downed it in one gulp. "So, we're going back tomorrow." He wiped his mouth with the back of his sleeve, and rolled over in his bed to go back to sleep.

Mitchell shook her awake at 3:30 a.m.

"Let's go get some fish to bring on the plane!"

She had no idea what Mitchell was talking about, but she duly got out of bed and threw on some clothes. "We're going to Tsukiji?"

"We have an 8 a.m. flight. So we'll have to do Tsukiji takeout style!" He was full of energy. Maybe four straight days of sleep and eight bottles of sochu, not to mention the wine chasers, had reinvigorated him.

Even though the vendors at Tsukiji only sold to retailers, Mitchell and his companion were able to convince a few to sell them some trays of uni and ana-go. Better than raw fish, these delicacies might actually travel well to the airport.

There were no cabs outside the fish market at 4 a.m., so they began to walk back. At some point, Mitchell's demeanor began to change. He seemed to become increasingly angry, paranoid, and frustrated. Maybe it was alcohol withdrawal. Maybe he was just crazy.

"I'm really unhappy, Link!"

Great. He was calling her Link again.

"Why are you unhappy, Mitchell?" She feigned concern. She really didn't care.

"Everything in my life is awful. I have nothing. I have no one. I'm alone."

"You have me." She meant that.

"And what do you do for me? Consume? Exhaust me? Make me deal with your fucked-up parents? Bring me mediocre pussy? Seriously, what do you do for me?" Mitchell was fidgeting as he walked.

"I guess just those things, Mitchell."

"That's right!" His voice was now booming, and he stopped walking. "All you do is take! All anyone does is take! But who cares about me? You don't care about me!" He grabbed her by the hair and she fell to her knees. "You don't care about me!" He kneed her in the jaw and walked away.

Crumpled in a pile on the sidewalk in Tokyo, she lay crying in the fetal position. Luckily, it was so early in the morning that there were very few passersby. Regardless, she didn't have the energy to be embarrassed.

Her body shook from physical pain, mental exhaustion, and, above all, her broken spirit. There was no reason to get up off the sidewalk.

"Link! Link! You stupid bitch! You're embarrassing yourself!" Mitchell yelled from the far end of the block. "Get up before you end up in the Tokyo version of Hillside. *Get up!*"

She slowly dragged herself to her feet. She touched her face to check for bleeding. There was none. She brushed the dust off her pants and staggered toward Mitchell.

"What was that about?" Mitchell yelled more than asked.

"What?"

"You falling down on the sidewalk! Imbecile! What was that melodrama?"

"You threw me to the sidewalk! You hit me! You—" His face was blank. Was it possible that he had forgotten so quickly? Or was this part of his strategy for making her think that *she* was the crazy one?

"I what?" Mitchell grabbed the back of her neck firmly with one hand and squeezed. "Go on. Finish your sentence. Your accusation. I *what?*"

"Nothing." Her voice squeaked. "Let's just go to the airport."

"Yes." Mitchell brushed off his sportscoat as though pushing away the filth that had just transpired. "Let's."

When they arrived back at JFK, it was the middle of the night. She was hoping that Mitchell would tell the driver to make two stops, but instead he gave only the address to his apartment. It looked like she'd have to spend another night with him. And he wasn't even drunk enough now to pass out. She thought for a moment whether there was wine in the wine fridge. Maybe Mitchell would begin drinking in the living room and leave her in peace to sleep in the bedroom.

She had no such luck. The moment they walked through the door, Mitchell instructed her to get Betty on the phone.

"I want that bitch here first thing tomorrow morning!" Mitchell screamed.

"Did Betty do something wrong?" She momentarily wished that Mitchell had kept her more up to date on his dealings with Betty so that she'd be better prepared to handle this sort of fallout.

"Just get her here!" Mitchell slammed the door to his office.

Betty arrived early in the morning, carrying the *New York Times*, as per the instructions left in voicemail the night before. Betty and Mitchell exchanged harsh words.

She was impressed with Betty's strength in combating Mitchell. She strained to hear what the fight was about.

Apparently, Betty had cleverly stolen several hundreds of thousands of dollars from Mitchell in a failproof legal manner. It seemed that Mitchell had made an oversight in one of his business dealings with Betty, and Betty was smarter than he had anticipated.

Knowing that he wasn't going to see the money again, Mitchell decided that Betty needed to be punished. She was stripped of her clothes and forced to kneel in the bathtub. Mitchell put his flaccid cock in Betty's mouth and pinched her lips closed around it. When he urinated, it squirted out of Betty's mouth.

When Mitchell finished the punishment, he left Betty naked in a pool of his piss in the bathtub. He found his companion, and with a simple instruction, made her carry out the rest of the punishment. "Toilet time."

She made Betty kneel in front of the toilet with her head through the seat. In order to keep the lid from falling, one must keep one's head up in perfect posture. The knees and feet fall asleep from the pain of pressure against the tile floor, and the back aches from the pose that is necessary to avoid a blow to the head from the seat cover. It's an ideal punishment if sadism is the goal.

"One hour," she told Betty dryly. She liked Betty. She really did. But if Betty stole from Mitchell, she didn't like Betty so much anymore. If anyone were getting that kind of cash out of Mitchell, it should be her. Besides, didn't Betty have a fortune to look forward to inheriting? Bitch.

Forty

"I've decided that I drink too much." Mitchell made a grand proclamation as he refilled his wine glass at lunch at Tino's.

"Really? And?"

"After seeing what happens when one consults doctors—thank you for that insight, by the way—I have decided to try a less medical approach." Mitchell waved his wine glass around. The irony was obviously lost on him.

"So, AA?"

"Pfft! AA! Those crazy, poor, pathetic assholes!" Mitchell took a swig of Chianti. "No! I'm not playing those pathetic games. I'm not an alcoholic. I just drink too much."

"So, what's the plan?"

"Hypnotism."

"Hypnotism. Really." This was even too crazy for her to process.

"Yes. I found a hypnotist who specializes in alcohol. He's going to treat me so that every time I think I want wine, I'm going to drink water."

"Water?" She knew that Mitchell wasn't drunk now, so she was trying to figure out why he sounded so crazy.

"Yes, water!" Mitchell seemed exuberant. "Lots of different water. Think of all the water there is!"

"Water," she repeated incredulously.

"Remember how much you liked the tap water in Athens?"

"Yes—"

"Well, let's find that here!" Mitchell really was excited. She had to give him credit for that.

"Okay, so the wine into water program," she tried to make a joke. "We'll call it the anti-Jesus."

"I love it!" Mitchell loved anything that overtly displayed his Judaism.

"Okay, so the anti-Jesus drinking program starts when?"

"Tomorrow." Mitchell reached into his fag bag and handed her five hundred dollars.

"What's this for?"

"To buy water!" Mitchell said this like it should have been obvious.

"You want five hundred dollars' worth of water? What's wrong with the tap?"

Mitchell ignored her comment. "I want to find my favorite water. I'm going to try every bottle of water there is." He turned and looked at her. "I want you to empty my wine refrigerator and fill it with water."

"You're serious?"

"I'm serious. And I'm excited. Maybe I'll get less fat. Then I can wear my good clothes!"

If she didn't know better, she would have thought Mitchell was high.

She was impressed that Mitchell was trying to stay sober. His apartment was filled with every brand of bottled water available for purchase in New York City. He even had bottles of Ensure for her in the wine refrigerator.

Instead of ordering in or going out to eat, Mitchell had begun cooking for her. Unfortunately, the lack of alcohol in his brain had clouded his judgment even worse than when he was drunk. He would cook her up two pounds of dry pasta, cover it with an entire bulk-size jar of sauce, and then serve it to her on an enormous platter.

He'd then scream at her to eat all of it. "I'm not letting your crazy family blame me for starving you. Eat everything!"

Unfortunately, her stomach would become hyperinflated and unable to process it. She would almost surely begin to retch and throw most of it up.

"That's okay! Puke out half. I'm sure some must be sticking inside anyway!" Mitchell would yell from the living room while she dealt with her misery in the bathroom. "Come here and drink Ensure!"

Sobriety made Mitchell mean and aggressive.

As September settled in, the Jewish holidays approached. Sober, pious Mitchell gave her a diatribe on the importance of reconciling with her family. She had her suspicions that Mitchell had ulterior motives, but she did want the chance for her extended family to see that she had survived her stay at Hillside. Especially because she knew that her parents had most definitely advertised her committal to everyone they saw at her cousin's July wedding.

To celebrate the Jewish New Year, Rosh Hashana dinner was being hosted by the wife of one of her father's many first cousins in Scarsdale. It was an easy train ride and a good excuse to get out of the city for an evening. Even though she had RSVPed, her extended family was clearly surprised to see her.

But her parents were the most surprised of all. So surprised, in fact, that they blatantly ignored her the entire night. She tried to say hello but was swiftly countered by the cold shoulder of their loathing and disappointment.

The evening was a failure. She spent most of the night sitting alone in a corner. No one wanted to speak to her. It may have been due to their fear and ignorance, but she felt like she had been stricken with leprosy, and they were acting as though she had broken out of quarantine.

"Rosh Hashana was awful, Mitchell," she told him as they sat in his living room watching Fox News.

"It couldn't have been that bad. I'm sure everyone was happy to see you alive."

"No one would even speak to me. So much for 'sweetness' in the New Year." She began to cry.

"Oh, baby, come here and sit on my lap."

She sat across his knees, and Mitchell put his arms around her in a big bear hug.

"I just don't get it, Mitchell. I don't know what more they want me to do. I think my family has washed their hands of me. Now they're just resentful that I'm not dead yet."

"It's true, baby. Some families can't deal with a family member in crisis." Mitchell buried his head in her back. "Especially when they are so much to blame for causing the crisis."

"How do you mean?"

"Well, for all of the years that they abused you mentally and physically, now they have to see how that manifested itself." Mitchell squeezed her more tightly. "They're ashamed and embarrassed. And they wish that you would just go away. It's easier for some people to talk about the child they lost than to confront the child they failed to fully destroy."

She buried her head in his neck and cried hard. "They didn't destroy me. I'm not destroyed. I'm a person, and they treat me like a freak."

"They don't understand. They don't understand your lifestyle, they don't understand the wealth you've been exposed to, they don't understand the power you have over women. So they hate you."

"I don't want them to hate me."

"I know. But they do." Mitchell held her head in his hands. "Who loves you, baby?"

"You do." She said it, but it didn't offer her any more comfort.

"That's right. I love you. Only I love you. Fuck the rest of them. Bring in the New Year with sweetness."

"Sweetness," she repeated, her voice barely audible. "Sweetness."

Forty-One

In the two days immediately following Rosh Hashana, her weight plummeted by six pounds. She felt lifeless, and even walking down her stairs was a challenge.

"My dear, you're looking positively frail."

"I feel positively frail." She tried to think of any changes in patterns in her behavior that could have accounted for such a rapid weight loss, but she could think of none.

"My dear, I think you're dying of a broken spirit." Sober Mitchell made a lot of sense.

"But how do I restore a broken spirit? Where do I turn? I feel out of options."

"I think it's time to go to see Dr. Kaala."

She was due for a follow-up appointment anyway. And a rapid decrease in her already small frame was definitely a red flag worthy of a trip to the psychiatrist.

She was able to get a time slot for later that afternoon. She filled out the questionnaire left for her in the office while she waited for the doctor.

How do you feel today? Please circle one.
She circled *sad*.
How did you sleep last night?
She circled *not well*.
How tired do you feel when you go to sleep?
She circled *exhausted*.
How rested do you feel when you wake up?
She circled *not at all*.
How are your current relationships with your loved ones?
She circled *strained*.
Is there anything else you would like me to know as we commence today's visit?
She wrote into the blank slot, *I have lost 6 pounds in two days. I feel defeated. Defeated by myself, defeated by others, defeated by my surroundings, and defeated by the world. Please advise.*

Dr. Kaala skimmed the answers on the clipboard and then cut to the business.

"You have lost weight."

"Yes. I was doing pretty well. But then I went to Rosh Hashana, and I lost my positive forward force."

"I see. Family holidays can be very difficult. Is there anything specific that happened at the holiday that affected you?" The doctor was taking notes.

"Nothing ostensibly evil. I was just ignored. My presence seemed to be a burden. On everyone. And there were a lot of people there." She really had no precise moment of evil doing to point out.

"I see. So, you felt abandoned? Unloved?"

"Leprous," she clarified.

"So, you were aggressively avoided by your family?" Dr. Kaala made some notes.

"As an understatement."

Dr. Kaala put down the notepad. "You have a very precarious condition. As I have told you before, your mind is cannibalizing your body. You show no outward signs of mental distress; instead you internalize and will eventually destroy yourself."

"So, you're saying that I should outwardly express my feelings? I don't think that I'm in tune enough with my feelings to do that."

"No, you're not in tune. But your body is. And it wants to feel as small as your heart feels." Dr. Kaala was speaking matter-of-factly but was being truly compassionate.

"So, do I make my heart feel bigger to make my body bigger?"

"It's not that simple. I am going to increase your dosages."

"You're going to further medicate me?"

"I am going to try to make your body and your mind play on the same team." Dr. Kaala left the room and returned with one of her signature goody bags. "The instructions for taking everything are inside."

"You really think that medication is the answer?"

"There is no amount of talk therapy or exercise that can heal the disconnect between your mind and your body. First we heal that, then we make you whole. Okay?" Dr. Kaala held the door to the room open in a signal of dismissal.

The patient left with no more answers than the ones that Mitchell had already given her; when her brain hurt, it destroyed her body. She just wished that she could process feelings like a normal person. If ever one existed.

"So? What did our good friend Dr. Kaala say?" Mitchell had been eagerly awaiting her return.

"Basically what you did. That my heart and mind got heavy, so they worked to destroy my body."

"And? What's in the bag?"

"Higher doses of the same medications she provided last time."

"You don't seem happy."

"I'm not. I don't feel like Dr. Kaala listens to me any more than anyone else. She just gives me bags of medications and sends me on my way."

"Dr. Kaala doesn't need to listen to you. Your problems aren't mental. They're physical manifestations of angst."

"Have you been talking to Dr. Kaala?" she asked, only half-kidding.

She flopped onto the sofa and pulled the blanket up over her head. There had to be a better road to wellness.

Forty-Two

Mitchell spent the next couple of weeks traveling. She wasn't really sure to where, and she really didn't care.

Since he had both stolen and gifted so much money from and to her at varying times throughout the past few months, she had come to the conclusion that money was transient. She decided to spend what she had before she died.

She went online and booked a cruise for a week and a half in October. It was 2004, and there was no Internet access on any of the ships. A cruise seemed like a good excuse to be completely incommunicado from the rest of the world.

She found a trip that left from New York and returned to New York. It didn't really go anywhere, but that didn't matter to her. It was a cold fall, and she didn't plan to spend much time outside the ship. The cruise went up to Nova Scotia and Newfoundland, then down to Bermuda, and then back to New York. The price was fair, and the trip was easy.

Mitchell called her at least four times a day to check in, and she let him know of her cruise plans.

"That's great!" Mitchell sounded genuinely excited for her. "You can get out of your crappy apartment, have a little time to rest. You won't have to worry about food. I think that a cruise is a great idea."

"I'm glad you think so." She was happy to have Mitchell's support.

She had never been on a cruise, but she liked the idea of disappearing for a while. Maybe she'd even get lost in the Bermuda Triangle.

Mitchell returned to New York in the beginning of October for a few days.

"So, tell me about your upcoming trip?" He seemed genuinely interested.

"Well, it doesn't really go anywhere, but it will give me the chance to re-group. Just sort of be alone with myself for a while."

"Well, I think that sounds great."

"Good. I'm looking forward to it."

They sat in silence and watched Fox News. They picked at the sushi lunch that had been delivered.

Mitchell had lost weight. Not a lot, but at least 20 pounds. She was surprised that he had even lost that much considering he still polished off at least two bags of fun-size Kit Kats a day. But who was she to notice anyone else's diet?

At some point, her cell phone rang. She ignored it and kept nibbling on the sushi platter.

"Aren't you going to answer that?" Mitchell asked, his mouth full, with rice dribbling out.

"It's just my uncle."

"Someone from your family is calling you? Answer it, you fool!"

She pressed the button on her cell phone. "Hi, Uncle Norman." Pause. "Uh huh." Pause. "Yes, I'm doing great." Pause. "Right." Pause. "Okay, love you too." She hung up.

"Call him back." Mitchell instructed.

"What?"

"I said, call him back. Now!" Mitchell was losing his temper.

"Why do you want me to call him back? He just called to check in."

"And you lied to him. You are *not* doing great." Mitchell's face was red. "Why didn't you tell me that you had a member of your family who cared about you?"

"Norman does not care about me. My grandmother, his mother-in-law, probably called him and nagged him into calling me."

"I don't care why he called. He's your first family member who seems to give a shit about you. *Call him back.*"

She redialed Norman's number. "Hi, Uncle Norman? I'm actually not do-ing so well. Can we talk?"

Mitchell took the phone from her. "Hi, Norman? This is Mitchell Durman. I think that we should work together to make something happen positively for your beautiful niece." Pause. "Yes, she's here in my home." Pause. "You're in Atlanta?" Pause. "Are you aware of the Hillside and Rosh Hashana debacles that transpired?" Pause. "You are?" Pause. "And you hate your brother-in-law, her father, too?" Pause. "Great, I'll see you Wednesday."

"What just happened?" she asked as Mitchell handed back her cell phone.

"Your Uncle Norman and Aunt Dawn are coming for a visit."

"What?!"

"You heard me. Now, shut up and eat your sushi."

Norman and Dawn came right up to Mitchell's apartment after arriving from the airport. They hadn't even checked into their hotel yet.

All three were sitting in Mitchell's living room when she arrived. Aunt Dawn had a glass of wine in front of her. She wondered where Mitchell had been hiding his wine. Maybe he wasn't as sober as she had thought.

She kissed everyone hello, then took a seat in the center of the couch.

Mitchell jumped right in to begin the dialogue. "As you know, your niece has been abandoned by her immediate and extended family. You are the final two who still seem to care about her fate."

"We do. We do," her aunt and uncle echoed in unison.

"Well, she and I have come up with some various plans to make her well and end this nightmare."

"We want to help!" Uncle Norman seemed sincere.

"Good, good." Mitchell passed Norman a folder containing the printouts of emails Mitchell had been exchanging with her parents in the past month. She hadn't ever seen them.

"What's that file, Mitchell?" she asked.

"These are the road blocks to your path to recovery." Mitchell nodded toward Norman and Dawn. "These good folks are stepping in to help."

She watched with apprehension as Norman and Dawn rifled through the emails. Those two had never expressed an interest in her before. In fact, the last time that either of them had had any communication was when their son had been elected to the Georgia state senate, and she had flown down for the inauguration. Such a big deal was made of the fact that she was a fitness model that she quickly felt like a prop for her cousin's campaign. She not-so-secretly resented Norman and Dawn. She was going to have to keep an eagle eye on these two. They were not to be trusted.

After they finished sorting through the emails that Mitchell had apparently been exchanging with her parents, Norman said, "So, what do we do now?"

"You tell me, Norman." Mitchell leaned in and gave one of the best acting jobs she'd seen yet. "You're her family. I'm just a friend and adviser. What do you and Dawn want to do?"

"We should get her into a facility." Norman made his intentions known.

Slack jawed, she stared at Mitchell. This must be joke. Mitchell was the one who had said so many times that it was the institutionalization that had broken her in the first place. Mitchell didn't even look directly at her and pretended not to notice her expression of disbelief.

"Do you have any institutions in mind?" Mitchell was playing her aunt and uncle right into his game.

"Well, we found one nearby in Connecticut. Silverhill." Norman slid a pamphlet onto the glass coffee table.

"Silverhill!" Mitchell looked right at her. "Isn't it wonderful that your aunt and uncle came prepared?"

"What's going on, Mitchell?" A dialogue had clearly transpired that she had not been privy to. She repeated, "What's going on?"

Mitchell ignored her question. Instead, he said, "Isn't this great! Look at this brochure. Don't you want to go to Silverhill?"

"Mitchell, what's going on?!"

Mitchell turned his attention back to her aunt and uncle. "What's going on is that she's going to go away and get well. Then she'll come back to New York, move into a nice apartment building, start a happy life." Mitchell signaled to his living room furniture, including his giant plasma television. "And all this will be hers! The couches, the entertainment wall, all of it! My contribution to her recovery!"

"Mitchell, can I talk to you alone for a minute?" She tried to collect her thoughts as quickly as possible.

"Not now." Mitchell dismissed her request. "Right now I'm entertaining company."

This wasn't entertaining at all.

She went home that night and stared at the ceiling as she tried to fall asleep. She was going to have to go back to Mitchell's early the next morning to see her aunt and uncle. Before she did, she wanted to try as hard as she could to figure out their modus operandi.

Norman and Dawn were uneducated and easily impressionable nouveauriche. Aunt Dawn embodied the negative stereotype of the Jewish American Princess. Their niece found it hard to believe that their intentions toward her were selfless. Mitchell must have sensed that, and he was playing them as pawns in his scheme. But his scheme to do what? Divide her family? Destroy whatever sense of belonging she had? Steal money? All sorts of thoughts raced through her head.

Sitting on Mitchell's sofa the next morning, Uncle Norman unveiled his plan. "We are prepared to drive her up to check in at Silverhill right now."

"I can't go to Silverhill now!" she protested. "I'm leaving on a cruise next week!"

Norman looked at Mitchell.

"It's true," Mitchell affirmed. "I've seen the travel itinerary." He threw up his arms in a way that spoke, *What can we do?*

Uncle Norman addressed her. "We will reimburse you for the cost of the cruise." Norman turned to Dawn. "Hand me the checkbook."

"I don't want your money," she said flatly. "I need to go on this cruise."

"How much are you out of pocket? I'm writing you a check." Norman persevered.

"No. I'm not sure why you're here, or what your intentions are, but no," she repeated.

Norman wrote a check for $1,600. It was just under the cost of the cruise. Obviously, Mitchell had told them how much she had spent.

"No," she said again.

"Please take the check," Aunt Dawn pleaded. "Come with us to Connecticut. We'll make sure you're okay!"

She raised an eyebrow. "How will you do that?"

"We'll stay with you for the entire month of rehab," Norman said.

"We'll never be more than five minutes away," Dawn added.

"I'm going on the cruise," she stated.

Mitchell pretended to mediate this dispute. "How about we have everyone sign some papers, some commitments and contracts to one another?"

Norman said, "I'm listening."

"She will go on her cruise. It can be a last hoorah, if you will. Upon return, she'll go with you to Silverhill." Mitchell nodded at her.

"Why should I trust them to take me to Silverhill? I don't know them! They haven't expressed any interest in my life before!"

Norman nodded. "It's true. We haven't been the family we should have been toward you."

"See!" Mitchell said. "They want to fix things. They want to try to help you!"

She found this all a little contrived and hard to believe.

Norman sensed her apprehension. "I've spoken with your grandmother. If you complete the twenty-eight-day program, she will give you fifteen thousand dollars. No questions asked."

"Really?" Now they were speaking her language.

"And I will match it," Mitchell declared.

She processed this information. "So, I go to Silverhill for twenty-eight days, and I get thirty thousand dollars?"

"That's the deal," Mitchell said.

"Will you do it?" Norman asked.

"Can I trust you?"

Mitchell addressed her hesitation. "We will all sign, and have notarized, contracts agreeing to this plan. Okay?" Mitchell looked at each person on his sofa individually.

Everyone nodded.

Mitchell disappeared into his office for a little while and returned with some documents.

"Here we go. I'm a lawyer, so I know how to draft these things. I need everyone to sign."

"What does the contract say, Mitchell?" she asked.

"On the day that you enter into Silverhill, I deposit ten thousand dollars into your bank account. On the day that you complete the program, whether successful or not, Norman and Dawn give you Grandma's fifteen thousand dollar check, and I give you the remaining five thousand dollars." Mitchell looked at her. "Sounds like a good deal to me."

She didn't trust any of the three people in the room, but the contract did look binding. Everyone signed.

"Good," Mitchell said, as he scooped up the papers. "Now, just for added security, I'm going to have her read the contract to my video camera. The two of you will state and spell your names in understanding and commitment to the clauses."

Everyone agreed. The video was made. She thought that the deal was set. She hoped she wouldn't get burned. Again.

Forty-Three

The cruise was not exactly as relaxing as she had hoped. There were terrible storms in the north Atlantic, and the seas were so high that the captain closed all the dining facilities and common areas and advised passengers to stay in their rooms.

She actually enjoyed rocking boats. Years of sailing training had given her strong sea legs. She tried staying in her cabin, but the dresser drawers and closet doors kept opening and banging shut, and the arrhythmic pattern was a bit unsettling.

She walked through the corridors of the ship all day and never saw another human being. There were emergency vomit bags lining the hallways and individually wrapped packets of saltine crackers strewn about. It occurred to her that she may be one of the few people aboard the ship who was not ill. That was irony at its finest.

By the time the ship pulled back into the harbor, she was ready to sign herself into the facility that her uncle and Mitchell had chosen. It couldn't be as boring as the cruise had been.

Plus, she stood to earn thirty thousand dollars just by agreeing to attend a month-long program—one thousand dollars a day seemed like a fair enough deal.

Uncle Norman flew up to New York without Aunt Dawn. He took a suite in an expensive hotel on the Upper East Side, within walking distance from her apartment, and literally across the street from the Metropolitan Museum of Art, though she doubted that a philistine such as he had ever actually crossed the street and entered the front doors of the Met.

She admonished herself for being such a snob.

She packed her bags and spent the night with Uncle Norman in his hotel. They planned to drive up to Connecticut in the morning. Instead, however, they took a detour to Mitchell's apartment.

Mitchell gave her the heavy television from his office as a present to look forward to when she completed her program. Because Uncle Norman had rented a car, Mitchell said that it was a good time to get the TV back to her apartment.

She knew better, however. Mitchell was giving her the TV in front of Uncle Norman to make a show of his supposed benevolence and generosity. But whatever. She took the TV.

Mitchell also asked to make a copy of her bank ATM card so that he could wire her the funds he had promised her. On top of the photocopy, he handwrote, *I, Mitchell Durman, promise to deposit $10,000 upon entry to Silverhill, and an additional $5,000 upon completion of the 28-day program.* Mitchell signed it. She signed it. Uncle Norman signed his initials as a witness. Additional copies were made. One went to her, one went into the safe, and Mitchell and Uncle Norman each palmed a remaining copy.

Everything seemed set, and the process seemed to be in motion. She was nervous; her experience at Hillside had been less than reassuring. But Uncle Norman promised that he and Aunt Dawn would be within five minutes of Silverhill's campus at all times and would be accessible at any hour, day or night.

She had no reason not to believe Uncle Norman. He wasn't a particularly astute man, but he gave her no indication that he was a malfeasant or a cheat. He reminded her of Forrest Gump. Not too bright, but totally reliable, and a real sweetheart at the core.

After they dropped the television off at her apartment, uncle and niece had a three-hour drive up to New Canaan, Connecticut. As they got closer to the campus, she grew more and more nervous.

"Uncle Norman, I really don't feel comfortable with this plan."

"This is the best thing for you. Plus, you'll come out with lots of money for a fresh start. And Aunt Dawn and I will be there for you the entire time."

"The entire time? Promise?"

"Every minute. We will be there for you." Uncle Norman looked at her, letting his eyes leave the road for a minute. "Your parents let you down, but your aunt and me never will. Your father is a wimp, and your mother is a meanie. But your aunt and me will be your rocks. Plus, you're lucky to have Mr. Durman. He is a solid friend. He don't mess around."

It was funny that Uncle Norman referred to Mitchell as "Mr. Durman," considering that Norman was more than twenty years Mitchell's senior. But this didn't surprise her much; Norman responded to Mitchell the way that most people in the service industry did. It was a bit unsettling.

She kept her mind on the thirty grand.

They had a lot of time together on the car ride. She couldn't remember spending so much time alone with Uncle Norman since she was a little girl. She used to spend every Passover holiday with Norman and Dawn in their home in Atlanta. Uncle Norman used to take her out on his boat to go fishing on the lake. They never caught anything, but he always bought her a big bag of candy to make up for it. He used to sneak her cheeseburgers, too, even though they were prohibited during the Passover holiday. Norman used to be her hero, the father for whom she had so yearned.

Uncle Norman also used to iron all her clothes, including her underwear. Even as a little girl, she found it odd that her uncle-by-marriage ironed her underwear. But she didn't think it was creepy. She just thought that Norman was weird.

All this passed through her mind as they drove to New Canaan. She kept trying to bring her mind back to the thirty thousand dollar payout.

"Uncle Norman, can I ask you a question?"

"Anything. We have lots of time to talk."

"How is it that you're able to suspend your life for an entire month while I'm in treatment? Isn't that a long time? What about your business?" She was surprised that the thought hadn't occurred to her sooner.

"Sweetheart, I'm going to level with you." Norman took a deep breath. "I don't have much else going on in my life right now. My brother fired me from my business."

"Your brother fired you from *your* business?" This didn't make much sense.

"Yes, my brother fired me, and Aunt Dawn and me are deeply in debt," Norman confessed.

"Does anyone else know this?"

"Well, I don't advertise that my family is splitting apart at the seams. But with your relationship with your parents, I figured you'd understand."

"I don't understand. But I empathize." She sighed. "Family relations are a delicate balance. At all times teetering on the abyss of mistrust and cruel malfeasance."

"I only understand about half the words you just said." Norman chuckled. "But I think you get it."

"So you're using my stay at Silverhill to get away from your own life for a while?"

"Well, no." Norman realized that he may have said too much. "It just happens to be doable right now. Getting away, I mean."

"Gotcha. A vacation staying with the crazy niece in rehab."

"Hey, we love you. No one else loves you. Your crazy bitch mother certainly doesn't. And your father's got no spine."

"You don't think my father loves me?" She thought Norman might be putting his foot in his mouth.

"Well, your father won't listen to Dawn. And she's his big sister."

"So?"

"So, she told him that I was taking you to Silverhill, and your father made a big stink about it being a bad idea."

"Did you tell him that you bribed me?"

Uncle Norman took his eyes off the highway again and looked at her. "We did not bribe you. We made a promise, and we are delivering money to help you make a fresh start. It's not our money, remember. It's Grandma's."

"And Mitchell's," she added.

"You're very lucky to have Mr. Durman," Uncle Norman repeated.

"Yep. Lucky. That's my word of the day."

They arrived at Silverhill at dusk. It was hard to see the campus in the darkness, but it looked like a beautiful estate on several acres of rolling hilltops. Not a bad place to be.

Intake at Silverhill was very different from Hillside. There were beautiful antique armoires, plush sofas, and gorgeous tapestry as wallpaper. No design detail had been overlooked; even the window treatments were fabulous antique curtains.

"It looks good, right? Nice?" Uncle Norman was trying to rally her spirits.

"I'm still nervous. I don't think I want to do this. I think I want to go home." She felt herself gasping for air. She hoped she didn't have a panic attack.

"You'll be fine. We just drove this far. It'll be good." Norman squeezed her arm. "And I'm at a small motel just down the street. You have my number. You can get me anytime."

"You know they're going to take my phone, don't you?"

"They're not going to take your phone!" Norman seemed surprised by the worry.

"You forget. I have experience. They're going to take my phone."

"Whatever. I'm coming every day anyway. You won't need to call me, because I'm going to be right here."

"Promise?"

"How many times do I have to keep saying it?"

"Until it's over, and I know it was true."

Silverhill didn't want to admit her. She was way below recommended body weight, and they stressed that they did not have round-the-clock medical care.

However, she knew that though there were probably better facilities available, Silverhill was one of the few decent ones that actually took her insurance policy. So, it was either here or nowhere.

She was actually hoping that she would be turned away so that she could go home and sleep in her own bed that night. But Uncle Norman pleaded with the staff, and she was finally presented with the intake documents. Damn it.

As she signed, she focused on the fact that just her mere signature equaled ten thousand dollars from Mitchell. And she had the contracts signed by all parties to prove it.

There was a golf cart waiting on the other side of the intake building to shuttle her up to her ward. She shivered as they drove up to the main building at the top of the hill.

"It's colder up here than I thought," she said to Norman.

"Do you think you packed enough?" Norman asked her as they zipped through the brisk autumn night.

"Definitely not."

"Well, Aunt Dawn is coming tomorrow. She likes to shop. I'll make sure she gets you some fall clothes for a month in Connecticut."

"Okay." She couldn't even say "thank you." She felt very little gratitude for any part of this current situation.

The golf cart stopped at the front steps of a grandiose colonial mansion. "We're here." The driver/security guard got out of the cart.

"This is a dormitory?" she asked in disbelief.

"Yep," the guard said. "'Cording to my paperwork, you were assigned to Mainhouse. Well," the guard swept his arm along the view of the building, "this is the main house. Mainhouse."

"It's nice!" Uncle Norman poked her in the ribs with his elbows.

It was definitely different from Hillside. But its *niceness* was yet to be determined. "Let's go in first, okay? Then we can decide whether it's nice or not."

Norman shrugged. "Well, I think it's nice."

The guard interjected, "Ain't nothing nice about rehab. Welcome to Silverhill."

When they entered through the front door, signs instructed them to go up the stairs to the residence floor.

"No elevator?"

"This house was built two hundred years ago, Uncle Norman."

"But really, no elevator?" Logic sometimes escaped Norman. It was a good thing that he was a sweet man. Because he had very little else going for him.

They ascended the wooden staircase, and she admired the mahogany banister. If nothing else, this building was a beautiful structure. She was just nervous about what would meet her at the top of the stairs.

What she found was a narrow carpeted hallway with lots and lots of doors. It reminded her of a fraternity house. There was a door open and several people inside at desks wearing staff identification tags. It seemed like this was the place to check in.

"Hi, I've just been admitted?" she said to no one in particular.

A young Hispanic female staff member put down a doughnut, wiped the sugar off her lip, took a gulp of coffee, and stood up to meet the new arrival. "Okay, let's get you checked in."

She was led down the hallway to a huge private room with a tiny single bed. The bed was made, and a corner was turned down as a welcoming gesture.

"This is my room?" It reminded her of a top-of-the-line budget hotel.

"Yep, just you," the staff member said. "There's a closet over there for your clothes, and a dresser for whatever else." The Hispanic woman pointed to a closed door in the corner of the room. "You have a private bathroom, too, but it stays locked because you're EDO."

"EDO?"

"Eating disorder. You don't get bathroom privileges through the day. Ten minutes, every morning, you get free bathroom. Take a shower, whatever." The staff member pointed toward her luggage. "Open everything up. Give me your razor blades, cell phone, computers, pillows, blankets, water bottles, and all that. Keep your books and your clothes."

She had brought her own pillow and was hoping to sleep with it. "You're taking my pillow?"

"You heard me," the woman reiterated. "I need to collect everything but clothes and books. Okay?"

"Do you need my shoelaces and belts?" It was an honest question.

The staff member looked shocked. "This ain't the lockdown ward, girl. This is Mainhouse. You keep your shoelaces. Why, where have you been?"

She didn't answer.

After sorting through her luggage, she unpacked everything that wasn't contraband and put it in the dresser. She handed over the duffle bags filled with her bedding and other prohibited items.

"All set?" Uncle Norman asked.

She looked at the staff member to answer the question. She was met with a nod. She looked back at Norman. "I guess so. This is it. Day one."

"You'll do great. It's nice here." Norman gave her a big hug. "I'll see you in the morning."

Norman went down the stairs, and the Hispanic nurse asked, "Do you need to use the bathroom before bed?"

"I do. Can you unlock it for me?"

The woman crossed the room, reached for a large string of keys, and then turned on the light and entered the bathroom. The staff member took a seat on the edge of the bathtub next to the toilet.

"I have to go to the bathroom," she told the woman.

"I know. Go." The woman pointed to the toilet.

"I don't get any privacy to pee?"

"Not in rehab."

"But I have a shy bladder."

"I'll wait."

"It's going to take a while, then."

"Maybe the first time," the woman stated matter-of-factly, as though this issue arose all the time, which it probably had. "But you'll get over it. Everyone does. So, are you going to pee, or what?"

Forty-Four

The next morning, she was jostled awake by a male nurse wheeling a cart filled with needles and other items.

She rubbed her eyes and looked at him. "Is it time to wake up?"

"No," he said in a soft voice, "it's only 5 a.m. Keep sleeping. I just need your left arm for blood."

She pulled her left arm out from under the covers and let it flop out on top of the blankets. She was so groggy that she didn't even feel the plastic band tourniquet or the prick of the needle.

The phlebotomist left the room, and she rolled over and went back to sleep.

What seemed like minutes later but was actually an hour and a half, another male nurse flung open her door and yelled, "Wake up! I'm unlocking your door! I need you for meds and vitals in ten minutes. Then change into your clothes. I'll see you at breakfast in one half hour. Go! You're wasting your bathroom time!"

She jumped out of bed and went into her bathroom. It was nice to pee without someone perched on the bathtub watching. She turned on the shower and brushed her teeth as the water warmed up. She was about to enter the shower when the male nurse burst in through the bathroom door and yelled, "Meds! Vitals! Move! Now!"

"But I didn't shower yet," she protested, naked but for a towel covering herself.

"Well, then, you had better budget your free bathroom time better in the future," He snapped.

"Can I shower later?"

"EDO patients only get the ten minutes free in the morning. Now move it! You're late for vitals."

"Can I get dressed first?" She wasn't trying to be difficult, but she didn't want to make her first impression on her housemates in the nude.

"After vitals and meds! You have time to dress and smoke before breakfast!" He was like a drill sergeant.

"I don't smoke."

"Good! Then no outside time. You'll have more time to dress."

"I can't go outside if I don't smoke?"

"Why would you go outside if you don't smoke?"

"Ummmm." She tried not to be obnoxious. "Fresh air?"

The male nurse laughed. "There are only smokers outside. Not a speck of fresh air in that yard. It's cold anyway. You're better off inside." He actually seemed momentarily compassionate and attentive. She might grow to like this guy.

"But for now, you want me naked in the hallway?"

He laughed. He was warming up to her. "Yes. Naked. In the hallway. Don't drop the towel."

The other patients outside her bedroom door were in various stages of undress too, so she didn't feel too out of place in her towel. She joined the line in front of the meds room and waited for her name to be called. She was given a paper cup containing all the medications that had been prescribed by Dr. Kaala. She felt comforted knowing that her doctors were communicating with each other, even if no one was communicating with her.

She swallowed her pills with a swig of water and began to walk away.

"Uh uh uh," the meds nurse chided. "Come back."

"What did I do wrong?" She was confused.

"Open your mouth and say 'ahhhh.'"

"Ahhhh."

"Now, flip your tongue both directions. I need to make sure you're not hiding your pills."

Given that she was almost completely naked, she supposed the only place she could have hidden her pills was in her mouth. And, after all, this was the place that made her pee with a bodyguard. She wasn't even subjected to that at Hillside. Silverhill was going to take some getting used to.

She got dressed and went downstairs. Breakfast wasn't served yet, but through the large patio window, she saw a big group standing around smoking. She wanted to go outside too.

She opened the door, and the guard on the other side looked up from his coffee. "You a smoker?"

"Yes," she lied. Then she realized that she had better procure a cigarette before she was banished back inside. She asked a random stranger for a cigarette.

"Here you go." A beautiful blonde woman about her age offered a smoke from a nearly full pack.

"Thanks."

"I'm Brigette. Are you new?"

She liked that she was immediately approached. "Yes, I'm new. Got in last night."

"Ooooh. Still detoxing?" Brigette asked.

"Um, no. No detox. They said I'm EDO."

"Oh yeah." Brigette looked her up and down. "You look thin. But you could have been a junkie."

"No, not a junkie."

"Oh." Brigette took a drag. "I'm a junkie. Meth and heroin. But I'm good now!"

"Congratulations." She didn't know what else to say.

"Yeah. You're lucky you don't have to detox." Brigette looked at her sincerely. "You don't have to deal with the seizures and the fevers and the vomiting." She sucked hard on the cigarette. "Nope, you just have to eat what they give you and play the game."

"Let's hope it's that simple."

"Better than detox. Gotta be better than detox."

The guard assigned to the smokers stood up and yelled, "Breakfast!"

There was a buffet set up, and she got in line behind everyone else. She felt someone poke her in the shoulder. It was the man who had awakened her in the morning.

"You're at the EDO table. In the other room." He nodded his head toward the huge table of food. "Away from the sight of the buffet."

She followed him and sat at a table with other women. Some were thin; some were not. One woman looked high. This was a strange place.

She sat to the immediate left of the man who had led her over. He sat at the head of the table. He introduced himself to her as Marcus. Everyone else at the table already seemed to know him.

Marcus had an egg timer and a cup of coffee in front of him. He told her that she was allowed to get one cup of coffee, no sweeteners, and one plastic cup of water with a lemon wedge.

"From the buffet?" She wanted to follow instructions to the letter—thirty thousand dollars kept swimming through her mind.

"From the buffet," Marcus affirmed. "And hurry back. They'll be bringing breakfast soon."

She returned with her cups. She didn't normally drink coffee, but if it was budgeted into her meal, she didn't want to question it. Hell, she didn't smoke either, and she had just had her first cigarette since she was seventeen and messing around her freshman year in college. She could allow for coffee too.

The cafeteria staff came out of the kitchen doors all at once. The trays they carried had Post-it notes with the names of the patients who would be receiving them. As soon as the trays were placed down, Marcus turned on the egg timer.

"You have exactly thirty minutes to eat all the contents off your tray," Marcus said.

Everyone had something different, but in general, all the meals were variations on the same theme. They each had a container of vanilla soymilk or cow's milk, a banana or an orange, a hard-boiled egg or a fried egg, a piece of multigrain toast, and a box of cereal. This was a much better breakfast than the stale rolls and bowls of dry Cheerios at Schneider's.

Marcus was watching all the women closely, so she watched them too. She wanted to make sure that she ate exactly as they did.

She poured most of her soymilk into her bowl of cereal and put the rest into her coffee. She sliced her banana on top of her bran flakes. She placed her fried egg on her toast and ate those together while they were still warm. She liked her cereal a little soggy.

Even with her methodical eating, she was still one of the first to finish. She folded her napkin and waited for her next cue from Marcus. He made small talk about the view from the dining room window, which was magnificent, and about the crappy institutional coffee.

When the egg timer chimed, all the women at the table had finished. The staff returned to collect the trays.

"Okay, I'm going to take each of you into your rooms to get a book or a magazine, if you don't already have one. Then we'll go to the time-out room."

"The time-out room?" she asked.

One of the other girls answered, "It's where they stick us for an hour after we eat. So we don't puke."

"Or do jumping jacks," another girl said.

"So we sit in a room?" This didn't sound like much fun. "And do what?"

"We read. We talk. We kill time until group starts."

She followed the herd up to the dormitories. She took a book from her dresser and met back up with the rest of them in the hallway. Marcus led everyone into the time-out room.

They all sat, uncomfortably, in the silence. One of the girls broke the silence to make an introduction. "So, you're new to the EDO?"

"I guess so. But I'm not sure it's where I should be. I'm thin, but I'm hungry."

"Oh. I purge," the girl said.

She was surprised to hear someone speak so frankly about an eating disorder. She couldn't even imagine voluntarily throwing up. She hated the feeling of vomiting. Ick.

"I obsessively exercise," another woman offered up.

"What do you do?" The first girl asked her.

"I get punched in the head."

They laughed. She was serious.

When an hour had passed, they were shuffled downstairs to join the big group from all of Mainhouse. The topic of group that day was the effects of alcohol in the body.

She liked science, and they had given her a notebook, so she took notes. She tried to pretend that she was in college attending a lecture.

After about an hour, Marcus appeared with a paper sack. The lecture was still going, so he whispered into her ear. "This is your snack. Pre-lunch. You have thirty minutes. I'll sit with you while you eat it."

She opened the bag and pulled out a plum, a container of soymilk, and an egg salad sandwich. This was a good snack. It beat the protein muffins she was sent at Hillside. The muffins that the staff ate. Every day. Maybe they were good muffins, but who knows? At least here, no one ate her sandwich.

She finished her snack, and then realized that she may be escorted off to the time-out room again. She looked at Marcus, and he understood the question in her eyes.

"You still have two hours' worth of group, so you can stay here." Marcus took her garbage and left the room.

When group time was finished, it was time for lunch. She had actually enjoyed group time. She had learned a lot about alcoholism. She had filled two pages in her notebook with notes from the lecture.

After lunch, and at the end of the hour-long time-out period, all the EDO patients met with the staff nutritionist. They were given folders filled with photocopies of meal plans and food charts. Then they were subjected to a short film on nutrition.

Some of the women had questions. She didn't have any.

"You don't have any questions?" the nutritionist asked.

"No, I know all this material," she responded, failing at her attempt to sound deferential.

"Really? How's that?"

"I was a licensed nutritionist at one point."

"Really?"

"Yes." At her slight weight, she was almost embarrassed to admit that she should have known better.

"How many calories in a gram of protein?"

"Four."

"Fat?"

"Nine."

"Formula for BMI?"

"Do you want me to write it out for you?" She couldn't understand the purpose of a pop quiz. She was here for help, not to be challenged on her credentials.

"No, that's all right." The nutritionist looked at her quizzically. "If you know so much about nutrition, why are you in the EDO program?"

"I just checked in last night. I haven't met with any doctors yet."

"So, do you think you belong in the EDO program?"

"I'm hoping that I belong at Silverhill," she replied honestly. "I'm in an abusive relationship." It was the first time she had said those words aloud.

Forty-Five

After dinner, Uncle Norman and Aunt Dawn came into the time-out room to visit.

"So, how's your first day?" Aunt Dawn asked in a singsong voice. Forty years of living in Atlanta had not killed Dawn's New York Jew accent.

"It's fine. The people are nice."

"How are the doctors?" Uncle Norman asked.

"I haven't met with any doctors. I'm hoping to meet some tomorrow."

"Well, I went shopping after I got off the plane," Dawn singsonged. "I put a bag in your room. It's what Uncle Norman told me you needed. There are pajamas, a heavy coat, some T-shirts and sweatpants, and lots of pairs of underwear." Dawn leaned in close toward her niece. "In case you can't do laundry, you need lots of underpants."

Laundry had never occurred to her. Maybe Dawn and Norman were more on top of things than she had given them credit for.

"Thank you." She meant it.

"We're coming back tomorrow, so let us know if there's anything else you need." Norman had a notepad, just in case.

She thought for a few moments. She thought that she had everything she needed. Then she thought of something. "I need a carton of cigarettes."

"I didn't know you smoked?" Norman asked.

"Let her smoke!" Dawn slapped Norman's hand.

She interrupted the potential marital bickering. "I don't smoke. But if I want any outdoor time, I need to start."

"They're making you smoke in *rehab*?" Norman sounded incredulous.

Dawn smacked him again. "Don't question their methods. Maybe smoking is a good substitute."

"Substitute for what?" Norman and Dawn were about to bicker again.

"I don't know. Substitute for binging, injecting needles, whatever," Dawn said, as though this were an actual explanation.

Again, their niece broke up the argument. "I don't think that it's a substitute for anything. But I think that they think you're crazy for wanting to go outside in the freezing cold for no reason."

"You need a reason for air?" Dawn was exhaustively combative.

"I don't know, Aunt Dawn. I'm just telling you what I've seen. Okay?"

"Okay." Norman held his pen to his pad. "Any particular brand?"

"I don't know. I don't smoke, Uncle Norman!"

"Then I don't get why you need cigarettes." Dawn looked at Norman. "Do you understand why she needs cigarettes?"

Norman and Dawn were the most draining visitors she could have imagined. She put her head in her hands.

As though someone read her mind, an attendant entered the room. "Visiting hour's up! All out."

Thank God she didn't need to sit through any more of Dawn and Norman going back and forth. For a fleeting moment, she felt sorry for her first cousins, having to grow up with such annoying parents.

Her parents were just plain cruel. They weren't exhausting in the same manner as Dawn and Norman. Her aunt and uncle had made an art form of back-and-forth competitive dialogue. She felt relieved when they left. But she also looked forward to seeing them the next day.

As draining as they were, she took comfort in knowing that Dawn and Norman were nearby, and she convinced herself that they had her best interests at heart.

The next morning, after meds were distributed and vitals were recorded, she heard her name being shouted from downstairs.

She found Brigette holding the receiver to the payphone. "It's *Mitchell*." Brigette said his name as though they were all in high school, and a teasing chant was about to follow.

"Thanks, Brigette." She picked up the phone. "Hi, Mitchell."

"Hi. Hey, is Brigette as hot as she sounds?" Mitchell was always thinking about pussy.

"She's an addict, Mitchell. She's my housemate in *rehab*."

"Whatever. I can get her what she wants. What's she on? 'Ludes?"

"You are so old, Mitchell." She laughed. "She's a meth and heroin addict. Successfully detoxed, by the way."

"I am old. I don't even know what meth is." Mitchell laughed.

"I think people cook it in their trailers."

Mitchell got back to the point of the phone call. "Brigette said that you have breakfast in a few minutes, so I know that you don't have a lot of time to talk."

"Nope."

"Okay, you'll probably meet with some doctors today. I want you to write down exactly what you need to say to them." Mitchell paused. "After the Hillside thing, you remembered to carry a pen and paper with you everywhere, right?"

"I have a notebook right here."

"Good. Write this down." Mitchell dictated a whole speech on primary conflicts and comorbidities.

She took careful notes and read back the statement. Marcus appeared in the phone booth and tapped the face of his watch.

"I have to go, Mitchell."

"You got what you have to say?"

"Got it."

"Okay. Bye. I love you." Whenever Mitchell said that, she found it incredibly unnerving.

"Yep. Talk to you later." She returned the receiver to its cradle and followed Marcus into the dining room.

She was pulled out of the group meeting to meet with her team of doctors. Dawn and Norman were there too. Everyone sat around in what must have been the parlor room when the Mainhouse had actually been a family estate.

She had her notebook open to the page with the notes from Mitchell. Dawn and Norman shifted uncomfortably in their seats. The head of her team of doctors was an elderly Eastern European woman with a thick accent and a slight frame. Her patient activist and nutritionist also sat with open notebooks, ready to write the minutes of the meeting.

"I've spoken with Dr. Kaala. She advised me that you are a special patient, with hypomania," the psychiatrist said. "Have you been informed of this?"

"Yes. Hypomania. What is that though?"

Norman and Dawn sat silently, taking in the information.

"Hypomania is an interesting chemical imbalance. It is defined by a basic dissociation with external factors. For example, you would have the same reaction if I told you that your house burned down as you would if I told you that you won the lottery."

"Okay, so I'm nonreactive?"

"That's too simplistic," the psychiatrist continued. "Patients with hypomania tend to not have mental and emotional reactions, as would a bipolar patient, for example. So, the effects of stress tend to be measured physically."

"Like an eating disorder?" Aunt Dawn chimed in.

"I don't think that we're speaking in terms of black and white. An eating disorder is black and white."

"So what are you saying, doctor?" Uncle Norman interrupted.

"I'm saying that our fear with this patient is that the hypomania can only survive in a flat-lined state for so long."

"And then?" Uncle Norman was disruptive.

"And then a patient can crash."

"Crash?" Aunt Dawn wanted clarification.

"Severe depression. Beyond any magnitude imaginable. Often resulting in suicide."

"I'm not suicidal!" Now it was her turn to interrupt.

"No. You're not. And you may not be." The doctor looked around the room at everyone present. "But I think that we are all in agreement that you walk a fine line?"

"So, my question to you, then, doctor, if I may, is whether you think that Silverhill can help me?"

The doctor avoided answering the question directly. "It can't hurt. What we can offer you here is a foundation of structure: a steady schedule, regular meals, group work."

"But it's not going to help her eating disorder?" Aunt Dawn was getting annoying.

"We haven't determined if an eating disorder is present. We have her with the EDO group because of her low body weight. And she doesn't fit in with the other patients, anyway."

"What do you mean, she doesn't fit in?" Uncle Norman was getting antsy.

"I mean, she doesn't have a chemical dependency. She's not an alcoholic. She's not a drug addict—"

"She's addicted to food!" Aunt Dawn was determined to neatly put her condition into a box with a name.

"No, I don't think so." The doctor was skilled at maintaining composure.

"But she's bulimic!" Aunt Dawn cried out.

"Or anorexic," Uncle Norman added.

She glared at both of them. They had come with an agenda, and they weren't listening to the doctor.

"Well, let's ask the patient, shall we?" The doctor was still remaining calm. "You've been monitored for the past two days, and you have complied with eating, in full, all the meals you have been given, correct?"

"Yes, doctor."

"Right, and the attendants monitoring you have made notes of your compliance." The doctor addressed Norman and Dawn. "That's not anorexia." The doctor turned back toward the patient. "Have you ever, now or in the past, induced vomiting?"

"No, doctor."

Aunt Dawn made a guttural sound of objection. She was being a bitch.

"Have you vomited after a meal?" the doctor continued.

"Yes, but always involuntarily."

"You mean, there was no way to avoid the vomiting? There was no inducing?" All the doctors present were taking notes.

"No. It has been uncomfortable, unpleasant, and unavoidable."

"I see." The doctor kept writing. "You have been monitored during and after every meal here, correct?"

"Yes, ma'am."

"And you have your bathroom locked, and an attendant with you every time you enter, right?"

"Yes, doctor." It was as though she were on trial.

"Are you aware that you have unusually large bowel movements?"

She stared at the doctor with her mouth open. "Um, I guess I've never compared them to other people's."

"Okay, well, you do." The doctor kept writing. "And do you know that you've lost four pounds since you arrived here two days ago?"

"Four pounds!" Aunt Dawn yelled, in shock.

"Shh, let the doctor speak." Uncle Norman tried to quiet Aunt Dawn.

"No, they've weighed me, but the numbers on the scale face away from me," she responded honestly.

"Okay, well, we are going to put you on a round-the-clock watch. Just to make sure that you're not doing something to purge. No exercising, no free breaks, nothing. And a two-hour rest after each meal."

"Two hours!" To her, this was cruel and unusual punishment. At six meals a day, that added up to twelve hours every day in the timeout room!

"It has to be done. Protocol." The doctor looked at Norman and Dawn. "Any questions?"

"So you don't think she's making herself sick?" Dawn didn't like to be wrong.

"We've already covered that." The doctor obviously didn't realize how mentally slow Norman and Dawn truly were. "So, I guess that's it. Next family meeting in one week, okay?"

"Okay," she said.

Norman and Dawn said nothing.

She turned to address them. "The doctor is meeting with us in one week, okay?"

Again, silence.

"Well, I can see that you three need some time to come up with a family strategy. We'll leave you to your visit." The three staff members left the room.

"Why didn't you say anything?" she asked her aunt and uncle.

"Sit down, sweetheart." Uncle Norman said.

She sat, not wanting to hear what was coming.

"New Canaan is more boring than we thought," Aunt Dawn said.

"What are you telling me?" She felt her heartbeat rise.

"We're old. This place is unfamiliar. There's nothing for us here. We're going back to Atlanta," Norman explained.

"What?!" Another betrayal for her to add to the list. "But you promised to stay a month. You've lasted less than three days!"

"Well, we tried." Norman shrugged.

"You *tried?!*" She couldn't believe what she was hearing. "I don't get to try! I don't get to leave! What happens if something goes wrong? What do I do? Whom do I call?"

"You can call Mr. Durman," Uncle Norman said.

"Mitchell? Mitchell pisses in my mouth! Do you really think that he's my safety net? He's my abuser! I do what he says so that he won't hurt me more than he already does!" It felt good to say it out loud.

"Look." Uncle Norman was trying to keep the peace, but the flat tone in his voice only sounded patronizing. "We're only your aunt and uncle. Don't you think that your father should be here? Aren't you his responsibility?"

"My father? My father told you this was a bad idea. You said so yourselves!"

"Well, if it was a bad idea, you wouldn't have come," Aunt Dawn said.

"You promised me thirty thousand dollars. Anyone would take that offer!"

"Well, that's when we thought you had an eating disorder," Aunt Dawn said.

"That's right, sweetheart. Now the doctor is saying it's not that. So we're going to leave," Uncle Norman continued.

"So, because I don't fit your diagnosis, you're jumping ship?" This was just too fucked up.

"Well, why do you need us if you don't have an eating disorder?" Aunt Dawn asked.

"Because I'm stuck here, alone, for the next month! And I have a Mitchell disorder!"

"Don't say that!" Aunt Dawn admonished.

"Shame on you!" Uncle Norman said. "Mitchell Durman is your lifesaver. You should be grateful."

"Mitchell makes me fuck strange girls I meet on the Internet. In front of him. With a strap-on. In the ass!" She was exasperated.

"You really are crazy if you believe that. You're lucky to have Mr. Durman." Uncle Norman sounded brainwashed.

She felt like her life had become a bad remake of the *Manchurian Candidate*. "Are you not listening to me? I'm begging you to hear me! Please!"

"We're going back to Atlanta. I don't like New Canaan. There's nothing to do." Aunt Dawn stood, purse in hand.

"Of course there's nothing to do. You're not here on vacation. You promised to be here to support me!"

"We think you're in good hands. We'll see you when you get out." Uncle Norman led Aunt Dawn through the front door of Mainhouse.

She stood, in shock, in the middle of the parlor room floor.

Marcus came to find her a few minutes later. "Ready to come to group?"

"Marcus, if the definition of insanity is doing the same thing twice while expecting a different outcome, then I have completely lost my mind."

"The meeting didn't go so well?" Marcus was a good man; he was genuinely concerned.

"The meeting went fine. My support network just went back to Atlanta, though."

"What does that mean?"

"It means it's just you and me, Marcus. I fell for someone else's bullshit. Again. And again. And apparently one more time." She looked Marcus straight in the eye. "If Einstein's definition of insanity is true, than I am truly fucking nuts."

Forty-Six

In group, the patients were asked to draw pictures of how they were feeling during their stay. Her favorite was a teenage addict who drew pictures of himself "throwing up in a field of opium while it's raining oxycodin." It was funny, but the delivery of the humor wasn't shielded by the severity of the statement.

Her drawing was less amusing. She drew herself scrunched into a small box. There were bricks on top of the box, weighting down the lid. And there were figures with their backs toward the box, pretending not to notice that she was inside.

After presenting her drawing to the group, she folded it up and stuck it in her notebook.

She ate her snack when Marcus brought it and tried to avoid speaking to him about the abandonment by her aunt and uncle. He took the cue and didn't mention it.

After lunch, the whole group from Mainhouse went down to the gymnasium. They were going to swim, and play basketball and ping pong, and all the other fun activities that were outlined in the brochure. She wasn't allowed to leave Mainhouse until she weighed over one hundred pounds. So she had to stay in the time-out room. Alone.

Silverhill was going to suck.

She learned three things very quickly during her tenure at Mainhouse. First of all, recovering addicts were very friendly and eager to bond with the people around them. Second, the mandatory AA meeting for all the residents of Mainhouse meant that she got the TV in the living room to herself for the primetime hour of eight to nine every evening. And third, no matter how many times she told her doctors and the rest of the staff that Mitchell was her biggest obstacle, they still interrupted her wherever she was to make her take his phone calls.

Every phone call from Mitchell was the same. He'd give her a list of things to tell the doctor, she'd write it down, and she'd tried to repeat it as best as she could during her interviews. She didn't want to play the game Mitchell's way, but she trusted his judgment better than her own. She didn't want to get stuck in *the system* again. Especially being in a different state than her residence. She didn't need mental health extradition on her record, too.

Felicia called her, and so did Betty. Mitchell obviously wanted her to remember her loyalties to her fucktoys.

In a way, she didn't want to leave Silverhill. It was boring, but it was safe. A return to Mitchell meant certain disaster.

Her father visited her twice. He seemed uncomfortable, but knowing that his older sister had abandoned his daughter in a facility in Connecticut, he acted out of a basic sense of obligation.

His visits were short and unproductive. They weren't necessarily counter-productive, but they certainly didn't contribute to any potential progress on her road to mental health recovery.

She told her father that Mitchell called her every day. She secretly hoped that her father would act in her honor and have Mitchell killed. She didn't really want Mitchell dead; she loved Adam, and he deserved to have a father. She just wanted Mitchell out of her life.

Her father was too spineless to take any action, no matter how small, to support her. But she gave him credit for making the drive up to Connecticut the times that he did.

At one point, a woman her parents' age was admitted into the EDO program. Beth had five children and weighed fifty-six pounds at the date of admission.

Her father saw Beth and realized how bad his daughter's condition could have actually been. Maybe misery loves company. Or maybe it's just easier to deal with horrific realities when one sees someone else suffering even more.

Every day was the same. Sometimes new people came into Mainhouse. Sometimes old people left. One woman completed the program and died the night of release of an overdose. But nothing really changed in the day to day.

She spent the bulk of each day in the time-out room, staring at the stored boxes containing reams of paper. At first, other patients kept her company. They played board games and told stories. But then the staff decided that it was better she be left alone.

One of the girls she befriended at Mainhouse tried to cheer her up. When she said that sitting in the time-out room felt like a punishment, the girl told her to think of it as "constructive isolation." That girl could have been a politician after kicking her heroin habit. Good use of spin.

Each morning, Mitchell called right before breakfast. Sometimes he called again in the evening, to make sure that she had repeated just what he had told her to say to the doctors.

She looked forward to the hour she spent in control of the living room television every night. Even the other EDO patients were forced to go to the AA meetings. She found comfort that at the very least, the staff at Silverhill had ruled out alcoholism as one of her morbidities.

Her snacks every day were a tuna salad sandwich, a turkey sandwich, or an egg salad sandwich. She had one of each for her three snacks every day. It was exciting to guess which came first each day. The little brown sack delivered by Marcus always held a surprise.

Life was becoming completely not worth living.

❧

It was getting colder outside. One day there was a frost on the grass in the smoking area. What few flowers were there died.

She had lost track of the days, but judging by the giant change in temperature, she figured that she must have been there for almost the full month. It must have been the end of November.

One morning, there were paper turkeys and pumpkins taped to the wall. It was Thanksgiving. A lot of people's families came to eat a mid-afternoon Thanksgiving feast with their loved ones at Mainhouse. Her family didn't come.

The EDO table was taken by patients who had visitors. She ate her turkey dinner at a folding card table with Marcus. And his egg timer.

Friday morning after Thanksgiving was strangely quiet at Mainhouse. All the psychiatric staff was off for the holiday weekend. Most of the therapists and other staff members were off too.

She sat in group, drawing yet another picture of herself in a box. She had a large collection of crayon drawings now. She amused herself by thinking that she'd show them at a gallery exhibition in the city. Maybe someone would find all her old song recordings, and her drawings would become valuable posthumously.

The show could be called *Girl in a Box*.

She wasn't even creative anymore.

Her mind was dulled. She wondered if her brain cells were dead or just dormant. The Ivy League graduate who had once occupied her mind had clearly checked out of residence. She wondered if soon she'd beginning drooling and speaking incoherently. She wondered at which point institutionalization completely destroyed one's soul.

She was disrupted from her aimless reverie that Friday morning.

"Upstairs. Your bags are on your bed." A managerial staff member stood over her as she sat, drawing on construction paper splayed out on the floor.

"What?" She looked up at the woman, confused.

"You're out!" Marcus clapped his hands. "You completed the program!"

She shook her head in an effort to think through the cobwebs. "I'm finished? I can go?"

"Twenty-eight days. Insurance is up, and we've done all we can for you." The staff member made a thumbs-up sign to indicate that she should rise to her feet.

"I can go?" she repeated.

"Up and at 'em. Let's move it." The staff member disappeared.

She turned to Marcus. "I'm done?" she asked, then reaffirmed, "I'm done! I'm leaving!"

"Let's go get you packed!" Marcus was just as excited as she was.

She sprinted up the stairs two at a time and flung open her bedroom door. All her confiscated belongings were on her bed, along with her duffle bags and her discharge papers.

"I'm out! I'm out, I'm out, I'm out, I'm out!" She put her arms in the air and skipped around her room.

"Okay, well, you get packing. I have to get back downstairs to group." Marcus backed out of the room. "But don't you forget to come say goodbye!"

"I promise!" She had a smile plastered across her face. She was beginning to come back to life. Maybe her spirit wasn't dead; it was sleeping.

She neatly organized everything she had into her two duffle bags. She hugged her old pillow from home. She had missed the down feathers.

After everything was put away, she went down the hall to get a cup of coffee. She wasn't a patient anymore, so she wasn't on fluid monitoring. She even put sugar and milk in her coffee. It felt like thumbing the nose at the law.

With her coffee in hand, she skipped back to her room. Some splashed out of the cup and burned her hand. She didn't even notice.

She sat on the end of her bed and waited for her pickup.

Wait. Who was going to pick her up?

"I'm sorry. You're going to have to unpack." The same staff member who had made her so happy only moments ago was now delivering shattering news.

"I can't go?" Her voice was almost a whisper.

"There's no family member willing to take you into custody. And we can't discharge you in the streets."

"I don't live on the streets. I have an apartment on the Upper East Side. And I miss it very much."

"I understand that. But protocol dictates that we have to discharge you into some sort of custody." The nurse actually did sound apologetic.

"Did you call my father?"

"He said no."

"Did you call my aunt and uncle?"

"They said no, too."

"So now what?" Tears began to stream down her face. Her aunt and uncle had promised not to abandon her. They had signed a contract! "What happens now?"

"Well, we're looking into other facilities that will take you for long-term care."

"But I thought I was done with the program? You said I had completed the program!"

"Yes, and you did. But the fact is that you haven't gained weight, and we know you're not purging. You draw pictures of yourself in a box for every group exercise. And during your after-meal time outs, you just stare at the wall." The nurse had read her file.

She didn't want to argue, but this assessment made no sense. "I had people to pass time with in the time-out room, but the staff said they couldn't stay with me anymore. And the group exercises are geared toward substance abuse. I'm sorry if I'm not drawing pictures of pills and hypodermic needles. That's out of my frame of reference. And I eat everything you give me. I piss and shit with attendants watching! I've played the game! I've played it perfectly!" She caught herself getting negatively excited.

"Yes, you have been a model resident of Mainhouse. We know that. But it doesn't explain why you haven't gained any weight."

"Maybe it's because I feel trapped in a box!"

She sat on her bed and waited for whatever was going to come next.

"We need you to sign some release forms so that we can send your medical and psychological records to other facilities." The nurse returned with HIPAA release forms.

"But why? Why do I have to transfer? If I've completed the program, why can't I go home?"

"Because no one will sign for your custody. Maybe we can find an institution that will." The nurse handed her the paperwork and a pen.

"So, I sign this, and then you send me someplace else?"

"By tonight. Your insurance won't cover another day at Silverhill."

"So, is this for my well-being or insurance purposes?"

"Both. Just sign the paperwork so that we can expedite this process."

Her hand shook as she signed the release. She knew that a transfer almost certainly meant three to six months in another care facility. And one not covered by insurance, which meant that as bad as Silverhill had been, anywhere else would be worse.

She penned half her signature, then looked up at the nurse. "What happens if I don't sign?" She wasn't being argumentative; she was legitimately curious.

"Then we have no choice but to put you into the involuntary lockdown unit on Silverhill's campus."

She had heard of the lockdown, but she had thought it was a rumor. "But I signed into Mainhouse voluntarily. Why would you put me into involuntary?"

"Because involuntary is operated by the State. So no insurance is necessary."

She couldn't believe that once again, she was being screwed by financials. "But I have a document from a judge that says that I'm mentally fit and cannot be involuntarily institutionalized."

"I know. We have it."

"So?" This was confusing and tremendously upsetting.

"So, that court order is only valid in New York State. You're in Connecticut now." The nurse was getting tired of debating. "Sign that release and go someplace nice, or don't sign it. Then you'll go to lockdown, and we'll stick you in the first place that will have you."

Her hand shook violently as she signed the last name to her signature. Her life really was a nightmare. She was all alone in the world. Even contracts meant nothing to anyone but her. A single tear fell to the page and blotted the ink in her name.

She lay on her bed, wringing her hands, waiting to hear word on what was going to happen to her next.

After several hours, the nurse returned.

"Well? Where am I going?" Her voice rattled; she was scared.

"It's Thanksgiving weekend. We can't get hold of anyone with any jurisdiction over any of the facilities we sent your file to," the nurse explained.

"So I can go home?"

"We can't get in touch with anyone on your Silverhill treatment team, either."

"What does that mean?"

"It's a holiday. There's no one on staff who has the authority to release you."

"But my insurance is up today. You won't get paid to hold me." She really, really wanted to leave.

"We know that. And I've spoken with the bursar and the lawyers." The nurse was trying to the relay the pertinent information in layman's terms. "If we release you, and something happens, the cost of that suit would be much greater than the cost of keeping you here through the weekend."

"So I'm staying here for free?"

"This was our oversight. No one had written your discharge plan, and the date of your insurance expiration unfortunately coincided with a holiday. This was our fault. We'll keep you here until we can get in touch with your treatment team to figure out the next step." The nurse said this as though her staying at Silverhill through the weekend was a great favor they were doing her.

"But why can't I just go home?"

"I've already told you. No one is willing to sign for your custody, and there is no one at all of Silverhill with any authority to override that." The nurse gestured toward her bags. "Better unpack. I need those duffle bags back in storage before dinner."

She pulled everything out of her bags. Feeling sneaky, she remade her bed with her own pillow and blanket. It was a pathetic act of rebellion. But it gave her a fleeting sense of power.

There was no group work or any treatment meetings that weekend. It seemed that a holiday weekend at Silverhill was more about keeping the patients stable till Monday and less about actually doing any forward work with them.

There was hardly any staff around. She had to spend twenty minutes tracking down an attendant each time she had to pee to get her bathroom door unlocked.

A lot of her friends had gone home, or on to other transitional facilities. And, being a holiday, no new people checked in. Mainhouse was eerily quiet.

On Sunday, she was told that her doctors had been contacted, and she was free to go after lunch.

"Do you mean it this time?" She was careful not to prematurely celebrate.

"Yes, we've spoken with an excellent caregiver who has faxed over an agreement to take you into custodial care."

"Really? My doctors aren't sending me to another facility?" She felt relieved.

"No. They have spoken at length with a gentleman who has promised to care for you."

A red flag popped up in her mind. "What gentleman?"

The nurse shuffled through the paperwork. "A very nice man. His name is . . . Mitchell Durman."

She protested at the office room on the residential floor of Mainhouse. "Please, let me speak with my doctors! Please!" She was in tears.

"You have to calm down. You don't want to be put in lockdown, do you?" The staff was dismissive.

"Please, you don't understand! I've told my doctors at length of the physical abuse that I've suffered at the hands of Mitchell Durman. Please don't send me to him!" She was sobbing, and her body shook. "Please! I'll go to a facility. Any facility. Please don't send me to Mitchell."

"Really, you need to calm down." No one was listening to her.

"But you don't understand!"

"We understand. We know that Mr. Durman has called you every day, like clockwork," one of the nurses explained. "And now he's spoken with your doctors. He seems to be the only one close to you who is willing to participate in your recovery."

"In my recovery?" She gasped for air. "But I was healthy before I met him. He made me this way. He's a monster! Please believe me. Mitchell Durman is a monster!"

"Now you're just projecting." The nurse was issuing psychobabble. "You're just upset because you know that Mr. Durman is integral to your path to recovery."

"Please! He's a monster! A monster! He makes me fuck young girls with a strap-on, and they drink his piss, and he makes girls lick shit out of his asshole, and he—"

"Stop. You're embarrassing yourself." The nurse looked directly at her. "You should be ashamed of yourself. You're very lucky to have a friend like Mr. Durman."

She packed her duffle bags, for the second time that weekend. She sat on the bench in the vestibule with one of the attendants, waiting for her pickup.

Two hours passed, and as each car sped up the circular driveway and then back down, she would at once get nervous, then relieved. She didn't want Mitchell to pick her up. But she didn't want to stay at Silverhill either.

A black car with New York license plates pulled up in front of the front door of Mainhouse. There was a handwritten sign hanging in the passenger window that read *Miss Durman*.

The attendant stood and picked up one of her duffle bags. "This is your ride. Let's go." The attendant was tired of waiting too.

"But, he's not even in the car. This is a taxi!" She couldn't believe that after all the bullshit they had subjected her to on Friday, Silverhill was going to release her into the custody of a livery cab driver.

"Whatever. Grab your bags." The attendant opened the front door and walked down the steps.

"It's a taxi! A taxi!" She yelled in the vestibule.

The managerial nurse who had given her so much trouble on Friday was walking by at that moment and overheard the exchange. "Is that really a taxi?"

"Yes!" she affirmed to the nurse, exasperated. "You told me on Friday that I had to be released into someone's custody. And now you're sending me off in a taxi?" The whole concept was bizarre and contradictory.

Apparently, the nurse thought so too. With one finger extended, as though to say "hold on," the nurse sent a message through the JobCom. "Do you know that the patient is being released into a taxi?"

There was a muddled response on the other end of the walkie-talkie.

"Yes, I know that the forms were signed and faxed over to us. But this is a taxi!" The nurse seemed just as concerned as she was.

There was another scrambled reply from the radio.

"You're not hearing me! We cannot release a patient into the custody of a taxi driver!"

More static.

"But it's a taxi!"

Now there was a lengthy, scrambled reply.

Defeated, the nurse turned to her and said, "Well, it looks like you're going home in a taxi." She turned and walked back into the foyer. "Safe trip."

The newly released patient stood in the driveway. She looked at the taxi. She looked up at Mainhouse. She had no choice.

She didn't even imagine to what hell the taxi would be delivering her.

Forty-Seven

"So, I had to bail you out again, huh?" Mitchell was standing in his living room, holding a glass of wine when she arrived.

"You started drinking again?"

"Hypnosis is bullshit." Mitchell took a gulp of wine. "How was rehab?"

"Ha ha."

"Hey, don't I even get a hug? Maybe even a thank you?" Mitchell was drunk.

"A thank you for what? I spent an extra weekend in that dungeon in limbo, and for what?"

"I just had to make sure you realized that I'm all you got." Mitchell extended his arms.

"I'm not going to hug you."

"Aw. Come on, babe. Say it!" Mitchell goaded her. "Say it! I'm all you got!"

"As much as it sickens me," she said.

"That's the spirit!" Mitchell laughed, ignoring her insolence. "Come on, have a glass of wine. Talk to me!"

"I don't want any wine. I just want to go home."

"But, my dear, you are home." Mitchell smiled maniacally. He was implying something.

"What are you saying, Mitchell?"

"I'm saying, welcome home!" He pointed toward the bedroom. "You get the bed. I'll stay on the couch. I love you that much."

"Mitchell, you're not hearing me." She crossed her arms, with her duffle bags at her feet in the foyer. "I want to go home."

Mitchell slammed down his glass on the art deco table in the foyer. Wine splashed all over the wood, but he didn't notice. His eyes grew red, and he gritted his teeth. With both hands, he grabbed all the hair on the back of her head and pulled her down to her knees.

"No, you crazy imbecile. You're not hearing me." He spat on her face as he spoke. "I signed the papers for you. I am obligated to keep you here for at least a week." He leaned down so that his nose was touching hers. "You don't understand. I own you."

She tried to focus on keeping strong. "You don't own me! I'm solid! I'm autonomous! I'm my own person!" She refused to cry.

"You are most certainly not your own person," Mitchell snarled. "You're my person. I faxed the paperwork to Silverhill. They sold you to me."

"They didn't sell me!" She continued to be obstinate. "No one can sell me!"

"They sold you, you fool! You became a financial liability and a legal nightmare to them. They were happy to sell you to the lowest bidder." Mitchell's voice was almost devilish.

"You didn't pay for me."

Mitchell slapped her across the face. "I've paid enough for you. You stupid, ugly consumer. Look at me!" Mitchell grabbed her face in both hands. "I'm drinking again because of you. Because of your stupidity!"

Against her will, she began to cry.

"Don't cry! Don't you dare cry!" Mitchell grabbed her hair again and yanked upward. "On your feet!" His voice boomed.

"Please don't hurt me!" She was afraid that she was pleading for her life.

"Don't give me that bullshit!" Mitchell slapped her again, hard. Her face burned, but she dared not raise her hand to touch it. "I'm the only one who hasn't hurt you." Mitchell slapped her again. She was afraid her face was going to bleed.

"Please, Mitchell," she whimpered.

"Don't 'please, Mitchell' me, you ungrateful little bitch!" Mitchell slapped her again. "I'm the only one who loves you. I'm the only one on your team."

"Please, Mitchell!" She repeated her plea, this time as a moan.

Another hard slap. "Where are your parents, huh? Where are your freakishly stupid aunt and uncle, huh? Who stayed with you toward the end? Who?" Mitchell stuck his face directly into hers.

"You did, Mitchell," she whispered.

"That's right. I did. I'm Mitchell the fucking saint. I'm a fool to have stayed by your side, but I did. I fucking did! Don't you realize that?"

"Yes, Mitchell." She sniffled.

He slapped her once more, this time even more powerfully. She spun around on her feet. Mitchell grabbed her hair and held her up so that she wouldn't fall. "Now, you stupid idiot, put on your pajamas and get into bed. I'm your fucking caretaker!" Mitchell threw her toward the master bedroom.

She fought to stay upright, but her hands hit the floor. She struggled back onto her two feet. She longed to be back in the safety of Silverhill.

"I said put on your pajamas. I'm your goddamned custodian. I have to fucking take care of you!"

She reached for one of her duffle bags and dragged it into the master bedroom.

Feeling physically unstable, it took all her concentration to shimmy herself into her pair of pajamas.

"When you're finished changing, come out here and have a glass of wine. I want to see if you remembered how to suck cock while you were on your month-long vacation!"

She shuffled her feet as she walked into the living room. She kept her eyes on the floor. She couldn't bear to look at Mitchell.

There was an overflowing glass of wine on the coffee table.

"Chug it," Mitchell ordered. "Chug it down now. You need a drink!"

She hadn't been around any alcohol in a month, and it was difficult to swallow the glass of wine. Through her tears and her sniveling, she did her best.

When the glass was almost empty, Mitchell instructed her, "Good. Now come here and suck my cock. Let me know how much you want to thank me."

Mitchell kept her hostage for a week. It wasn't too bad. Mostly, he drank heavily and snored loudly on the sofa. She stayed in the bedroom and watched the projection television on the wall. It was just as boring as being in Silverhill.

Eventually, Mitchell let her go home. He claimed that he had completed his legally obligated custodianship, and that she was then free to leave. She had no idea if this was true or not. Nor did she care. She was just happy to go home.

When she finally got back to her apartment, she was once again overwhelmed by an oppressive feeling of emptiness. Maybe the thirty thousand dollars would make her feel better.

She called Uncle Norman.

"Hi, Uncle Norman." She greeted him flatly. There was no emotion in her voice.

"Hello? Ummmm. . . ." Uncle Norman couldn't even bring himself to speak her name. He must have been truly ashamed of himself. "Where are you?"

"I'm back at home."

"You're . . . at home?" Uncle Norman seemed confused.

"Of course I'm at home. My treatment was twenty-eight days, remember?"

"No, yeah, no. I remember. Twenty-eight days." Norman was stuttering.

"That was the agreement, right?" She was getting agitated.

"Yes. No. Right. Okay. Twenty-eight days. Right."

"Well, twenty-eight days are up, and then some." She tried to listen for a reaction. Norman was silent. She continued. "Anyway, I'm back at home."

"How are you feeling?" Uncle Norman feigned concern.

"I feel great. Really happy to be home." She tried to keep the conversation on track. "Anyway, I'm calling about our agreement."

"What agreement?" Uncle Norman played dumb.

She wanted to attack him for abandoning her, but she forced herself to keep her eye on the prize. "You know. I did my twenty-eight days. Grandma sends me fifteen thousand dollars. I get back on my feet and away from depending on Mitchell."

"Right. Yeah. Okay. I remember." Uncle Norman paused. "Hey, can I call you back in like two minutes?"

She had no idea why Norman was hemming and hawing, but she had already learned that he was a cad and not a man of honor. So it didn't surprise her that he had to collect his thoughts before speaking to her. Norman's mind wasn't sharp enough to have a difficult conversation without ample preparation time.

"Sure, Uncle Norman. I'll be waiting by the phone." She meant it.

After almost an hour, her phone rang. She didn't even need to look at the caller ID.

"Hi, Norman."

"Hi. Right. Sorry about that." Norman's voice sounded like his body was fidgeting.

"No worries." She steered right back to the point of the phone call. "So, the money? When can I expect it?"

Norman made a pathetic attempt to change the subject. "So, did you get better?"

"Better when? Better than what?" She was legitimately confused.

"Did you get better at Silverhill?"

"Better than what?" she asked again.

"Better than when you checked in?" Norman was trying to avoid answering the money question for some reason.

"Ummm, it was a disturbing experience," she said honestly.

"So, then, you're not better," Norman stated.

"Like I said, it was disturbing." She didn't like having to repeat herself.

"What was disturbing? Facing your problems?" Norman was desperately trying to deflect blame from the truth.

"No. It was disturbing to find out who I can't trust in this world from the tiny pool of people I thought I could."

"I don't know what that means, sweetheart."

She was getting tense, but she struggled to maintain her composure. "It means, Norman, where the hell did you go?"

"When?"

"When? When I was fucking abandoned in Connecticut! Where were you? In your getaway house in Hilton Head?"

Silence.

"You were! You left me there to rot and went on vacation!" She really hated Norman now.

"We weren't on vacation. But yes, we were at our house in Hilton Head. But that doesn't matter!" Norman feebly tried to defend himself. "Your father should have taken responsibility for your care once you were in Silverhill. My mission was just to get you in."

"So you tricked me?" She wasn't surprised.

"We didn't *trick* you. We were just trying to get your father to take notice."

"This was all about a power play with Dawn trying to control the actions of my father?" This made sense. Sibling rivalry that lasted more than half a century. Again, she was a stupid pawn.

"No. It's not like that." Norman's voice sounded whiny. He didn't even speak like a grown man, even though he was more than sixty years old. It was embarrassing to witness him so pathetic, even just to hear it.

"So, what is it, then, Norman?"

"We just wanted your father to take some responsibility."

She changed the subject. This conversation could only go in circles. "Forget my father. Let's talk about the money. You know, the other part of the deal."

"Grandma's money," Norman stated, mostly to himself.

"That's right. Grandma's money." She took a deep breath. She didn't want to have to involve her grandmother. "I don't have to call Grandma, do I?"

"No, no, Grandma agreed to the plan and sent a check." Norman was confessing more than he had intended.

"Great!" She felt momentarily relieved. "Well, you know my address. Just send it over."

"It's gone." Norman's voice was barely audible.

"I'm sorry. I couldn't hear you. Can you repeat that?" She wanted to jump through the phone line and beat Norman senseless.

"It's gone. The money's gone. I have to go now."

"Don't you dare hang up!" she commanded. "If the money's gone, where did it go?"

"Well, . . ." Norman was trying to compile a lie, but his mind just wasn't sharp enough. Why didn't her aunt marry someone even slightly intelligent? It was difficult to communicate with a dolt. "Well, . . . Grandma sent Dawn and I the check." His poor grammar always made her cringe.

"Right. Okay. So you have the check."

"Well. . . ." Norman's pauses were intensely aggravating.

"Where is my money, Norman?!" she shouted.

"It's gone. Spent. Expenses." Norman sounded like he was on the verge of tears. "I told you that I lost my job, right?"

"So you stole my money?!" Now she was yelling. "I have nothing. *Nothing.* You stole from your niece who has nothing!" She took a deep breath. "What expenses, Norman?"

"Well, it was expensive going up to stay with you in Connecticut, and—"

"And what? And what?!" She couldn't tolerate this conversation any longer. "You stayed for three days, Norman! Three fucking days!"

"It was expensive," Norman repeated.

"You're telling me that you spent fifteen thousand dollars on three days in Connecticut?"

"Well, and airfare, and. . ."

"Okay, stop fucking making shit up, Norman. You are pathetic. There is no way that you spent fifteen thousand dollars in three days. And even if you did, that check from Grandma was not to cover *your* expenses, remember?!"

"It was only ten thousand dollars that Grandma sent—"

"You're not helping your fucking case, Norman! Grandma is your ninety-two-year-old mother-in-law, you son-of-a-bitch! You took from her. You stole from me. You are a disgrace!"

"But. . . . I lost my job." Norman sounded like a whimpering puppy that had just peed on the rug.

"So you take from an old woman and an ailing girl?"

"I don't want to talk about this anymore."

"No kidding." She breathed for a moment. "I could deal with you being a liar. But I'm shocked that you're also an outright thief. God is sending you straight to hell, Norman. You're going straight to hell."

"But, I lost my job. . . ." His voice trailed off as she slammed down her phone.

Damn it! She was so fucking naïve. Was there anyone in the world who was not out to get her? This was ridiculous. She had always thought that Mitchell was paranoid. Maybe she wasn't paranoid enough.

Forty-Eight

"I'm going to be leaving the country for a while. I'd like to take you to lunch before I go." Mitchell called her in the morning.

"Do you want me to come by with the newspaper?" She knew her role in this system.

"No need." Mitchell surprised her by saying, "I've already been out for a walk this morning."

"You've been out?"

"I'm turning over a new leaf. I can't stop drinking, so forget that. But it doesn't mean that I have to rot away." Mitchell sounded sincere.

"I agree. You shouldn't rot."

"I have been rotting. And you have contributed to it, by the way." Mitchell accused her. "You consume way too much of my energy."

If Mitchell wanted to blame her for his miserable life, so be it. She was just happy that he was going to be gone for a while. Maybe now she could piece her life back together.

"Okay, Mitchell. So where shall I meet you?"

"At Tino's, of course!"

"Of course."

When she got to Tino's, Mitchell had already finished off most of a bottle of Chianti. It wasn't even noon. He must have been the first customer in the restaurant and had begun drinking early.

"Hello, Mitchell." She took her usual chair.

"Hello, beautiful."

"Cut the crap, Mitchell. What's going on?"

"Oooooh. . . ." Mitchell filled her wine glass. "What happened to the lady? Where's my little Jackie O?"

"They beat the civility out of me during my institutionalization. Seriously, Mitchell, what's going on?"

"Well," Mitchell spoke in a soft and patronizing tone. "As I said on the phone, I'm going to be leaving the country for a while."

"You said that. Where are you going?"

"Who knows? Who cares? I need to focus on me." Mitchell leaned in toward her and snarled, "I'm tired of focusing on *you*."

She ignored the slight. "Good, Mitchell. I think that you should focus on you. I think that's a very healthy approach to the future."

"I'm glad you agree." Mitchell pointed toward the table. "Now drink your wine."

She had a clear agenda for that lunch. She wanted to get her promised monies. But she didn't want to lay her cards on the table too soon.

They had a luxurious though brief lunch. They ate in relative silence.

"I'm going to have an espresso. Will you join me?"

She realized that he wasn't going to let her out of the lunch anytime soon. Since Mitchell had consumed almost all of the three bottles of Chianti he'd ordered, she realized she needed a drink.

"I'll pass on the espresso." She turned to Claude. "I'd like a Vin Santo, s'il vous plait."

"Bien sûr." Claude disappeared into the kitchen.

"Vin Santo, huh?" Mitchell furrowed his brow. "You only drink dessert wine when you mean business."

"I do mean business, Mitchell." Her Vin Santo arrived, and she took a gentle sip. "Before you leave for your trip to . . . somewhere, I'd like to settle the financials."

"And what financials are those, my dear?"

"Well, the contract we signed when I entered Silverhill."

Mitchell took a sip of his espresso and suspended the demitasse cup in mid-air. "Well, of course I remember that contract."

"Great." Maybe she would finally see some of her due.

"Not so fast." Mitchell put the cup back on the saucer. "Did Norman and Dawn give you the money?"

"My grandmother gave them the check."

"And?" Mitchell was waiting for the rest of the story so that he could taunt her.

"And they, um, reappropriated it." She was trying to be diplomatic. She didn't want to call Norman and Dawn thieves, even though they were.

"They reappropriated it?" Mitchell repeated. "You mean, they pocketed it."

"I don't want to talk about Norman and Dawn. They're despicable enough. I'm talking about your promise to me."

"And I don't lie to you, do I?" Mitchell chided.

"I like to think that you don't."

"Well, I spent more than five times that amount to get you out of Schneider's!" Mitchell took a big swallow and finished his espresso. "The legal fees were ridiculous."

"You didn't get me out of Schneider's!" She was shocked.

"I most certainly did!"

"Okay, I'm sorry. You're right. Your lawyers got me out of Schneider's. And deposited into Hillside."

"Wasn't Schneider's!" Mitchell's voice was childish and singsongy.

"So that's it? You're saying that the money that you owe me went to repay a debt by which you had me involuntarily committed into a state psychiatric ward?"

"Your parents had you committed."

"Your lawyers didn't help."

"They got you out of Schneider's, didn't they?"

She couldn't believe they were even debating this. "So, you never intended to make good on your promise?"

"I'd give you the money if Dawn and Norman did." Mitchell leaned in toward her. "But I knew they were shit people with no morals. It was a safe bet on my part."

She had nothing left to say. She folded her napkin and stood to leave the table. "Goodbye, Mitchell."

"Not even a thank you as you walk away?" Mitchell called out after her.

"Thank you for once again teaching me that all people are shit."

Forty-Nine

With Mitchell gone, she could finally relax. She had no demands on her time, no threats to her health, no pussy hunting to do.

She also had no job, no friends, no purpose.

She had some nice jewelry. She had some nice clothes. She had great shoes. She sat in her apartment in sweatpants.

She almost wished that she were an addict like her fellow inmates at Silverhill. At least they had drugs and alcohol and enjoyable sex to fill their days. Her days were empty. Hollow.

Everyone she trusted had lied to her. Stolen from her. Abandoned her.

She didn't think that she was a bad person. But maybe she was. How could so much anguish befall a good person?

Maybe she was too mercenary. Maybe she was too naïve. Maybe she was too stupid. Maybe she was too smart. Maybe she was too weak. Maybe she was too strong.

Maybe all her assets were flaws.

The days leading into winter ticked by slowly. She slept rarely and fitfully when she did. She took walks to nowhere. She treated herself to lonely restaurant meals. She wanted to speak to someone, if only to say "hi," but she had no one to call.

The speed dial on her cell phone was filled with numbers of women she never intended to call again. And her friends from before Mitchell had all moved on with their lives and forgotten her. This may have been the point at which many people give up entirely.

But suicide sounded like more effort than relief. The thought never even crossed her mind. Instead, she tried to think of ways to fill her days. She needed things to look forward to, new adventures to fill her days.

She really, truly, felt crazy to her core. Her thoughts were fuzzy, her nightmares disassociated, her days a scramble. She gained no pleasure from eating or drinking or sleeping or waking. She wasn't even tuned in enough to be depressed. She was the living undead.

On one Friday morning, she did two things. The first thing she did was post an ad on Craigslist to find a male dinner date. She didn't want to deal with the email process of regular dating sites. She wanted immediate gratification. She needed to prove to herself that there were good men out there in this world. As for Craigslist, it had been a great resource to meet women instantly, so why wouldn't it work just as easily for men?

The second thing she did was call her father.

"Dad, I know you don't want to speak to me, and I know you left me to the will of the system back up at Silverhill. But I need your help. I don't want to die." She spoke from the heart.

"Sweetie, I don't want you to die either. But at this rate, I think you know you're going to."

"Dad, I don't think I'm going to die. And I think that it's disgusting and defeating that everyone has settled on that as my ultimate fate. Because it's not. It's just not." She was defiant.

"Where's Mitchell?" Her father hated Mitchell, and he had always suspected that Mitchell was in the background, orchestrating every exchange she had with a member of the outside world. Which was, for the most part, true.

"Mitchell's gone. I don't know where. But he's going to be gone for a while. So I have a window." She spoke earnestly. "I have a real window, Dad. I can beat this." She didn't know what "this" was. Maybe it was Mitchell, or her abusive childhood, or her low body weight, or even her disdain for the general population of people around her. *This.*

"You really want to do the work?" Her father wanted to hear affirmations.

"I checked myself into Silverhill, didn't I?"

"Only because you were bribed." Her father knew the story, maybe from her grandmother.

"Yeah. I was bribed. But I was lied to. I did my end. Everyone else cheated me."

"I know. I could have told you that. My sister is an abominable human being." Her father liked the word "abominable." "If you had asked me, I would have told you that Dawn was a meddler. Her only pleasure is in feeling that she's controlling everyone else's world."

"A meddler is different than a thief, Dad."

"Well, I didn't know that my sister was a thief until she stole from you. But I'm never speaking to her again. She's a horrid person."

"And Uncle Norman?"

"Norman's just an idiot. Not in a malicious way." Her father was qualifying the statement. "Norman is sweet, but he's too stupid for his own good. He bumbles through life." Her father paused. "I think that Norman may have hit his head. No man can be that dumb. I don't know how my sister has stayed with him all these years. She can't enjoy being married to a man with no brain."

"Norman has a brain. I think he just doesn't understand it." She tried, half-heartedly, to defend Norman.

"Sure he has a brain. He found a way to scam you out of fifteen thousand dollars, right?"

"I don't have strong defenses."

Her father sighed. "That's what I'm afraid of. So, lay it out there. What are you asking me for?"

"I don't know yet. I'm going to see my psychiatrist, Dr. Kaala, and ask her for some advice and referrals. But, before I pass any information on to you, I have to ask: Are you willing to get with the program?"

"As long as it's not something ridiculous and inappropriate. Like Silverhill. Or that bulimia safari that Mitchell emailed us."

"Mitchell sent you information on a bulimia safari?" She hadn't heard about this.

"Oh yeah. He was very excited. It's a program in Africa call *Anorexia, Bulimia, and Safari.*"

"Really? That actually sounds cool."

"I think the idea is that when you're fighting for your life against nature and predators, you don't have time to think about attacking yourself."

"That sounds like a good program, Dad."

"Well, I'll tell you what. Let's address your basic, most immediate issues. Then we can send you to the lions' den. Deal?"

"Deal."

She made an appointment to see Dr. Kaala that Monday. In the meantime, she had a weekend to fill.

Her posting on Craigslist, which was 100 percent honest and direct, had received several hundred responses. And more filled her inbox every minute. She wondered if all girls received this multitude of replies, or if only she did because she wrote so candidly. The one thing she had learned from Mitchell was that truth and honesty trumped all, even if deception and deceit immediately followed.

Skimming through her responses, she made dates for Saturday brunch, Saturday dinner, Sunday brunch, Sunday dinner, and Monday breakfast. That would lead her into her appointment with Dr. Kaala. The rest of her dates could be planned after that.

The men that she met were nice, but not memorable. The meals that she had were nice, but not memorable. She was filling her days in a way that was nice, but not memorable. She was looking forward to meeting with Dr. Kaala.

"I need structure. Foundation. Talk therapy." She spoke candidly with her doctor.

"Silverhill was not the right place for you," Dr. Kaala affirmed.

"No kidding."

"You don't function when stifled." Dr. Kaala pulled some books off the shelf. "These books are case studies of people who function well when stifled. You are not one of them." Dr. Kaala dropped several books at her feet.

"So, what are you telling me?" She really wanted to know her prognosis.

"I'm telling you that being in an institution or a facility or whatever makes you more crazy."

"More crazy than what?"

"More crazy than not crazy." Dr. Kaala was not providing any insight.

"I'm confused."

"The doctors at Silverhill took you off almost all the medications I had prescribed." Dr. Kaala shuffled through her file.

"All but what?"

"Everything but your sleeping pills, basically." Dr. Kaala slammed the folder shut. "They were more interested in sedating you than treating you."

"Maybe. I mean, I guess so. That makes sense. At least, from an economic standpoint."

Dr. Kaala interrupted. "Everything makes sense from an economic standpoint. But you are not a source of profit, no?"

She shrugged her shoulders and dropped her head. "Maybe not to you, but to some people."

"Well, that is not my business. It is my business to heal you." Dr. Kaala leaned against the edge of the desk and looked at her intently. "How may I heal you?"

"I guess I need someone to talk to. I need an advocate. A friend in my court. Even if it's just a paid therapist."

Dr. Kaala walked around the side of her desk and pulled out some business cards from her desk drawer. "I can send you to such a person."

She palmed the cards that Dr. Kaala laid out in front of her. "Thank you."

"Don't thank me. Find the therapist that works for you. Get well. Feel well. Do well. Yes?" Dr. Kaala had a disarming, trustworthy accent.

"Yes. I will make some calls. Yes. I will find my advocate."

"Good." Dr. Kaala opened the office door. "You have good things for you, if you find the right support."

She walked to the reception desk to submit the cash to cover her copay. She was surprised when the receptionist handed her one of Dr. Kaala's notorious goody bags of medications.

"I'm getting more meds?"

"The doctor wrote in her notes that she was very upset that you were taken off the medications she had prescribed." The receptionist was all business. "Your copay is twenty-five dollars."

She had received mixed signals from Dr. Kaala. She was given referrals for psychoanalysis, but she was also given a bag of medication.

Did Dr. Kaala want her to get better? Or just mask the signs of how crazy she really was?

She sorted through the stack of business cards that Dr. Kaala had given her and made a therapist selection based on geographical proximity to her apartment. It seemed as good a system of selection as any, since she really had no fundamental frame of reference for an educated choice.

The therapist she chose had a completely unpronounceable last name. It looked like a mess of consonants thrown together on a business card. When she called the number, she was half-hoping that she would get an answering machine recording so that she could hear how the name sounded. She didn't want to embarrass herself.

Unfortunately, the therapist answered the phone. So she avoided slaughtering the name by just bypassing a formal greeting.

"I was given a referral by Dr. Kaala on Park Avenue. May I please schedule an appointment?"

"Can you come in this evening?" Wow, this therapist wasted no time.

"Sure, okay." She had nothing else to do.

"Okay. 6:30 p.m. Bring your insurance card."

"Okay." She hung up the phone. That was easy.

At 6:15, she left her home to walk to the therapist's office, which was located only three blocks away. She had vastly overestimated the time she'd take to get there.

"I'm going to see Dr. Tshks—" She couldn't even begin to try to say it correctly.

The doorman seemed to recognize the struggle; he must have gotten it from patients all the time. Instead of pronouncing it, he just said, "15J. The elevator's on the right." He pointed through the small lobby.

She rang the doorbell at apartment 15J and a tiny, middle-aged Jewish woman opened the door. "You can call me Dr. T."

Okay. Dr. T was a manageable name. She understood now why so many Jews had shortened and otherwise altered their last names when immigrating to the U.S. If the original names were anything like Dr. T's, alterations were necessary.

They didn't cover very much during that first session. But Dr. T did ask her if her parents would be willing to come in for a session. The doctor wanted to meet her parents to make an unbiased evaluation of them before addressing the parental issues with her patient. It made a lot of sense.

When she got home that night, she immediately called her parents. They agreed to meet with Dr. T in the morning. She would have a session soon after. A debriefing of sorts.

She was a little nervous and a little excited to hear what Dr. T would have to say after sitting with her parents for forty-five minutes. She arrived on time to her appointment and sat on the sofa, wringing her hands.

"Well?" She asked Dr. T, anxious to hear all the details.

"Well, what?"

"My parents. Please tell me everything."

"Okay. Well, let's start with your father." Dr. T leaned forward. "Your father. Your father loves you very much. He feels very helpless, and very scared. He's a very weak man."

"Weak?" She didn't like to hear her father referred to as "weak."

"Weak in that he has strong convictions, but he does nothing to actualize anything." Dr. T made sense. This sounded like her father exactly.

"Okay. And my mother?"

"Your mother is pure evil. Let's focus on your father." Dr. T dismissed the question.

"I'm sorry. Can we go back? Did you say pure evil?"

"I did. Pure evil. Now, your father on the other hand—"

"No. Seriously. I can't believe you just said that!" She didn't want to defend her mother, but how could someone say that after a forty-five-minute encounter? "Is pure evil even a real clinical term?"

"I'm not being clinical. I'm telling you that there is no reason to discuss your mother because it is impossible to forge a relationship with pure evil. Now, can we go back to your father?"

"Yes. Okay. Sorry. So, my father?"

"I think that your father is a good man. I also think that he's severely afraid of your mother. He's also afraid of you. He's often paralyzed by fear." Dr. T took a sip from a soda bottle and continued. "So, your father, when he does try to do something, often does the wrong thing. Not for want of good intentions. But he's just not good at fathering and dealing with interpersonal relationships."

"So, you're saying that I should give my dad a shot?"

"Definitely. Give up on your mother though."

Dr. T and her father made arrangements for her to have therapy appointments every single day for a month. The appointments were usually late in the morning, and Dr. T scheduled at that time so she could feed her lunch before she went home. She also had appointments on Saturday nights, after the sunset that ended the Sabbath. Dr. T was a religious Jew.

The introduction of routine was paramount to the patient's everyday life. Now she had someplace to go each day, and someone to whom to be accountable. Dr. T was a positive influence.

The doctor had uncanny insight. The patient had never before met someone who was so able to analyze and interpret situations and people. When Dr. T addressed the Mitchell issue, it was as though she channeled Mitchell's voice exactly. It was a bit unnerving.

"I'd like you to see the movie *Gaslight*. I think that it will help you to better understand the hold that Mitchell has on you."

"You want me to watch a movie? Is it a new movie? I haven't heard of it." She thought it strange that psychoanalysis indicated the necessity of movie watching.

"There is a psychological condition called gaslighting that got its name from the movie." Dr. T wrote the title on a Post-it note and handed it to her. "It's a black-and-white movie from the 1930s. Angela Lansbury's first film. I think you'll find the plotline disturbing."

"How so?"

"The young woman in the movie is a strong, confident, intelligent woman. She marries a manipulative, deceitful man who is motivated by evil. Through mind games and scare tactics, he convinces her that she is losing her mind. When she is fully convinced that she is indeed crazy, he is able to control her by fear."

"Fear of what?"

"Fear of losing him. You see, he makes her believe that he is the only one who will stand by her as she falls into an abyss of insanity."

"But she's not really insane?" She was trying to process this information. "If she's not really crazy, why does she stay with him?"

"Ding ding ding." Dr. T smiled. "And that, sweet girl, is the purpose of your therapy."

"To find out why I'm with Mitchell?"

"That, and why you were so vulnerable to gaslighting in the first place."

"And then?"

"And then, through our sessions, hopefully you'll be able to break free from Mitchell's strong grasp."

"So I'm not really crazy?"

"Of course not! If you were crazy, would they have let you out of Hillside? Would they have let you out of Silverhill? Would I allow you to come into my home every day to sit in my office?" Dr. T made a good point.

"I guess I understand what you're saying. But I do legitimately feel crazy." She sighed.

"That's because you were the perfect candidate for gaslighting. That's why Mitchell found you. That's probably how Mitchell found you. Don't underestimate the efforts of the evildoer."

Her days were structured around meetings with Dr. T. But that still left her with twenty-three vacant hours in every day. To fill her time, she dated different men she met on Craigslist.

Most of the men invited her on conventional dates. There were a lot of brunches and lunches and dinners. She avoided drink dates because they seemed to often play out as interviews for real dates. And she had enough invitations for real dates to make the formality of the noncommittal drink dates invalid.

The men all ran together, lumped into a chasm of superfluousness and superficiality. Some of the men kept her attention for the duration of a meal. Most did not.

As much as she had been abused by Mitchell, she had been spoiled by him, too. It wasn't that she expected all men to be as inherently wealthy and well educated as he, but she had grown used to a man who was a power player in his life and not merely a follower in abject happenstance.

Almost all the men asked her out for second dates. But her schedule was so filled with first dates that she had little room to allow for follow-up. It wasn't that she didn't want second dates; in fact, she welcomed and embraced the idea that there could be the chance for her own happily ever after. At the same time, however, she was trying to prove to herself that Mitchell was a fluke, an anomaly among men. And the only way to do that, in her confused mind, was to surround herself with other men.

Fifty

Dr. T knew that she was spending her evenings with a rotating door of potential suitors. But at the moment, the therapy was focusing on her unhealthy attachment to Mitchell. The other men would have to wait.

She wasn't sure if she was expecting some sort of instantaneous "ah ha" breakthrough moment, or if psychotherapy was not an instant gratification sort of system, but she felt more as though she were simply going through the motions than actually making any gains. Nonetheless, she showed up every day, on time, at Dr. T's home office, ready and willing to move forward.

She had watched *Gaslight*, as she had been instructed, but she'd found the movie to be confusing and fragmented. And she failed to see how it compared with her life.

"I was afraid that you would say that." Dr. T sighed.

"What do you mean?"

"Well, when the topic of a movie hits so close to home, it's common for someone to just miss the plotline entirely," Dr. T explained.

"You think that I missed the plotline?"

"Well, did you like the movie?"

"Not really."

"Then yes, I think you missed the plotline," Dr. T said flatly.

"Oh."

"Oh, exactly. But we can work on that. That's why we're here, isn't it?"

She nodded.

Dr. T added, "By the way, you owe me three dollars for the movie rental."

Again she nodded. But this affirmation was contrived. She liked and respected Dr. T. But she also knew that her month of psychoanalysis was costing her father upwards of forty thousand dollars. To ask for a reimbursement of three dollars she thought was in poor taste.

But she did think the doctor had some keen insights, and a strong understanding of what was happening in her world.

"So, what do you do every night?" Dr. T listened but never took notes.

"I go out."

"Out where? Out to clubs? To bars? Where?"

The men she attracted were always deeply entrenched in the world of food and fashion, not unlike Mitchell. And her keen knowledge of wine was appreciated by a certain worldly, wealthy, hedonistic demographic. As long as no one hit her, she always felt that she was trading up from Mitchell.

"Mostly to restaurants. Sometimes to the theater or the opera, or to art galleries. But most men want to take me out to eat."

"And why do they want to do that?"

She wasn't really ashamed of the answer, although she wasn't exactly proud of it either. "I think they're using me for my knowledge of wine. Plus, I'm good company."

"I can see that. You're intelligent, well informed, and pleasant to speak to." Dr. T probed deeper, "but do you think that any of them want more?"

"More, how?"

"Sexually, emotionally, longer term?"

Maybe it was from her experience with all of the women she had met for Mitchell, or maybe she was just good at recognizing immediate red flags. "I'm sure they do. I hope they do!" she emphasized.

"So, you think that if you meet a good man, an honest man, a good fit, you can be the woman he's looking for?"

She dropped her head. "Not now, no. But I know that I am that woman to someone."

"I know that you are, too." Dr. T spoke with true compassion. "But you're useless to anyone until you break free from Mitchell. You know that, right?"

"I do," she said sheepishly.

"I'm a little disturbed by the fact that you didn't recognize any of your own life in *Gaslight*," Dr. T said.

"I didn't like that movie. I didn't get it."

"I know that. You've said that." Dr. T leaned in close and looked her in the eye. "The fact that you don't recognize a mirror image of yourself is the foundation for your necessary psychotherapy."

❧

The men came and went. She was attracted to some, bored with others. She never felt that she was using or abusing anyone; she was good company, cordial, and appreciative at worst.

She saw some men twice, but never any more. She slept with some. Her sex was a bit mechanical but not contrived. She was a good lay. Perhaps a bit robotic, but good nonetheless.

She was also a great dinner companion. She had lots of stories to tell. Lots of adventures and lessons learned that she could relay. There was nothing a man could resent or regret about an evening out with her.

Except that some did. When she didn't accept follow-up dates with men to whom she felt no attraction, she was often confronted with hostile and hateful emails and voicemails, which only reconfirmed her thoughts that those men were not good suitors.

Her therapy sessions really focused on her dealings with Mitchell, not the other men in her life. Dr. T just didn't have enough hours in the day to dissect all her problems.

Her mother voluntarily came into the city for a couples' therapy session. The hour was spent with her mother in tears and not many issues actually brought to the table and addressed.

It was easy and convenient for her mother to define her daughter as unbalanced and destructive. But her mother was so narcissistic and self-centered that she didn't look any deeper, maybe for lack of desire, maybe for lack of intent, or maybe for validation of her daughter's craziness. But regardless, the one and only therapy session with her mother was a wash.

"I just don't understand why she's doing this to me!" Her sobbing mother blew her nose into a tissue.

"What is she doing to you?" Dr. T tried to get clarification.

"She's killing herself because she hates me!"

Dr. T handed her mother the entire box of tissues. "Is it possible that your daughter is in this state because she hates herself?"

"No." Her mother blew her nose again. "She's a crafty little bitch. She's destroying herself to make me look like a bad mother." Her mother repeated, "Why is she doing this to me?"

The daughter and the doctor exchanged a pregnant glance. Her mother was more insane than she was. And openly admitting it.

"I don't think that your daughter is this thin because she hates you. I don't think that she's so generous as to sacrifice her soul for her parents," Dr. T stated.

"But she's hurting me!" Her mother protested.

"When a child is in harm's way, it's often difficult for a parent to come to terms. But I guarantee you, your daughter is not thinking of you when she's hurting herself." Dr. T was an excellent diplomat.

It was lost on her mother. "But she's doing this to me! She is a horrible, manipulative bitch!" Her mother sobbed hard. "She'll kill herself just so I look like a bad mother!"

"Um, I think you may be missing the point. Your daughter needs your support, not your crass accusations. She's dealing with an abuser, and she needs a safe foundation network to leave him."

"But why is she doing this to me?!" Her mother raised her arms upward, like a martyr seeking salvation. Too bad her mother was a Unitarian. There was no evangelical presence to witness her melodramatic prayer.

"Okay. I think this session is done. Until you see beyond yourself, and empathize with your daughter's pain, you cannot, will not, be a safe place for her to find healing."

"But she's hurting me!" Her mother repeated, while backing out of the office.

"I know. I heard you." Dr. T closed the door.

"Wow" was all the daughter could say to Dr. T.

"My lord, your mother is one stubborn bitch." Dr. T sat back down. "What kind of deranged parent looks at a child in crisis and makes the entire situation about them? Your mother is either ridiculously paranoid or fiercely self-absorbed."

"So, what do we do moving forward?" she asked earnestly.

"Well, we don't meet with your crazy, evil, crying mother again, that's for sure." Dr. T took a swig of soda. "Your father's scheduled to be coming in this week, isn't he?"

"Tomorrow."

"Good." Dr. T leaned back in the armchair. "Hopefully your father isn't as vain as your mother. Weak, I can work with. Vain is a hard shell to penetrate." Dr. T took another swig of soda as though it were vodka. "My lord, your mother is a selfish bitch."

The session with her father the next day was a complete counterpoint to the session with her mother. Her father was humble, nervous, and open to criticism.

Whether or not he took the criticism was irrelevant. He listened and nodded.

"Well, my first observation is that you and your daughter communicate very well." Dr. T looked at her father. "I point this out because yesterday, when I met with your wife, your daughter didn't say a word."

"Well, she doesn't speak to my wife that much."

"No. No. No." Dr. T waved a finger. "I didn't say that your daughter didn't *try* to speak. I said that she didn't. Because she was unable. Because your wife controlled the session."

"Well, did you make any progress yesterday?" her father asked earnestly.

"The only thing that happened yesterday was that your wife destroyed an entire box of tissues in an effort to make me feel sorry for her."

Dr. T really was on her side. God, she liked Dr. T.

"I don't understand—"

"I mean that your wife has mastered the art of fake tears." Dr. T looked him straight in the eyes. "Do you really think that your daughter cares about your wife enough to harm herself out of spite?"

"I think that my daughter is a brilliant, troubled little girl."

"Woman," Dr. T corrected.

"Woman." He looked at his daughter. "Sorry, woman."

"So, this strong, intelligent woman. The one sitting next to you on the couch. Do you think she hates your wife enough to destroy herself?"

Her father looked at her intently. "My wife has problems. I know that. My brother-in-law and my mother-in-law also had problems."

"What are you telling me?" Dr. T was skilled at cutting through bullshit.

"I think that my daughter is stronger and smarter than my wife. So, no. I don't think that my daughter is self-destructing out of spite."

"What do you think about Mitchell Durman?" Dr. T cut right to the chase.

Her father's face turned almost purple in anger. "Mitchell has sent my wife and me several dozen emails. I think that he is an awful man, and he is doing terrible things to my daughter. That's all I know."

Dr. T nodded. "So you know this? You feel this, you believe this?"

"Absotively," her father affirmed with one of his favorite made-up terms.

"Great. So what are you actively doing to change it?"

Her father was caught off guard. "Excuse me, what?"

"What actions are you taking to change the status quo?"

"Umm. . . ." Her father hesitated. "Well, I'm sending her to therapy with you, right?"

"That's a Band-Aid. How are you, her father, actively fixing this situation?"

"Uh. . . . Well. . . . I haven't written her off like her mother has."

She was surprised at her father's candor, and his astuteness.

"So, your wife has washed her hands of your daughter?" Dr. T asked her father.

"In a manner of speaking, yes," he admitted.

"But you haven't?" Dr. T pressed harder.

Her father shifted uncomfortably on the couch. "No. I love my daughter. I love both of my children."

"To what end?" Dr. T asked.

"Well, I love them more than I love my wife."

Wow. She had always felt that her mother had been competing with her for her father's affection, and for the first time in her life, she understood why.

"So why have you abandoned your daughter?"

Her father was defensive. "I haven't abandoned her! I'm paying for this therapy, aren't I?"

"I'm not asking what you pay for. I'm asking why you've abandoned your daughter. Why do you go along with all the crazy requests of your wife?"

Her father turned toward her on the couch and looked her in the eye. In a sheepish voice, he said, "Because at the end of the day, you'll be gone. You'll be off on your own, living your own life. I have to go to bed next to her every night. I have to keep the peace. Please forgive me."

It was tremendously painful to hear her father admit to being a giant, spineless pussy. It was one thing to suspect it. It was an entirely different thing to hear him confess to it. Crap.

❧

"So, have you been on any interesting dates?" Dr. T knew how to illicit information by playing into her weaknesses.

"I had a tasting menu at Jean Georges' last night."

"And?"

"And the food was good. The wine was spectacular."

"You know that I'm not asking about that." Dr. T looked at her. "How was the man?"

"He didn't make an impression," she admitted.

"Tell me, do any men make an impression?"

"Mitchell made an impression."

"Mitchell is a bad guy. Anyone else?"

"Phil made an impression."

"Right. Phil, the married man who left his pregnant wife for you?"

"'I didn't say that Phil left a *good* impression." She tried to feign a laugh, to diffuse the heaviness of the situation.

"Okay, so you go out every night, right?"

"Sometimes more than that."

"Okay, so you're dating, we'll say, two dozen times a week?" Dr. T was so good at getting to basics.

"It's about there. Often more, sometimes less. I schedule two or three dinner dates in one evening, if the timing allows," she confessed.

"And to what end? What do you want from these men?" Dr. T asked.

"Marriage and children."

"I'm being serious." Dr. T pushed.

"So am I."

"You want someone to give you the life that Mitchell has given you, minus the beatings and lesbian sex," Dr. T stated. "Is that what you're saying?"

God, Dr. T was good at this job. She dropped her head to her knees. "I think you may be right."

Fifty-One

She spent Christmas Eve and Christmas with two Craigslist dates. Dr. T had relayed the message that her parents did not want her in their home for the holidays.

The men with whom she spent the holiday had seemed angry with her. Apparently, she had seemed distant and unapproachable during the social parts of the holiday festivities. Plus, one sent her an email saying that she had eaten too much of the communal shrimp cocktail and owed the hostess an apology. Her feeling was a mixture of shame and resentment. So she pretended that the email never existed.

Maybe she didn't understand the subtleties of portion control. But she had been caught up in the tangible excitement of families that actually enjoyed being together. She had never experienced that.

Okay, so Christmas wasn't spent with her family, as she had hoped. But a new year arrived, and there was no reason why the tattered relationship couldn't be patched in the next twelve months.

Plus, she had proved to herself that she could have a great Christmas season without spending it with family or a current boyfriend. Even if her hosts regretted inviting her.

Even though she thought that her therapy with Dr. T had given her some insight and helped her toward recovery, her father thought otherwise. He decided before the first month was up that seeing Dr. T was a waste of her time and his money. Mitchell was still out of the country, so her father mistakenly thought that Mitchell was gone for good.

He wanted some form of tangible evidence to prove that she had made great strides. He didn't understand that psychoanalysis is a long and arduous process. Without satisfying his need for instant gratification, he pulled the plug.

She felt abandoned, and she told Dr. T that. Dr. T tried to convince her that she was cared for by people in the world. Dr. T invited her to a bat mitzvah, in the hopes that she would come to realize that she was loved, and that her presence was valued.

At first, she thought that maybe several patients had been invited to Dr. T's daughter's bat mitzvah. But upon arrival, she was embarrassed to find that she was the only one. She was embarrassed because other guests asked how she knew Dr. T, and she wasn't sure how to answer.

At the same time, she was thrilled that Dr. T had selected only her to attend such a special, personal event. She knew that she wouldn't be seeing the doctor as a patient anymore, but their professional relationship ended on an uplifting note. To Dr. T, she wasn't just another case number on a shelf of patients' dossiers.

Since she had nothing better to do, she made dating a professional sport. She would challenge herself to see how many men she could go out with in one day. Breakfast, coffee, lunch, late lunch, drinks, drinks, dinner, drinks. She could line up a string of men back to back.

Dating men was even easier than dating women, and women were sluts who opened their legs to her without her having to even buy them a cup of coffee. It was amusing to her, in a pathetic way, that men were even more vulnerable to her prowess.

Even though she was still frighteningly thin, working with Dr. T had given her back her confidence. And with that, she had regained her youthful beauty. She had always been told that she looked like a cross between Jackie O and Audrey Hepburn, and now she did again. Both women were notoriously bulimic. A dubious honor to share with the icons.

Her strikingly piercing green eyes and perfect creamy skin had returned to her beautiful face. And she had that classic sexiness that was rare in current times. Her hair was full, and thick, and sculpted to her long, sleek neck.

She had never personally thought that she was beautiful. Not because she judged her appearance harshly, but because she had never been a visually driven person. And she didn't feel like she had a beautiful heart, so she assumed that its ugliness manifested itself physically too.

But she was wrong. Men were visually driven creatures. They chose not to see her cold heart, but instead were melted by the radiating beauty in her face. This made them vulnerable to her, and they were putty in her hands.

Not that she intended to take advantage of their weakness. She really, truly had a longing to make a deep and lasting connection with a man. And she secretly hoped that one of the men she dated would be the fabled man of her dreams.

After all, the biggest cliché is that love makes one want to be a better person. And she desperately wanted to be a better person.

Unfortunately, most of the men she met were weak and pathetic and willing to submit to her desires entirely. All this did was foster a contempt for men that was rapidly growing in her mind.

She began to push them, to see how far they'd let her take them. Some men would take her to outrageously expensive dinners. Others would take her to overnight getaways in the mountains in New York. One man even took her to trapeze school.

Her days were now filled with activities, but she was growing more and more bored. Keeping busy and feeling alive were not the same thing.

She almost felt sorry for the men who genuinely liked her. She was not whole enough to like anybody back.

Mitchell returned to New York toward the end of January. He called her up and demanded that she come to his apartment immediately. Like a remote-controlled robot that had just been switched on, she obeyed.

Mitchell had lost a lot of weight on his trip ("Running from lions will do that to you," he said). He almost looked handsome. He was wearing a gorgeous white suit that was perfectly tailored to his now smaller frame. His hair was neatly trimmed, and even his goatee was manicured.

"You look well, Mitchell. Very handsome."

"You look fat. What happened to you?"

"I look fat?"

"Well, not fat, but fatter than I expected. What, are you a little piggy now?"

"I feel good, Mitchell. I'm feeling very well. I think that I look nice."

"I think that you look fat. Oh well." Mitchell sat on the couch and patted a spot for her to sit next to him. "Come. Sit. Let's reconnect."

She sat down, and Mitchell grabbed her face in both hands. He gave her a big, wet kiss on the mouth. "Ick," she said, wiping off his spit with the back of her hand.

Mitchell laughed. They could still be playful. "So, how much did you miss me?"

"Well, I—"

"Hold that thought. Let me open a bottle of champagne to celebrate this reunion." Mitchell walked over to the wine fridge. The water and Ensures were replaced with rows of fresh wine bottles. She held her tongue. Who was she to judge?

Mitchell poured them each a glass of champagne and sat back down next to her.

"So, you asked if I missed you, and—"

"Wait!" Mitchell stood up and spun around in a circle. "Tell me, don't I look great?"

"I told you when I came in, very handsome." She tried not to roll her eyes.

"I do look great. I really do! I used to be very dashing and handsome when I was young. Maybe I'm getting back my youth." Mitchell had the exuberance of a little boy. He sat back down.

"When you were young? Mitchell, you're only in your forties. When was 'when you were young'?" She was serious. In the past month, she had dated men well into their sixties, and all looked better than Mitchell. Age was not his enemy. He was.

"Young, you know. Young. Like, in my thirties."

"So, like five years ago?" she teased.

"Okay, let's not do the math. The point is, I look great, right?"

"Right. You look great, Mitchell."

Mitchell took a big swig of champagne. "Speaking of getting older, isn't someone turning twenty-four next week?"

"Yes, Mitchell. My birthday is Sunday." She also took a sip of champagne. "You know what that means, don't you?"

"No, tell me."

"It means that you and I have now known each other for a year." She couldn't believe it.

"Only a year? God, it feels like an eternity." Mitchell looked at her. "It feels like a fucking eternity. Being with you is so draining that I want to kill myself." Mitchell wasn't being facetious.

"I'm sorry, what are you saying?"

"I'm saying, look how great I look after a month away from you, piggy." So much for the happy reunion. "You're obviously the reason that I hurt myself." Mitchell pointed to the champagne bottle on the coffee table. "Look, you're even making me drink again."

There was no point in arguing with him. She just stared at him with a completely blank expression on her face.

"Aren't you going to say anything?" he asked.

"What do you want me to say, Mitchell? How am I supposed to respond?"

"Give me a reason for feeling okay that I haven't abandoned you yet. Tell me why I'm still your friend. Tell me why I love you and why I'm loyal. Make me not feel like an asshole for not squashing you like bug yet." Mitchell sounded sincere.

"I don't know why you don't release me from your friendship." She really hoped that he would. Mitchell was toxic.

"Tell me how much you missed me while I was gone."

"Well, I—"

He cut her off. "Stop. I know you didn't miss me. You've been very busy, haven't you?" It was a statement, not a question.

"I don't know what you mean."

"I mean that now you've worked your way through the entire population." Mitchell looked her in the eye. "I mean, is there any single man in New York who hasn't taken you to dinner? Is there any girl that you haven't fucked? Is there anyone left?"

She was not entirely surprised that he had been monitoring her activities.

He burst into laughter. "I'm teasing you, fool. I know that you can have any man or woman that you want. That's why I found you in the first place." He waved his glass in the air, and some champagne splashed to the floor. "I'm glad that you're out meeting every man in this city. It can prove to you how weak and pathetic they all are."

She wanted to disagree, but she honestly couldn't.

"What, you're not going to respond?" Mitchell looked at her intensely. "Tell me, honestly. Have you met one man, one single man, who wasn't a weak pussy who rolled over to you?"

She couldn't think of any. This was a somber moment. "No."

"No. Exactly. And that, my dear, is why you always come back to me."

Mitchell finished off his glass of champagne and poured a refill. "That's why you always have come back, and why you always will. Because I am not a weak pussy like the other men in this city. I'm strong. I don't find you beautiful. Your heart is ugly. And that's why I'm your friend." He offered his glass in the air, soliciting a toast.

She clinked glasses with him. She hated him.

"To the first year of a most unholy friendship."

"Right, to a year," she mumbled. She stood to leave. "I think I'm going to go now." Maybe she could still reinstate some of her dates in the evening. She had to prove Mitchell wrong and find a good man out there.

"Okay. Are you sure that you won't join me for lunch?" Mitchell asked as she put on her coat.

"No, thank you. I've lost my appetite." She meant it.

"You never lose your appetite," Mitchell chided. "You are a consumer, remember? The biggest little woman consumer in the world."

She walked toward the door and didn't turn around to respond.

As the door closed behind her, she heard Mitchell shout, "By the way, we have reservations for brunch on Sunday at Per Se. I thought that's where you'd like to spend your birthday."

Damn it, he knew her so well.

Fifty-Two

She went back to her dating schedule. But all the men were disappointing. They were boring, mostly unraveled, drones at their jobs, cogs in the wheel of Wall Street. She found herself sighing a lot.

She also, as much as she fought it, looked forward to spending her birthday at Per Se. It had been ages since she and Mitchell had gone out for fine dining. And Per Se was the newest and finest restaurant to have opened in the entire world. It hadn't been open for long, and reservations were being taken months in advance. She wondered how long ago Mitchell had booked their table for her birthday? For an asshole, he was quite often surprisingly thoughtful.

She didn't see him much in the week leading up to her birthday, and she was happy about that. She didn't even like knowing that he was back in the city. She kept bumbling through her busy days of dating and aimless first encounters.

Mitchell called her early Sunday morning. "I'm sick" was all he said.

"Sick? Sick how?" She was concerned. Not for his well-being but for the prospect of having her birthday ruined.

"I have diarrhea. I've been vomiting all night. I think I have food poisoning." Mitchell really did sound awful.

"You think you ate something bad?" She feigned concern.

"I must have." Mitchell sniffled. "I feel miserable. Like death."

"Oh—"

"I know. You're thinking about your birthday." Mitchell knew her too well. "You're still going to Per Se."

"I am?" She tried not to sound as relieved as she was. Was Mitchell being generous?

"I've already put down a five hundred dollar deposit to reserve our table, so yes, you're going." Okay, so he had been strong-armed by the reservationist to be generous. It was still nice.

"Alone?"

"Well, I sure as hell can't go." Mitchell sounded like he was choking. "I have to go throw up again. Come to my house and get my Amex card." He abruptly hung up the phone.

She got dressed up to go to brunch, carefully selecting her outfit to be at once properly formal but not inappropriate for the early hour of the day. When she was satisfied with her wardrobe, she left for Mitchell's.

His door was propped open in anticipation of her arrival. She found him draped across the couch in his boxer shorts, moaning.

"Happy birthday," Mitchell gurgled. He didn't look up.

"Mitchell, are you sure that you don't want me to stay with you?" She had a flashback to the scene in Bangkok when he had accused her of abandoning him when he was sick. She didn't want a repeat.

"I'm sure. Even if I wanted you to stay, I'd be so pissed that I'd have to pay Per Se for a meal that no one ate." Mitchell shook his head. "No, I want you to go. Eat for two. I've paid for it." Mitchell tried to laugh, but he felt so sick that even his laugh sounded like a strained moan.

"Okay. Well, I have to leave now to make the reservation." She kept her eye on the clock.

"I've put my credit card and a note granting you permission to use it on the table in the foyer. In an envelope. Do you see it?"

She turned and saw the envelope. "Yes, I'll get it."

"There's also cash in there. Take a cab. It's your birthday." Mitchell shifted on the couch.

"Okay. Thank you, Mitchell."

"You're welcome." As the door shut behind her, she heard Mitchell mutter, "Happy birthday. By the way, you look gorgeous."

She arrived at Per Se just on time, and the hostess promised to make it a special day. She sat alone, relaxed and composed. This was the perfect setting in which to spend her birthday. And it was even better because she had no one to distract her from an afternoon in pure hedonism. She had the fleeting thought that all her recent dates would have been much more pleasant if all the men had just remained silent. It was what they said that always soured her to them.

She ordered two tasting menus. After all, Mitchell had already paid for two. The captain returned a moment later. "I've spoken with the chef, and he is not going to send two tasting menus. He's going to do much better." He seemed pleased with himself.

"Better?"

"Yes, madam. In light of it being your birthday, and you being . . . well, who you are in the food and wine world, the chef would like to offer you a forty-course menu." The captain smiled ear to ear.

"Forty courses?" She was tremendously excited, but maintained her composure. "But won't that take all day?"

The captain nodded. "It will take all the way into dinner service. But it's your birthday. Also, the chef values your opinion and would like to test some new dishes on you, if you'd oblige."

She couldn't help but smile. "I think that this is going to be a wonderful birthday. Thank you."

"No, madam. Thank *you*." The captain poured her another glass of champagne from the communal bucket near her table. "I should also tell you that the sommelier is very nervous and excited to do your pairings."

"Because it's forty courses?"

"No, madam. Because he holds your opinion in high regard. He doesn't want to disappoint you."

"I'm sure that it will be lovely."

"You're very kind." The captain bowed. "But chef and the sommelier are very eager to charm yours, one of the most discerning of palates."

She knew that she was well respected in the fine dining world, but she had almost forgotten how highly she was regarded. It had been a while since she had been so overtly honored. This was going to be an amazing birthday.

Her meal concluded at around 7 p.m. She was perfectly sated. She wasn't overly stuffed or overly drunk. The staff at Per Se had mastered the art of correct portion size and pacing.

The check arrived, and she tried not to let her face betray her sticker shock at the price. She had never seen so many zeros on a bill. She was sure that she had had more expensive meals, but this was the first time that she had actually signed a bill herself.

Gratuity was included, but she added an extra hundred dollars for good measure. She signed her signature and added Mitchell's initials right after it.

She was given a gift of fresh muffins and chocolate truffles in a bag, and she decided to bring them to Mitchell to cheer him up. She had to stop off at his apartment on her way home anyway, to give him back his credit card.

Mitchell looked a little better when she got to his apartment. He was still in his boxers, but at least he wasn't shivering and vomiting. He looked comfortable on the couch. He also looked a little drunk. And there were Kit Kat wrappers strewn everywhere.

"Feeling better?" she asked as she put the Amex card back into his wallet.

"I think that whatever made me sick is out of my system." Mitchell didn't get up to greet her. "Did you have a nice birthday?"

"It was wonderful, thank you." She was careful to understate her enjoyment. She wanted him neither jealous nor resentful. "Your presence was missed."

"I'm sure." Mitchell rolled his eyes sarcastically.

She didn't say anything in response. She hadn't missed him at all, so it was best not to drag out the lie.

Mitchell just stared at Fox News in silence. He drank from an oversized goblet filled with wine. She had seen enough.

"Anyway, Mitchell, I'm going home now. I'm sure that I have phone calls to return from people wishing me a happy birthday." She tried to back up into the foyer.

"Who?" Mitchell got aggressive. "Who would call to say happy birthday? Not your parents. Not your imaginary friends. Who, but me, is saying happy birthday?"

She knew that the restaurant staff at Per Se didn't count. "I'm sure my grandma called."

"Right! Of course. Grandma. The one who let Norman and Dawn steal from you. That grandma, right?" Mitchell was trying to get her angry.

"Okay, Mitchell. I'm just going to go now."

"No one cares that it's your birthday. No one cares when it's my birthday either. We're all alone, don't you get it yet?" Mitchell seemed on the brink of tears.

"I'm not alone."

"Really? How many people were at your table to celebrate your birthday?"

"One," she replied sheepishly.

"Isn't 'one' the definition of 'alone'?" His voice got louder. "No one cares about us. No one loves us. We only have each other. And I know that you hate me. So where does that leave me!"

"I don't hate you, Mitchell," she lied.

"You hate me," Mitchell snarled. Then he began to sob. "And you should hate me. I hate me too." He was crying like a small boy.

She was uncomfortable. She had no idea what to say. "Mitchell, please don't cry." It was the best she could muster.

"How can I not cry? I'm nothing. *Nothing!* I'm a shell of a man. All I have is you, and all you have for me is contempt."

It was true. But she still didn't like to see a grown man cry. "Really, Mitchell, please. Don't cry. You have a great life. A son who loves you, and—"

"And what? My son doesn't love me. My son doesn't even know me! Pamela won't even let me hardly see Adam!" Mitchell's body heaved with tears.

"Adam will get to know you. You just have to give it time." Compassion was not her strong suit, but she was trying her best.

"No. *No!*" Mitchell pounded his fist on the coffee table. "No one will love me, and anyone who says differently is a liar. *A liar!*" Mitchell got to his feet. "My life is empty. Worthless! People only speak to me because I have money!"

"That's not true—"

"Not true? Do you think that Pamela would contact me if I weren't supporting her? Do you think she would have even given birth to Adam if she didn't want my money?"

It sounded like paranoia, but Mitchell's paranoia was often well founded.

"Mitchell, please sit down. Relax. You were sick today. Maybe you're running a fever."

"I hope it kills me, then." Mitchell walked over to the window. "Fuck it. I won't wait for the fever to kill me." He opened the window and let in a gust of cold February air. "I'm going to kill myself first."

"You're not going to kill yourself, Mitchell." She struggled to remain calm. "Please sit down."

He put one leg out of the window, and then wedged out his head. Muffled, she could hear him yelling, "I'm going to kill myself. I have nothing to live for. Everyone hates me. I'm going to die. *I want to die!*"

She was afraid that he was serious. Even if he weren't planning to jump, he could now very easily fall. She ran over to the window and grabbed Mitchell by the leg that was still in the apartment, and she pulled as hard as she could.

"Mitchell! Get back inside! You are not going to jump and splatter yourself on East Sixtieth Street!"

"And why not? Give me a reason why not!"

"Well, fuck you if you want to die!" She was losing her cool. "But I'm sure as hell not going to let your 250-pound body land on someone down below! You have no right to kill anyone else too. If you're going to kill yourself, take pills. Get a gun. Don't jump out of a fucking building. You asshole!"

Mitchell stopped resisting her pulling on his leg. He brought his head back inside the apartment, and then lifted his leg back in over the sill. He fell to the floor and leaned against the wall.

He began to sob again. "You wouldn't let me die." He sounded surprised. "You wouldn't let me do it."

"I didn't want you to kill anyone else, too."

"I know. I know you say that. But even so, you wouldn't let me die," Mitchell repeated. Then he looked up at her. "Thank you. You can go now. I won't jump."

She believed him. She put on her coat and walked out of the apartment.

"Happy birthday!" Mitchell called out as she left.

Maybe she would have been better off if she had let him die.

Fifty-Three

She didn't see much of Mitchell for the rest of February. She assumed that he was still alive, but it wasn't as though anyone would have called to inform her otherwise.

She continued on her whirlwind of dating. She had devised a system when she posted online: she would place two ads at exactly the same time. One would be a serious posting, looking to meet a real suitor. The other she would post as a prostitute. If any men responded to both postings, she could tell that they were just responding to every W4M posting there was. Those men were instantly deleted.

Most of her dates went well. They were always pleasant, genuine-seeming men who took an interest in her immediately. But, on average, she found them to be dull and boring, with little to contribute to the conversation. She wondered if the man for whom she was destined even existed.

She had two bad dates in a row, though. One was a dinner date who got drunk and threatened the waiter. While the screaming match ensued, she excused herself to the bathroom and instead ran out of the restaurant and into a bus waiting at a stop just outside the door. It wasn't her practice to dine-and-dash, but if the man was going to become violent, she didn't want the violence to become directed at her.

The second bad date was a drinks date the next night. The guy immediately admitted to lying about his age, his marital status, and his current state of employment. She should have just left, but she was morbidly curious. He confessed that he was just fascinated by the world of online dating and wanted to see what could transpire. Then he pretended to take a phone call and walked out of the bar, leaving her with the bill.

She began to sour toward the idea of meeting any more new people. Maybe she had already met all the available bachelors in New York and had missed her chance to grab onto a good one when she'd had the opportunity. She decided not to date anymore for a while. It was a waste of everyone's time and money, and it was just making her lose faith in the goodness of other people overall.

When Mitchell called her the next morning, she agreed to meet him for lunch at Tino's. After lunch, they went back to Mitchell's apartment to have a little more wine and spend some time together before she disappeared to jury duty.

They ordered in some dinner from the expensive Italian delivery restaurant around the corner and settled on the couch to watch a pay-per-view movie and eat truffle pizza.

Mitchell had just finished his first slice of pizza when his cell phone rang. He listened intently for a minute, and then got up to leave the room. She could hear the voice on the other end of the phone call. Whoever it was, was screaming.

"Calm down. Calm down. I can't understand you. Stop crying. Calm down." Mitchell began to pace in the kitchen.

She knew better than to interrupt, but she tried to eavesdrop to find out what was happening.

"So, are you telling me that he's dead? . . . Right, okay. . . . And where are you now?" Mitchell kept pacing. "Okay. . . . Right, . . . I heard you. . . . Can you put the police on the phone? . . . I don't know, whichever one you want me to speak to. . . . That's okay, I'll wait." Mitchell cupped the receiver and said to her, "Can you put my food in the oven to keep warm? I think I'm going to be on the phone for a while."

When he hung up, his face was completely expressionless.

"Do you want to tell me what's going on?" She was trying to be supportive.

"Let's go have our dinner. I'll tell you over some wine."

She pulled the food out of the oven and carried it over to Mitchell, who was now sitting in the living room, drinking wine directly from the bottle.

"Whenever you want to speak."

"It's no big deal." Mitchell took a slice of truffle pizza. "You remember my oldest and dearest friend, Abraham?"

She had heard Mitchell mention Abe several times, even though she had never met him. "Sure. You've spoken of him."

"Well, apparently, he flew some hookers out from LA to his home in Maui. They had a nice little party, and Abe did a little too much meth."

"Too much meth?" she repeated. It didn't seem like a choice drug for a wealthy Jew. Although her time in Silverhill had taught her that addicts came in all packages.

"Abe did too much meth and died."

"He *died?*" She couldn't believe that Mitchell was so devoid of emotion. "Abe is dead?"

"Yes. One of the hookers found my name and number in his wallet. It was she who called." Mitchell was unnervingly matter-of-fact.

"It was the hooker who called?" She found herself repeating a lot of this information. It was a lot to process.

"Yes. One of the hookers. They were sent by an ex-girlfriend of mine who I guess is now a madam. Abe knew to call to get reliable hookers from my ex. They were flown out to spend the weekend with him."

"And they killed him?"

"That's for the court to decide." Mitchell took a bite of pizza. "Anyway, Abe is dead. What's on TV? Can you rewind the movie?"

She stared at Mitchell in disbelief. She knew that he was a cold person, but she thought that he would have some reaction to the death of his oldest friend. "Mitchell, are you sure you're all right?"

"I'm fine. Pass me the remote." Mitchell extended his hand. "Hey, maybe you'll be selected for the jury. How funny would that be?"

"It would be hysterical. Are you sure you're okay?"

"I'm fine. Seriously, stop asking." Mitchell pointed toward the bags with the remaining takeout food. "Why don't you take your dinner to go? I have the feeling that I'm going to be dealing with a lot more phone calls tonight. Goddamn asshole, Abe!" Mitchell pounded a fist toward the sky.

She gathered her belongings and picked up one of the food bags. "Okay, I'm leaving. But you know how to get me if you need anything."

"Hey, just don't send the stupid fucking hookers to jail if you get a meth case. Abe was the asshole. Not them."

"Got it. Exonerate the hookers." She tried to make light of his request.

"That's right. Exonerate the hookers. Blame the dead guy. That can be your purpose at jury duty." Mitchell raised one hand and wiggled his fingers in a show of dismissal.

As she walked toward the subway, she thought about how unaffected Mitchell had been about learning of Abe's death. She had always tried to convince herself that Mitchell really did care for her and wanted to keep her alive. But if he responded with such indifference to the news of Abe's death, wouldn't he care even less if she were to die? Were these Mitchell's true colors? She shivered in horror. God forbid.

In a way, jury duty was a blessing. It kept her off the Internet and gave her a solid reason for not seeing Mitchell. In another way, jury duty was a lot like Hillside. There were a lot of people sitting in a holding room in silence, staring at a wall. Maybe the next stop after jury duty was, in fact, a psychiatric hospital. Bureaucracy had a way of driving people insane after all.

She had five days of reporting to the holding room. By the fifth day, she still hadn't been selected. There was still a chance that she could be taken in the afternoon, however. They were looking for jurors for a trial against a Colombian drug cartel that had been busted downtown. She was an ideal juror. She was totally clueless and free to submit to the two-month sequester. What irony if Mitchell had correctly predicted her fate.

As it turned out, the building was evacuated when she returned from lunch that Friday. Apparently, a bomb threat had been called into the courthouse. All the jurors who had reported since Monday were excused and not required to make up the lost day.

While she was walking up the block to her apartment, Matt, the owner of the bar under her apartment, came running out onto the sidewalk.

"Fuck, you're famous!" Matt was smiling.

"Famous?" She had no idea what he was talking about.

"You haven't been online recently?" Matt asked.

"I've had jury duty all week. Why? What's going on?"

"Well, apparently two jackasses you met last week found each other and have started a really nasty strand of Internet postings using your name."

"I don't understand. What are you talking about?"

"Well, these guys were trying to say some bad shit about you, and then a whole bunch of other guys responded in your defense. A lot of people like you, by the way."

"Great. Whatever, Matt. Keep going. How am I famous?"

"Well, after these two guys said shit about you, like thousands of people posted stories of bad dates."

"Bad dates with me?" She was shocked.

"No, silly. You have a team of guys writing about how awesome you are." Matt took a sip from his can of soda. "No, basically everyone who has ever had a bad date is posting, using your name. Guys, girls, people in other fucking countries. It's insanity! You really haven't heard about any of this?"

"Like I said, I was in jury duty all week."

"Well, if you want to read some, I've been printing everything out. There are like twenty new postings with your name every minute."

"But they're not about me?"

"No! That's what's hysterical. I mean, the first couple are. But then some people said some really nice things about you. That's when other people just started writing about their bad dates with other people in general. It's really amazing! A reporter came by to ask me some questions so that you can be included in the next publication of *Urban Legends*. How cool is that? I know an urban legend. Hey, are you sure you don't want to read some of the printouts I made for you?"

"I'm going to pass. But thanks for letting me know." She started walking toward her front door, and then turned back around toward Matt. "Hey, you don't think I'm in any real danger, do you?"

Matt thought for a minute. "Some people put pictures up of you that I don't think you knew were taken."

"Like what?"

"Like walking down the street, running errands, standing on the subway. Stuff like that. And there was one creepy picture that some guy took of you from under a table while you were out with him."

"Are you kidding me, Matt? 'Cause if you are, this is a horrible joke."

"Babe, I'm like your big brother. I'm looking out for you."

"So, as my big brother, what do you think I should do?"

"Honestly?" Matt sighed. "I'd get the fuck out of New York."

Back in her apartment, she listened to her answering machine. There were several messages from her father.

"*Some reporter from the* Washington Post *called our house early this week. Now there are reporters all over. At our home, at my office. Please call me and let me know what the hell is going on. Please call me now. This is Dad, by the way."*

She didn't even have the stomach to turn on the computer and look to see what was happening. There were messages on her machine from reporters too, so she knew that her father wasn't exaggerating. This was a media feeding frenzy, and it looked like she was the prey.

"Hi, Mitchell." Who else was she going to call?

"Hi. How was jury duty?" Mitchell asked.

"Boring. I wasn't selected."

"I'm not surprised. You're too smart for a jury, and the lawyers know that. They weed you out when they think that—"

She cut him off. "I'm calling because I think that I'm going to go away for a while."

"Really?" Mitchell seemed interested. "And where are you going to go?"

"Somewhere. Anywhere. I think that I've overstayed my welcome in New York."

"Well, let me know if you need any help in the travel department. Like booking or finding a destination. You know. Whatever. I'm here to help."

"I appreciate that Mitchell. But I think I'll do this one on my own."

Fifty-Four

"Let's go to Ibiza"

She was confused by Mitchell's middle-of-the-night phone call. "When?"

"I don't know. Next week, maybe? We'll talk about it when you get here in the morning. Good night." Mitchell hung up.

The next morning, she delivered the newspaper, sucked Mitchell's cock, went out to purchase a case of wine, and then sat on the couch and addressed the phone call. She had almost dismissed it as a dream, especially when he hadn't mentioned it.

"Right. Ibiza. Well, I was online looking for pussy and I got bored so I started looking for travel. Which, really, my dear, you should be doing. But since I already have to do all your jobs—" Mitchell stopped himself before he went off on a tangent. "Anyway, I found this website. It's like eBay, but for travel. And the trips have no minimum bids. I can't remember how I found it—"

"I told you about it."

"Yes! I knew that it was someone. Thank you. Anyway, I put in one dollar bids for some timeshare apartments in Spain, and I won the auctions!"

"For a dollar?"

"For a dollar!" Mitchell was genuinely excited. He took another big gulp from his glass of wine and swallowed poignantly. "So, we have three weeks in Marbella, and three weeks in Ibiza. In two-bedroom apartments."

"Really? We do?"

"Well, I do. I've decided that you should pay for your travel. I'm tired of footing the bill for everything."

"What's the catch?" Mitchell was acting a little manic.

"No catch. I want a companion, and you need someplace to go. So, the deal is, you get yourself to Spain, and I'll cover all land costs."

"Land costs?"

"Car rental, food. You know the drill."

She knew the drill. "I'll have to think about it." She stood to leave. She had fulfilled her obligations to Mitchell for the day anyway. They had nothing more to talk about.

"What's to think about?" Mitchell looked surprised that she was being so noncommittal. "I'm offering you two months in Spain, free of charge. Didn't you tell me yesterday that you wanted to leave New York?"

"I did." And she really did want to leave New York as soon as possible.

"So? Do you have the money for two months in the Med?"

She said smugly, "I have two dollars."

"That's funny. You're funny." Mitchell laughed like a crazy person.

"I'm going home now, Mitchell." She began to walk away.

"I'm leaving for Paris tonight!" Mitchell yelled after her. "So don't be a fool."

She got home and sat in front of her computer. Two months in Spain did sound like a good plan. But two months with Mitchell sounded awful. And what would they do together in a timeshare apartment that whole time?

She had a lot to think about. To distract herself, she began searching the Internet for last-minute travel deals.

Like Kismet, she found a one-way cruise to Europe. It sailed from Ft. Lauderdale to Lisbon, and it left the next day. The ship was heading out on a repositioning cruise; the boat was leaving winter in the Caribbean for summer in the Mediterranean. These trips weren't popular, which meant they were very cheap.

She made a few inquiries and played around with a few more search engines. The cruise was cheaper than airfare to Europe. She picked up the phone.

"Okay, Mitchell. I'm going to meet you in Spain."

"Great!" Mitchell sounded patronizing, but it was probably because her voice made it sound like she was doing him a favor. "So, what airline are you traveling? Are you flying into Barcelona or Madrid? Keep in mind that we're staying in the south."

"I'm not flying. I'm taking a boat."

"A boat! Of course you are!" Mitchell laughed. Nothing she did surprised him. "Of course you would be taking a boat." He tried to catch his breath through his laughter. "So, what is the boat itinerary?"

"The ship leaves Ft. Lauderdale tomorrow afternoon."

"We don't have the timeshare until late next week, my dear. Where will you stay in the meantime?"

"There is no 'meantime,' Mitchell. The boat is sailing across the Atlantic. I think it takes ten days."

"And it gets you to Spain?" It sounded like Mitchell was writing this information down.

"It gets me to Portugal. I'll take a bus to Spain." She had mostly thought this through.

"Good! Great! I think that is an excellent idea." Mitchell shuffled through some papers, and she could hear the rustling through the phone. "I'm giving you the phone number to the place in Marbella. Call me when you're in Europe."

"Will do."

"Bye bye." Mitchell used his baby voice because he knew it irritated her.

She hung up the phone and began to pack for two months in Europe.

In Ft. Lauderdale, there was a massive line of people waiting at the pier to check in. This didn't surprise her. It was a huge ship and a long trip. There was bound to be a lot of luggage and a lot of passengers who didn't speak English. The check-in process was going to take a while.

As she stood in line, she decided to call Grandma. Not because she actually wanted to speak with her, but she knew that Grandma had a big mouth and would let the whole family know that she would be gone for a couple of months. She figured that it would be bad form to leave the country for that long and not tell anyone.

Grandma was a pain in the ass about her going on the trip, but after a bit of protest, she wished her bon voyage.

When it was finally her turn in line, she felt like she had been waiting an eternity. All she wanted to do was board the ship and find something to eat. It suddenly occurred to her that in all the time she had spent booking the trip, she had completely forgotten to eat. She was starving, and she felt herself beginning to get irritable.

She just had to last through check-in.

She presented her passport and waited for her welcome aboard package. She had watched hundreds of her fellow passengers complete this process already, and she knew that it would only take a minute. So when the agent was gone from the post for twenty minutes, she began to get nervous.

Was there a problem with her booking? Was it bad that she had booked only one day in advance? Was there some sort of visa she had neglected to procure? A million thoughts raced through her head.

"I'm sorry that took so long." The agent apologized upon return. "There was a problem with the booking of your stateroom."

"A problem with my stateroom?" She was going to lose her cool. "I spent a long time selecting room—" She looked at her hand. "Room 5014! That's the room I want. That's the room I chose."

"I know. And I apologize. But that room is not available. You've been reassigned."

"Reassigned? I don't want to be reassigned! I deliberately requested—"

The agent cut her off. "You've been reassigned to 12007."

She stopped her rant. "12007?" She had seen the floor plans. "Isn't that a honeymoon suite?"

"I believe it is, ma'am, yes." The agent handed her a few forms for her signature.

"I have a honeymoon suite?" She repeated, totally shocked.

"Yes, ma'am. And again, we apologize for the mix-up." The agent tapped the documents with a pen. "Please sign, ma'am."

She signed the papers, accepted her room key, and boarded the ship. Even though she was starving, she needed to make a detour to the room. She had to see what the suite was like.

It was as though she had a little palace on the water. She had a large living room area with a pullout sofa bed, half-bath, and a balcony. Past the refrigerator and minibar area, she found the master bedroom. There was a king-size bed, plasma TV, and a marble bathroom with a tub. This was the opposite of her crappy interior stateroom on her last cruise.

She took a bottle of water out of the refrigerator and stood on the balcony. This cruise was going to be so wonderful that it didn't even matter to her that Mitchell would be waiting for her at the other end.

There were lots of solo passengers on the ship. It wasn't so much a pleasure cruise for people as a cruise of necessity. There were people on the ship who were moving to Europe but couldn't fly. There were large families who found that taking a ship to Europe for a summer in St. Tropez was easier than wrangling children on a flight. There were backpackers who had also discovered that taking a boat was cheaper than taking a plane. There were some old people who were just sailing over and then flying back to the States for the mere fact that they had nothing better to do.

Several passengers on the ship were about her age. She became friendly with lots of different people. And with her large suite, she was even able to entertain. She would order up trays of hors d'oeuvres and cheese, and her guests would bring wine and bottles of liquor. She even made a couple of love connections. And she met Kay, a thirty-one-year-old Finnish woman. Kay was traveling by boat because sinus problems prohibited air travel. She was going to spend the summer with her family back home. Before going to Finland, Kay would spend a week in Marbella. Meeting her was serendipitous.

At night, she'd go to the casino. One of the sexy, older married men spent every night buying her cognac and teaching her to play craps. She liked craps. It was social, and fun, and the energy was electric.

The cruise was bringing her back to life.

When the boat arrived in Lisbon, all the passengers seemed disappointed that the trip was over. It had been better than she, or anyone else apparently, had imagined. She felt relaxed and revived.

She got off the ship, found her luggage, and looked at the taxi line. She was about to join the line when it occurred to her that she hadn't planned this far in advance; she didn't have anywhere to go.

She found Kay smoking a cigarette on the pier, looking blankly at the water lapping the bulkheads.

"Hey, Kay." She sat down on her suitcase.

"Hey, beautiful." Kay had a bit of a platonic crush on her.

She lit a cigarette too. The two girls smoked in silence.

She asked Kay, "Hey, where are you going tonight?"

"No plan. You?"

"No plan either."

"Wanna stick together?" Kay asked, reading her mind.

"That makes the most sense. I still have a few days before I have my place in Marbella." She tried not to think about Mitchell being there too.

"Yeah, I have some time before my resort is booked." Kay put down the cigarette. "Maybe we should hang out in Lisbon?"

"Sure. I haven't been to Portugal. Let's check it out." This was the way she had grown accustomed to traveling with Mitchell anyway. She liked flying by the seat of her pants.

"So you want to stay in Lisbon?" Kay needed more of a set itinerary.

"Well, for like a day. Then we can go south to Faro, maybe drink some port along the way."

"I think you know more geography than I do. Mind if I follow your lead?"

"Sure." She squeezed Kay's arm to reaffirm the union. Then she looked over at the taxi line. It was more than one thousand people long. "One thing I can tell you, though. I am *not* getting in that line."

"Even if we got on the line, and got in a cab, we don't even have a plan for where we're going."

"Good point." She smiled at Kay, and the two girls laughed.

She left Kay with all the luggage and began to walk away.

"Where are you going?" Kay called after her.

"I'm going to find us a plan. We need a place to go, right?" She was a seasoned traveler, to put it lightly. She'd find something for her and Kay.

"Do you even speak Portuguese?" Kay yelled.

"I speak Spanish."

"Do you think that will help?"

"Nope."

She found a group of baggage handlers standing around smoking cigarettes. They had already distributed all the luggage from the ship and were now just loitering until the end of their shift.

The boys were all in their late teens, so she felt safe walking up to them by herself. Who can be intimidated by a boy in a reflective orange safety vest and coveralls?

"Hola. Alguien habla español?" She asked if any of the boys spoke Spanish.

One of the boys stepped forward. In a thick Portuguese accent, he said, "Yo, sí. Por qué? Necesitas ayuda?" He asked her if she needed help, and then pointed toward her luggage and Kay.

She looked at her bags too and realized what he was asking. "No. Con mis maletas, no. Estoy bien. Lo qué pasa es qué no tengo donde qué irme. Necesito ideas." She explained that she was fine with her luggage, but she needed some tips on where to go now that she was here.

"No tienes ni idea?" The boy seemed surprised that she had no plan.

"Ni idea. Me ayudes?" She asked if he'd be willing to help her.

"Sí, pues." He extinguished his cigarette and extended his hand. "Soy Joao." He introduced himself.

She returned the greeting, and then walked him over to Kay. "This is Joao. He's going to help us."

"You just picked up the baggage handler?" Kay looked a little unsettled.

"Sure. Look at him. He's a good guy." She sized him up.

Joao was a short guy, maybe about 5' 1", and stocky in a muscular way. Probably from moving luggage at the pier. He had a full head of spiky light brown hair and an incredible tan that one can only get from working long hours on the dock. If she had to guess, she'd say that Joao was about nineteen years old. And absolutely adorable.

"So, what is Joao going to do with us?" Kay stared at him, clearly looking for a reason not to trust him, but he was just so cute and earnest that it was hard to find fault.

"I don't know. I'll ask him." She turned to Joao. "Oy ye. A donde vamos?"

"Ahorita?"

"Sí, pues."

"Vamos al hospital por un ratito."

"Al hospital?"

"Sí, pues." Joao lit another cigarette.

"Apparently, we are going to the hospital," she said to Kay.

"Why the fuck are we going to the hospital?"

"I don't know. But it's gotta be more interesting than standing in the taxi line." She pointed toward the wall of people. It looked like the line hadn't even moved.

"Okay, let's go." Kay sighed and stood up. "Are we really going to the hospital, though?"

She ignored Kay and said to Joao. "Bueno. Vamanos."

Joao picked up the girls' luggage and walked them toward his car in the employee parking lot.

He drove a tiny little two-door hatchback. Because Kay's only languages were Finnish and English, she got into the backseat.

Kay's companion sat in the front seat and tried to get more information out of Joao regarding the hospital visit. Her Spanish was far more fluent than his, and he struggled to explain the situation.

She turned to Kay in backseat. "Okay, the best I could understand is that we have to visit one of his friends who had a liver transplant."

"A liver transplant?" Kay repeated.

"That's what he said. I don't know if that's what he meant, but that's what he said." She was sort of excited to see the hospital in Lisbon. Hospitals in other countries fascinated her; they were a cross-section of the socioeconomic effects of politics, and she thought that they provided insight into the climate of society.

Joao parked the car in the lot at the hospital, and the girls followed him into one of the small one-story buildings that scattered the campus. Unlike in the United States, there wasn't one massive structure.

Once inside, Joao signed in, and the three of them milled about in the chairless waiting room. After about ten minutes, a nurse called Joao's name.

She didn't understand why Joao was being called in by the nurse, so she questioned him, and without saying anything, he lifted his shirt. He had a huge new scar reaching all the way across his belly. She was speechless.

She and Kay went outside to have a cigarette while Joao had his appointment.

"So, tell me again. What's going on?" Kay asked in between drags.

"Apparently something was lost in translation. Joao is not visiting a friend who had a liver transplant. *He* had the liver transplant, and we're just joining him for a follow-up appointment with his surgeon."

"He had a liver transplant? What is he, like, twelve?"

She didn't respond. They sat in silence in the warm spring sunshine on the steps of the hospital in Lisbon and waited for Joao.

Back in the car, they were once again met with the reality that they had no destination. Some men on the ship had invited her to have drinks with them at their hotel on one of the hilltops surrounding Lisbon.

She asked Joao if he knew where the hotel was, and he sort of nodded and shrugged at the same time. It seemed that maybe he knew of the general vicinity but not the actual location.

"So, where are we going?" Kay was becoming increasingly stressed out and kind of annoying.

"Road trip. Enjoy it, babe."

By what could only have been divine intervention, they found the hotel about two hours outside of Lisbon. The two girls got out of the car and left Joao with the luggage. She found her hosts, the men from the cruise ship, and knocked on the door.

The man who answered seemed surprised to see them.

"Hi. It's great to see you." He was wearing a robe, fresh out of the shower. "But what are you doing here?"

She was unfazed. "You invited me for drinks."

He looked Kay up and down and said. "I invited you. Not you plus guest."

She looked at Kay. Maybe Kay was a little homely, but she wasn't entirely unattractive. Plus, she was Finnish. Didn't guys like that blonde-haired, blue-eyed, tall look?

"Well, I'm traveling as a team now," she stated matter-of-factly.

"Okay. Well. . . ." The man hesitated.

"Never mind. We're not wanted. We're on our way. Enjoy your stay." She took Kay by the arm and marched down the hallway.

"What just happened?" Kay was totally confused. Obviously, she did not have a lot of experience with men.

"Nothing happened. We just don't have the standing invitation."

"Did he just reject me?"

"No!" Kay's companion lied. "Don't worry about it. We had a beautiful drive into the countryside, and now we're heading back to Lisbon."

Kay was stuck on the facts. "I can't believe that guy just rejected me, on sight!"

"Guys are assholes. Joao's a good guy. Let's not keep him waiting." She quickened her pace as they walked out of the hotel.

"Qué fue?" Joao asked what happened.

"Vamos a regresar a Lisboa. Conoces a algunes lugares parar quedarnos a dormir?" She asked Joao if he had any ideas for places to stay back in Lisbon.

They got into the car and drove into the main section of the small suburban town. Joao stopped the car near what seemed to be the Main Street vicinity and got out. "Tengo hambre." He told her that he was hungry.

Kay looked upset. "I'm sorry. This is all my fault. I'm too fucking ugly to travel with you."

"Don't say that! That's not true!" She lied.

"It is true. Tell Joao that dinner is on me."

They found a little restaurant and had a carafe of port and some hot sandwiches. Joao had coffee though. He couldn't drink since his liver transplant, which, according to him, was a result of alcohol abuse. One must drink a lot of alcohol to need a new liver before age twenty. Maybe Joao should have gone to Silverhill.

After dinner, they drove back into the city. It was dark now, and Lisbon was beautiful at night. They still had no hotel booked, but she wasn't worried.

Kay was a little less easygoing. "Do we have a place to go? What are we doing with this strange man in his little car?"

"Joao is not a strange man. I trust him." She looked at Joao and winked. He didn't understand a word of the English conversation, but he winked back.

They drove through narrow little side streets and back alleyways.

"Where is he taking us?" Kay was beginning to panic.

"Relax. Maybe he knows a good cheap hotel."

"If someone tries to murder us, I'm blaming you." Kay wasn't kidding.

"That's okay. At least we know where the hospital is."

Joao parked the car in one of the tiny, dark alleyways and got out. He disappeared.

"What's happening? What's going on?" Kay was getting frantic.

"Relax. If he was going to kill us, would he have left us in his car with the keys and the engine running?"

"I guess not." Kay wasn't really confident.

After about ten minutes, Joao reappeared and began to take their luggage out of the hatch.

"Is he unloading us?" Kay was panicking again.

"Relax. I'm sure we're just at some small hotel. Stay calm." But she had no idea what was happening either.

Joao opened a small door to a narrow building and began running up the stairs, carrying the girls' luggage.

"What's happening?" Kay was on the brink of tears.

"Oy ye! Joao! A donde vamos?" She asked Joao what the story was.

"Ustedes se van a quedar con mi abuelita. Es muy buena gente."

"What did he say?" Kay demanded.

"He said that we're going to spend the night with his grandmother. Don't worry, he says she's good people."

Kay exhaled a giant sigh. She was not used to companion's incongruous system of travel.

Joao's grandmother lived on the fifth floor of an old walkup building. It wasn't too different from her building back in Manhattan, except that it didn't have running water. But who cared?

Joao's grandmother seemed thrilled to have guests. There was no common language between them, but his grandmother shut off the television when the girls entered the apartment. Kay's companion took that as a hospitable sign.

Joao's grandmother offered them some tea and showed them where they would be sleeping. Two cots were side by side in a spare room off the living room. It was perfect.

Joao kissed his grandmother, said a few words in Portuguese, and left. The three women looked at each other in silence, holding their respective mugs of tea. Maybe the language barrier was going to be more difficult than they had thought.

It was late, though, so the uncomfortable silence was broken when Joao's grandmother announced that it was time for bed. At least, that's what they assumed was said since the old woman left the living room and closed the bedroom door.

"So, what now?" Kay asked.

"Well, I guess now we sleep. See you tomorrow!" She opened her suitcase and pulled out her pajamas, changed, and got into one of the cots.

"What the hell did you get us into?" Kay asked as the two lay side by side.

"Hey, you wanted to experience Lisbon, right? Well, welcome to Lisbon."

❧

The great thing about crossing the Atlantic in a boat is that there is no risk of jetlag. The time zones change once a day or once every other day by an hour.

She and Kay woke up at dawn and found Joao's grandmother in the kitchen boiling water. The three women all kissed hello, but she felt bad that she didn't know the old woman's name. She didn't even know how to say "grandma" in Portuguese.

At first, she thought that the water was being boiled to brew coffee or tea, but through a complicated dialogue of hand gestures, she realized that the water was for bathing. She and Kay each took a bucket of hot water and began to clean themselves up, as best as they could figure out was customary.

"You don't think that that poor old woman carried all of this water up the stairs for us, do you?" She didn't want to be a burden of a houseguest.

"I saw a weird medieval-looking pump in the kitchen," Kay replied.

"So she pumped it up? Like from a well?"

"How the fuck should I know?"

"Hey, Kay. Our mission today is to learn how to say 'thank you' in Portuguese."

The girls finished their bathing and found Joao's grandmother sitting at the small round dining table with three mugs of hot instant coffee and a plate of hard baked biscuits. She wondered if the old woman had already left the house that morning and gone to the bakery? It didn't seem as though any food was stored in the home.

They finished breakfast and got dressed for the day. Joao's grandmother walked them over to a large wall clock in the sitting area and pointed to the hour hand. Through sweeping hand gestures, they understood that they were to be back at 1 p.m.

"What's at one?" Kay asked as they descended the stairs.

"I'm guessing lunch." She referenced her experience with other cultures with histories of Iberian colonialism.

"She's cooking us lunch?"

"It's a big deal in these cultures. Lunch is an important family meal."

"Why do you think that woman was so happy to take us in?" Kay was still trying to piece together the details of what was happening.

"I think that it's an honor for her to have us as guests."

"Really?"

"Really."

They wandered through the narrow streets of Lisbon. It was a gorgeous spring day. There were people everywhere, enjoying the outdoors.

They walked through the main square, wandered into a few shops, and basically enjoyed their free time.

"There are things we need to buy," she said to Kay. "Let's make a mental list."

"European phone card," Kay said.

"Definitely. Oh, and maybe a bottle of wine to bring to lunch?" She wasn't sure if it was commonplace to bring alcohol as a gift to a meal, but no one ever turned down the gift of wine.

"And flowers. Don't you think Grandma's house could use some flowers?"

"You're calling her 'Grandma' now, Kay?" She teased.

"Do you know anything else to call her?" Kay laughed.

They pooled some Euros and bought a decent bottle of port, a bouquet of flowers, and phone cards.

Kay seemed excited to be making her calls. She happily chatted in Finnish.

Kay's companion wasn't so excited. She was calling Mitchell.

"I'm sorry, Mr Durman is not here," the receptionist responded to her request to speak to him.

"Of course he's there. Mr Durman is a guest of your resort. He has an apartment. I have the confirmation number right here." She read the confirmation number to the receptionist.

"Mr Durman *was* here, but now he's gone."

"Gone? Gone where?" She was relieved and panicked at the same time. She didn't want to see Mitchell, but she also didn't want to be stranded in Europe. There were only so many grandmothers to take her in.

"Would you like me to take a message? In case he calls us."

"Please let him know that his companion has arrived in Lisbon."

"Yes, ma'am. Anything else?" The receptionist was friendly, though not helpful.

"No. That is all." She hung up. Where the hell was Mitchell?

Joao's grandmother was surprised and delighted by the gifts. Apparently, they were entirely unexpected. The flowers were put in a vase on the dining table, the bottle of port was opened, and three glasses were poured.

Lunch was an incredible rabbit stew. Joao's grandma seemed thrilled to be able to feed the houseguests with such an elaborate spread.

"I think Grandma was cooking all morning," Kay said, embarrassed.

"So, be grateful. Oh, that reminds me, we have to learn how to say thank you," she said, ready to dig into a beautiful plate of Portuguese home cooking. "You know how they say 'it's like Grandma used to make in the old world'? Well, this is Grandma."

They tried not to speak too much during the meal. Joao's grandma smiled and radiated warmth and love, but Kay's companion could tell that the English being spoken was a source of discomfort.

After lunch, she and Kay insisted on washing the dishes. It took both of them nearly fifteen minutes to figure out how to produce water from the pump. But Joao's grandmother was watching some sort of Portuguese game show in the sitting room, and they didn't want to disturb her moment of relaxation.

When water finally came out of the pump, they filled the entire sink. They were afraid they wouldn't be able to figure it out twice, so better safe than sorry.

With the dishes washed and put away, the three women all settled in for a little nap. It was a good day.

She and Kay went out for a walk in the evening. They made some phone calls. She still couldn't find Mitchell. She really didn't care.

They went to bed early that evening, to the sound of Joao's grandmother watching television in the adjoining room.

The next morning was basically exactly the same as the first. Lisbon was pretty boring. The girls were ready to go, before they overstayed their welcome.

Kay's companion went down to the payphones alone and this time was given a message with a phone number attached. She braced herself and dialed.

"Where are you, you moron?" Ahhh, Mitchell's pleasant greetings.

"I'm in Lisbon. Where are you?"

"I'm in Marbella, at a sister resort. The first resort was under construction, so I was moved." This made sense.

"Okay."

"Okay? Not okay. Why are you not here?"

"Because until two minutes ago, I didn't know where 'here' was."

"Great. Well, now you do. So, when will you arrive?"

"I don't know. When should I arrive?" She played with the phone cord between her fingers.

"You should have arrived yesterday. I shouldn't be wasting my life waiting on you."

"Well, now that I know where you are, I can figure out how to get to you."

"Okay. Don't come to Marbella. I'll meet you tomorrow in Seville," Mitchell instructed.

"Tomorrow in Seville. Got it. What time?"

"Imbecile, there is probably only one bus a day from Lisbon to Seville. So I'll meet that bus. Got it? Got it?"

"Yes, Mitchell. Got it," she confirmed. "I'll see you tomorrow."

Damn it. She had really wanted a little more time before she had to go to meet Mitchell.

She wandered the streets of Lisbon alone for a few hours. She'd duck into a port shop here and there, sampling the tastings being offered. She watched a few street performers for a while. She basically killed time.

When it was approaching the afternoon, she headed back to her hostess's home.

Kay was reading a book in the sitting room. Joao's grandmother was in the kitchen, stirring a pot on the stove.

Kay looked up from the book. "That was a long phone call. You were gone all morning."

"Yeah, well, I had to figure out some details."

"Why didn't you come to get me?"

"Who am I, your fucking tour guide?" She put her hands over her mouth. She had just accidentally channeled Mitchell. "I'm sorry. I didn't mean that. I'm a little tense."

"No worries." Kay lied. "So do you have a plan?"

"Yes, I'm taking a bus to Seville tomorrow."

"I thought you were going to Marbella?" Kay was confused.

"I am. My friend is picking me up in Seville, and then we're driving to Marbella together."

"Can I get a ride?" Kay asked.

"I'm sorry, what?" She hadn't even mentioned Kay to Mitchell.

"A ride. I'll take the bus with you to Seville. Do you think I can get a ride to Marbella?" Kay looked at her hard. "We are traveling together, right?"

"Um. Yeah. Sure. We will take the bus together to Seville."

"And then drive to Marbella." Kay finished her sentence.

"It's not my car, Kay. I'll do my best."

Kay didn't look pleased with that answer. But before the two girls could elevate the tension level, lunch was served.

It was difficult to communicate to Joao's grandmother that they needed to get bus tickets. They must have indicated something correctly because at one point, the old woman threw on a jacket and led them down the stairs.

The old woman disappeared for a moment, and then returned, sitting in the backseat of a taxi. The two girls got in.

In what seemed to be the outskirts of the city, there was an enormous, expansive outdoor bus terminal. The taxi left them at a ticket booth, and Joao's grandmother waited in the back of the cab.

The girls purchased tickets for the following day and were told by the agent in English that they were extremely lucky tickets were still available.

They got back into the cab and returned to the apartment house. Joao's grandmother put out her hand, and they each handed over ten Euros. They had surrendered more than the cab cost. Grandma handed them each five Euros in change.

As they were drinking their coffee the next morning, Joao came in through the door. His grandmother must have called him.

In Spanish, he asked them if they were ready to go meet their bus. He carried down their luggage, and the girls kissed his grandma goodbye.

When he came back up the stairs, she finally remembered to ask him how to say thank you.

Kissing the grandma a little more, and backing out the front door, she repeated to the old woman, "Obrigada."

Joao's grandmother blushed and kissed her face one last time, hard.

Then it was down the stairs and off to Seville.

The bus route to Seville covered much of the landmass of Portugal. The countryside was beautiful if not a little repetitive. There didn't seem to be many cities in Portugal, and if there were, the highway bypassed most of them.

Several hours later, they were deposited at the bus depot in Seville. After claiming their luggage, the two girls wheeled their belongings up the long and winding ramps to the main lobby.

"Is your friend here?" Kay asked, out of breath.

"Yes, he should be right . . ." She saw Mitchell at the top of the ramp. "There." She pointed. Mitchell waved, pretending to be excited to see her.

She got to Mitchell, and hugged and kissed him hello. It was more of a show for the strangers in the bus depot than an actual heartfelt reunion.

"And what is this?" Mitchell motioned toward Kay.

"This is Kay. We met on the ship and stayed together in Lisbon."

"I see." Mitchell's voice grew cold. "I'm Mitchell Durman." He extended a limp handshake toward Kay. Then he turned to her. "May I speak with you for a moment?"

Mitchell grabbed her upper arm in a vice grip and pulled her the rest of the way up the ramp.

"Mitchell, please. You're hurting me," her voice squeaked.

"No, imbecile. You're hurting me." Mitchell put his face close to hers. "Why is this fat pig following you?"

"I told you. We met on the ship. Kay is my friend."

Mitchell slapped her firmly across the face. "*That* is not your friend. Get rid of it."

"But Mitchell, can't we give her a ride to Marbella? She's going there too."

Mitchell pinched her cheek and twisted. It hurt. "You are treating me very badly right now. You go over to that fat Nordic whore and get rid of her."

"But Mitchell, where is she supposed to go?" She didn't want to fight with Mitchell, but she would feel terrible about abandoning Kay.

"I don't give a fuck where she goes. Where do fat pigs go? Tell her to go off to slaughter. But she's not coming with us." Mitchell was serious. But did he have to be so cruel?

She left her luggage with him and walked back over to Kay, who was still waiting halfway up the ramp.

"I'm sorry, Kay. We're unable to give you a ride. Mitchell has other obligations and engagements to fulfill in Seville," she lied.

Mitchell had sneaked up behind her. He interjected, "I do not have other obligations. But I have no desire to drive you to Marbella." He looked back at his companion. "We have to leave now."

"I'm sorry, Kay."

"Do not apologize to that!" Mitchell once again grabbed her firmly by the upper arm.

They left a shocked and abandoned Kay waiting in the middle of the ramp at the bus terminal.

Once inside Mitchell's rented car, he began his punitive diatribe. "What the fuck was that?"

"What was what?" She really didn't understand why he was so angry.

"That disgusting growth that you apparently sprouted on the ship and allowed to cling to you this far."

"Kay is not a disgusting growth that clung to me." She knew that she shouldn't be defending Kay. This would only infuriate Mitchell more. But she thought that he was being unnecessarily cruel to the woman who had kept her company for the past two weeks.

"That is not what you should be attracting." Mitchell spat in disgust.

"I didn't attract her. We were traveling together," she tried to explain. "Kay and I are friends."

Mitchell slammed on the brakes. "You and that are *not* friends. I am your friend. Kay is a leech."

She said nothing. Any more words would most certainly bring further trouble.

"I was going to take you to some nice places in Seville. I was going to show you a good time." Mitchell spat out the window. "But now, you've hurt me so badly. . . ." Mitchell's voice trailed off.

He parked the car on a side street and got out, indicating for her to follow.

"Where are we going, Mitchell?" She ran behind him. He had an incredibly long gait.

"*I* am going to have a coffee and a bite to eat. *You* are going to watch and work on shutting the fuck up." Mitchell seated himself at a little table at an outdoor café. She sat down next to him.

Mitchell ordered a meal for himself and made a big point of telling the waiter that there would be nothing for her.

"I can pay for my own meal, Mitchell." She was starving.

"I'm sure you can. I bet you squirrel away all sorts of money." Mitchell tucked his napkin into his shirt collar. "But you will not be eating this meal. You have behaved very badly."

"Just because of Kay?"

"Because of that, and because you should have been in Marbella several days ago." Mitchell glared at her. "And you know that. I don't know what took you so long, but I have better things to do than to track you down in the only third-world country left in Europe."

Mitchell's food arrived, and they sat in silence.

It wasn't that long a drive from Seville to Marbella, but it felt like an eternity. She could almost feel the contempt building inside Mitchell. Their arrival to the resort was not going to be a pleasant homecoming. That much she knew.

They parked the car in the dirt lot across the street from the resort. There were several staircases leading to their rental apartment, and Mitchell left her to fend for her own luggage.

She lost sight of him but found one of the apartments with the door ajar.

She entered and found Mitchell in the middle of the room, leaning against the back of the couch, watching the door.

"That's your bedroom." Mitchell pointed toward the doorway nearest to the entry foyer. "Go put your bags down and undress. Meet me in my bathroom."

She knew what was coming, and she also knew that delaying the punishment would only make it worse. She tossed her clothes onto the small single bed and walked naked into Mitchell's bedroom.

He was waiting near the tub, with his pants unzipped and his cock out and in the palm of his hand. "Get in the tub and lie down."

She hesitated in the doorway for a moment, and Mitchell grabbed her firmly by the hair and dragged her to the tub.

"I said *lie down!*"

She lay on her back in the tub and closed her eyes as she began to cry.

"Open your mouth!"

She forced her jaw open and braced herself.

Mitchell pissed all over her body. A lot in her mouth, but also in her hair and down her stomach to her legs. It was a long, full piss. He must have been saving up since lunch.

When he was finished, Mitchell said, "Stay there for a while. I want you to bathe in my piss for a while. Really let it seep in."

She spit the piss out of her mouth when he had left the bathroom and sobbed violently. Her shaking body against the hard tub made her bones hurt. She saw the pool of yellow around her and smelled the stench. She couldn't stop crying.

A few minutes later, Mitchell returned. He acted caring and concerned. He extended his hand and helped her to her feet. He turned on the shower and placed a bottle of shampoo in the corner of the tub.

"Wash yourself off. I'll take you to dinner."

She spent no less than an hour in the tub. She was trying futilely to get herself to feel clean again, but she felt so disgusting that all the soap in the world was not going to help.

When her fingers got prunish, she knew that it was time to get out of the shower. She wrapped a towel around herself and walked into the main area.

Mitchell was sitting on the couch in the living room, drinking a bottle of wine. He offered her a glass.

"Have some wine, my dear. Get the taste of piss out of your mouth."

She accepted the glass and sat down on the couch next to Mitchell.

"You understand why I had to punish you, right?"

She nodded, but she honestly didn't understand.

"You brought someone else into our world. Someone who didn't belong. And you tried to dump that someone on me. Like it's my responsibility to give a pig a ride just because you shared a boat trip?"

Her eyelids were stiff from crying. She didn't respond. She just looked blankly straight ahead.

"And that crap about you staying in Lisbon for a few days?" Mitchell scoffed. "Well, that was just stupid."

She remained silent.

"You know the thing I respect most about you, though, imbecile?" Mitchell put his arm around her bare shoulder. "I like that you take your punishments. You are very good at that."

She didn't fight off his embrace, but she didn't change her posture in any way to accept it, either.

"Okay. I'm sure you're hungry. Why don't you go and get dressed, and we can take a walk around the resort?"

She stood up and marched into her small bedroom. She got dressed as best as she could, considering her hands were shaking. She had no idea what had just happened. But she knew that two months in Spain with Mitchell were going to be a nightmare.

When they got back to the resort after taking a brief walk, Mitchell offered to unpack her bags. She politely refused, but it seemed that his motives were less to be helpful and more geared toward taking an inventory of her belongings. Saying no was just going to make the confrontation more intense.

"What the fuck is this?" Mitchell screamed from her bedroom.

"What?"

"You have plastic bags of cheese in your luggage!"

"Oh, yeah, I took some snacks from the ship. I didn't know how long it would take to get here from Lisbon, and I wanted to be prepared," she explained.

"So you stole cheese?" Mitchell was standing in the living room now, holding one of the bags.

"Well, yeah." She saw nothing wrong with this.

"How sick in the head do you have to be to steal cheese from a boat?" Mitchell was one to talk.

"Well, you told me that I'd be responsible for my own expenses. I'm cutting costs."

"With *cheese*?" Mitchell clicked his tongue in disgust. "Who does that?" Mitchell walked the bag over to the garbage and ceremoniously dumped it in.

"You didn't have to throw it out, Mitchell."

"Really? And what, pray tell, should I have done with your bag of cheese?"

"You could have put it in the refrigerator." She was being serious.

"My lord, you are mentally ill. Why would I put stolen cheese into my refrigerator?" Mitchell walked over to her. "What else do you have in your bags?" He asked accusatorily.

"Nothing," she answered honestly.

"Nothing? So if I search your bag, I'll find nothing?"

"That's right." There was nothing particularly interesting in her luggage.

Mitchell called her in to join him in her room. All her belongings were splayed out on the bed. He had a fistful of papers. "What's this?" He barked.

"Those are names and addresses of people I met on the cruise over."

"You smoke now, right? Give me your lighter." Mitchell extended his one empty palm. She could only guess at his intentions.

Very slowly and methodically, Mitchell set fire to all her new contacts' information. He let the ashes float in the air and flitter about on the tile floor.

"You didn't need to burn those."

"Why? You don't need them, right? Those losers aren't your friends," Mitchell cackled.

"They were very nice people. I enjoyed making some friends for once," she said defiantly.

"Don't be stupid! I'm your friend! Your only friend. Not those fat Finnish girls you found on the boat."

"There was only one Finnish girl, and she surely doesn't count me as a friend after I abandoned her at the bus depot in Seville."

"Say it properly. *Sevilla*." Mitchell was just trying to pick a fight with her about anything.

"Okay. Sevilla. Where I leave young Finns to die."

Mitchell laughed. He liked sardonic humor. "Now you're talking."

She walked out of the room, calling after her, "Keep the lighter. Burn what you like. I'll be in the living room." So much for her attempt to cultivate new friends.

Mitchell remained alone in her room. "Ah ha!" He came back into the living room, holding a bottle. "What's this?"

"It's cognac, Mitchell."

"I know it's cognac. Why is it in your luggage?"

"It's a gift for my dad. I'm trying to be nice. I bought it duty free."

"Fuck your father! That asshole has done nothing but make my work with you more difficult." Mitchell opened the bottle. "This cognac is now a gift to me." He swigged from the bottle and glared at her. "Thank you for the cognac."

"You don't drink hard alcohol, Mitchell."

"Don't tell me what I do and don't do, you pathetic cheese thief!" Mitchell grabbed a glass from the wet bar and filled it to the brim with cognac. "I drink cognac now!"

She didn't want him to piss on her again, and he was clearly on a mission to get drunk. She hadn't seen him drunk on hard alcohol before, so she thought it best not to test his boundaries. She didn't want to poke a monster.

Fifty-Five

They didn't have much to occupy their days. Mitchell had switched from drinking wine to drinking straight whiskey, ever since his romance with her cognac bottle. He drank it with the same voracity that he drank wine, so he was more or less useless most of the time.

When he was awake, Mitchell would cook for her. The restaurants in Marbella were mostly British run and generally awful. They ate out a few times but regretted it. Mitchell's cooking was actually fairly decent.

He had decided that she should pay for her own groceries, and she was surprised at how high the prices were for basic staples in Marbella (ten Euros for a kilo of tomatoes!). She bought the cheapest produce and ingredients she could find. Mitchell spared no expense in buying fancy pieces of fish and nice cuts of steak and parading them around in front of her while refusing to share.

She had lost track of the days, and she could only hope that their time in Marbella would be over soon.

Sometimes, she'd walk along the marina and see all the yachts owned by Mitchell's contemporaries. She'd watch the beautiful young women sunning themselves on the bows. She remembered when she had first been seduced by this lifestyle. She used to be beautiful and carefree, too.

Now she was jaded and malcontent. She'd pass her reflection sometimes in a shop window. She looked hollow, and her bitterness showed through. She hated her reflection. After a week of passing out drunk on the couch in the apartment, Mitchell decided that he wanted to lose weight. She was beginning to realize that he was the one with the eating disorder.

Mitchell offered to pay her ten Euros for each session of her training services. It was the first time he had really acknowledged her life before meeting him. She jumped at the chance to oblige.

Unfortunately, Mitchell seemed particularly interested in working out when he was drinking heavily. This rendered him obstinate and uncooperative. He would just lie back on the weight-training bench and nap. Then he would accuse her of being a lousy personal trainer and refuse to pay her.

She didn't really care that he was withholding funds. His torture tended to coincide with the amount he drank. And the more he drank, the harder he slept when he passed out. So she would take small bills out of his fag bag to make up the amount that he would stiff her.

All the days were rolling into one mass of vacant subexistence.

❧

"How would you like to go to Morocco today?" Mitchell was in the kitchen cooking them a breakfast of bacon and eggs.

She was standing on the living-room balcony smoking a cigarette. "Sounds great. When?"

"After breakfast." Mitchell delivered her a plate of scrambled eggs.

"Is Morocco that close?" she asked.

"Are you really that stupid? I'll tell you, your public school education really shows every so often. Even with the extensive travel I've shown you, your knowledge of geography is abysmal." Mitchell poured a glass of wine and ate his eggs.

"So, that means that yes, it's close?" she asked earnestly.

"It means shut the fuck up and eat your breakfast." They drove in silence from Marbella to Gibraltar to find the ferry docks. They had just missed the express ferry, so they opted to take the slower, larger car carrier from another company. It was still going to get them to Tangiers faster than if they waited for the next express to leave.

Even though the ferry accepted vehicles, they had had such bad luck with rental cars in the past that they both agreed it was wiser to pay to park the car in the lot on the European side of the voyage.

"How long are you leaving the car, sir?" the parking attendant asked Mitchell.

"I don't know. Maybe three or four days," Mitchell replied.

She waited until they were walking away to ask, "We may stay in Morocco for a while?"

"Aren't you as bored as I in Marbella?" Mitchell asked.

"Depends on your definition of boredom." She was trying to be playful.

Mitchell picked up on her humor. "Just get your bony ass on the boat." Soon, they were tying into the port at Tangiers. They joined the other passengers in line to disembark. When it came their turn to leave the boat, they walked up to the Moroccan customs official at a podium and extended their passports.

The official shook his head. "No stamps. Stay on."

"I'm sorry." Mitchell sought clarification. "Stay on? We can't leave the boat?"

The agent continued to shake his head. "No leave. No stamps."

Mitchell turned to her and said, "Did you know anything about a passport stamp?"

"No, Mitchell. I don't even know when and where we were supposed to get them." She was hoping that Mitchell would refrain from throwing a hissy fit in front of the Moroccan government officials.

Mitchell turned back toward the agent. "I'm sorry, officer. I'm understanding that we need our passports stamped, but I'm not understanding when that was supposed to be done?" So far, Mitchell was staying calm.

"On the boat. On the way over, officer stamps your passport." The agent said matter-of-factly.

Mitchell turned back toward her. "Are you sure that you knew nothing about this?"

"This is the first I've heard of a passport stamp," she said honestly.

Mitchell leaned in close to her face. "This sort of shit is supposed to be your responsibility. I can't believe you let me down again!" Mitchell then turned back toward the agent. "If the officer stamping passports was on the ship, doesn't it stand to reason that the officer is somewhere around on the dock."

"The officer is still on the ferry," the agent said.

"Good!" Mitchell said in his irritatingly patronizing sing-songy voice. "So, can we get him please?"

After about fifteen minutes of Mitchell and the agent bickering, the agent gave in. The officer with the stamps came out onto the dock. Without even looking at either passport, the officer slammed a stamp on each one.

The fact that the officer didn't even bother to open either one of their passports to the identification page wasn't lost on Mitchell. She watched his face grow beet red in fury. But he held his tongue. This was neither the time nor the place to make trouble.

As they walked away from the ship, Mitchell leaned in toward her and hissed, "This is all your fault."

"How was us not having a stamp my fault?"

"They probably would have let it slide with our American passports, but you! You have that goddamn Arab last name."

"It's a Jewish name, Mitchell, and you have a Jewish last name too." This was the most ridiculous argument.

"My name isn't in Arabic, though. My god, imbecile. Is there anywhere in the world where you don't stick out? Are you ever going to stop causing me problems?"

There was no point in responding to Mitchell when he was being this nonsensical. She just walked beside him in silence down the pier to the street.

They hailed a taxi, and Mitchell instructed the driver to take them to the souk. Once they were seated in the backseat and in transit, he began to chastise her further.

"Do you know what you did wrong back there?"

"You mean back on the boat?"

"No, you fool. When we were walking to the taxi."

"What did I do wrong when we were walking to the taxi?"

"Didn't you see the group of street urchins following us?"

She hadn't. "No, Mitchell. There was a group?"

"A posse of young boy thieves. They were sizing you up to rob you." Mitchell was sounding paranoid.

She hadn't seen anyone at all on the pier. After all, they were the last to leave the boat. They weren't even amid other passengers. "I'm sorry, Mitchell. I didn't see any street urchins."

He grabbed her hair and shouted into her ear. "This is the problem with you, imbecile. You don't notice danger. You step into foolish situations!"

She braced herself under the pain of the pull and tried not to wince. "I don't want danger."

"You say you don't want it, but you invite it!" Mitchell spat out the words. "You move in with baggage handlers; you pick up stray backpackers. You are an idiot! Your stupidity is exactly what gets you into situations like Hillside. And Silverhill. I don't care if you get yourself killed, but stop trying to bring me down with you!" He screamed.

"I'm sorry, Mitchell. I'll try not to invite danger." He was being ridiculous.

Mitchell let go of his grip on her hair. "You can't help it. You're a natural-born victim." The taxi let them off at the entrance to the souk, and they wandered through the marketplace. It was still pretty early in the morning, and the pulse of the marketplace was palpable.

They passed all sorts of stalls filled with dolls and hookahs and gold and clothes. It wasn't so much a market of tchotchkes; there were many amazing pieces of beauty.

Mitchell caught her looking at the merchandise. "If you were still my girl, and I actually liked you, you would be having a field day right now. I'd be buying you clothes and gold and treats."

She kept walking.

Mitchell kept talking. "But you're not my girl. You're my burden. And I hate you for that."

It was the first time that Mitchell had ever said that he hated her. "You hate me?"

"No," Mitchell said. "But I'm getting really sick of being stuck with you."

"You're not stuck with me, Mitchell."

"Then why do you keep appearing?" Was this a joke? She had been punished for arriving in Marbella too late, and now she was being accused of just randomly showing up. She couldn't win. They left the souk, having made no purchases, and walked into town and looked through shop windows.

"Let's find a travel agency, shall we?" Mitchell quickened his pace. "We'll see if we can rent a driver to take us to another location for a night on the Med. Sound good?"

"Sounds good." She felt herself almost moving into a run just to keep up with Mitchell.

They found a travel storefront and went inside. She lit a cigarette and sat on a chair, out of the way, while Mitchell spoke with the travel agent.

After a few minutes, Mitchell returned to her and beckoned for her to follow him out. "Never mind."

"Never mind what?"

"Never mind, I'm not taking you on a nice drive through Morocco. I keep catching myself about to do these really nice things for you, as though you were my girl. I have to stop myself from being so nice." There was not an ounce of irony or sarcasm in Mitchell's voice.

She ignored the comment. "So, what now?"

"I think that I would like to buy something for my son. Adam deserves something nice." Mitchell began looking for a suitable store for some gift shopping.

There was a child-sized mannequin in a window draped in gold silk robes. Mitchell paused to stare at the mannequin for a minute, and then entered the store.

"I'd like to buy that outfit in a size suitable for a seven-year-old," Mitchell said to the clerk.

"Um, Mitchell? Adam is eight." She tried to mumble it under her breath.

He turned to her with a face of fury. "Don't tell me how old my own son is!"

She thought that it was funny that she had remembered that Adam's birthday had passed but Mitchell had totally forgotten.

Mitchell turned back toward the clerk. "I'd like that to fit an *eight*-year-old young man."

While Mitchell dealt with his transaction, she browsed some of the women's fashion. A pair of amazing gold-knit shoes caught her eye.

Mitchell caught her staring. "Stop shopping for yourself! We are in here for my son, you selfish bitch. Don't even think of looking at something for a woman. You're barely a woman yourself!" Mitchell snatched his package from the clerk's hand and then turned back toward her. "Let's go. We're leaving. Selfish bitch."

She followed Mitchell down the street, and he walked into a large café. "What are we doing here, Mitchell?"

"*I* am eating lunch. *You* are clinging onto me and following me everywhere."

"Well, I don't want to be attacked by street urchins."

The wit was completely lost on Mitchell. "That's true. Those boys would have a field day with you. They could mug you and rape you. Hey, maybe they'd hack you into little pieces. Then you would finally leave me alone."

"Maybe." Actually, being hacked into little pieces didn't seem like such a bad alternative to another moment with Mitchell.

They returned to Marbella later the same day. The trip to Morocco was outrageously short. She did end up buying a pair of shoes, but not nice ones from a store. She bought a beautiful blue pair from a street vendor on the pier while they waited for the boat. The shoes cost only five Euros.

Back in Marbella that evening, Mitchell announced that the next day they would leave to begin their journey to Valencia. He sent her to her room to pack.

She began to inventory her belongings and place everything into her luggage. One of her bags was still wet, since Mitchell had decided in a drunken fit that he wanted to wash the cheese smell out of it.

But something was missing. She had been wearing a gold bangle that Mitchell had brought her as a gift, from a weekend he had taken in Dubai back when he had still "liked" her. And now it was gone. She was usually so good at watching her things. She couldn't imagine that she had lost something. Especially something as nice as a solid 22-carat gold bangle.

"Mitchell?"

He was sitting on the couch, not yet drunk, but well on his way. She wanted to catch him before he lost consciousness.

"Mitchell, have you seen my gold bangle?"

"You lost the beautiful bangle that I gave you? How dare you!"

"I don't think it's lost, Mitchell. I'm sure it's in the apartment. I was wearing it today, but I took it off to change and bathe, and it disappeared." She was mentally retracing her footsteps.

"I cannot believe you were so careless!" Mitchell's voice boomed. "How dare you make excuses. You and I both know that the bangle is not in the apartment. You must have been pick-pocketed by one of the urchins on the dock!"

"Mitchell, the bangle was on my wrist, not in my pocket."

"You fool! You cannot actually be so stupid. They are skilled at removing jewelry without the victim noticing. That's how they make their living. They steal from stupid victims like you!" He was screaming at her.

"I really don't think that I was robbed, Mitchell." She kept moving her eyes around the room. "I know it's around here somewhere."

"You are crazy, and you are careless. And you look like the perfect target. Of course you were robbed!" he scoffed. "You're so nuts that you probably wouldn't even remember it while it was happening!" Mitchell pointed his finger toward her room. "Now go finish packing. And try to think of how you're going to make it up to me that you lost something so valuable. Stupid bitch."

She dragged her feet out of the room. "Okay," she said under her breath. She couldn't believe that she would have allowed something so valuable to her to be lost. That bangle reminded her of happier times with Mitchell. Back when she was still a princess. But those days were gone, and now so was the bangle.

"I'm not kidding, either!" Mitchell continued his tirade. "I want restitution. *Restitution*! One of your pathetic 'I'm sorries' isn't going to get you out of this one!"

She went into her bedroom and closed the door. She flopped onto her bed, on top of her clothing piles, and stared at the ceiling until she fell asleep.

She woke up long before dawn to the jackhammer sounds of Mitchell snoring. She rubbed the sleep from her eyes and looked down at her body to realize that she had slept the night in her clothes.

Standing up, she rubbed the wrinkles out and put all her other clothes into her still soggy luggage. The bag hadn't been designed to be soaked in the fashion that Mitchell had wet it.

After everything was put away, she sat on the foot of the bed and looked at her watch. It was just about 4 a.m. She listened to the drone of Mitchell snoring in an alcoholic stupor in the living room. She wasn't going to be able to get back to sleep at this point.

So she decided to act on a hunch that she had. She went into the living room, stepping as softly as she could, and found Mitchell's fag bag. Trying not to make a sound, she unzipped it slightly and stuck in a couple of her fingers. She felt the bangle.

But she had awakened the slumbering monster. Mitchell leaped off the couch and grabbed her simultaneously by the hair and the back of the belt. He body slammed her to the floor.

The fag bag fell to the ground, and the bangle rolled out. A familiarly folded wad of money that he had told her she had lost early that week also came out.

She was in too much pain to cry or protest. She tried to feel around for any broken bones, and then tried to bring herself back up to her hands and knees. Mitchell once again grabbed her by the hair and belt and lifted her all the way into the air.

He carried her in this way into his bedroom and slammed her onto the bed with such force that she rolled off onto the floor and was wedged between the bed and the wall. Mitchell got onto the bed and grabbed her hair.

"Get up! Get up! Get back on the bed. You thief!" Mitchell roared. "You worthless, piece of shit little thief!"

She worked with the force against her hair and pulled herself onto the bed.

"Look at me! Damn you, look at me!" Mitchell palmed her bottom jaw and squeezed with his fingers. She was afraid that he was going to pop out some teeth.

She moaned. She could barely open her eyes, her face was in so much pain.

"What were you doing with your dirty paws in my bag!" Mitchell's face was scrunched into a satanic rage.

"I was . . . checking for my lost bangle." She panted as she spoke.

Mitchell backhanded her across the face. Hard. "Why would you check my bag for your bangle? Why would it be in there?"

"I don't know." She was crying now. "But it was."

Mitchell backhanded her again, on the same side. She felt her face swelling.

"Your bangle was *not* in my bag!"

She knew better than to protest, yet she whimpered, "but it was."

"It was *not!* Your bangle was stolen by street urchins in Tangiers. And you're so crazy that you're thinking that you saw it." Mitchell slapped her again, mercifully not as hard as before. "You're losing your mind! You're losing your mind."

"I saw it." She sniffled.

"Really? In the dark, you think you saw it in my bag?" Mitchell's face was inches from hers.

"I felt it. I was . . . holding it."

"So, you admit that you were stealing from my private bag!"

"No. I was looking for my bangle."

"Your bangle is gone, you crazy bitch! Your bangle is gone." Mitchell grabbed her by the hair and dragged her off the bed. She hit the floor with a thud. He dragged her across the floor and through the apartment. She tried to use her hands and feet to move with the pressure, but he was pulling too fast.

She couldn't help but moan.

Mitchell opened the front door with one hand while not letting go of his grip on her hair with the other. He threw her onto the concrete entranceway. "Now stay here and wait until it's time to go!" He slammed the door. "Stupid bitch" was muffled as she heard him walk deeper into the apartment.

She lay on her side on the cold concrete. She couldn't sit up. The first signs of dawn were peaking through the darkness. She used to love to watch the sunrise.

Fifty-Six

They drove in silence through the arid landscape of southern Spain. She looked out the passenger side window at the desert landscape, watching the monotony of the passing olive trees.

The road map was in her lap. Mitchell had handed it to her when they first got into the car. Her big dark sunglasses served two purposes. They cut the glare of the blazing sun from the sandy landscape. They also hid the dark bruises that had formed around her eyes. She didn't look in the mirror to see the bruises. She could just feel that they were there.

"I'm about to treat you too well again," Mitchell muttered.

"What?" she asked without actually turning to look at him.

"I'm going to treat you too nicely. I'm taking you to places you don't deserve to go," Mitchell continued.

"Where are we going?" She still didn't look at him.

"I'm not your fucking tour guide!" Mitchell screamed, as though the mean switch in his brain had been flicked back on. "Look at me!"

She turned her head before he could turn it for her.

"I can't even see your fucking eyes!" Mitchell grabbed her metal-framed sunglasses off her face and crumpled them in his fist. He dropped the twisted frames and lens into her lap.

She looked at her broken glasses. She picked up the frames, and began to unfurl them.

"Don't try to fix them. They're dead. They're gone!" Mitchell yelled. He grabbed the sunglasses with one hand, let go of the steering wheel for a minute, and rolled down his window. He threw the sunglasses onto the highway.

They drove for another hour in silence. With the blazing morning sun, she had to squint her eyes just so they wouldn't hurt from the harsh light.

After a while, they passed through a town. Mitchell pulled the car over on a side street, left it idling, and said nothing as he left her in the car.

She pulled down the sun visor, which she hadn't dared do while Mitchell was in the car. She saw her reflection in the mirror. She didn't mean to, but she did. Her face was red and swollen. Her hair was matted to her head. Her eyes were black and puffy. She closed the sun visor, deciding it was better to look into the light than to look into a mirror.

Mitchell returned after about twenty minutes. He said nothing as he entered the car, and she chose not to ask him where he had just gone.

Mitchell backed the car out of the side street and drove back onto the highway. As soon as they were under way, Mitchell tossed a black box into her lap. His eyes didn't leave the road as he did it.

She looked at the black box. It was more like a hard pouch with a zipper.

She opened it up and inside was a pair of Armani sunglasses. The original price tag for six hundred Euros was still attached. She put on the sunglasses.

She looked at Mitchell. She knew better than to say thank you, lest she set him off again. Instead she looked straight ahead at the windshield.

Mitchell appreciated her not acknowledging the new sunglasses. He said flatly, "Since you asked, we're going to spend the night in Granada. I'm going to treat you to a trip to Alhambra. I purchased the tickets this morning."

They arrived in Granada and checked into a modest hotel. The bathroom was so small that Mitchell had to keep the bathroom door open to fit on the toilet. She looked at his feet, firmly planted in the hallway, and at the top of the newspaper sticking through the doorframe. It was hard not to find the scene amusing.

When they were satisfactorily settled in, Mitchell decided that it was time to head into downtown Granada. He parked the car in a large lot, put the Euros in the meter at the end of the street, put the ticket in the windshield, and then motioned for her to get out of the car.

They walked through the city, and Mitchell spotted a little sidewalk café that looked appealing. "That's where we'll be meeting."

"What's where?" she asked.

"Don't you listen? I'm going to meet you at a table at that café. At 5 p.m."

She looked at her watch. "It's only 11 a.m. now."

"I know that, imbecile. But you have work to do in Granada," Mitchell explained. "I have three tickets to the Alhambra. Granada is a major university city. Your job is to find some pussy worthy of that third ticket. Think you can handle that?"

There was always a catch with Mitchell. She sighed. "Okay, so you want me to find some pussy and deliver it to you?"

"Shouldn't be too hard in Granada." Mitchell walked away. "Okay, I have some work to do. So do you. Bye bye."

She wandered through the main square in Granada and surveyed the quality of available young women. She didn't want to pounce on any one girl too soon though, because she couldn't imagine how she would entertain someone for six hours before meeting up with Mitchell.

Sitting on a marble bench, she watched people go by. She was bored, but she knew that she couldn't show up to meet Mitchell empty handed.

She spotted a young blonde sitting alone, haplessly skimming through a book. She saw her chance. By this time in her career with Mitchell, she had the game down to an effortless science. She walked over to the girl, made an introduction, and invited the girl to come to the Alhambra that night after an evening of fucking.

The girl, a Dutch student spending a year at the university in Granada, eagerly agreed. The girl had something to do in the afternoon but wrote down an address and a phone number and asked to be picked up at 7 p.m.

Satisfied that her work was completed, she took her time wandering over to the designated café meeting spot. She knew Mitchell well, and she knew that he would be there well ahead of schedule. He was.

"Why are you alone?" He didn't even bother to greet her.

"We have a date for later this evening." She pulled out one of the chairs at the table and took a seat.

"How do we have a date if there's no one with you now?"

"I have a phone number and an address."

"That means shit." Mitchell slammed down his coffee. "How do you even know that's real?"

"I've been doing this for a while, Mitchell. It's real."

"It had better be. I'm tired of putting up with your bullshit all the time. I want something in return." Mitchell finished his coffee. "Let's go to the car. I'm bored with Granada."

They killed time until 7 p.m., and then they searched for the address the girl had given. It was fairly easy to find, and judging by the shabby neighborhood, it was student housing. It was definitely a legitimate address.

She found a payphone down the street while Mitchell idled the car. The girl answered the phone and a few minutes later exited the building.

Once everyone was inside the car, Mitchell became the charming personality that he always was when in the presence of a possible sex object. She took that as a sign that he approved of the girl she had found.

Mitchell drove them back to the hotel, and the three of them went up into the tiny room. At some point during the day, Mitchell had stocked the room with wine. He poured three glasses.

The Dutch girl gulped the first glass down, clearly feeling nervous. Mitchell gave his accomplice a sideways glance, and she knew that it was her job to make the fucktoy feel comfortable.

Feigning affection and arousal, she ran her fingers through the girl's long blonde hair and set her other hand on the girl's thigh. She could feel the girl relax under her touch.

She took her hand out of the girl's hair and lightly brushed the girl's face in a way that turned the head toward her. Delicately, but firmly, she gave her a kiss. The girl released a guttural moan. She was primed and ready for play.

The domme instructed the girl to disrobe and then kneel in front of Mitchell. Slowly, the girl undressed, as though to give them a strip tease. Mitchell pulled down his slacks and took is cock in his right hand.

As the girl kneeled down, Mitchell slowly stroked himself. His feet twitched with delight. The domme hoped that he didn't notice that she rolled her eyes. She really hated this sex play.

She instructed the girl to begin giving Mitchell a blowjob. While this happened, she opened her luggage and found her strap-on.

She took off only her pants and underwear. She wasn't in the mood to be naked.

She entered the girl from behind and was greeted by a whimper of delight. Again, she rolled her eyes.

Rhythmically, almost robotically, she pumped the dildo in and out of the girl's asshole. As the girl gyrated more enthusiastically, she pumped harder and faster. Mitchell began to groan.

Mitchell and the girl orgasmed and groaned loudly at the same time. The girl even emitted a little scream.

The domme pulled the dildo out of the girl's asshole and rose to her feet. She walked into the small bathroom, released the harness, and let the tool fall to the floor. She picked it up by the harness cord and threw it into the sink. She turned on the hot water to full blast and left it running, then went back into the bedroom.

The girl was already mostly dressed. Mitchell had fastened his pants. Playtime was over.

"Our friend here is ready to go home, so I've offered her a ride," Mitchell said in his annoying gentle voice.

She gave him a look as though to ask what had happened to the plan of going to the Alhambra. He read her look and shot one back, as though to figuratively silence her. She left the issue alone. It was always best not to question Mitchell or his motives.

The trio piled into the car and drove back to the Dutch girl's home. Without much ado, the girl got out of the car and entered the house.

Mitchell turned to his companion. "I promised you a night at the Alhambra. I'm incredibly exhausted, but I always make good on my promises, right?"

"Right." She felt that it was in her best interest to just agree.

"Okay, so we'll drive up that way now. Believe it or not, this pussy you found is actually on the way to the Alhambra anyway." He turned to her as they began to drive. "By the way, thank you. Excellent work."

She stared off into the dark Spanish night.

The Alhambra was only lit up at night and open to visitors once a month. Mitchell must have been planning this evening for longer than he had led on.

It was a beautiful evening, but they were both far too tired to walk around. So they looked at the majestic structure, agreed that it was magnificent, and then left to go back to the parking lot.

Back at the hotel, she slept soundly. She knew that every time she presented Mitchell with an enjoyable fucking session, she bought herself a few days of peace.

She had breakfast on her own in the hotel lobby. Mitchell was still fast asleep. The previous evening's activities must have worn him out.

When she let herself back into the room, Mitchell was in the bathroom. His feet were planted on the floor in the hallway, and as she passed to enter the bedroom, she avoided looking at him sitting on the toilet.

"Are you all packed?" Mitchell called from his throne.

"I never unpacked," she replied.

"Good. Because we're going to Ibiza today."

"How are we getting there?" She wasn't really sure how one accessed Ibiza.

"I don't know yet. We'll drive to Valencia and figure it out from there."

"Okay. Sounds like a plan."

"Imbecile, that is not a plan. We are going to wing it." Mitchell laughed playfully.

She ignored the slight and mentally prepared herself for the trip to Ibiza.

Once in Valencia, they opted for the air route to Ibiza. The boat options all seemed to take too long and required a bit of advance planning.

Plane tickets were only about fifteen Euros, and the flight was little more than half an hour.

In Ibiza, they took a cab to their timeshare resort. It was a long cab ride, almost an hour. Mitchell made a note that once they were settled into their apartment, they would find a place to rent a car.

Ibiza seemed relatively quiet, especially considering the insanity she had anticipated at the world's craziest club destination. But it was only the end of April, so it was still the off-season.

They were pleasantly surprised to find that the resort was right on the water. Their apartment had a large balcony overlooking the Med, with a view of the resort pool right beneath them. It wasn't as big or as fancy as the timeshare they had rented in Marbella, but it was a much nicer location.

They set down their bags and left the hotel in search of a rental car.

"You can't drive standard, can you?" Mitchell had never asked her about her driving before; he had always driven everywhere.

"Not well," she replied honestly.

"How much for an automatic?" Mitchell asked the rental clerk.

The automatic cars were almost three times the rate of the standard transmission vehicles, but Mitchell agreed to the price.

"You're getting an automatic?" She asked Mitchell, as they were led out to their Chrysler PT Cruiser.

"No, you're getting an automatic," Mitchell explained. "I expect you to go out to the clubs every night, and I don't want you getting into trouble driving in the middle of the night in a vehicle you can't control."

"I'm going out alone?"

"Of course. I'm too old and fat to go to the nightclubs."

"So, why do I have to go to the clubs?"

Mitchell glared at her. "Why else would we be in Ibiza? Your purpose here is to go out to the clubs and come home with pussy." Mitchell sighed. "Really, imbecile. I thought you would have understood your role in this relationship by now."

Mitchell tossed her the car keys, and she got into the driver's seat. "Where to?" she asked.

"Let's go into town. Since you're driving, I feel like going to have a few drinks."

Ibiza was a lot larger than either of them had anticipated, and the drive into town was long. But it was a straight shot on a road along the water, so it wasn't too bad.

She parked the car in the first available spot in the center of town, and they got out to find a place to sit.

"You're a better driver than I thought, imbecile. I had incredibly low expectations." Mitchell tousled her hair playfully. "If I had known that you could drive so well, I would have had you play chauffeur all this time. I would have saved a fortune on taxis."

"You never asked," she said.

"That's because you're so incompetent with everything else in your life, I figured that you'd kill us if you ever got behind the wheel."

"Thanks." She rolled her eyes.

"You're not incompetent?" Mitchell dared her to object to the accusation.

"I guess I am."

"That's right."

She changed the subject. "So, do you see anything you like?"

"Pussy-wise or venue-wise?"

"Either." She didn't really see much of anything. Ibiza was pretty dead in the off months.

"Let's sit in that café and have a drink." Mitchell paused. "Well, I'll have a drink. You're driving." He laughed. "I like the way that sounds."

They whiled away the afternoon, and then headed back to the resort for a nap.

At around midnight, Mitchell woke her up.

"It's time to start the day." He shook her out of her sleep.

"It's the middle of the night."

"This is Ibiza, silly! It's time to start the day." He shook her a little more firmly. "Come on. We'll go to dinner and then we'll find out which clubs are the hot spots this time of year." He shook her again to let her know that he meant business. "Come on! Let's go!"

She was still wearing her clothes, so all she had to do was put on her shoes.

"We're really going out now?" she asked.

"I don't have the patience for your foolishness. Let's get in the car. I'll even do you a favor and drive."

"Gee, thanks."

Mitchell slapped her lightly across the face. "Are you sassing me?"

She dropped her gaze to the floor. "No."

They had a modest pizza dinner at a restaurant near the waterfront. Mitchell grilled the wait staff and some of the other diners to find out which clubs were worth a visit. Everyone agreed that Pacha was the place to go.

After dinner, Mitchell drove back to the hotel. Once inside the room, he tossed her the car keys.

"Why are you giving me the keys now?" She should have known better than to ask.

"You're going to Pacha," Mitchell said, matter-of-factly.

"Now? But I don't even know where it is. And this is a huge island!" She had an image of being lost forever, driving in circles in the PT Cruiser.

"I'm sure you'll figure it out." Mitchell replied. "You're smarter than you look."

To her surprise, Pacha was incredibly easy to find. It was about forty minutes away from the resort, but it was a really obvious destination.

It was also empty. She was the only car in the parking lot. She looked at the clock on the dashboard. It was 3 a.m. She had heard that Ibiza's nightlife didn't really kick into gear until almost dawn, so she decided to wait for a little while in the car.

Sure enough, by around 4 a.m., the parking lot began to fill up and club goers began crowding into the entrance. She got out of the car and joined the group to enter.

Women didn't have to pay a cover charge, and because she was alone, she was able to bypass the line of couples and mixed groups.

She was underwhelmed; there weren't that many people, and there were almost no attractive, unattached women.

She bought a Coke at the bar and sat in a chair in the lounge. And she fell asleep.

She was awakened by a kiss on the cheek. Startled, she looked up to see a giant security guard hovering over her.

The bouncer yelled over the loud, pulsing music, "I think it's time for you to go home."

She agreed. Satisfied that she wasn't leaving of her own resolve, she got into the car and prepared for the drive home.

As she drove along the highway, she began to feel ill. Her hands were cramping, and her chest felt as though it were vibrating. At the first available place to pull over, she stopped the car.

She thought that maybe she was having a heart attack. She could barely breathe, and she was having trouble unclenching her fists. Something was terribly wrong with her.

But after about a half hour, the episode passed. She got back onto the highway and drove the rest of the way back to the resort. She was just happy to make it back alive.

She didn't know what was wrong with her, but she could tell that it was bad. Still wearing her clothes, she threw herself onto her bed. She wasn't sure if she'd even live to see the morning.

Mitchell awakened her at about noon. Her body felt weak. It was difficult to get out of bed. She told Mitchell that she thought she may be sick. A parasite from Morocco, perhaps? But he dismissed her concerns.

Mitchell wanted to know everything about her evening at Pacha, but she didn't have much to say. And she didn't dare tell him about her episode on the highway; she didn't want her health to be used against her.

In the afternoon, they took a drive around the island. Mitchell was sober enough to drive, so he did. She didn't want to drive anymore anyway.

They weren't really looking for anything in particular, and in the off-season in Ibiza, there wasn't much to find anyway.

What they did find, however, was a girl waiting at a bus stop, looking bored. Mitchell pulled the car over.

"Get that girl to come home with us," Mitchell commanded.

"The girl at the bus stop?"

"Quit acting stupid. You know the drill." Mitchell rolled his eyes.

She got out of the car and walked back toward the bus stop. The girl was American, so she wasn't sure how the encounter would play out.

She said to the girl, "My friend and I would like to take you to lunch and fuck you."

The girl replied, "I'm waiting for the bus."

She said, "Well, of course, afterward we'll take you wherever you'd like to go."

The girl thought for a minute and then stood up. "Okay, can we go to lunch on the beach?"

The two girls walked back toward the car. The fucktoy got into the backseat, and the domme sat in the front next to Mitchell.

"Our guest would like to have lunch on the beach," she said to Mitchell.

"But of course!" Mitchell proclaimed, as he put the car into gear and sped off.

Because it was far from the peak season in Ibiza, finding open restaurants on the beach proved to be difficult. But the girl had obviously been on the island for some time and was able to direct Mitchell toward an area of open venues.

They parked the car in a sandy lot and walked along the shore. All three removed their shoes, and she and Mitchell followed as the girl led the way.

They stopped at a nice pizza shack set in the sand and sat under one of the big umbrellas. They had lunch (although at that late hour it would have been dinner anywhere else in the world).

They asked questions, pretending to get to know the girl, and pretending to listen to the answers. After they had finished the meal, they walked back to the car and drove off to the hotel.

She still was feeling awful; she was afflicted with diarrhea now and was convinced that she had contracted something in Morocco. But she tried to power through her misery. She felt void of energy, and severely dehydrated, but she didn't want to give Mitchell any fuel for an attack.

It was easy to get the girl naked and ready for play. In fact, it was too easy. The girl sat next to her on the bed in her room while she laboriously pulled on her strap-on. But she was just too drained to fuck.

Essentially, she lay lifeless on the bed, trying in vain to conjure enough strength to fuck the girl.

The girl, thinking that the problem was a lack of stimulation, went down on her. But even having her pussy eaten could do nothing to rouse her from her physical misery.

She instructed the girl to suck Mitchell's cock, and the girl did so happily. But try as she might, she couldn't even get into position to fuck the girl.

After Mitchell came, he left to drive the girl back home.

When he returned, he had little more to say than "What the fuck was that?!"

"I'm sorry, Mitchell. But I really don't feel well."

"Of course you don't feel well. You are literally moments away from death. But does that mean that you have to ruin the fun for everyone?" Mitchell scoffed. "How does it look when you pick up a girl to fuck, and then you lie lifeless on your bed, unwilling to do any fucking?"

"Unable," she corrected.

"Don't sass me. You could find the energy if you really wanted to." Mitchell began to walk out of her room. "Take a good nap. You're going out clubbing again tonight."

With barely enough strength to put on her shoes, she forced herself to get ready to go out that night. She got into the car and drove the distance to Pacha. She knew that Mitchell wouldn't accept her return without a story of possible pussy, so with the strength she had left, she began to hunt women.

Her target became a Slavic bartender named Blanka, who was absolutely stunning. She had another clubgoer take pictures of her kissing Blanka, and she worked Blanka up to the idea of a fuck session.

The pictures she showed Mitchell seemed to keep him interested for a few days, and she continued to go out every night to Pacha to talk to Blanka.

Try as she might, though, she couldn't get Blanka to go home with her. This may have been for the mere fact that Blanka worked long into the morning. Or it may have been because she just felt too exhausted to work her normal charm on Blanka.

But Blanka was beautiful to the point of being statuesque, and after a few nights, and several digital photos, Mitchell decided to make a trip to Pacha to check out the scene for himself.

She and Mitchell arrived at Pacha at around 1 a.m., with the intention of having dinner in the main restaurant before the nightclub officially opened.

It was the first great meal that the two of them had had in a long while, and Mitchell made sure not to let her forget it. They had a great tasting menu, and then went onto the dance floor so that she could introduce him to her conquest.

Mitchell was intrigued, but he could also tell that his companion was losing her edge. The fatigue of spending every night out, coupled with her physical mal-being, was becoming pervasively evident. Even Mitchell couldn't deny that she couldn't maintain the pace. He resented her for being human.

Fifty-Seven

She sat out on the balcony smoking a cigarette while Mitchell worked in the kitchen cooking her a late lunch. She hadn't been awake yet when he had left the apartment to shop for groceries, so she had no idea what to expect. Her expectations were low.

But they weren't low enough. Mitchell came out onto the balcony with a large bowl of brown goo.

"What's this?" she asked, hoping that it sounded better than it looked.

"It's gruel." Mitchell chuckled.

"Seriously, what is it?"

"It's gruel." Mitchell placed the bowl of slop in front of her with a big wooden spoon protruding. He sat down across the table. "Eat it. It's all you're getting today."

"I can't eat this, Mitchell. Even the smell is making me sick." She really hoped for mercy.

"Well, it's that or nothing. And I know that you've been feeling low on energy lately, so you had better fuel up."

"Maybe I'll just buy something while I'm out tonight." She hoped to avoid picking up the giant wooden spoon.

"*Eat it!*" Mitchell's voice boomed. "I cooked it, so eat it!"

"But, Mitchell, I don't even know what it is."

"It's a little of this, a little of that. Whatever was cheapest at the store." Mitchell laughed. "It's slop. But really, you don't deserve better, do you?"

"Why not?" She confronted him honestly. "Why don't I deserve better?"

"Well, you've wasted almost a week trying to land Blanka, and I think that we both know that that's not going to happen."

"So, I'm being punished?"

"Crazy girl, at this point, anything bad that happens to you, you've brought on yourself." Mitchell pointed at the spoon. "Now eat the meal I've cooked for you, before things really get ugly."

She tried to eat, but the stench was overpowering. The texture of the food was like an awful, gristly stew. She couldn't even tell what the main ingredients were.

She fought her way through the bowl, but before she finished it, she couldn't help the convulsions in her stomach. She threw up off the side of the balcony. And when she was finished throwing up, she heaved some more. Nothing but air came out.

Mitchell sat and drank his wine. He seemed proud of the misery he had caused. When she couldn't throw up anymore, he handed her a napkin to wipe her mouth.

"You deserve no more than gruel. But you've worked hard this week. I know that, and I appreciate it. Even if you couldn't deliver Blanka."

She collapsed into the plastic patio chair. She had nothing else to purge. There was nothing else inside her. Her spirit was dead; her soul was cold; her body was limp. She couldn't respond to Mitchell.

He said, "I think that we're done with Ibiza, don't you?"

She nodded, limply.

"Good. I think that I'll fly to Valencia tomorrow. We still have lots of time at this apartment. You should stay and maximize the investment."

She shook her head.

"Okay." Mitchell said, reading her body signals. "You can fly with me to Valencia tomorrow. We'll figure out where you're going from there."

She stared at the vomit that dripped from the side of the balcony. Mitchell seemed not to notice.

He said to her, "I think it's time for you to go to bed now, isn't it?"

She nodded, happy that he was showing some mercy.

"Good." Mitchell said. "Go to sleep. Valencia in the morning."

She staggered off to her bedroom and collapsed. They left for Valencia early in the morning, and because it was such a short flight, they arrived soon thereafter. Mitchell was pleased to discover that the airport had free WiFi throughout; it was the first airport that they had encountered internationally with Internet access. It just showed her how far technology had evolved since she had first met Mitchell. It seemed forever ago.

They sat in the airport, and Mitchell pulled out his European MacBook from his bag. He played around with his email and looked into flight itineraries.

Then he slammed his computer shut and stood up. "Okay, I'm ready to leave. I think that I'm going to take an afternoon flight to Milan."

He hadn't said anything about her, so she asked him, confused, "And me?"

"And you what?" Mitchell scoffed. "Didn't I tell you that on this trip, you're on your own?"

She concurred. "You did, but even if I left now, there are no flights to the U.S. from Valencia. Not that I have anything booked anyway."

"Well, whose problem is that?" Mitchell clucked his tongue. "I took you to the sexiest island on Earth, and you couldn't even deliver me quality pussy. So what do I care how you get back to New York?"

"You're leaving me?" As much as she loathed him, she didn't want Mitchell to abandon her.

"Let's not talk about that. I booked a flight for myself online. I still have time before it leaves. I'll buy you lunch before I go."

She had a knot in the pit of her stomach. She knew that this situation was not going to end well. But because she couldn't think of anything better to do in the tiny airport, she followed Mitchell over to the elevator leading one flight up to the food court.

When they entered the elevator, a beautiful blonde girl was already inside, presumably from a lower floor. The lone girl was also apparently en route to the food court.

She accidentally hit the girl with her suitcase, and Mitchell simultaneously poked his companion in the ribs. Under his breath, he said, "Fuck that girl."

She had grown tired of these missions, but the girl was looking at her lustfully, and she knew that this was an easy task. Plus, judging from the tags on the girl's luggage, the girl was British. So language wasn't a barrier.

Even so, she didn't say anything to the girl during the ride up in the elevator, save for a mumbled apology for the whack from her suitcase. Mitchell didn't seem pleased. She didn't care.

Mitchell bought two sandwiches from a vendor and placed them on a tray. She waited with the luggage at one of the food court picnic tables. He dropped the tray on the table, aggressively. She pretended not to notice.

He decided to rehash the issue. "You missed an opportunity to fuck that Brit from the elevator."

"And where did you want me to fuck her, Mitchell?"

"In the ass." Mitchell laughed, pleased with his play on words.

"Ha ha," she said flatly.

Mitchell passed her her sandwich off the tray and leaned in toward her. He said, "Look, that girl is sitting alone eating her lunch. She's at the table over there." Mitchell pointed with his thumb.

"So?" She picked up her sandwich and began to unwrap it.

"So, if you fuck her today, I'll buy you a ticket to Milan." Mitchell took a bite from his sandwich.

"But your flight leaves soon. There's no time to get me on that flight." She was trying to understand what Mitchell was saying.

"No." He agreed. "You can't be on the same plane as me. But I'll buy you a ticket for the flight directly afterwards, and I'll meet you at Malpensa."

"And all I have to do is fuck that girl?"

"That's the deal." Mitchell spoke with his mouth full.

"Where? Where do you want me to fuck her?" She was already so indebted to the devil, what was one more offense?

"How many times have I told you that all of the action takes place in the ladies' room?" Mitchell took another bite of sandwich.

"A million times," she replied, then added, "but we're in an airport."

"Are there not bathrooms in airports?"

"There are."

"Good. So you fuck the girl in the bathroom, and you earn yourself a flight to Milan."

"That's it?" She was waiting for the catch.

"That's it. Go fuck her." Mitchell stood, not having finished his lunch. "I have a plane to catch. You may, too, if you figure this out."

Mitchell left.

She looked at the girl, who was eating alone, and tried to determine the best way to approach.

Eventually, she decided to forsake all tact and just walk directly up to the girl.

"When you finish with your lunch, I need a few minutes of your time to fuck you." She was almost expecting the girl to hit her, or at least dismiss her in an aggressively defensive way.

Instead, the girl stood to dispose of the lunch tray. "Where are you taking me?" She was earnest.

"All the action takes place in the ladies' room."

When Mitchell's companion turned around, Mitchell was already long since gone to make his flight. But she had learned that Mitchell seemed to observe all her actions. She didn't want to piss him off.

After the two girls had collected their respective luggage, they took the elevator back down to the main floor of the Valencia airline terminal. She led the girl into the handicapped restroom in the ladies' room so that all their luggage could fit in the stall.

She pulled off her slacks and pulled her strap-on out of her bag. She instructed the girl to get on all fours for the receipt of the fucking. "Where do you want me?" The girl asked.

"I really don't give a fuck," she responded, already bored.

Naked, the girl climbed onto all fours on the toilet seat.

With saying a word, she entered the girl from behind.

The act of sex may have been lost on the others who milled about in the ladies' room, awaiting their turn to use the stall, but what she hadn't factored in was that the toilet had been set to an automatic flush; every time she pounded in the girl's asshole, the toilet flushed.

The girl seemed excited to be desired. The orgasm she had was insane. As the toilet flushed uncontrollably, the domme tried to muffle the girl's screams with one hand. The girl bit her. Downplaying the intensity was no use.

After the girl climaxed hard, several times, the domme climbed off and let the strap-on fall to her feet.

The two girls exited the handicapped stall. There was a long line of women waiting to use the bathroom.

Unceremoniously, and with disregard for the shocked expressions of the onlookers, she dropped the strap-on dildo into one of the communal sinks, rinsed off the filth, and then wrapped the appendage in paper towel and put it in her purse.

She gave the girl a look of dismissal and exited the ladies' room to find a ticketing agent for the intercontinental flights. There was a ticket waiting in her name.

Mitchell was waiting for her in the baggage claim area of Malpensa. She didn't know how long he'd been waiting, but he had already rented a car. This was a good thing; it was very late at night, and the car rental counters had all closed.

As they walked to the car, Mitchell said, "I was going to stick you in a hostel tonight. But because it's so late, and I don't have a hotel room yet myself, I'll be nice. You can stay with me. Tonight." He opened the car door and got in.

The car was a manual transmission. She was relieved that he wasn't expecting her to drive.

"You're the navigator." Mitchell tossed a map of Milan and surroundings into her lap.

"Where are we going?" She opened the map.

"You tell me! You're the navigator. Get us to Milan!"

She looked at the map and noticed the tremendous distance between Malpensa and Milan. She looked at her watch. It was after midnight.

"Mitchell, I don't think that we'll get into town before one or two in the morning. And we still don't have a hotel room." She wanted him to have enough information on which to base a judgment for a destination.

Mitchell exhaled a long deep breath and buzzed his lips. He was thinking. "I was afraid of that. Okay, here's our plan. First hotel we see, you get out and get us a room."

"Okay, I'll keep an eye out for hotels."

"Don't keep an eye out, imbecile! You're the navigator." Mitchell shook the map violently in her face.

"Mitchell, this is a road map. There's no topography, and no hotels on it either. Just streets."

"Are you sassing me?" Mitchell hit her in the side of her head with the palm of his hand.

"No, sir." She tried to get as close to the door as she could. She wanted to be out of Mitchell's reach."Okay." Mitchell calmed down again. "We'll keep an eye out for hotels. In the meantime, tell me all about the British slut in the Valencia bathroom."

She told him all about the bathroom escapade. She made sure to highlight the repeated flushing of the automated bowl. Mitchell laughed. She knew that he would. It was pretty funny.

She wanted to tell the story in a sexy way, but a physical encounter in an airport bathroom wasn't very hot. There wasn't much she could do to make the story erotic.

"Her asshole was ready and willing for you?" Mitchell liked to ask leading questions to get himself aroused.

"My purple cock slid right in."

"No resistance?" Mitchell's breathing was getting more shallow. He was turned on.

"None. And a couple of massive orgasms."

"All over a flushing toilet." Mitchell liked that part of the story.

"All over a flushing toilet."

"And a crowd of people standing outside, hearing all of this?"

"A huge line. Lots of people waiting."

"And listening!" Mitchell belly laughed. "I have to hand it to you, young lady. When you do it, you do it well."

"Trained by the best." She was being facetious, but Mitchell took it as a compliment.

"You're welcome." He meant it.

She looked out the windshield onto the dark highway. She saw lights in the distance and pointed. "Hotel!"

Mitchell swerved the car across the traffic lanes and pulled off at the exit to the hotel. It was a Holiday Inn.

The parking lot was dark, and there was no light on in the lobby. Mitchell idled the car in front of the entrance.

"Are they closed?" She had never seen an entirely dark lobby at a major hotel chain before.

"How can a hotel close?" Mitchell said in disbelief. "There are lights on upstairs. There are obviously guests here tonight." Mitchell turned to her. "Okay, get out. See if you can find someone in there."

She walked over to the front door, but it was locked. She could see a large deadbolt hanging from a chain on the inside of the doors.

She walked back to the car and leaned over to stick her head into the open driver's side window. "The door is chained shut."

"You mean to tell me that this hotel locks its customers in at night?" Mitchell chortled.

"I guess so." She smiled. "That must be a fire hazard, huh?"

Mitchell scoffed. "Fucking Europeans." He pointed back to the door. "Bang on the glass. Try to see if you can get someone's attention."

She banged on the glass for several minutes, and finally she saw a light go on in the office behind the front desk. A sleepy young man in hotel uniform rubbed his eyes and walked over to the door. Through the glass, the young man yelled, in Italian.

She didn't speak Italian, but she hoped that because it was a hotel near an international airport, the man would understand English.

"May we have a room for the night, please?" She shouted through the glass.

Her voice must have been too muffled through the door. The man shouted back, "What?"

"I need a room. For tonight. You have vacancies?" She was tired of shouting.

"Hotel is closed. No check-in." The man yelled back.

"We pay cash!" She had learned long ago that any special service could be accommodated for the right price.

The man stood and stared at her through the glass for a minute. He looked out and saw Mitchell sitting in the car. The man walked away from the door, went back into the office, and reemerged holding a set of keys.

He unchained the door and motioned for her to enter.

Mitchell saw her go inside, so he parked the car and came back carrying nothing but his fag bag under the crook of one elbow.

"Thank you for accommodating us." Mitchell handed the man three one hundred-Euro bills. Mitchell knew the system.

They were given a room key, and in the dark, they went up into their suite. They both fell asleep in their clothes.

Mitchell woke her up by shaking her. Groggily, she opened her eyes. She looked at the clock and noted that they had only had about two and a half hours' sleep. She needed more.

"Mitchell, I'm tired. Can't we sleep a little longer?" she asked.

"No time! No time!" He pulled the blanket off her. "Get up! We're driving down to Portofino, and if we wait too long, we won't be able to get in."

"Get in where?" She was confused.

"We won't be able to get into the city of Portofino!" He said this like it should have been obvious to her.

"We won't be able to get into the city?"

"They only allow a certain number of visitors in a day. If we don't leave now, we won't make the cut!"

"They limit the number of people?" She rubbed the sleep out of her eyes.

"That's what I said." Mitchell was antsy. "So get up. I have a craving for fish soup!"

They hadn't brought anything up into the room with them, so getting ready to leave took only a moment.

Once in the car, she hoped that Mitchell wouldn't ask her to play navigator again. Luckily, he seemed to know the route to Portofino. He drove at a ridiculously high speed.

But as fast as he drove, it wasn't enough. When they arrived near Portofino, there was already a line, several hundred cars deep.

"Damn it! Damn it, damn it, damn it!" Mitchell pounded the steering wheel with his fist. "We're too fucking late!"

"We can't get in?" She thought this seemed like an odd system.

Mitchell turned toward her and shook his fist in her face. "This is your fault! You didn't get out of bed fast enough!"

She couldn't imagine that if they had left the hotel ten minutes earlier that there wouldn't be this line of cars. But, to keep the peace, she apologized.

"I'm tired of your sorries!" Mitchell did a U-turn to get out of the car line and go back from whence they came. "Your sorries mean nothing! And now I don't get my fish soup!"

She found it strange that Mitchell was focused on a bowl of soup, and that the fixation had been the sole reason for driving to Portofino. She wanted to get him focused on something else. "Is there any other soup that you'd like to have?"

Mitchell cocked his head in thought. "I once had an amazing bowl of cheese soup in Parma. So thick, the spoon stood upright in it."

"Great, let's get you that soup." She was glad that Mitchell was calming down.

They drove north to Parma at a normal pace. Parma wouldn't have a line for entry.

But Mitchell drove right past the exit.

"Mitchell? We're not going to Parma?"

"I have decided that you are not worthy of a bowl of cheese soup. Since you made me forgo my fish soup, you don't deserve to be treated any better than the piece of shit that you are."

She said nothing.

They passed under a large overpass with a structure on it. Mitchell pulled the car off the highway.

"What's here?" she asked. "Do you have to pee?"

"No, I do not have to pee." Mitchell mocked her with a childlike voice. "But this is where we'll have lunch. You deserve no better than a rest stop meal."

"This is a rest stop?"

"There is a store on top of the overpass." Mitchell pointed upward. "Pretty cool for a highway, right? You can eat your lunch and watch cars pass beneath you."

The concept did seem kind of cool. She followed Mitchell up the stairs and began to walk toward the restaurant, but he grabbed the back of her shirt collar and pulled her toward him.

"Not there, imbecile. You haven't earned a restaurant privilege." Mitchell clucked his tongue. "Come, we'll buy some provisions at the general store."

She remained silent as Mitchell wandered through the aisles of the store. There were certain things on the shelves that she would have been happy to eat, but she knew not to ask.

After a few minutes, Mitchell carried his arm full of groceries up to the cashier. He was purchasing several bottles of wine, some bread, dried salami, some sliced prosciutto, and a brick of parmesan.

She followed him down the stairs toward the parking lot. But Mitchell didn't walk to the car. Instead, he walked over to the grassy area near the lot.

He sat down in the grass, and she followed suit. Mitchell spread the food out on the grass and cut himself a big slice of salami and a hunk of cheese. He then passed her a small piece of cheese with the end of the knife.

The cheese was amazing, but they were only a few miles outside of Parma, so the quality made sense. She extended her hand to ask for more.

Mitchell looked at her with her open palm. Then he looked at the unopened bottles of wine. "I'll tell you what, if you can find me a corkscrew and some cups, I'll share my lunch with you."

His lunch? If she had known that he wasn't going to share, she would have bought something for herself. But she didn't argue. Instead, she walked around the grassy area to other picnickers.

She returned with a corkscrew and two plastic cups.

"Well done, imbecile." Mitchell began to open one of the bottles. "Every once in a while, you prove that you are good for something."

She sat back down in the grass. "May I please share your lunch?"

Mitchell opened two more bottles of wine, then handed the corkscrew back to her. "First, go return this to the nice family that lent it to you."

She returned the corkscrew and came back to Mitchell. He was staring at her oddly. "What's wrong, Mitchell?"

"Strange. I was just about to ask you the same thing."

"What do you mean?" she asked.

"I was just watching you walk. Are you feeling okay?" Mitchell put his hand to her forehead. "You could barely walk in a straight line. You looked like you were about to fall over."

She was embarrassed that she looked as terrible as she felt. "I'm not feeling well, Mitchell. I've told you that."

"Yes, but I thought you were just faking to shirk your responsibilities." Mitchell pointed at her, with his mouth full of salami. "But now I look at you, and I realize you're dying."

"I'm not dying, Mitchell. I just don't feel well." She looked at the spread of food. "Maybe I'm just hungry."

Mitchell shook his head and pointed his finger into the distance. "Walk over to that bush. I want to see you walk."

She stood up and walked to the bush and back. She did feel incredibly rickety. She hoped that Mitchell would give her some food.

Mitchell said, "Yep, you're dying." He cut himself another hunk of cheese. "Won't be long now. Then you'll be out of my hair for good."

She didn't get anything to eat. She was so hungry that she was in pain, but she didn't want to set Mitchell off on a violent tirade.

Watching the cars go by on the highway, she longed to be in any one of them. She didn't want to get back into the car with Mitchell.

They drove back toward Milan. The city was confusingly laid out, and she had trouble interpreting the map. There were a lot of roads that seemed to go in circles.

"Where are we going, navigator?" Mitchell asked.

"I'm not sure. It's a tough map to read. This may be a difficult city to drive in," She replied.

"It's only difficult because you're a moron who can't read a map," Mitchell snapped at her.

They were in the middle of city traffic, and she had no idea where to direct him. They came to an intersection, and Mitchell inadvertently stalled the car.

He pounded the dash with his fist and turned the engine back on. "Do you see what you made me do?" Mitchell screamed. "Because of your incompetence as a navigator, you're making me drive badly!"

"I'm sorry," she said softly. She rotated the map in her hands and picked a direction. "Let's go left."

"Are you sure? Left?" Mitchell was still yelling.

"No, I'm not sure. But all these roads go in circles, so I guess if we go the wrong way, we'll just end up back here."

"That's it? That's your navigational skills at work? You're leading me in circles?" Mitchell's voice got louder.

"I'm not leading you in circles," she explained. "But all the streets go in circles."

"What did I tell you about sassing me? Enough sass! Enough!" Mitchell grabbed her hair to pull her toward him. Then he punched her hard in the side of the head.

Her head bounced off Mitchell's fist and slammed against the doorjamb on the passenger's side.

Instantly, her body curled itself into the fetal position. Try as she might, she couldn't unclench her muscles. Her hands locked into little clawlike hooks, and she could feel her toes lock up as well.

She tried to open her eyes, but they were rolling so far back in her head that she couldn't see anything but a greenish darkness.

She tried to speak, but the only sound she could make was choking. She was having a seizure.

Mitchell could see that something was wrong. He had predicted that day that she was going to die, and maybe he was right.

"Okay, drama queen." Mitchell pulled the car off to the side of the road. "Enough faking."

Her body spasmed out of her control. Her jaw was locked.

"Seriously, I don't have the patience for one of your pretend episodes of a run-in with death." Mitchell shook her by the shoulder. "I said enough! Snap out of it."

Her body continued to shake. She could feel drool falling from the corner of her mouth. She was unable to lift her hand to wipe it away.

"I said enough!" Mitchell shook her again hard.

She tried to muster all her strength. She tried to speak, but only a gurgling sound came out.

Finally, she was able to say the word "hospital." It was barely audible, and she hoped that it wasn't just a sound in her head.

"What was that you said?" Mitchell kept shaking her. "Did you say hostel? Do you want me to leave you at a hostel?"

Again, she choked out the word "hospital."

"I heard you. We'll find you a nice little hostel." Mitchell pulled the car back onto the road.

All of her body hurt. It was a pain so intense, and so all consuming, that she hoped that she would die. She needed the relief.

Again, she whispered, "Hospital."

"I hear you! I said that we're looking for a hostel." Mitchell laughed. He was making fun of her.

Once more. "Hospital." It was a plea; the wish of a woman soon to die.

Mitchell looked at her. He took one of her hands in his own and tried to unfurl the fingers. They were solid like rocks in the claw shape.

Mitchell said, "You look awful. Are you sure that you want to go to a hostel?"

She repeated the only word she could speak. "Hospital."

Why was he torturing her? Finally, he said, "Oh, you're saying *hospital*."

She tried to nod but instead emitted a choking sound from the bottom of her throat.

"Well, I'll give you credit, imbecile. You are a phenomenal actress. This is an excellent performance." Mitchell pulled the car to the side of the road. "Okay. Get out. Here's twenty Euros for a taxi ride to the hospital." He tossed a crumpled bill into her lap. "Get out!" He repeated.

She couldn't get her body to move. Every muscle and tissue inside her was locked into spasm. She gurgled again.

Mitchell glared at her. "I guess you're not taking a taxi to the hospital. Fine. I'll take you." Mitchell made it sound like he was doing her a favor.

She couldn't breathe. She couldn't move. She couldn't speak. She knew that she wasn't going to live.

Fifty-Eight

Mitchell found the Metropolitan Hospital and pulled into the emergency room lot. EMTs raced out and put her onto a gurney. They were unable to get her out of her fetal position. Her body was like a rock.

She was wheeled into an emergency room, and several doctors ran onto the scene.

Mitchell stood in the room with the doctors and asked if anyone spoke English. None did. So Mitchell asked if anyone spoke French. One of the doctors said that he did.

Her understanding of French was better than her speaking. She heard Mitchell tell the doctor that she was crazy. Mitchell said that she needed a full psychiatric analysis, and that anything that she might say would be a blatant lie.

The doctor told Mitchell that she was in a coma. She heard this and tried to object. But she couldn't move, and no sound came out of her mouth.

She was given several shots and an IV drip of glucose and potassium. She felt the familiar burn of the potassium, but she couldn't even moan in pain.

She was also administered several shots. She felt a charge in her system and assumed that she had been given adrenaline.

She kept trying to move her body, but it was as though her brain had disconnected. She was aware of everything happening around her, but she was unable to participate.

Mitchell handed one of the doctors her passport. Then he left.

She tried to stay focused on what was happening around her, but eventually her brain checked out too. She was nothing now.

❧

She awakened the next morning in a room filled with about ten beds. She had an IV sticking out of the back of her hand. Her luggage was placed against the wall, next to her bed.

She had to pee, so she got up and wheeled her IV stand into the bathroom. When she came out, there was a doctor waiting for her.

The doctor spoke English and introduced himself as the psychiatric evaluator.

He asked her a series of questions as he wrote the answers down in her chart.

"Do you know what happened to you?" The doctor asked.

"I was hit in the head, and then my body stopped working," she responded.

"And do you know where you are?"

"I'm in the hospital."

"Do you know which hospital?" The doctor was scribbling away.

"Hospital Metropolitano," she replied.

"In which city?"

"Milan."

"And where are you from?"

"New York."

The doctor stood next to her and said, "You've suffered a blow to the head. We sent the police out to find your friend."

"My friend?"

"Yes, the man who brought you here. Mitchell Durman."

She tried to brace herself for the rest of this report. "And?"

"And I'm sorry to say that we were unable to arrest Mr. Durman. When the police finally tracked down his whereabouts, he had already left on a plane to Dubai." The psychiatrist looked apologetic.

"Can't you get him out of Dubai?"

"I'm afraid that emirates don't participate in extradition." The psychiatrist sighed. "It seems that your friend has gone into hiding."

"So, that's it?" she asked.

"Well, that's it for him. We can't arrest Mr. Durman there."

"So, that's it." If Mitchell had run from the police, was he finally gone from her life forever? Was this finally the end of the nightmare? He wouldn't dare recontact her for fear of the international legal repercussions. She sighed in relief; she may have hit rock bottom, but her life with Mitchell was over. Finally. In that strange hospital, in a large communal room, with doctors who didn't even speak her language, she felt safe. Free. Done.

"Well, that's it for now. But I have to finish my psychiatric profile on you before your release." The doctor looked back at her chart. "How old are you?"

"Twenty-four."

"And when is your birthday?"

"In February."

"And in what country do you reside?"

"In the U.S."

"Okay, all of these questions seem to indicate that you have no lasting brain trauma." He flipped through the chart again. "Can you say your name in full?"

"Evelyn Celia Dahab."

"Good." The doctor wrote something down. "And the last question. Do you know why you're here?"

She didn't understand what he was asking. "You mean here in Milan? Or in the hospital?"

"No, we know the answers to those questions, right?" The doctor leaned in toward her. "Do you know why you're here? Do you know what purpose you have being in Europe? Do you know why you came? Do you know why you're *here*?"

She mouthed the words and shook her head. She confessed honestly. "No."